U.S.
Flea Market

DIRECTORY

U.S. Flea Market
DIRECTORY

THIRD EDITION

*A Guide to the Best Flea Markets
in All 50 States*

Albert LaFarge

St. Martin's Griffin ❧ New York

www.stmartins.com

Library of Congress Cataloging-in-Publication Data

LaFarge, Albert
    U.S. flea market directory : a guide to the best flea markets in all 50
    states / Albert LaFarge.—3rd ed.
        p. cm.
    Includes index.
    ISBN 0-312-26405-4.
        1. Flea markets—United States—Directories. I. Title: U.S. flea
market directory. II. Title: United States flea market directory.
III. Title: Flea market directory. IV. Title.

HF5482.15.L34 2000
381'.192'02573—dc21

                                                        00-024869

First St. Martin's Griffin Edition: June 2000

10 9 8 7 6 5 4 3 2 1

Contents

Acknowledgments

The author would like to thank the hundreds of flea market owners, managers, and employees who have generously offered their time, in person and through thousands of written questionnaires, E-mail exchanges, and telephone interviews (often interrupting the press of business to do so) to provide the information for this guide. The author is also grateful to the large number of readers whose comments (in letters, faxes, E-mails, and phone calls) have provided useful information on flea markets.

In particular, the author wishes to express his thanks to the following people who have helped considerably in making the third edition of this book not just possible but better than ever: Jerry Stokès, Executive Director of the National Flea Market Association, for his unflagging support of this book and his commitment to improving the flea market industry; Greg Cohn and Kristen Macnamara, my editors at St. Martin's, for their energy, enthusiasm, and editorial guidance; my agent, Jim Fitzgerald, for his encouragement and infectious confidence in this project; Avery Moody; and the Tifts, especially Ann, Hal, Kippy, Maysie, and my wife Jeanne, who heroically endured detours at flea markets even during our honeymoon.

Also, Magnus Bartlett; Rip Hayman; Ray Huie; Christopher Johnsen; Jack Kelly; komodo@javanet.com; Ann LaFarge; Tildy LaFarge; Elizabeth Montague; Helen Robinson; Steve Rosston; shelly@navicom.com; Michael Sussman; Peter J. Tampas; Bill Webb; and mwhite@whitesguide. com (Mark White).

The author remains grateful to the following individuals and institutions for their help in the preparation of the past editions of *U.S. Flea Market Directory*: Robert Allen; Christopher Artis; Bandicoot; Peter Becker; Amanda Beesley; Claire Bocardo; Craig Boyce; Karol Ann Boyce; Kathryn Brennan; Elizabeth Burns; Katharine Butler; the California State Library, Sacramento; Ricardo Chiong; John and Jean Cole; Columbia University, particularly the staff at Butler Library; Lisa Considine; John Farley; John Grant; Martha Gross; Dorothy Harris; Dan Herbert; Alan Kaplan; Antoinette LaFarge; John Pendaries LaFarge; Louisa LaFarge; the Library of Congress; Louisiana State Library, Baton Rouge; Grace Macmillan; Jack

Macrae; Tia Maggini; Doug Mendini; Ray Meyerson; Allie Middleton; Mushroom (Rock Island, Illinois); the New Mexico State Library, Santa Fe; the New York Public Library; Nota Bene, Inc. (especially John Oldham and Richard Holmes in Technical Support); Marian Oaks; Jay Ottaway; Beverly and Dean Pallozzi; Peter Perez; Rusty Rhoades; John Ryan; Jim "Smitty" Schmidt; Bruce Sherwin; Victoria Shoemaker; Mark Sweeney, the Tennessee Flea Market Association; the Texas State Library, Austin; Lane Unsworth; Katrin Velder; the late Chuck Von Berg, his widow, Sarah, and his daughter, Shelley (we miss you, Chuck); and Craig West.

Introduction

Welcome to the fascinating and profitable world of flea markets! With this guide in hand, you can choose from a wide variety of the best flea markets across the country and instantly learn how to find them, when to visit, what you're likely to discover when you get there, and how to go about setting up your own stand if you want to be a vendor.

What Is a Flea Market?

The term *flea market* normally brings to mind a place where shoppers can go "off the beaten track" to find bargains on antiques, collectibles, or "junque." Flea markets tend to escape precise definition, but you generally know one when you see one. Flea markets come in many shapes and sizes, indoors or outdoors (or both), and can be found everywhere from rural back roads to the center city. For the purposes of this book, I have defined a flea market as any regularly recurring event involving several independent vendors of used merchandise, antiques, collectibles, discounted new merchandise, what have you—but not exclusively new merchandise at list price, because then what you have is an ordinary shopping mall ("discount malls" are a not-too-distant relative of flea markets). Given these criteria, I have tried to be inclusive in judging what is and isn't a true flea market.

In my view, the best flea markets offer a diversity of merchandise and accommodate a wide range of vendors, including transients who show up only sporadically, perhaps to sell the surplus of an attic or garage. In my travels around the country I have come across any number of fine little antiques shops that call themselves flea markets, but regrettably there is not room for them in this guide. I have also chosen not to include upscale antiques malls, auctions, and specialty shows. The distinctions can seem hazy at times, and in some instances I've just had to "go with my gut."

A Brief History of the Flea Market

Today's American flea market is the modern incarnation of a feature common to civilized societies throughout history—wherever there is a high concentration of people, there will be market days when they assemble for the exchange of goods and services. The ancient Greek *agora* was a central place of assembly where farmers, fishmongers, bakers, and all manner of tradespeople had their stalls. Bankers and money changers set up tables where today one might find automatic teller machines (indeed, ATMs are now common at flea markets). The ancient agora was a central meeting place for friends and acquaintances, a place to exchange news, hear speeches, even vote. The Roman *forum* began as a humble market and eventually became the focus of political and social life as civic buildings grew up around it during the city's rise to greatness; throughout the Roman Empire, towns were established on a plan that incorporated a centrally located forum for a variety of civic functions. Lively central markets such as these have grown up naturally in communities around the world since the dawn of time.

The term *flea market* is derived (literally) from the French *marché aux puces,* after those pesky little parasites of the order Siphonaptera (or "wingless bloodsucker") that used to infest the upholstery of used furniture brought out for sale. Indeed, at many American flea markets you will still find that old upholstered furniture is either strictly inspected or banned altogether from the sale floor precisely in order to prevent a bug problem.

A flea market by any other name is still a flea market in my book. Americans refer to them variously as swap meets (a term prevalent on the West Coast), trade days, and a host of other colorful names, including Swap-O-Rama, Swap 'N' Shop, Peddlers' Fair, Trading Center, Flea Emporium, and Flea Mall. Naturally, at any of these places you will find people coming from far and wide hunting for bargains on antiques, collectibles, new and used merchandise, and good old-fashioned "junque."

A flea market can operate just about anywhere there is available space—in vacant parking lots, drive-in movie theaters, speedways and racetracks, sporting facilities, fairgrounds, self-storage facilities, and converted retail spaces (including revamped supermarkets and shopping malls that went bust!). They are held mostly on weekends, but many also happen on the odd weekday (especially Friday or Monday). Some are open daily (in which case the weekend days tend to draw the highest turnout). A newly opened market may meet as infrequently as once or twice a year and grow over time to monthly, weekly, or even daily operation, depending on demand and availability of the space, which is often determined by the primary user. Parking garages, for example, may accommodate commuters' cars during weekdays and yield to bargain hunters on weekends; drive-in theaters often feature vendors' wares by day and a feature film after dark. Fairgrounds have flea markets that operate regularly *except* when the fair is in town. This aspect of secondary use can be a flea market's greatest asset in its struggle to compete with higher-rent retail businesses, since the lower rent means lower prices for consumers.

A few words on the "first Monday" phenomenon, which is exemplified by First Monday Trade Days in Canton, Texas, one of the country's oldest and biggest flea markets. The origins of this sprawling monthly event go back to 1873, when the district judge set aside court days on which stray horses would be auctioned off. Before long, people were coming from all over Texas for these auctions, some bringing their own goods to trade or sell (back then it was known as "Hoss Monday"). As the tradition grew, the streets of downtown Canton were soon overflowing with animals, supplies, and produce. Like other, similar "court days" around the country, especially in the South, Canton's First Monday event grew until residents began to dread the horde that descended upon their city for one weekend each month. The city eventually passed an ordinance against trading in the street, but the crowds had grown too large to control.

With the rise of the mass-produced automobile in the 1930s, the importance of the horse began to decline, and it was presumed that "Hoss Monday" would slowly die out. That prediction never came to pass: First Monday had developed into a "horse of a different color," with a reputation for great bargains on all manner of things. In 1965, the city of Canton purchased six and one half acres of land and designated it a trading area with spaces for vendors to rent for a nominal fee; this area soon filled to capacity, prompting the city to buy more land. Today, First Monday Trade Days completely overtakes the town, and hotels are booked for miles around. In this guide you will find many events that have grown out of this same tradition and that regularly attract vendors and shoppers by the thousands.

Flea markets have matured and flourished into a major recreation option for travelers throughout America. America's passions for collecting, shopping (especially for bargains), and leisure travel have fueled an explosion in the flea market industry over the past decade. In 1993, Ed Spivia, owner of the Lakewood Antiques Center, a monthly collectibles market outside of Atlanta, described on CNN how flea markets were "so popular that they are becoming a scheduled part of vacation plans." This trend accelerated dramatically in the late 1990s as entrepreneurs responded with improved merchandise and entertainment options, food concessions, and other amenities. As the flea market industry gets bigger and savvier, management companies have begun to take over and operate highly profitable flea market "franchises" with sophisticated marketing.

In 1997, the National Association of Flea Markets (NFMA) was launched to help owners and operators network and form alliance with suppliers. NFMA has seen a rapid increase in its membership and continues to grow by leaps and bounds. The association is a vital resource for sellers, shoppers, and suppliers alike. (For more information, visit NFMA's official Web site at www.fleamarkets.org, which describes member benefits, provides information on the annual convention, and offers links to individual flea market sites.)

There are now several on-line auction services where buyers and sellers can get together to exchange goods in the virtual marketplace. The most popular is currently Ebay (www.ebay.com), which was launched in 1995 and currently has more than two million registered users with hundreds of thousands of new items added daily. (The site attracted 6.5 million unique visitors in February 1999.) Registering is free, and anyone who is registered can bid or sell. Auctions usually take about a week to complete. Sellers pay an insertion fee, which ranges from twenty-five cents (for items with an opening bid of ten dollars or less) to two dollars (for opening bids of fifty dollars and higher), plus a "final value fee" ranging from 1.25 percent to 5 percent of final bid, depending on the price realized. (For more information, go to http://pages.ebay.com/aw/agreement-fees.html.)

Recent Ebay Listings

Prices realized from auctions conducted in May and June 1999.

1946 Wurlitzer 1015 Jukebox: Bidding started at $2,500, and it sold for $5,710. Seller shelly@narvicom.com was pleased to report that the item went to another collector and will be in good hands.

Vintage Miller Bros 101 Ranch poster: Seller mwhite@ whiteguide.com (Mark White) got a final bid of $976 (the opening bid was $1, with no reserve).

1977 Aladdin Welcome Back Kotter Lunchbox and Thermos: Thermos was described as perfect (in unused condition), with original handle and hardware. Final bid: $162.50 (opening bid was $19.99). The buyer, komodo@javanet.com, comments, "It's always a pleasure finding and being able to purchase mint lunch boxes."

Elvis Presley's Young Face Rubber Stamp: Listed as "brand new, never used mounted rubber stamp of The King. Measures $3\frac{3}{4}$"×$3\frac{1}{4}$"." Winning bid for this item was $23.69. Bidding began at $5.00 and attracted a total of twenty-seven bids.

Two-ounce Cobalt Irregular Hexagon "Blue Coffin" Poison Bottle: Embossed stars on each side panel, "NOT TO BE TAKEN" on the front; $4\frac{1}{4}$ inches tall, "great +++" condition. Winning bid: $19 (opening bid: $12.50). Seller: robkay@globalnet. co.uk.

Ebay has spawned a whole new generation of World Wide Web addicts. A friend got carpel tunnel syndrome just by surfing Ebay for hours on end. You can find just about anything (that's legal) in their catalog, from cars to Hummel figurines.

Other major players in the arena of electronic auctions and secondary market sales are Amazon (www.amazon.com), which has recently partnered with Sotheby's auction house; Yahoo Auctions (www.yahoo.com), and Edeal (www.edeal.com). There are many specialized sites, but the early players have an advantage in that sellers and buyers are naturally attracted to the sites with the highest exposure. For a list of on-line auction sites, visit www.yourguide. net/buyandsell/links_online_auctions.html.

Though the World Wide Web will never be able to offer the tactile experience of flea markets in the so-called real world—the sights and smells, the human interaction, the excitement of turfing through dusty piles of junk in pursuit of hidden treasures—the "searchability" offered by on-line commerce has significantly expanded the horizons of collectors who are seeking out particular items, and the Web has attracted a whole new generation of hobbyists and small-time entrepreneurs into collecting. While some of these people may be couch potatoes who are too lazy to go out and get their hands dirty at flea markets, most collectors are active both in cyberspace and in the "real" world of physical stuff. These two "forums" are complementary, and the upshot is more and better flea market shopping.

Tips on Buying and Selling

Standard lore has it that the best bargains are to be found by showing up early and staying late in the day. A good start, but the main objective is just to get there, whenever you can. The next order of business is for buyer and seller to agree on a fair price for an item of interest to the buyer. Sellers vary widely in their pricing strategies and their willingness to negotiate, but for the most part, you will find that if you tell the seller your true estimate of what an object is worth to you, you can get the item for substantially less than originally listed. By being honest and cautious, knowing what you want, and relying on your own good judgment, you are poised to succeed in the marketplace.

Some Tips on Buying and Selling

- Be the early bird—and get the worm.
- Stay late. Some of the best bargains can be had around closing time, when dealers tend to exhibit added willingness to sell you that mahogany table rather than pack it up and truck it home themselves.
- Find a flea market near you and swing by regularly, even if for a quick once-over. Vendors and merchandise tend to change regularly.
- Take the road less traveled. The more out-of-the-way the area, the lower the prices. (But don't give up on the metropolis, there's lots of great stuff there.) Stray down side aisles where other people don't seem to be going: where better to find that neglected treasure?
- Find out as much as you can about your favorite collectibles.

- Keep moving and don't stand still unless/until you're absolutely transfixed by an item.
- Go ahead and haggle. Be respectful, and enjoy the lively interaction of bartering, which can be pleasant for both parties if done in the right spirit. Dealers expect it, and may even respect you more for it.
- There can be good deals in bad weather. Open-air markets "live and die by the weather," says Michael Santulli, of New York City's Annex Antiques Fair and Flea Market, and vendors get spooked when the rain comes. Shoppers who brave the elements are often rewarded—why not take advantage? I once got a great deal on a rug at an auction held during a sloppy snowstorm in New York City. Hardly anyone else showed up to bid.
- Bring a tape measure. If you're shopping for furniture (even if you don't admit you are), have the dimensions of your doors and interior spaces handy.
- Bring a magnifying glass. You'll be surprised what you'll find under the extreme close-up.
- Bring a magnet (to test metal objects).
- Bring a flashlight even if you aren't planning to arrive before dawn or stay past dusk. A flashlight will come in handy for inspecting identifying marks such as manufacturer's serial numbers, which are often located in darkened areas. Learn to use such markers to determine authenticity, especially if you are preparing to pay high prices.
- When shopping for large items, prepare for success by bringing a vehicle big enough to hold your payload; if not a truck, then a large car, preferably with a roof rack, and a good supply of bungee cords and moving blankets.
- Don't be afraid to give a vendor your business card; write down what you're looking for and ask for a call (or E-mail) if anything turns up. Experienced collectors and professional "pickers" print up cards listing their interests. Also, ask a vendor for his or her card, and call them to follow up if they say "try next week."
- Watch out for repair jobs, repaints, mixed-and-matched parts, and the like, especially in the more valuable stuff.
- An old object that has never broken down may be a better bet than an item of more recent vintage that has already fallen apart and been repaired.
- Talk to the vendors, who are often affable schmoozers and knowledgeable collectors.
- Don't let your better half talk you out of something you really love.
- Let your better half talk you out of something you don't really love.

Rules and Regulations

Overall, flea market operators strive to make available the widest variety of products possible within the parameters of safety, the law, and good taste. For varying reasons, many flea markets place restrictions on the sale of certain types of merchandise. Almost all markets categorically forbid the sale of illegal weapons (switchblades, throwing stars, unlicensed firearms, and the like; illicit drugs; and stolen, counterfeit, or "gray market" products whose sale violates copyright or patent laws. The vast majority of flea markets ban pornography, liquor, or any distasteful or potentially harmful items. Many markets restrict the sale or even presence of dangerous animals such as vicious dogs or poisonous snakes; chemicals or gases (some ban propane indoors for safety reasons); and fireworks. As mentioned earlier, some market operators submit old upholstered furniture to inspection for insects or even ban such merchandise from the sale area altogether in an effort to ward off the eponymous fleas and other pests. A flea market operator may feel the need to restrict the sale of cheap new merchandise such as costume jewelry, socks, sports shoes, sunglasses, or T-shirts, especially if they are present in excess. Such items are occasionally confined to one area of the market or limited to certain days.

Some managers will not tolerate "subversive" literature on the sale floor; others ban "racially denigrating" items, palm readers, games of skill, gambling, and carnival-type operations. Managers undertake these measures in the name of protecting the consumer as well as themselves and other vendors.

Taxes and Licensing for Flea Market Vendors

In general, the vendor assumes responsibility for obtaining any applicable licenses and remitting sales taxes directly to the state. Flea market operators are generally cooperative in advising prospective vendors about local taxes and licenses. Market operators sometimes demand proof of a state tax identification number and any required permits before allowing vendors to set up, since the state requires the operators to furnish such information in their tax returns. Prospective vendors are advised to contact the department of taxation and finance (or the board of equalization) for the state in which a particular market is located. Each state has a toll-free number to call for an application for registration as a sales tax vendor, which will include information on filing procedures and regulations. The state will grant a certificate of authority allowing vendors to collect applicable taxes. Vendors buying from wholesalers can obtain a state-issued resale certificate allowing them to avoid paying sales taxes until these taxes have been collected from the consumer. Some states allow sellers of household items to bypass sales tax registration altogether, but vendors should inquire before proceeding, just to be sure. Systematic record keeping is important for tax reasons, since it will enable a vendor to prepare complete and accurate tax returns, which must show gross sales, taxable sales, and sales taxes due, among other things. An unexpected tax audit will be much less stressful if transaction records have been kept up-to-date and neatly organized. Flea market vendors should protect themselves by maintaining organized and detailed records from the outset.

State or local licensing may be required for the sale of prepared foods and other items. When in doubt, check with the flea market manager and/or the state's department of business permits (again, there should be a toll free number). Generally, vendors who purchase prepackaged food items from a wholesaler will not need a separate license—the wholesaler or initial preparer bears that responsibility—but a vendor who prepares and packages food for resale will probably be subject to safety inspections and licensing through the state's department of agriculture and markets or the county department of health. (Food items that are not subject to rapid microbial growth of bacteria, such as canned foods, bread, cookies, and cakes, may not require such a license, but it is wise to check, since rules can vary by county.) Most flea market operators regulate the sale of food or grant exclusive concessions to responsible chefs.

How to Use This Directory

The following explanations are offered to help the reader understand the elements that make up the listings in this guide.

The term *weekend* has been used consistently throughout this book to mean Saturday and Sunday; weekdays are thus indicated separately wherever applicable. **Hours of operation** are sometimes estimates, since many flea markets begin as soon as the first seller sets up and continue until the last one leaves. It is always a good idea to call ahead to make sure a market will be open when you arrive—especially if you are going out of your way to visit.

Information concerning the average **number of vendors** is based primarily on estimates offered by the market operator. For most listings, a range indicates the number of vendors in low and high season. Although many flea markets operate year round, virtually all have seasonal fluctuations in attendance. Open-air markets in particular are naturally dependent upon good weather, and visitors should expect a lower vendor turnout (and, correspondingly, fewer shoppers) in bitter cold, oppressive heat, or otherwise inclement weather. At many outdoor markets in the South, as in the resort communities of Florida, the busiest part of the season coincides with the peak tourist season in midwinter, and summer is the low season as a result of the heat. For indoor markets in extremely cold or hot climates, the phrase "climate-controlled" becomes a key part of advertising and promotion.

The description of **types of merchandise** is based mainly on operators' recollections of what they have seen regularly over time; these generalizations therefore represent merely *trends* rather than any kind of guarantee of what items will be available on a given visit. Seasonal items (especially fresh produce) may be in abundant supply from several vendors one month and altogether absent the next. Flea markets are by nature unpredictable—which is, of course, a big part of the excitement.

Vendor space rental rates are intended to be accurate as of press time but can change without notice. Prospective vendors seeking to confirm rates are advised to inquire directly to the markets.

Addresses, phone and fax numbers, E-mail addresses, and World Wide Web sites are listed where available at press time.

The best flea markets (in my view) are listed up front in this book's main section, alphabetically by state and town, with a map for each state. Several hundred other markets that may well be worth visiting—markets with fewer than fifty vendors or which were contacted by phone, mail, or E-mail and did not furnish complete and satisfactory information by the publisher's deadline—are listed in an **appendix of brief listings** at the end of this book. An alphabetical **index** of all listings is also supplied for ease of reference.

The following symbols indicate that a market

♿ is wheelchair accessible.

🚹 provides public toilet facilities.

To the Reader

Past editions of this guide have benefitted enormously from the strong support you have shown both at the bookstore and through your suggestions about the constantly evolving world of flea markets. I have made every effort to incorporate any new information received from readers across the country, and I continue to welcome your input. If you would like to share your opinions, offer new information, or participate in upcoming surveys, please feel free to contact the author:

U.S. Flea Market Directory
c/o St. Martin's Press
175 Fifth Avenue
New York, N.Y. 10010
E-mail: alafarge@aol.com

Elephants are always drawn smaller than life, but a flea always larger.
—Jonathan Swift

Wherein could this flea guilty bee,
Except in that drop which it suckt from thee?
—John Donne

So naturalists observe a flea
Hath smaller fleas, that on him prey;
And these have smaller still to bite 'em
And so proceed *ad infinitum*.
—Jonathan Swift

MAIN
LISTINGS

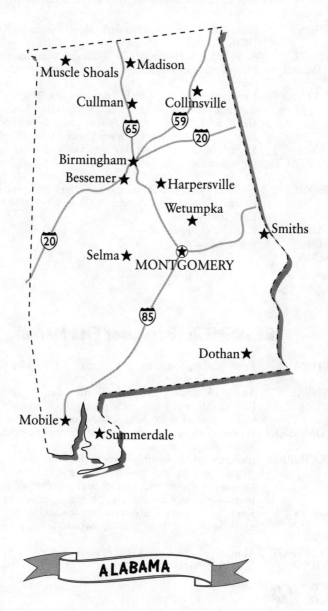

ALABAMA

ATTALLA: Mountain Top Flea Market

WHEN	Every Sunday, 5:00 P.M. to dark. In operation since the early 1970s.
WHERE	At 11301 U.S. Highway 278 West, six miles west of Attalla.
ADMISSION	Free admission; ample free parking; indoors and outdoors, year-round.
FEATURES	Variety of offerings including antiques and collectibles, clothing, crafts, new and used merchandise, fresh produce, and tools. Averages up to 1,000 vendors. Nine food concessions. Draws nearly two million visitors annually.
RATES	$7 per 10'×22' space per day. Reservations are not required.
CONTACT	Janie Terrell, 11301 U.S. Highway 278 West, Attalla, AL 35954.
PHONE	(800) 535-2286 (reservation office hours are Monday, 12:30 P.M. to 4:00 P.M. and Tuesday, 8:00 A.M. to 4:00 P.M.)
FAX	(205) 589-4119
E-MAIL	mtopflea@hopper.net
WEB	www.lesdeal.com
NFMA	Yes

BESSEMER: Bessemer Flea Market

WHEN	Every Friday, Saturday, and Sunday, 8:00 A.M. to 5:00 P.M. In operation since 1980.
WHERE	At 1013 Eighth Avenue North. Take exit 112 off I-59 to Highway 11, then go right (south) about three blocks; market is just behind McDonald's.
ADMISSION	Free admission; acres of free parking; indoors, outdoors, and under cover, year-round.
FEATURES	Antiques and collectibles, yard-sale stuff, crafts, furniture, sporting goods, and tools. Averages 400 to 600 vendors. Concession stands with cotton candy, fresh fried pork skins, peanuts, etc. An old-fashioned, "honest-to-goodness" market.
RATES	From $6 per space. Reservations for sheds and buildings must be prepaid; reserve up to two outdoor spaces without prepayment.
CONTACT	Manager, 1013 Eight Avenue North, Bessemer, AL 35020.
PHONE	(205) 425-8510

BIRMINGHAM: Birmingham Fairgrounds Flea Market

WHEN
First weekend of every month, plus three weekends in December: Friday, 3:00 P.M. to 9:00 P.M.; Saturday and Sunday, 9:00 A.M. to 6:00 P.M. In operation since the early 1970s.

WHERE
At the Alabama State Fairgrounds; take exit 120 off I-20 and follow signs to State Fair Complex.

ADMISSION
Free admission; free parking for more than 2,000 cars; indoors year-round and outdoors, rain or shine.

FEATURES
Antiques and collectibles, books, new and vintage clothing, coins and stamps, kitchenware, crafts, dolls, furniture, jewelry, lamps, new and used merchandise, Oriental rugs, porcelain, fresh produce, toys, "and lots more." Averages 400 to 450 vendors. Snacks and hot meals are served on the premises.

RATES
From $55 per indoor space for three days or $25 per outdoor space. Reservations are recommended two weeks in advance.

CONTACT
Manager, 621 Lorna Square, Birmingham, AL 35216.

PHONE
(800) 362-7538 or (205) 822-3348

COLLINSVILLE: Collinsville Trade Day

WHEN
Every Saturday, 7:00 A.M. to 2:30 P.M. In operation for more than forty-four years.

WHERE
On Highway 11 South. Take Route 68 from I-59, then turn right onto U.S. 11; or go left from Route 68 after leaving Route 411 at Leesburg, AL.

ADMISSION
Free admission; parking available at 50¢ per car; indoors and outdoors, rain or shine.

FEATURES
Antiques and collectibles, books, new clothing, coins and stamps, kitchenware, crafts, furniture, jewelry, livestock, new and used merchandise, fresh produce, and toys. Averages close to 1,000 vendors. Snacks and hot meals are served on the premises. The original "big one in Collinsville" draws more than 30,000 shoppers weekly.

RATES
$8 per 10'×12' space indoors per day or $5 per 15'×20' space outdoors. Reservations are not required.

CONTACT
Manager, P.O. Box 560, Collinsville, AL 35961.

PHONE
(888) 524-2536 or (256) 524-2127

CULLMAN: Cullman Flea Market

WHEN	Every weekend, 8:00 A.M. to 5:00 P.M. In operation since 1989.
WHERE	On Route 278 off I-65 (take exit 308).
ADMISSION	Free admission; over nine acres of free parking; indoors year-round and outdoors, weather permitting.
FEATURES	Antiques and collectibles, baked goods, books, new and vintage clothing, kitchenware, crafts, furniture, jewelry, new merchandise, porcelain, fresh produce, tools and hardware, and toys. Averages 250 to a capacity of 500 vendors. Snacks and hot meals are served by two food concessions on the premises. Advertised as one of the nicest and cleanest in the South.
RATES	From $20 to $30 per weekend depending on location; call for monthly rates. Reserve from two weeks to a month in advance.
CONTACT	Del or Gene Bates, 415 Lincoln Avenue S.W., P.O. Box 921, Cullman, AL 35055.
PHONE	(256) 739-0910
FAX	(256) 739-5352

DOTHAN: Sadie's Flea Market

WHEN	Every Friday, Saturday, and Sunday, 8:00 A.M. to 5:00 P.M. In operation since 1990.
WHERE	At 1990 U.S. 231 South, five miles south of Dothan, just past the Olympia Spa Country Club; eight miles north of the Florida line.
ADMISSION	Free admission; sixty acres of free parking; indoors year-round and outdoors, weather permitting.
FEATURES	Antiques and collectibles, books, new clothing, coins and stamps, kitchenware, crafts, furniture, jewelry, livestock, new and used merchandise, fresh produce, and toys. Averages 300 to a capacity of 350 vendors. There are two snack bars on the premises. Average of 2,000 shoppers per weekend. There is a shower and an RV park on the premises.
RATES	$3 per outdoor space or $6 under cover on Saturday or Sunday (free setup on Friday); electricity is available for RVs at $4 per day. Reserve a week in advance.

CONTACT Sarah or Kenneth West, 105 Olympia Drive, Dothan, AL 36301.
PHONE (334) 677-5138

HARPERSVILLE: Dixieland Antique and Farmers Market

WHEN Every weekend, 9:00 A.M. to 5:00 P.M. In operation since the 1980s.
WHERE On Route 25 between Wilsonville and Harpersville.
ADMISSION Free admission; ample free parking; indoors and outdoors, year-round.
FEATURES Antiques and collectibles, furniture, new and used merchandise, and fresh produce. Averages close to 200 vendors. Plenty of good food and refreshments. Under new ownership; weekend traffic is about 5,000 shoppers.
RATES From $5 per 11'×12' space per day outdoors, $7 per covered space, $12 indoors (Friday setup OK with prepaid weekend). Reservations are recommended; call Wednesday through Friday.
CONTACT Manager, 3000 Highway 25 South, Harpersville, AL 35078.
PHONE (205) 672-2022
FAX (205) 672-2203

MADISON: Limestone Flea Market

WHEN Every weekend, 9:00 A.M. to 5:00 P.M. In operation since 1991.
WHERE At the intersection of Highway 72 and Burgreen Road between Athens and Huntsville.
ADMISSION Free admission; free parking; indoors, rain or shine.
FEATURES Antiques and collectibles, books, new and vintage clothing, crafts, furniture, household items, jewelry, new and used merchandise. Averages 300 to a capacity of 455 vendors. Five food concessions on the premises. North Alabama's largest indoor market.
RATES $41 per 10'×10' space per weekend, including table and electricity. Reservations are required.

CONTACT   Rosa Isbell, Manager, 30030 Highway 72 West, Madison, AL 35756.
PHONE   (256) 233-5183
FAX   (256) 233-1415

People Collect Everything . . .

- Kitchen sinks
- Bathtubs
- Lunch boxes
- Plastic handbags
- The little plastic bags that grocery-store carrots come in
- Fast-food memorabilia
- Telephone calling cards from around the world: Singapore, Croatia, Poland, Japan, and Italy, where they originated in 1976; one card fetched 5,000 deutsche marks ($3,300) at an auction in Germany in the mid-1990s, according to the *Wall Street Journal*
- Varieties of sawdust
- Typewriters (manual or electric)
- Early personal computers
- Locks of Ringo Starr's hair
- Old transistor radios (Bakelite, Japanese minis, etc.)
- Hubcaps and other car parts

MOBILE: Flea Market Mobile

WHEN   Every weekend, 9:00 A.M. to 5:00 P.M. In operation for over four years.
WHERE   At 401 Schillinger Road North. Take I-65 to Airport Boulevard West to Schillinger Road North, one and a half miles on the left.
ADMISSION   Free admission; free parking for up to 1,000 cars; indoors and outdoors, rain or shine.
FEATURES   Full spectrum of antiques, collectibles, new and used mer-

chandise, new and vintage clothing, kitchenware, crafts, furniture, jewelry, livestock, pets, fresh produce, tools. Averages up to a capacity of 700 vendors. Concessions serving a variety of foods and beverages (try the boiled and roasted peanuts and the roasted corn on the cob). Overnight security throughout weekend.

RATES $25 per space for one day or $35 for both days. Reservations are recommended.

CONTACT Daryl Thompson, General Manager, 401 Schillinger Road North, Mobile, AL 36608.

PHONE (334) 633-7533 (office is open daily)

 NFMA Member

MONTGOMERY: Montgomery's Gigantic Indoor Flea Market

WHEN Every Friday, noon to 6:00 P.M., and Saturday, and Sunday, 9:00 A.M. to 6:00 P.M. In operation since 1999.

WHERE At 2270 East South Boulevard, one block west of the Wal-Mart.

ADMISSION Free admission; ample free parking; indoors, year-round.

FEATURES A variety of antiques and collectibles, new, used, and garage-sale merchandise. Averages 200 to 250 vendors. Food is served on the premises. The management is friendly here and the merchandise is worth checking out.

RATES From $10 per 10'×10' space per day. Reservations are not required.

CONTACT Barbara Gene Butler, 2270 East South Boulevard, Montgomery, AL 36116.

PHONE (334) 286-5005

FAX (334) 281-2404

MUSCLE SHOALS: Fairgrounds Gigantic Flea Market

WHEN The second weekend of every month (except September), Saturday, 8:00 A.M. to 6:00 P.M., and Sunday, 10:00 A.M. to 5:00 P.M. In operation since 1994.

WHERE At the Fairgrounds, on Highway 43 South.

ADMISSION	Free admission; thirty-three acres of free parking; indoors and outdoors, rain or shine.
FEATURES	Antiques and collectibles, designer clothing, tools, and quality new and used merchandise. Averages 300 to 600 vendors. Food is served on the premises. This market draws over 25,000 shoppers per event.
RATES	$95 per 10'×10' space indoors and $75 outdoors. Reserve a month in advance for outdoor space; there is a waiting list for indoor space.
CONTACT	Michael or Richard Epperson, Sale-a-Rama Promotions, 254 Seville Street, Suite 3, Florence, AL 35360.
PHONE	(800) 672-8988 or (256) 764-6400
FAX	(256) 764-6481

SELMA: Selma Flea Market

WHEN	Every Saturday, 5:00 A.M. to whenever. In operation since the 1980s.
WHERE	On Highway 80 Bypass at River Road.
ADMISSION	Free admission; free parking; indoors, outdoors, and under cover, rain or shine.
FEATURES	Antiques and collectibles, books, new and vintage clothing, kitchenware, crafts, furniture, jewelry, new merchandise, fresh produce, toys—and "bargains." Averages 300 to 400 vendors. Snacks and hot meals are served on the premises. RV parking is available.
RATES	$8 per 10' space per day under cover, $5 outdoors. Reservations are not required.
CONTACT	Gary Maluda, 606 River Road, Selma, AL 36703.
PHONE	(334) 875-0500

NFMA Member

SMITHS: Lee County Flea Market

WHEN	Every weekend, 7:00 A.M. to whenever. In operation since 1988.
WHERE	At the intersection of Route 431 North and 280 West at Lee County Route 379, about fifteen miles from Opelika and ten miles from Columbus (take exit 62 off I-85).

ADMISSION   Free admission; ample free parking; indoors and outdoors, rain or shine.

FEATURES   All kinds of stuff—new and old, collectible and "junque"—with lots of opportunity for the serendipitous find. Averages 170 to 200 vendors. Food is served on the premises; there is a vegetable stand.

RATES   From $3 to $12 per space per day. Reservations are required for spaces under cover of shed.

CONTACT   Ruth or Bryant Williams, P.O. Box 471, Smiths, AL 36877.

PHONE   (800) 835-0498 or (334) 291-7780

SUMMERDALE: Highway 59 Flea Market

WHEN   Every weekend, 8:00 A.M. to 5:00 P.M. In operation since 1985.

WHERE   On Highway 59 between Robertsdale and Foley.

ADMISSION   Free admission; twenty-seven acres of free parking; indoors and outdoors, rain or shine.

FEATURES   Full spectrum of antiques and collectibles, new and used merchandise, and fresh produce. Averages up to 300 vendors. There is a snack bar on the premises. Well advertised through TV, radio, and newspaper announcements. Mobile home parking facilities; hot shower facilities.

RATES $5 per space per day; $5 overnight fee. Reservations are not required.

CONTACT   Jeff Smith, 804 South State Highway 59, Summerdale, AL 36580.

PHONE   (334) 989-6642

FAX   (334) 989-6809

NFMA Member

WETUMPKA: Santuck Flea Market

WHEN   First Saturday of each month from March through December, from daybreak to 2:00 P.M. In operation for over nineteen years.

WHERE   Twenty-five miles north of Montgomery. Take Route 231 North to Highway 9; then turn right and market will be six miles down, on the right.

ADMISSION   Free admission; ample free parking; outdoors, rain or shine.
FEATURES   Antiques and collectibles, books, new clothing, kitchenware, crafts, furniture, jewelry, new and used merchandise, fresh produce, and toys. Averages 300 to 400 vendors. Snacks and hot meals are served on the premises. Operated by volunteers from Santuck community, and proceeds go to the local fire department.
RATES $20 per space per day. Reservations are required—check for waiting list on Friday (day before market) after 8:00 A.M.
CONTACT   Jack S. Johnson, President, 662 Dexter Road, Wetumpka, AL 36092.
PHONE   (334) 567-7400

Anchorage

JUNEAU

ALASKA

ANCHORAGE: Downtown Saturday Market

WHEN	Every Saturday from Memorial Day weekend through Labor Day weekend, 10:00 A.M. to 6:00 P.M. In operation since around 1990.
WHERE	In the parking lot at 3rd and E Streets, across from the Hilton Hotel and overlooking Ship Creek and Cook Inlet.
ADMISSION	Free admission; free parking; outdoors, rain or shine.
FEATURES	Antiques and collectibles, new and used merchandise, crafts, and local produce in season. Averages 300 to 400 vendors. Food is available on the premises.
RATES	from $25 per 9'×15' space. Reservations are required.
CONTACT	Bill Webb or Diana Arthur, P.O. Box 102440, Anchorage, AK 99510.
PHONE	(907) 272-5634
FAX	(907) 272-5635
E-MAIL	saturdaymarket@alaskalife.net

 NFMA Member

ANCHORAGE: Downtown Wednesday Market

WHEN	Nine Wednesdays from early July through the end of August (call for this year's dates), 10:00 A.M. to 8:00 P.M.
WHERE	On Fourth Avenue from C to F Streets and on D and F Streets between Fourth and Fifth Avenues, in downtown Anchorage.
ADMISSION	Free admission; ample free parking; outdoors, rain or shine.
FEATURES	Local merchants and vendors sell a mix of collectibles, crafts, new merchandise, household stuff, and local produce. Averages close to 150 vendors. Food is served on the premises. This market and its companion on Saturdays in Anchorage, are the biggest of their kind in Alaska.
RATES	Call for rates.
CONTACT	Diana Arthur, P.O. Box 102440, Anchorage, AK 99510.
PHONE	(907) 272-5634
FAX	(907) 272-5635
E-MAIL	saturdaymarket@alaskalife.net

NFMA Member

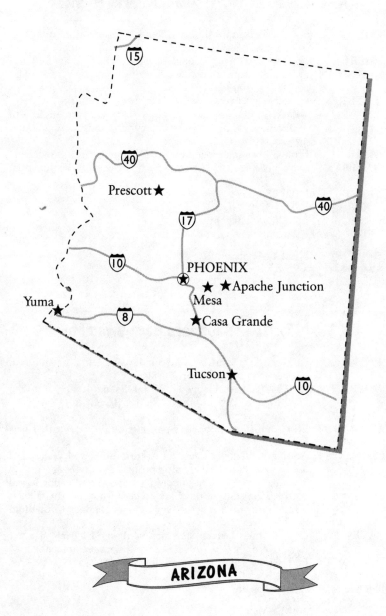

15

40

Prescott★

17

40

10

PHOENIX
★ ★Apache Junction
Mesa

Yuma
★

8

★Casa Grande

Tucson★

10

ARIZONA

APACHE JUNCTION: Apache Park 'N' Swap

WHEN	Every Friday, Saturday, and Sunday, 7:00 A.M. to 4:00 P.M. In operation since 1965.
WHERE	At 2651 West Apache Trail, at the Apache Greyhound Park.
ADMISSION	Free admission; ample free parking; outdoors and under cover, year-round.
FEATURES	Collectibles, overstock/discount items, "sundries," Southwestern crafts, used and garage-sale items. Averages 200 to 700 vendors. Food is served on the premises. Watch and jewelry repair on the premises.
RATES	From $8 per space per day. Reservations are recommended.
CONTACT	Steve Haskett, 2651 West Apache Trail, Apache Junction, AZ 85220.
PHONE	(602) 288-0571
FAX	(602) 982-8770
E-MAIL	ppns0010@aol.com
WEB	www.americanparknswap.com

NFMA Member

CASA GRANDE: Shoppers Barn Swap Meet

WHEN	Every Friday, Saturday, and Sunday, 7:00 A.M. to 4:00 P.M. In operation since the early 1980s.
WHERE	At 13480 West Highway 84 (at Selma Road), between Phoenix and Tucson. Take Exit 198 (C. G. Eloy) off I-10, then go south two miles.
ADMISSION	Free admission; ample free parking; outdoors, weather permitting.
FEATURES	Antiques and collectibles, crafts, furniture, jewelry, new and used merchandise, fresh produce—"anything goes." Averages up to several hundred vendors. Food is not served on the premises, but there are grocery stores nearby. This is a family-oriented market that attracts vendors throughout the Southwest.
RATES	Call for rates (which start at less than $10 per space per day); overnights are OK. Reservations are recommended.
CONTACT	Bud Gray, 13480 West Highway 84, Casa Grande, AZ 85222.
PHONE	(520) 836-1934

NFMA Member

MESA: Mesa Market Place Swap Meet

WHEN	Every Friday, Saturday, and Sunday, 7:00 A.M. to 4:00 P.M. A new market.
WHERE	At the corner of Baseline and Signal Butte Roads.
ADMISSION	Free admission; ample free parking; under cover, rain or shine.
FEATURES	Antiques and collectibles, new and used merchandise, clothing, produce, plants, and more. Averages up to its capacity of 1,600 vendors. Food is served on the premises.
RATES	$26.52 per 10'×30' space (includes parking space). Reserve well in advance (waiting list); call Wednesday at 9:00 A.M.
CONTACT	Tricia Curran, Manager, or Sharon Hooks, 10550 East Baseline, Mesa, AZ 85208.
PHONE	(602) 380-5572 or (602) 380-7467 (380-SHOP)
FAX	(602) 380-5578
WEB	www.mesamarket.com

NFMA Member

PHOENIX: Fairgrounds Antique Market

WHEN	Third weekend of every month (except October): Saturday, 9:00 A.M. to 5:00 P.M. and Sunday, 10:00 A.M. to 4:00 P.M. In operation since 1986.
WHERE	At the Arizona State Fairgrounds, at 19th Avenue and McDowell Road. Take the McDowell exit off I-17 and drive east one mile, or take the 19th Avenue exit off westbound I-10 and go north one-quarter mile.
ADMISSION	Admission $2 per person; free admission for children fourteen and under; parking for several thousand cars at $5 per car; indoors, rain or shine.
FEATURES	Antiques and collectibles, books, vintage clothing, coins and stamps, crafts, dolls, used furniture, jewelry, porcelain, toys, used merchandise, and a lot more. Averages 100 to 200 vendors. Snacks and hot meals are served on the premises. Arizona's largest monthly collector's market, with as many as 60,000 shoppers daily during the busy winter season.
RATES	$75 per 8'×10½' space per weekend, and $45 for each additional space. Prepaid reservations are required a week in advance.
CONTACT	Jack Black Enterprises, P.O. Box 61172, Phoenix, AZ 85082-1172.
PHONE	(800) 678-9987 or (602) 943-1766 (in Arizona)
FAX	(602) 997-4686

E-MAIL   arthur@jackblack.com
WEB   www.jackblack.com

NFMA Member

PHOENIX: Paradise Valley Swap Meet

WHEN   Every Friday, Saturday, and Sunday, 5:00 A.M. to 3:00 P.M.
           In operation since the mid-1970s.
WHERE   At 2414 East Union Hills Drive; go north on Cave Creek
           Road to Union Hills Drive, and the market is on the north-
           east corner.
ADMISSION Free admission; free parking for up to 150 cars; outdoors,
           weather permitting.
FEATURES   Antiques and collectibles, new and vintage clothing, furni-
           ture, jewelry, fresh produce, pets, and new merchandise; also
           real estate brokers and palm readers. Averages 50 to 125
           vendors. Snack bar on premises.
RATES $10 per space per day; $15 for a corner space. Reservations are
           recommended; call on Thursday or Friday between 10:00 A.M.
           and 1:00 P.M.
CONTACT   Viola Cirio, 2414 East Union Hills Drive, Phoenix, AZ
           85024.
PHONE   (602) 569-0052

PHOENIX: Phoenix Park 'N' Swap

WHEN   Every Wednesday, 4:00 P.M. to 10:00 P.M.; every Friday,
           6:00 A.M. to 2:00 P.M., and every Saturday and Sunday, 6:00
           A.M. to 4:00 P.M. In operation since 1961.
WHERE   At 3801 East Washington Street, at the southwest corner of
           40th Street.
ADMISSION Admission $1 per person (free on Friday); ample free park-
           ing; outdoors and under cover, rain or shine.
FEATURES   Collectibles, books, clothing, kitchenware, Southwestern
           crafts, jewelry, new merchandise, and garage-sale items—
           "everything you can think of from A to Z." Average 800 to
           2,000 vendors. Snacks and hot meals are served on the
           premises. The staff are friendly and run a "smooth opera-
           tion." An "in-house carnival" operates from October through

	May, and there is a classic-car swap the second Sunday of every month.
RATES	From $10 per space on Wednesday, $5 on Friday, or $15 on Saturday or Sunday. Reservations are recommended.
CONTACT	Karlene Wieland, Marketing Director, 3801 East Washington Street, Phoenix, AZ 85031-1796.
PHONE	(800)772-0852 or (602) 273-1250 (ext. 46)
FAX	(602) 273-7375
E-MAIL	ppns0010@aol.com
WEB	www.americanparknswap.com

  NFMA Member

PRESCOTT: Peddlers Pass

WHEN	Every Friday, Saturday, and Sunday, 8:00 A.M. to 4:00 P.M. In operation since 1987.
WHERE	At 2201 Clubhouse Drive, six miles east of Prescott on Highway 69.
ADMISSION	Free admission; free parking for up to 700 cars; outdoors, weather permitting (there is an indoor farmers market).
FEATURES	Antiques and collectibles, new and vintage clothing, coins and stamps, crafts, new merchandise, fresh produce, jewelry items. Averages 200 to 275 vendors. Snacks and hot meals are served on the premises. An old-time flea and farmers market.
RATES	From $8 per 20'×20' space per day; add $2 per day for corner spaces; electricity $4 per day, more for largest spaces. Reservations are recommended during peak season (April through October).
CONTACT	Robert H. Scott or Suzy Arnold, 2201 Clubhouse Drive, Prescott, AZ 86301.
PHONE	(520) 775-4117 (office) or (520) 778-5299 (home)

NFMA Member

TUCSON: Tanque Verde Swap Meet

WHEN	Every Thursday and Friday, 3:00 A.M. to 11:00 P.M. and every Saturday and Sunday, 7:00 A.M. to 11:00 P.M. In operation since the mid-1970s.

WHERE	At 4100 South Palo Verde Road. Take Palo Verde exit north off I-10 and go about one-half mile; market will be on the left.
ADMISSION	Free admission; ample parking; outdoors, year-round.
FEATURES	Antiques and collectibles, books, new and vintage clothing, coins and stamps, kitchenware, crafts, furniture, jewelry, new and used merchandise, porcelain, fresh produce, and toys. Averages up to a capacity of 800 vendors. Cafeteria and snack concessions are on the premises. More than 50,000 shoppers every weekend.
RATES	From $12 to $16 per space, depending on size and location (spaces start at 11'×26'). Reservations are not required.
CONTACT	Ken Fiore, P.O. Box 19095, Tucson, AZ 85731-9095.
PHONE	(520) 294-4252
FAX	(520) 294-2358
E-MAIL	tvsm@flash.net
WEB	www.flash.net~tvsm

 NFMA Member

YUMA: Arizona Avenue Swap Meet

WHEN	Daily, 8:00 A.M. to 5:00 P.M. In operation since the mid-1970s.
WHERE	At 1749 Arizona Avenue.
ADMISSION	Free admission; free parking for up to 150 cars; outdoors, weather permitting.
FEATURES	Antiques and collectibles, books, new and vintage clothing, kitchenware, crafts, used furniture, jewelry, new and used merchandise, fresh produce, and toys. Averages 75 to a capacity of 130 vendors. Snacks and hot meals are served on the premises.
RATES	$6 per 18'×20' space per day or $25 per week; tables are available at 50¢ each. Reservations are not required.
CONTACT	Bob Butcher, Manager, 1749 Arizona Avenue, Yuma, AZ 85365.
PHONE	(602) 343-1837
FAX	
E-MAIL	
WEB	
NFMA	No

File Under: Serendipity

Someone once bought a book in an Amsterdam shop and later found two Rembrandt sketches tucked inside.

In the late 1990s, a collector brought a painting of the HMS *Titanic* to an *Antiques Roadshow* appraiser and said he had purchased it at a shop in Southampton, England. It was an undistinguished painting, but the frame also contained an original *Titanic* luncheon menu from April 14, 1912, the day it sank. The appraiser said this menu is the only such menu known to have survived intact and estimated its worth at between $75,000 and $100,000. Even before the film, this *Titanic* find would have been an event.

YUMA: Yuma Park 'N' Swap

WHEN	Every Friday through Sunday, plus Thursday during winter, 6:00 A.M. to 4:00 P.M.
WHERE	At 4000 South Fourth Avenue.
ADMISSION	Ample free parking; year-round.
FEATURES	Just about everything imaginable. Averages up to a capacity of 900 vendors. This market claims to be the largest in southwestern Arizona and draws as many as 30,000 on weekends.
RATES	From $10 to $15 per 11'×21' space depending on location.
CONTACT	Bill Gresser, 4000 South Fourth Avenue, Yuma, AZ 85365.
PHONE	(800) 722-6811 (outside Arizona) or (520) 726-4655
FAX	(520) 344-0115
E-MAIL	bill@gresser.com
WEB	www.ypns.com
NFMA	Yes

★ Batesville

🛡️40

🛡️40

🛡️55

⭐ LITTLE ROCK

Hot Springs ★

🛡️30

ARKANSAS

BATESVILLE: The Market

WHEN	Every Friday, Saturday, and Sunday, 9:00 A.M. to 6:00 P.M. (opens 11:00 A.M. on Sunday). In operation since 1980.
WHERE	At 310 West Main Street (lower Main) in downtown Batesville.
ADMISSION	Free admission; street parking; indoors, year-round.
FEATURES	Treasure of all kinds; antiques and collectibles, new and vintage clothing, coins and stamps, kitchenware, crafts, fresh produce, and jewelry. Averages 100 to a capacity of 140 vendors. Snacks and hot meals are served on the premises. Where the buyers buy and the sellers sell. Air-conditioned comfort.
RATES	$10 per 10'×12' space per day or $25 for three days or $60 per month. Reservations are not required.
CONTACT	Mark Davis, 310 West Main Street, Batesville, AR 72501.
PHONE	(870) 793-7508

HOT SPRINGS: Hot Springs Flea Market

WHEN	Daily, 10:00 A.M. to 5:00 P.M. In operation since the late 1980s.
WHERE	At 2138 Higdon Ferry Road, less than one block off Highway 7, across from the Hot Springs Mall; follow billboards and directional signs.
ADMISSION	Free admission; free parking for up to 200 cars; indoors, outdoors, and under cover, rain or shine.
FEATURES	Antiques and collectibles, books, new and vintage clothing, kitchenware, crafts, porcelain, jewelry, furniture, coins and stamps, and fresh produce in season. Averages up to 100 vendors. Food is not served on the premises. A growing eleven-acre market with plans for additional booth space and parking; there are also plans for a summer farmers market.
RATES	About $7.50 per day for an outdoor stall or an 8-foot table indoors. Reservations are recommended.
CONTACT	Doyce Garner, 2138 Higdon Ferry Road, Hot Springs, AR 71913.
PHONE	(501) 525-9927 or (501) 520-4016

A Sampling of Flea-Bitten Vanity Plates

FLEAFXR
FLEA I
ANTEEKS
ARTFCTS
I REHAB
TINKER
MR SIGN

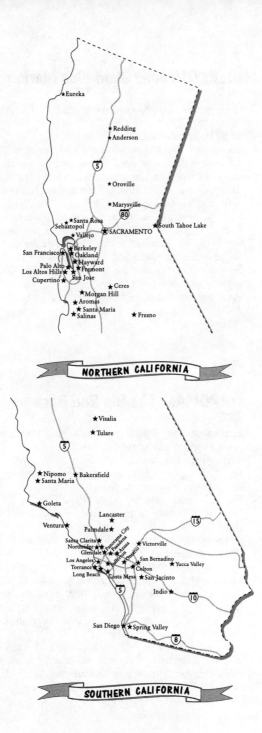

★ Eureka

★ Redding
★ Anderson

(5)

★ Oroville

★ Marysville

(80)

★ Santa Rosa
Sebastopol ★
★ Vallejo   ★ SACRAMENTO   ★ South Tahoe Lake

★ Berkeley
San Francisco ★ ★ Oakland
Palo Alto ★ ★ Hayward
Los Altos Hills ★ ★ Fremont
Cupertino ★ ★ San Jose
                     ★ Ceres
          ★ Morgan Hill
          ★ Aromas
          ★ Santa Maria
          ★ Salinas   ★ Fresno

NORTHERN CALIFORNIA

★ Visalia

★ Tulare

(5)

★ Nipomo   ★ Bakersfield
★ Santa Maria

★ Goleta

                 Lancaster
                    ★   (15)
Ventura ★   ★ Palmdale
Santa Clarita ★   ★ Victorville
Northridge ★ ★ Panorama City
Glendale ★ ★ Pasadena
              ★ Azusa
Los Angeles ★ ★ ★ Ontario   ★ San Bernardino
Torrance ★ ★ Fullerton   ★ Colton   ★ Yucca Valley
Long Beach ★ ★ Costa Mesa   ★ San Jacinto
              (5)   Indio ★   (10)

San Diego ★ ★ Spring Valley
                    (8)

SOUTHERN CALIFORNIA

ANDERSON: Jolly Giant Flea Market

WHEN Every weekend, 6:00 A.M. to 4:00 P.M. In operation since the 1970s.

WHERE At 6719 Eastside Road.

ADMISSION Admission 50¢ per person or $1.35 per family; admission for seniors 35¢; nine acres of parking (free with admission); indoors year-round and outdoors, weather permitting.

FEATURES Antiques and collectibles, automotive equipment, books, new and vintage clothing, kitchenware, crafts, furniture, jewelry, new and used merchandise, porcelain, and tools. Averages 150 to 200 vendors. Snacks and hot meals are served on the premises. A clean and friendly market and one of the biggest between Sacramento and Portland, Oregon.

RATES $6 per 10'×10' space on Saturday, $8 on Sunday. Reservations are not required.

CONTACT Patti or Jim Smith, 6719 Eastside Road, Anderson, CA 96007.

PHONE (916) 365-6458

AROMAS: The Big Red Barn

WHEN Every weekend, 7:00 A.M. to 5:00 P.M. (antiques shops are open every Wednesday through Sunday). In operation for over twenty-five years.

WHERE At 1000 Highway 101, seventeen miles north of Salinas and seventeen miles south of Gilroy.

ADMISSION Free admission; twenty acres of parking at $3 per car on Sunday (Saturday is free); indoors and outdoors, rain or shine.

FEATURES Antiques and collectibles (baseball cards, bottles, coins and stamps, Disneyana, etc.), new and vintage clothing, kitchenware, crafts, furniture, glassware, jewelry, new merchandise, tools, and fresh produce. Average close to 300 vendors. Snacks and hot meals, including outdoor barbecue, are served on the premises. Friendly, family-style flea market with indoor antiques shops, an antique carousel, and a small animal auction on Saturday.

RATES $10 on Saturday or $25 on Sunday; $35 for Saturday and Sunday. Reservations are recommended a week in advance.

CONTACT Debra Hagan, Director of Operations, 1000 Highway 101, Aromas, CA 95004.

PHONE (831) 422-1271 or (831) 726-3101

FAX   (831) 726-1108
E-MAIL   redbarn@pacbell.net

AZUSA: Azusa Swap Meet

WHEN	Every Sunday, 5:00 A.M. to 4:00 P.M. In operation for over twenty-eight years.
WHERE	At 675 East Foothill Boulevard, a mile north of the 210 Freeway (take the Azusa Avenue exit), then a half-mile east on Foothill Boulevard.
ADMISSION	Admission $1 per person (under age twelve or over age fifty-five are admitted free); free parking for up to 1,700 cars; outdoors, rain or shine.
FEATURES	Antiques and collectibles, books, new and vintage clothing, kitchenware, crafts, furniture, jewelry, fresh produce, and new and used tools; lots of new merchandise. Averages 590 to a capacity of 885 vendors. Snacks and hot meals are served on the premises. Real estate and loan offices on the premises.
RATES	$24 per space per Sunday or $85 per month. Reserve a week in advance.
CONTACT	James Edwards, Proprietor, 675 East Foothill Boulevard, Azusa, CA 91702.
PHONE	(714) 640-4603; evenings or day of market call Mr. Cisneros, manager, at (626) 334-8915.
FAX	(626) 334-4813

BAKERSFIELD: Fairgrounds Swap Meet

WHEN	Every Tuesday, Saturday, and Sunday, 6:00 A.M. to 3.00 P.M. In operation since 1983.
WHERE	At the corner of Union and Ming Avenues. Take Fairgrounds exit off Highway 99, or take Union Avenue exit off Highway 58.
ADMISSION	Admission 75¢ per person on Saturday, $1 on Sunday, and 50¢ on Tuesday; ample free parking; outdoors, year-round.
FEATURES	Antiques and collectibles, books, new and vintage clothing, coins and stamps, kitchenware, crafts, furniture, jewelry, new and used merchandise, porcelain, fresh produce, tools, toys, Western tack. Averages 300 to 350 vendors. Snacks

and hot meals are served on the premises. Just a neat market that appeals to all.

RATES $10 per space on Saturday, $12 on Sunday, and $6 on Tuesday (corner spaces $3 extra per day); electricity is available at $3 per day. Reservations are not required.

CONTACT Ed Murphy, 312 Stable Avenue, Bakersfield, CA 93307.

PHONE (805) 833-1733 or (805) 397-1504

BERKELEY: Berkeley Flea Market

WHEN Every weekend, 7:00 A.M. to 7:00 P.M. In operation for decades.

WHERE At the Ashby BART Station parking lot (at Martin Luther King Jr. Way and Ashby).

ADMISSION Free admission; limited parking in a nearby lot; outdoors, year-round.

FEATURES Antiques and collectibles, crafts, household goods, and produce. Average up to 300 vendors. An international selection of foods is served on the premises. This market claims to be the Bay Area's most diverse, and proceeds go "back to the community"; after all, it's Berkeley, right? Owned and operated by a consortium of nonprofit organizations.

RATES $20 per space per day. Reservations are recommended; call on Thursday between 5:00 P.M. to 7:00 P.M. or on Friday between noon and 3:00 P.M.

CONTACT Charisse at Community Services United, 1937 Ashby Avenue, Berkeley, CA 94703.

PHONE (510) 644-0744

FAX (510) 540-6970

E-MAIL findme@berkeleyfleamarket.com

WEB www.berkeleyfleamarket.com

CERES: Ceres Flea Market

WHEN Every weekend, 6:00 A.M. to 3:00 P.M. In operation for over fifteen years.

WHERE At 1651 East Whitmore Avenue, off Highway 99.

ADMISSION Admission $1.50 per carload on Sunday, free on Saturday; parking is free; outdoors and under cover, rain or shine.

FEATURES   Baseball cards, books, new and vintage clothing, kitchenware, crafts, furniture, jewelry, new and used merchandise, fresh produce, and toys. Averages 400 to 450 vendors. Snacks and hot meals are served on the premises. The motto of this flea market is, "People Pleasing People."

RATES   From $5 to $10 per space on Saturday, or from $22 to $30 on Sunday. Reserve a week in advance.

CONTACT   Joann Fluharty, P.O. Box 35, Ceres, CA 95307.

PHONE   (209) 537-9827

FAX   (209) 537-6852

COLTON: Maclin's Open-Air Market

WHEN   Every Thursday and Saturday, 5:30 A.M. to 3:00 P.M.; furniture auction every Thursday at 10:00 A.M. In operation since the 1930s.

WHERE   At 1902 West Valley Boulevard, between the Riverside Avenue and Pepper Avenue exits off I-10, just north of the freeway.

ADMISSION   Admission 50¢ per person; ample free parking; outdoors, rain or shine.

FEATURES   Antiques and collectibles, clothing, discount merchandise, kitchenware, crafts, furniture, jewelry, porcelain, fresh produce, toys, watches, and used merchandise. Averages 150 to 200 vendors. There is a Market Grill and an Outdoor Cactus Cantina on the premises. A high-volume market with good amenities—targeted to bargain hunters. Kiddie rides and ponies; live music for the market; antiques and furniture auction every Thursday, rain or shine.

RATES   From $15 per 10'×10' space on Saturday, and from $25 Sunday through Tuesday. Reservations are not required.

CONTACT   Paula Stevens, 1902 West Valley Boulevard, Colton, CA 92324.

PHONE   (800) 222-7467 (222-SHOP) or (909) 877-3700

FAX   (909) 988-8041

COSTA MESA: Orange County Fairgrounds Swap Meet

WHEN   Every weekend, except when the Orange County Fair is run-
                ning, 7:00 A.M. to 4:00 P.M. In operation since 1969.
WHERE   At the Orange County Fairgrounds, at 88 Fair Drive.
ADMISSION   Admission $1 per person; ample parking at $3 per car; out-
                doors, year-round.
FEATURES   Almost entirely new merchandise, though you can find "any-
                thing under the sun." Averages close to 1,000 vendors. Food is
                served on the premises.
RATES   From $47 per space per day. Reserve the preceding Tuesday.
CONTACT   Swap Meet Office, 88 Fair Drive, Costa Mesa, CA 92626.
PHONE   (949) 723-6660
FAX   (949) 723-6660
E-MAIL   telphil@earthlink.net
WEB   www.ocmarketplace.com

CUPERTINO: De Anza College Flea Market

WHEN   First Saturday of every month, 8:00 A.M. to 4:00 P.M. In
                operation since the late 1960s.
WHERE   At 21250 Stevens Creek Boulevard on the college campus.
ADMISSION   Free admission; ample parking at $3 per car; outdoors, rain
                or shine.
FEATURES   Antiques, collectibles, and new and used merchandise.
                Averages 700 to 925 vendors. Food is served on the prem-
                ises.
RATES $25 per space per day. Reservations are required.
CONTACT   Casey, Manager, 21250 Stevens Creek Boulevard, Cuper-
                tino, CA 95014.
PHONE   (408) 864-8946 or (408) 864-8414

A Sampling of Flea-Bitten Bumper Stickers

FLEA MARKET MANIAC
BORN TO SHOP
CAUTION: THIS CAR STOPS AT ALL GARAGE SALES
SHOPPER ON BOARD
LICENSED JUNK COLLECTOR

EUREKA: Flea Mart by the Bay

WHEN
Every Friday, Saturday, and Sunday, 8:00 A.M. to 8.00 P.M. In operation for over fifteen years.

WHERE
At 1200 West Del Norte. Turn off Highway 101 onto Del Norte (at the Motel 6) and head west to the market.

ADMISSION
Free admission; free parking for up to 500 cars; indoors, year-round.

FEATURES
Antiques and collectibles, books, vintage clothing, kitchenware, crafts, fishing supplies, used furniture, glassware, jewelry, new and used merchandise, records, and toys. Averages 50 to a capacity of 125 vendors. Snacks and hot meals are served on the premises. Near a public fishing pier and picnic area.

RATES
$5 per table per day, or $10 for all three days; monthly rates are $56 per 8'×10' booth or $112 per 8'×20' booth. Reservations are not required.

CONTACT
Leah Patton, Manager, 1200 West Del Norte Street, Eureka, CA 95503.

PHONE
(707) 443-3103

FREMONT: Ohlone College Super Flea Market

WHEN	Second Saturday of every month, 8:00 A.M. to 3.00 P.M. In operation since 1986.
WHERE	At 436000 Mission Boulevard; take the 880 Parkway east to Mission, then left to Ohlone.
ADMISSION	Free admission; parking at $1.50 per car; outdoors, year-round.
FEATURES	Garage-sale items, collectibles, and crafts—typical flea market fare. Averages 250 to 350 vendors. Food is served on the premises. This is a pleasant market in a clean, attractive setting.
RATES	From $25 per space per day if reserved, or $30 on same day. Reserve a week in advance.
CONTACT	Elaine Nagel, 436000 Mission Boulevard, Fremont, CA 94539.
PHONE	(510) 659-6285
FAX	(510) 659-6264
E-MAIL	enagel@ohlone.cc.ca.cc
WEB	www.ohlone.cc.ca.us/org

FRESNO: Big Fresno Flea Market

WHEN	Every weekend, 6:00 A.M. to 3:00 P.M. In operation for more than a decade.
WHERE	At the Fresno Fairgrounds, at 1121 South-Champ.
ADMISSION	Free admission; ample free parking; outdoors, rain or shine.
FEATURES	Miscellaneous collectibles and used merchandise. Averages close to 200 vendors. Food is served on the premises.
RATES	$17 per 20'×20' space per day. Reservations are recommended.
CONTACT	Manager, 1121 South Champ, Fresno, CA 93702.
PHONE	(209) 268-3646

FRESNO: Cherry Avenue Auction

WHEN	Every Tuesday and Saturday, 6:00 A.M. to 4:00 P.M. In operation since 1932.

WHERE	At 4640 South Cherry Avenue, between Central and American Avenues. From the south, take Highway 99 to Manning Avenue, then go west to Cherry Avenue, then north to market; from the north, take Highway 99 to Jensen off-ramp, then west to Cherry Avenue, then south about three miles.
ADMISSION	Free admission; parking for up to 2,500 cars at $1 to $2 per car; outdoors, year-round.
FEATURES	Antiques and collectibles, books, new and vintage clothing, kitchenware, crafts, furniture, fresh produce, tools, and toys. Averages 700 to 1,000 vendors. American, Mexican, and Chinese food is served on the premises. Auctions are held at 9:00 A.M. to 2:00 P.M.; a video arcade, pony rides, and a carousel are also nearby.
RATES	$8 for two spaces on Tuesday, from $10 to $20 for one space on Saturday; call for monthly rates. Reservations are required for monthly spaces only.
CONTACT	W. D. Mitchell, Owner, or Mitch Burson or Neil Burson, Managers, 4640 South Cherry Avenue, Fresno, CA 93706.
PHONE	(209) 266-9856
FAX	(209) 266-9439

FULLERTON: Trouble-Shooters Antiques and Collectibles Roundup

WHEN	Semiannually on the first Sundays in May and October, 9:00 A.M. to 3:00 P.M. In operation for over twenty years.
WHERE	At "Cal State Fullerton." Take Nutwood exit off 57 Freeway and go west (follow signs).
ADMISSION	Admission $5 per person; free admission for children under twelve; free parking; outdoors, rain or shine.
FEATURES	Antiques and collectibles of all types—no new or craft items are allowed. Averages close to 1,000 vendors. Snacks and hot meals are served on the premises. All profits benefit the *Register* Charities (*Orange County Register* newspaper).
RATES	$50 per 8'×18' space per day. Reservations are recommended; events regularly sell out.
CONTACT	R. G. Canning Attractions, P.O. Box 400, Maywood, CA 90270-0400.
PHONE	(323) 560-7469 (560-SHOW), ext. 15; office hours are Monday and Wednesday from 10:00 A.M. to 5:00 P.M.
FAX	(323) 560-5924

E-MAIL   rgc@rgcshows.com
WEB   www.rgcshows.com

GLENDALE: Glendale Community College Swap Meet

WHEN   Third Sunday of every month, 8:00 A.M. to 3:00 P.M. In operation since 1994.
WHERE   On the Glendale 2 Freeway (take Mountain Street exit).
ADMISSION   Free admission; ample free parking; outdoors, year-round.
FEATURES   Antiques and collectibles, used items, clothing, furniture, and toys. Averages 150 to 200 vendors. Food is served on the premises.
RATES $35 per space per day if preregistered, or $45 unreserved. Reservations are not required; call by Thursday to preregister.
CONTACT   Jane Harris, 1122 East Garfield Avenue, Glendale, CA 91205.
PHONE   (818) 240-1000 (ext. 5805) or (818) 548-0864 (ext. 5038), Monday through Thursday.
FAX   (818) 548-6216
E-MAIL   jharris@glendale.cc.ca.us
WEB   www.glendale.cc.ca.us/cse

GOLETA: Santa Barbara Swap Meet

WHEN   Every Sunday, 7:00 A.M. to 2:00 P.M. In operation for over twenty-seven years.
WHERE   At 907 South Kellogg (call for recorded directions).
ADMISSION   Admission $1 per person (free for children under twelve); parking for up to six hundred cars at $1 per car; outdoors, weather permitting.
FEATURES   Antiques and collectibles, books, new and vintage clothing, coins and stamps, kitchenware, crafts, used furniture, jewelry, new merchandise, porcelain, fresh produce, and toys—mostly garage-sale items and used merchandise. Averages 230 to 270 vendors. Snacks and hot meals are served on the premises. If it's legal, you can find it here.
RATES $17 per 16'×16' space per day; weekly and monthly reservation fees are an additional $10 and $25, respectively.

Reservations are not required; reserve on Sunday at the snack bar.
CONTACT   Manager, 907 South Kellogg Boulevard, Goleta, CA 93117.
PHONE   (805) 964-9050 or (805) 967-4591 on Sunday
FAX   (805) 967-4591

HAYWARD: Chabot College (ASCC) Flea Market

WHEN   Third Saturday of every month, 8:00 A.M. to 4:00 P.M. In operation since 1985.
WHERE   At 25555 Hesperian Boulevard. From the north, take Highway 880 South to Winton Avenue West exit, go to third light, then left onto Hesperian; from the south, take 880 North to Jackson Street, Highway 92, and go west toward San Mateo Bridge to Hesperian Boulevard North exit.
ADMISSION Free admission; ample free parking; outdoors, rain or shine.
FEATURES   Collectibles, crafts, and household items. Average 200 to 300 vendors. Food is served on the premises. Benefits the college's student activities.
RATES $20 per space per day when reserved in advance, or $25 per space on the day. Reservations are recommended—call for information packet.
CONTACT   Joanne Simonson, Manager, 25555 Hesperian Boulevard, Hayward, CA 94545.
PHONE   (510) 786-6918 or (510) 786-6914
FAX   (510) 265-5739
E-MAIL   jsimonson@clpccd.cc.ca.us
WEB   www.chabot.cc.ca.us

INDIO: Maclin's Indio Open-Air Market

WHEN   Every Wednesday and Saturday evenings, 4:00 P.M. to 10:00 P.M. Duration of market not reported.
WHERE   At 46-350 Arabia Street, directly behind the Riverside County Fairgrounds. Take Monroe Street off I-10 East, then go right onto Indio Boulevard (Highway 111) and then left to Arabia.
ADMISSION Free admission; ample free parking; outdoors, year-round.
FEATURES   New and used items, furniture, fresh produce, crafts, jew-

elry, and much more. Averages close to 100 vendors. Snacks are served on the premises.

RATES $17 per space on Wednesday and $15 on Saturday. Reservations are not required.

CONTACT   Mario, 46-350 Arabia Avenue, Indio, CA 92201.

PHONE   (800) 222-7467 (222-SHOP) or (909) 984-5131

FAX   (909) 988-8041

LANCASTER: Lancaster Chamber of Commerce Semi-Annual Flea Market

WHEN   Semiannually, on the third Sunday in May and the first Sunday in October, 9:00 A.M. to 4:00 P.M. In operation since 1966.

WHERE   At 155 East Avenue I. Take Avenue I exit in Lancaster and go east approximately five miles, then go one block north from the intersection of Division Street and Avenue I.

ADMISSION   Admission $4 per person, $2 for seniors; free for children under thirteen; ample parking at $2.50 per car; indoors and outdoors, rain or shine.

FEATURES   Antiques and collectibles, books, new and vintage clothing, coins and stamps, kitchenware, crafts, furniture, jewelry, new and used merchandise, fresh produce, and toys. Averages 500 to 600 vendors. Food is available on the premises. Pony rides and petting zoo for the kids.

RATES   From $60 to $70 per 10'×10' space or $50 per 15'×15' space indoors, and $20 per 20'×25' space outdoors. Reservations are on a first-come, first-served basis (usually sells out).

CONTACT   Lancaster Chamber of Commerce, 554 West Lancaster Boulevard, Lancaster, CA 93534-2534.

PHONE   (805) 948-4518 (office hours are Monday through Friday, 9:00 A.M. to 5:00 P.M.)

FAX   (805) 949-1212

E-MAIL   lcoc@hughes.net

WEB   www.lancasterchamber.org

LONG BEACH: Outdoor Antique and Collectible Market

WHEN	Third Sunday of every month (plus added events in May and October), 8:00 A.M. to 3:00 P.M. In operation since 1982.
WHERE	At the Long Beach Veterans Stadium, twenty minutes from downtown Los Angeles. Take Lakewood Boulevard North exit off Freeway 405, then turn right onto Lakewood Boulevard and continue to Conant Street.
ADMISSION	Admission $4.50 per person (early admission at 5:30 A.M. is $10); free for children under twelve; free parking for up to fifteen thousand cars; outdoors, rain or shine.
FEATURES	Antiques and collectibles only—a wide assortment of art deco, vintage clothing, dolls, furniture, glassware, jewelry, pottery, primitives, quilts, and toys. Averages close to 800 or more vendors. Snacks and "stadium food" are served on the premises.
RATES	From $50 to $70 per space per day. Reservations are recommended.
CONTACT	Donald or Lynn Moger, Americana Enterprises, P.O. Box 69219, Los Angeles, CA 90069.
PHONE	(323) 655-5703

LOS ALTOS HILLS: Foothill College Flea Market

WHEN	Third Saturday of every month, 8:00 A.M. to 3:00 P.M. in operation since 1983.
WHERE	At 12345 El Monte Road, Parking Lot F.
ADMISSION	Free admission; metered parking at $2 per car (bring quarters); outdoors, year-round.
FEATURES	Antiques, collectibles, garage-sale items, art, jewelry, and garden items. Averages 100 to 200 vendors. Food is served on the premises. Benefits Foothill College Theater Guild.
RATES	$15 per 16'×16' ($12 for students and seniors 65+, advance reservations only), or $20 per corner space. Reservations are recommended, but standby is also available.
CONTACT	Charlotte Davis, Manager, 12345 El Monte Road, Los Altos Hills, CA 94022.
PHONE	(650) 948-6417
WEB	www.secondhand.com/shops/foothillflea

LOS ANGELES: Alameda Swap Meet

WHEN	Daily (except Tuesday): weekdays, 10:00 A.M. to 7:00 P.M. and weekends, 8:00 A.M. to 7:00 P.M. In operation since 1985.
WHERE	At 4501 South Alameda Street, between 45th Street and Slauson.
ADMISSION	Free admission; free parking for up to 500 cars; indoors, year-round.
FEATURES	New merchandise only: clothing, kitchenware, crafts, electronics, furniture, jewelry, toys, and various merchandise, plus fresh produce. Averages close to 300 vendors. Snacks and hot meals are served on the premises. This one's not for used or antique merchandise. Live entertainment on weekends.
RATES	Call for rates (waiting list). Transient vendors are not accommodated.
CONTACT	Romeo Ramos, 4501 South Alameda Street, Los Angeles, CA 90058.
PHONE	(323) 233-2764
FAX	(323) 233-2688
E-MAIL	ramos6953@aol.com

MARYSVILLE: Marysville Flea Market

WHEN	Every Sunday, 6:00 A.M. to 4:00 P.M. In operation since the 1950s (under current management since 1980).
WHERE	At 1468 Simpson Lane, off Highway 20.
ADMISSION	Free admission; acres of free parking; indoors year-round and outdoors, weather permitting.
FEATURES	Antiques and collectibles, books, new and vintage clothing, coins and stamps, kitchenware, crafts, used furniture, jewelry, livestock, new and used merchandise, fresh produce, tools, and toys. Averages 75 to a capacity of 250 vendors. Snacks and hot meals are served on the premises. Friendly atmosphere.
RATES	$5 for two tables on Saturday, $10 on Sunday ($15 for a covered space on Sunday). Reservations are not required.
CONTACT	Betty Foster or Richard Sinnott, 1468 Simpson Lane, Marysville, CA 95901.
PHONE	(530) 743-8713

MORGAN HILL: Morgan Hill Flea Market

WHEN   Every weekend, 7:30 A.M. to 6.00 P.M. In operation since 1964.

WHERE   At 140 East Main Avenue. Take Dunne Avenue exit to downtown Morgan Hill, then right on Monterey Street to Main Street, then right on Main and one block from there to market.

ADMISSION   Free admission; free parking; outdoors, rain or shine.

FEATURES   Antiques and collectibles, new and used merchandise, new and vintage clothing, kitchenware, crafts, and fresh produce. Averages 100 to 125 vendors. There is a snack bar on the premises.

RATES $12 per space on Saturday, $13 per space on Sunday. Reservations are on a first-come, first-served basis.

CONTACT   Jim Ahlin, 140 East Main Avenue, Morgan Hill, CA 95037-3734.

PHONE   (408) 779-3809

NIPOMO: Nipomo Swap Meet and Buyers Mart

WHEN   Every Friday, Saturday, and Sunday, 6:00 A.M. to 6:00 P.M. In operation since 1974.

WHERE   At 263 North Frontage Road (101 Freeway); off ramp is Tefft Street.

ADMISSION   Free admission; ample parking at $1 per car on Saturday or $2 Sunday (free on Friday); indoors year-round and outdoors, weather permitting.

FEATURES   Antiques and collectibles, books, new clothing, coins and stamps, kitchenware, crafts, furniture, jewelry, new and used merchandise, fresh produce, and toys. Averages 300 to a capacity of 400 vendors. Snacks and hot meals are served on the premises.

RATES $3 per 14'×18' space on Friday, $6 on Saturday, and $9 on Sunday ($15 for all three days); monthly rates indoors. Reservations are recommended.

CONTACT   Carnival Marketplaces, 263 North Frontage Road, Nipomo, CA 93444.

PHONE   (805) 929-7000

FAX   (805) 929-7007

E-MAIL   Swapmeet@calcoast.com

WEB   www.swapmeet.hypermart.net

NORTHRIDGE: Northridge Antique Flea Market

WHEN
Fourth Sunday of every month, plus the fifth Sunday of the month (whenever there is one), 8:00 A.M. to 3:00 P.M. (early-birds admitted as early as 5:00 A.M.). In operation since 1995.

WHERE
At Cal State Northridge, on Devonshire at Lindley. From the 405 Freeway take Devonshire west to Lindley. From the northbound 5 or 210 take the 188 west to Balboa, then south on Balboa to Devonshire, then west to Lindley.

ADMISSION
Admission $3 per person (earlybird admission $5); free parking; outdoors, rain or shine.

FEATURES
Antiques and collectibles, crafts, clocks and watches, vintage clothing, furniture, jewelry, and toys. Averages 150 to 300 vendors. Food is served on the premises.

RATES
$50 per space. Reservations are recommended.

CONTACT
Manager, Antique Attractions, 17041 Lakewood Boulevard, Bellflower, CA 90706.

PHONE
(562) 633-3836

FAX
(562) 408-0496

OAKLAND: Coliseum Swap Meet

WHEN
Daily except Monday (weekends are the big days), 6:00 A.M. to whenever. In operation since around 1980.

WHERE
At 5401 Coliseum Way, one block north of the Coliseum Sports Complex. Take the High Street exit off Freeway 880.

ADMISSION
Admission $1 per person on weekends; free parking for more than 500 cars; outdoors, weather permitting.

FEATURES
Antiques and collectibles, books, new clothing, furniture, jewelry, new and used merchandise, fresh produce, and toys. Averages up to a capacity of 410 vendors. Snacks and hot meals are served on the premises.

RATES
$5 per space on Tuesday; $10 on Wednesday, Thursday, or Friday; $15 on Saturday; and $18 Sunday. Reservations are not required.

CONTACT
Manager, 5401 Coliseum Way, Oakland, CA 94601.

PHONE
(510) 533-1601

OAKLAND: Nor Cal Swap Meet

WHEN	Every weekend, 7:00 A.M. to 4:00 P.M. In operation since 1989.
WHERE	At Seventh and Fallon Streets in the parking lot (Laney College).
ADMISSION	Admission 50¢ per person; free for children under twelve; free parking for up to 500 cars; outdoors, year-round.
FEATURES	Collectibles, clothing, miscellaneous "junque," new merchandise, and fresh produce. Averages 250 to 400 vendors. Food concession stand on the premises.
RATES	$16 per double space (minimum), $9 per additional space. Reservations are on a first-come, first-served basis.
CONTACT	Manager, 1150 Ballena Boulevard, Suite 250, Alameda, CA 94501.
PHONE	(510) 769-7266
FAX	(510) 521-3972

ONTARIO: Maclin's Ontario Open-Air Market

WHEN	Every Tuesday, Saturday, and Sunday, 5:30 A.M. to 3:00 P.M. (vendors may show up as early as 5:30 A.M.) In operation for over fifty-seven years.
WHERE	At 7407 Riverside Drive at the corner of Campus Avenue, between Euclid and Grove. Go south off the Pomona Freeway (Route 60); freeway off-ramps are Euclid and Grove.
ADMISSION	Admission 50¢ per person; ample free parking; outdoors, rain or shine.
FEATURES	Baseball cards, books, new clothing, comics, kitchenware, crafts, new furniture, jewelry, knives, fresh fish and fresh produce, and baked goods. Averages 200 to 300 vendors. Snacks and hot meals are served at a restaurant on the premises; there is also a full bar with large-screen T.V. Experience shopping the old-fashioned way in laid-back family-style surroundings targeted to bargain hunters. "We're rustic, not backward." Kiddie rides and ponies; live music for the market. Livestock auction every Tuesday, rain or shine.
RATES	From $7 to $20 per 10'×10' space per day or $20 to $35 per 10'×20' space, depending on location, plus a $5 insurance fee. Reservations are not required but can be arranged by calling on the preceding Friday, between 1:00 P.M. and 4:00

P.M.; day of market spaces are rented on a first-come, first-served basis.

CONTACT   Marsha, 7407 Riverside Drive, Ontario, CA 91761.
PHONE   (800) 222-7467 (222-SHOP) or (909) 984-5131
FAX   (909) 988-8041

OROVILLE: Oro Dam Flea Market (aka Chappell's Flea Market)

WHEN   Every weekend, 7:00 A.M. to 4:00 P.M. In operation since 1978.
WHERE   At 1141 Oro Dam Boulevard West.
ADMISSION   Free admission; ample free parking; outdoors, year-round.
FEATURES   Odds and ends. Averages close to 50 vendors. There is a snack bar on the premises. Atmosphere hasn't changed much in twenty-plus years (but the merchandise comes and goes).
RATES $10 for three tables on Saturday, $8 on Sunday. Reservations are recommended.
CONTACT   Manager, 1141 Oro Dam Boulevard West, Oroville, CA 95965.
PHONE   (916) 533-1324

PALMDALE: Antelope Valley Swap Meet at Four Points

WHEN   Every Saturday, 7:00 A.M. to 3:00 P.M., and Sunday, 6:00 A.M. to 4:00 P.M. In operation since the 1970s.
WHERE   At 5550 Pear Blossom Highway at the intersection of Highway 138, 5 miles east of Palmdale.
ADMISSION   Admission $1 per person; free parking for up to 1,500 cars; outdoors, rain or shine.
FEATURES   Antiques and collectibles, books, new and vintage clothing, coins and stamps, kitchenware, crafts, furniture, jewelry, new merchandise, porcelain, fresh produce, and toys. Averages close to 400 vendors. Hot and cold meals (including homemade corn dogs, authentic Mexican food, and biscuits and gravy) are served on the premises. Live country and Western bands on Sundays; pony rides.
RATES $10 per 20'×20' space on Saturday; $15 on Sunday; $20 for both days. Reservations are recommended.

CONTACT   Joyce Bruce, P.O. Box 901807, Palmdale, CA 93590.
PHONE   (661) 273-0456
FAX   (661) 273-5465
WEB   www.swapmeetat4points.com

PALO ALTO: Music Boosters Flea Market

WHEN   Second Saturday of every month, 9:00 A.M. to 3:00 P.M. In
            operation since 1989.
WHERE   At 50 Embarcadero Road at corner of El Camino Real, across
            from the Stanford Stadium.
ADMISSION   Free admission; ample free parking; outdoors, rain or shine.
FEATURES   Collectibles, crafts, and various used merchandise. Averages
            close to 100 vendors. Band members serve barbecued hot
            dogs, hamburgers, etc. Benefits the schools's instrument
            music program.
RATES $20 per two parking spaces ($15 for senior citizens); special
            rates for nonprofit groups. Reserve a month in advance.
CONTACT   Phyllis Smith or Cathy Brown, Managers, 920 Boyce
            Avenue, Palo Alto, CA 94301.
PHONE   (650) 324-3532 (324-FLEA) for recorded message, or (650)
            321-0725 or (650) 321-6783
FAX   (650) 329-9953
E-MAIL   psmith@pausd.palo-alto.ca.us

PANORAMA CITY: Valley Indoor Swap Meet

WHEN   Every Wednesday through Monday (closed Tuesday), 10:00
            A.M. to 6:00 P.M. on weekends and 11:00 A.M. to 7:00 P.M.
            on weekdays. In operation since 1986.
WHERE   At 14650 Parthenia Street, accessible from both the 405 and
            the 101 freeways.
ADMISSION   Free admission; ample free parking; indoors, year-round.
FEATURES   Clothing, jewelry, fresh produce and baked goods, pets,
            and other merchandise. Averages close to 100 vendors.
            There are three snack bars on the premises. The atmos-
            phere is fun filled, with lots of food (and great prices)
            for the whole family. Arcade, beauty salon, carnival-
            style entertainment (including clowns and circus acts),
            music, etc.
RATES $500 per space for four weeks. Reservations are required.

CONTACT   Dena Weingardt or Nora Diaz, 14650 Parthenia Street, Panorama, CA 91402.
PHONE   (818) 893-8234 or (818) 892-0183 or (818) 893-5273
FAX   (818) 894-5676
E-MAIL   info@indoorswap.com
WEB   www.indoorswap.com

PASADENA: Rose Bowl Flea Market

WHEN   Second Sunday of every month, 9:00 A.M. to 3:00 P.M. In operation for over twenty-five years.
WHERE   At the Rose Bowl, at Rosemont and Arroyo, near the junction of Foothill Freeway (210), Ventura Freeway (134), and Pasadena Freeway (110). Follow signs posted in town.
ADMISSION Admission $5 per adult; children under twelve admitted free. Early admission (from 6:00 A.M.) is available at $10. Special group rates; ample free parking; outdoors, rain or shine.
FEATURES   Full spectrum of antiques, collectibles, new and used merchandise (such as furniture, clothing, household items, and "junque"), kitchenware, crafts, and just about anything else you can imagine. Averages close to 2,200 vendors. Hot meals are available. Unquestionably California's largest flea market, and among the largest and most colorful in the world, with an average daily customer attendance of approximately 20,000. Good celebrity watching!
RATES   From $30 to $90 per space per day. Reservations are recommended sixty days in advance for better locations.
CONTACT   R. G. Canning Attractions, P.O. Box 400, Maywood, CA 90270-0400.
PHONE   (323) 560-7469 (560-SHOW), ext. 11; office hours are Monday and Wednesday from 10:00 A.M. to 5:00 P.M.
FAX   (323) 560-5924
E-MAIL   rgc@rgcshows.com
WEB   www.rgcshows.com

Celebrity Spottings: Pasadena, California

Celebrity Spottings at the Rose Bowl Flea Market is like shooting fish in a barrel. Over the years, sightings have included the following:

★ Michelle Pfeiffer (haggled for pair of shorts . . . and won)
★ Geena Davis
★ John Malkovich
★ Cher (identified by tattoo)
★ Diane Keaton
★ Whoopi Goldberg (author of *Book*)

REDDING: Epperson Brothers Auction and Flea Market

WHEN	Every weekend, 7:00 A.M. to 5:00 P.M. Auctions are held every Wednesday at 6:30 P.M. In operation since 1962.
WHERE	At the end of Fig Tree Lane, off Airport Road, a mile south of the Redding Municipal Airport.
ADMISSION	Admission $1 per person on Sunday (free on Saturday); ample parking (free with admission on Sunday); outdoors, year-round.
FEATURES	"Everything and anything" from furniture to fresh produce and live animals. Averages one hundred to 300 vendors. Food is served on the premises. This established market boasts "twenty acres of trees and tables."
RATES	$5 per space on Saturday, $10 on Sunday. Reservations are on a first-come, first-served basis.
CONTACT	Keith or Karen Bloom, 21005 Fig Tree Lane, Redding, CA 96002.
PHONE	(530) 365-7242 or (530) 378-1266 (for inquiries about the auction, contact Jack Epperson)

FAX   (530) 365-3159
E-MAIL   bloom@jett.net

SACRAMENTO: Auction City Flea Market

WHEN   Every weekend, 7:00 A.M. to 5:00 P.M. In operation since 1964.
WHERE   At 8521 Folsom Boulevard, about eight-tenths of a mile west of Watt Avenue, between Howe Avenue and Watt Avenue, directly off Highway 50; two blocks from the light-rail station.
ADMISSION   Free admission; acres of free parking; indoors and outdoors, rain or shine.
FEATURES   Antiques and collectibles, books, new and vintage clothing, coins and stamps, crafts, electronics, new and used merchandise, porcelain, fresh produce, tools, and toys. Averages 250 to 500 vendors. Snacks and hot meals are served on the premises.
RATES $20 for one table, $30 for two (limit two tables per vendor). Reservations are recommended.
CONTACT   Manager, 8521 Folsom Boulevard, Sacramento, CA 95826.
PHONE   (916) 383-0880 or (916) 383-0950; office hours are Wednesday and Friday, 9:00 A.M. to 5:00 P.M.
E-MAIL   emagovac@aol.com

SACRAMENTO: Forty-niner Flea Market

WHEN   Every Thursday through Sunday, 7:00 A.M. to 4:00 P.M. In operation for more than five years.
WHERE   At 4450 Marysville Boulevard.
ADMISSION   Admission 25¢ per person; parking at 25¢ per car; outdoors, rain or shine.
FEATURES   A mix of antiques, collectibles, new and used merchandise. Averages 60 to a capacity of 125 vendors. There is a snack bar on the premises. Friendly, family atmosphere.
RATES $6 per space on Thursday, $9 per space on Friday, Saturday, and Sunday; call for monthly rates. Reservations are not required.

CONTACT   Bill Brancamp, Manager, 4450 Marysville Boulevard, Sacramento, CA 95838.
PHONE   (916) 925-4944; during swap-meet hours call Rafael Sanchez at (916) 920-3530.
FAX   (916) 920-1026

SALINAS: Salinas Flea Market

WHEN   Every weekend, 6:00 A.M. to 4:00 P.M. In operation since the 1970s.
WHERE   At 925 North Sanborn Road, at the Skyview Drive-in Theater.
ADMISSION Admission 50¢ per person on Saturday and $1 on Sunday; free parking for up to 700 cars; outdoors, rain or shine.
FEATURES   About half new, half used goods—antiques and collectibles, books, new and vintage clothing, kitchenware, crafts, furniture, jewelry, fresh produce, and toys. Averages 100 to a capacity of 180 vendors. Snacks and hot meals are served on the premises.
RATES $15 per space on Saturday and $22 on Sunday. Reserve a week in advance.
CONTACT   Art Jackson, 925 North Sanborn Road, Salinas, CA 93905.
PHONE   (831) 757-3532 (757-FLEA) or (831) 424-7490 or (831) 424-1477 (snack bar at the drive-in)

SAN BERNARDINO: Orange Show Outdoor Market and Swap Meet

WHEN   Every Sunday, 6:00 A.M. to 3:00 P.M. In operation for over thirty-seven years.
WHERE   At the National Orange Showgrounds in San Bernardino.
ADMISSION Admission $1; free for children under twelve; ample free parking; outdoors, rain or shine.
FEATURES   Garage-sale items, some antiques and collectibles, new merchandise, fresh produce, furniture, new and vintage clothing. Averages up to 1,000 vendors. Hot meals are available on the premises. Promoters call it the largest weekly outdoor flea market in San Bernardino County and "a fantastic place

for the average guy to clean out the garage and make a few bucks."

RATES   From $8 to $40 per space per day. Reservations are recommended.

CONTACT   R. G. Canning Attractions, P.O. Box 6103, San Bernardino, CA 92412.

PHONE   (909) 795-1884

FAX   (909) 795-1884

E-MAIL   rgc@rgcshows.com

WEB   www.rgcshows.com

SAN DIEGO: Kobey's Swap Meet at the Sports Arena

WHEN   Every Thursday through Sunday and most holidays, 7:00 A.M. to 3:00 P.M. In operation since 1980.

WHERE   At 3500 Sports Arena Boulevard, between I-5 and I-8. Take Rosencrans exit off I-5 and I-8, then turn right onto Sports Arena Boulevard, and market will be on the right in the Sports Arena parking lot.

ADMISSION   Admission $1 per person; 75¢ for senior citizens; free admission for children under twelve and handicapped persons; free parking for more than 2,500 cars; outdoors, rain or shine.

FEATURES   Antiques and collectibles, books, new and vintage clothing, kitchenware, crafts, coins and stamps, flowers, furniture, jewelry, new merchandise, records and tapes, toys, computer equipment, and fresh produce. Averages up to eight hundred or more vendors. Snacks and hot meals are served on the premises. San Diego County's largest open-air market, boasting 30,000 to 40,000 shoppers every weekend.

RATES $25 and up per day on Saturday or Sunday, $6 to $12 on Thursday, $8 to $16 on Friday for reserved spaces; $20 unreserved (day of market). Reservations are not required.

CONTACT   Chris Haesloop, General Manager, P.O. Box 81492, San Diego, CA 92138.

PHONE   (619) 226-0650 (24 hours) or (619) 523-2700 (weekdays)

FAX   (619) 523-2715

E-MAIL   webmaster@k-online.com

WEB   www.kobeyswap.com

SAN FRANCISCO: Alemany Flea Market

WHEN	Every Wednesday and Sunday (farmers market on Saturday), 7:00 A.M. to 3:00 P.M. In operation since 1995.
WHERE	At 100 Alemany Boulevard (at the intersection of Highways 101 South and 280 North).
ADMISSION	Free admission; ample free parking; outdoors and under cover, rain or shine.
FEATURES	Antiques, collectibles, clothing, crafts, household items, jewelry, and "funky" stuff. Averages 120 to 220 vendors. There are two caterers on the premises. This is a community-oriented market in the city.
RATES	$30 per space per day. Reservations are recommended— there may be a waiting list.
CONTACT	Sid Baker or Amalia Martinez, Managers, 501 Cesar Chavez, Room 109A, San Francisco, CA 94124-1243.
PHONE	(415) 647-2043 (leave a message); day of market contact Dave Frieders at (415) 285-5011.
FAX	(415) 643-9514
WEB	www.cl.sf.ca.us (the city's Web site)

SAN FRANCISCO: America's Largest Antique and Collectible Sale

WHEN	Three weekend events in February, May, and August: Saturday, 8:00 A.M. to 7:00 P.M. and Sunday, 8:00 A.M. to 5:00 P.M. In operation since August 1988.
WHERE	At the Cow Palace. Take the Cow Palace exit off Route 280 or Route 101 and follow signposts.
ADMISSION	Admission $5 per person; parking for up to two thousand cars is available at $3 per car; indoors, year-round.
FEATURES	Antiques and collectibles, vintage clothing, jewelry, and antique toys. Averages close to four hundred vendors. Snacks and hot meals are served on the premises. Upscale merchandise.
RATES	$90 per 10'×10' space (tables not provided). Reserve a month in advance.
CONTACT	Palmer, Wirfs and Associates, 4001 Northeast Halsey, Portland, OR 97232.
PHONE	(503) 282-0877 (office hours are Monday through Friday, 9:00 A.M. to 4:30 P.M.)
FAX	(503) 282-0877

E-MAIL   cpalmer@transport.com
WEB   www.palmerwirfs.com

SAN FRANCISCO: San Francisco Flea Market

WHEN   Every weekend, 6:00 A.M. to 4:30 P.M.
WHERE   At 140 South Van Ness at the corner of Mission Street, in the South of Market (SOMA) district. Take the Mission Street exit from Highway 101.
ADMISSION Admission 50¢ per person; street parking; outdoors, year-round.
FEATURES   Mix of collectibles, garage-sale stuff, and new merchandise; "hidden treasures." Averages up to 100 vendors. Food is available nearby. Heavily advertised.
RATES $25 per space (with vehicle) per weekend. Reservations are on a first-come, first-served basis.
CONTACT   Manager
PHONE   (415) 646-0544

SAN JACINTO: Maclin's Market in San Jacinto

WHEN   Every Saturday, 6:00 A.M. to 3:00 P.M. In operation since 1998.
WHERE   At 789 North Lyon Avenue.
ADMISSION Free admission; ample free parking; outdoors, year-round.
FEATURES   Antiques and collectibles, new and used goods and books, clothing, furniture, kitchenware, crafts, jewelry, pets, fresh produce, tools, and brand-name new and used merchandise. Averages up to 100 vendors. Occasional horse and dog shows, motocross, music festivals, rodeos, and more. Convenient RV parking is available.
RATES $15 per 20'×20' space per day. Reservations are recommended.
CONTACT   Linda, 789 North Lyon Avenue, San Jacinto, CA 92383.
PHONE   (800) 222-7467 (222-SHOP); Saturdays call (909) 654-2546.
FAX   (909) 988-8041

SAN JOSE: Capitol Flea Market (aka San Jose's Old-Fashioned Capitol Flea Market)

WHEN   Every Thursday through Sunday, 6:00 A.M. to 5:30 P.M. In operation since around 1980.

WHERE   On Capitol Expressway and Monterey Highway. Take Route 101 to Capitol Expressway exit west, and the market is four stoplights up on the right side.

ADMISSION   Admission 50¢ per person on Thursday and Friday, $1.25 on Saturday, and $1.50 on Sunday; free for children under twelve; acres of free parking; outdoors, rain or shine.

FEATURES   Mostly garage-sale items and a huge volume of produce, with lots of variety in new and used items. Averages close to 1,000 vendors. Snacks and hot meals are served on the premises. A gigantic garage sale includes a huge farmers market; used car and truck sale every Saturday and Sunday. Live music every Saturday and Sunday.

RATES $14 per 20'×20' space on Thursday, from $10 on Friday, from $15 on Saturday, and from $20 on Sunday. Reservations are not required.

CONTACT   Manager, 3630 Hillcap Avenue, San Jose, CA 95136.

PHONE   (408) 225-5800

SAN JOSE: The Flea Market

WHEN   Every Wednesday through Sunday, 7:00 A.M. to 6:00 P.M. In operation since 1960.

WHERE   At 1590 Berryessa Road, between Highways 680 and 101. From Route 680, take West exit onto Berryessa Road; from Route 101, take 13th Street exit west to Hedding, then left onto Hedding (which becomes Berryessa after crossing over Route 101), and follow signs.

ADMISSION   Free admission; eighty acres of paved parking at $1 per car Wednesday through Fridays, $5 on weekends; outdoors, rain or shine.

FEATURES   Collectibles, books, new and vintage clothing (including discount fashions and children's apparel), kitchenware, crafts, flowers, furniture, paintings, plants, pottery, tools ("from bonsai pruning shears to power miters"), toys, T-shirts, and all manner of new and used merchandise. Averages 2,000 to a capacity of 2,300 vendors. More than twenty-five snack bars and restaurants plus more than sixty roving snack and beverage carts. The quarter-mile-long

"Produce Row" is perhaps California's largest farmers market. This is surely one of the largest flea markets in the United States, with an estimated 80,000 visitors attending each weekend—more than four million visitors annually. Wednesday's the day for the best bargains; and compared with the weekend madness, Thursday and Friday are relatively calm. Visitor attractions include an old-fashioned carousel, two arcades, playgrounds, pony rides for kids, and many other special events, including the following monthly festivals: Family Pet Festival, Crafter's Boutique and Holiday Fair, Cinco de Mayo, Summer Brewfest, Oktoberfest, Salsa Festival, Children's Summer Funfest (call for dates).

RATES $15 per 17'×20' space on Wednesday, $5 per day on Thursday and Friday, $25 per day on Saturday and Sunday (first Saturday of each month is only $10); call for weekly and monthly rates. Reservations are recommended; Sundays are usually sold out.

CONTACT   Manager, 1590 Berryessa Road, San Jose, CA 95133-1003.

PHONE   (408) 453-1110; for vendor reservations call Patrick DeTar; for special events and festivals, call Rich Alvari at ext. 224 or via pager at (408) 308-8168.

FAX   (408) 437-9011

E-MAIL   rich@sjfm.com

WEB   www.sjfm.com

NFMA Member

Famous Flea Markets of Europe

London: Portobello Road
Madrid: "El Rastro"
Rome: Porta Portese
Paris: Marché aux Puces de Clignancourt
Brussels: Place Grand Sablon
Munich: Kunstpark

SAN JUAN BAUTISTA: San Juan Bautista Antiques Flea Market

WHEN	Annually, on the first Sunday in August, 8:00 A.M. to 5:00 P.M. The August event has been going since 1964, the June event since 1990.
WHERE	In the center of historic downtown San Juan Bautista, two miles off Highway 101 (30 miles south of San Jose).
ADMISSION	Free admission; free parking; outdoors, rain or shine.
FEATURES	Only antiques and collectibles are allowed. Averages up to a capacity of 400 vendors. Ten restaurants on the premises. Managed by the local chamber of commerce, this popular event draws about 20,000 shoppers. Entertainment is provided throughout the day.
RATES	$175 per 10'×14' space. Reserve by the end of May.
CONTACT	Terry Arburger, Chamber of Commerce, Events Department, P.O. Box 1037, San Juan Bautista, CA 95045-1037.
PHONE	(831) 623-2454 or (831) 623-0674
FAX	(831) 623-0674

SANTA CLARITA: Saugus Swap Meet

WHEN	Every Sunday and Tuesday, 7:00 A.M. to 3:00 P.M. In operation since the 1960s.
WHERE	At 22500 Soledad Canyon Road. From Los Angeles, take I-5 northbound to Valencia Boulevard, then go east on Valencia three miles, and market will be on right side.
ADMISSION	Admission $1 per person; free for children under twelve; free parking for up to 7,000 cars; outdoors, rain or shine.
FEATURES	Antiques and collectibles, kitchenware, crafts, new and vintage clothing, electronics, furniture, household and decorative items, jewelry, porcelain, fresh produce, auto accessories, lamps, and shoes. Averages 700 to a capacity of 800 vendors. Snacks and hot meals are served on the premises. One of the largest weekly swap meets in Southern California. Average attendance is estimated at 18,000 customers on Sunday and 3,000 on Tuesday.
RATES	From $25 to $60 per 16'×20' space on Sunday and $10 on Tuesday, depending on location; one vehicle per space; vendors must bring their own display equipment. Reservations are recommended for Sunday only.

CONTACT   Terri Burbank, 22500 Soledad Canyon Road, Santa Clarita, CA 91350.
PHONE   (805) 259-3886; office hours are 8:00 A.M. to 3:00 P.M., Sunday through Friday
FAX   (805) 259-8534
WEB   www.scvpages.com

SANTA MARIA: Hi-Way Drive-in Theatre Flea Market

WHEN   Every Sunday, 6:00 A.M. to noon. In operation since the 1980s.
WHERE   At 3170 Santa Maria Way (take the Santa Maria exit off the 101 Freeway).
ADMISSION   Admission 25¢ per person or $1 per carload; ample free parking; outdoors, year-round.
FEATURES   New and used merchandise, collectibles, crafts, and fresh produce. Averages 100 to 150 vendors. There is a snack bar on the premises.
RATES $8 per space ($9 for produce sellers). Reservations are recommended.
CONTACT   Bob Gran, Sr., 3170 Santa Maria Way, Santa Maria, CA 93455.
PHONE   (805) 934-1582
FAX   (805) 934-4992

NFMA Member

SANTA ROSA: Forty and Eight Flea Market

WHEN   One Sunday each month from May through September (call for dates), 7:00 A.M. to 3:00 P.M. In operation since the early 1970s.
WHERE   On Maple Avenue off Highway 12, on the grounds of the Santa Rosa Veterans Memorial Building (directly across from the Sonoma County Fairgrounds).
ADMISSION   Free admission; ample free parking; outdoors, rain or shine.
FEATURES   All sorts of stuff, especially garage-sale items (anything vendors wouldn't be ashamed to sell at a church or school bazaar). Averages up to 300 vendors. Food is served on the premises. Sponsored by the American Legionnaires 40/8

League, also known as La Société des 40 Hommes et 8 Chevaux.

RATES $15 per 19'×19' space; call for special rates for prepaid multiple rentals. Reservations are recommended.

CONTACT   Manager, P.O. Box 9191, Santa Rosa, CA 95405.

PHONE   (707) 522-9391

SEBASTOPOL: Midgley's Country Flea Market

WHEN   Every weekend, 6:30 A.M. to 4:30 P.M. In operation since the 1960s.

WHERE   At 2200 Gravenstein Highway South. Take I-101 to Route 116 west to Sebastopol, about eight or nine miles, and market will be on the left.

ADMISSION   Free admission; free parking; outdoors and under cover, rain or shine.

FEATURES   Household items, plants, antiques and collectibles, fresh produce, and new merchandise. Averages 150 to 250 vendors. Two snack bars.

RATES   From $13 per 4'×8' space, including one table; some spaces are covered. Reservations are not required.

CONTACT   Manager, 2200 Gravenstein Highway South, Sebastopol, CA 95472.

PHONE   (707) 823-7874

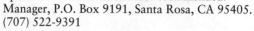

SOUTH LAKE TAHOE: Tahoe Flea Market

WHEN   Every Sunday from May through October (plus Saturday on Memorial Day, July Fourth, and Labor Day weekends), 8:00 A.M. to 5:00 P.M. In operation since the mid-1970s.

WHERE   At the Elks Lodge, 2094 Highway 50 (at Elks Club Drive), one mile south of the South Lake Tahoe Airport.

ADMISSION   Admission 75¢; free parking for up to 120 cars, plus additional street parking; outdoors, weather permitting.

FEATURES   Antiques and collectibles, books, new and vintage clothing, coins and stamps, kitchenware, crafts, furniture, jewelry, new merchandise, porcelain, fresh produce, and toys.

Averages up to 100 vendors. Snacks and hot meals are served on the premises. Indoor bar/lounge.

RATES From $12 per 10'×15' space; tables and umbrellas (for shade) are available at $5 each; dealers may set up the night before market. Spaces are assigned on a first-come, first-served basis.

CONTACT Randy Mundt, P.O. Box 10645, South Lake Tahoe, CA 96158.

PHONE (530) 541-3967

SPRING VALLEY: Spring Valley Swap Meet

WHEN Every weekend, 7:00 A.M. to 3:00 P.M. In operation since 1970.

WHERE At 6377 Quarry Road.

ADMISSION Admission 50¢ per person; ample free parking; outdoors, rain or shine.

FEATURES Everything from collectibles and garage-sale items to new merchandise. Averages close to its capacity of 1,049 vendors. Food is served on the premises. One of the best weekly swap meets in southern California.

RATES From $7 per space per day. Reservations are recommended—call a week in advance.

CONTACT Rich or Mike, Managers, 6377 Quarry Road, Spring Valley, CA 91977.

PHONE (619) 463-1194

FAX (619) 472-1435

TORRANCE: Alpine Village Swap Meet

WHEN Every Tuesday through Sunday, 6:00 A.M. to 3:30 P.M. In operation since the late 1970s.

WHERE At 833 West Torrance Boulevard.

ADMISSION Admission 50¢ per person; ample free parking; indoors and outdoors, rain or shine.

FEATURES All kinds of new, used, and collectible merchandise. Averages close to 500 vendors. There is a café and restaurant on the premises.

RATES $10 per 16'×18' day Tuesday through Friday, $35 on

Sunday; monthly rates available. Reservations are not required.
CONTACT Manager, 833 West Torrance Boulevard, Torrance, CA 90502.
PHONE (323) 770-1961 or (310) 327-4384

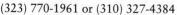

TORRANCE: The Roadium Open-Air Market

WHEN Daily except Christmas Day and New Year's Day: weekdays, 6:00 A.M. to 4:00 P.M., and weekends, 6:00 A.M. to 3:00 P.M. In operation since 1955.

WHERE At 2500 West Redondo Beach Boulevard, between Freeway 405 and the Harbor Freeway; take the Redondo Beach exit off either freeway.

ADMISSION Admission 50¢ on Monday, Tuesday, Thursday, and Friday; $1.25 on Wednesday; $1.50 on Saturday and Sunday; free parking for up to 12,000 cars in nearby lot, with shuttle service to market on weekends and holidays; outdoors, rain or shine.

FEATURES Antiques and collectibles, books, new and vintage clothing, coins and stamps, kitchenware, crafts, fresh produce, furniture, jewelry. Averages 450 to 480 vendors. Snacks and hot meals are served on the premises. The market features new, used, and antique goods Monday through Friday; on weekends the market is devoted to new merchandise; billed as well-advertised and clean.

RATES $16 per 10'×18' space on Monday, Tuesday, Thursday, or Friday; $30 on Wednesday; from $22 to $42 on Saturday or from $14 to $42 on Sunday, depending on location; all vendors must have a California resale permit. Reserve a week in advance, in person with cash; no mail or phone reservations are accepted.

CONTACT Maria Sanchez, Manager, 2500 West Redondo Beach Boulevard, Torrance, CA 90504.

PHONE (323) 321-3709 or, within California, (800) 833-0304
FAX (323) 321-0114
E-MAIL roadium@earthlink.net
WEB www.roadium.com

NFMA Member

TULARE: Tulare County Fairgrounds Swap Meet

WHEN	Every Tuesday and Wednesday, 6:30 A.M. to 3:00 P.M. (except during fair for several days a year in September and March—call for this year's fair dates). In operation for over nine years.
WHERE	At 215 East Alpine Avenue. Take Bardsley exit off Route 99 west to "O" Street, then north to Gate 8 for flea market.
ADMISSION	Free admission; unlimited free parking; outdoors and under cover, rain or shine.
FEATURES	Antiques and collectibles, books, new and vintage clothing, kitchenware, crafts, furniture, jewelry, livestock, new and used merchandise, porcelain, fresh produce, and toys. Averages about 10 vendors on Tuesday to 100 vendors on Wednesday. Snacks are available on the premises.
RATES	$5 per 20'×20' space on Tuesday, $10 on Wednesday. Reservations are not required.
CONTACT	Clifton Williams or Stacy Rianca, 215 East Martin Luther King, Jr., Avenue, Tulare, CA 93274.
PHONE	(559) 686-4707
FAX	(559) 686-7238
E-MAIL	tcf@jps.net
WEB	www.tularefair.org

VALLEJO: Napa-Vallejo Flea Market

WHEN	Every Sunday, 6:00 A.M. to 5:00 P.M. In operation for over thirty-eight years.
WHERE	On Highway 29, halfway between Napa and Vallejo.
ADMISSION	Free admission; parking for up to five thousand cars at $2 per car; indoors and outdoors, rain or shine.
FEATURES	Antiques and collectibles, books, new and vintage clothing, kitchenware, crafts, furniture, jewelry, new merchandise, porcelain, fresh produce, and toys. Averages 700 to 1,000 vendors. Snacks are available on the premises. Billed as one of the oldest and best flea markets in California.
RATES	$20 per table per day. Reservations are not required.
CONTACT	Tom Harding, 303 Kelly Road, Vallejo, CA 94590.
PHONE	(707) 226-8862

VALLEJO: Shoppers Carnival

WHEN	Every weekend, 10:00 A.M. to 5:00 P.M. In operation since 1997.
WHERE	At the corner of Redwood and Highway 29, off I-80.
ADMISSION	Free admission; ample free parking; indoors, year-round.
FEATURES	Specialty and used merchandise. Averages 60 to 250 vendors. Food is served on the premises.
RATES	$15 per 10'×10' space per day, or $25 for two spaces. Reservations are not required.
CONTACT	Dan Heckerman, 1074 Reed Avenue, Suite 69, Sunnyvale, CA 94086.
PHONE	(408) 247-8114
FAX	(408) 247-0984

VENTURA: 101 Swap Meet

WHEN	Every Sunday, 6:00 A.M. to 3:00 P.M. In operation since the mid-1960s.
WHERE	At 4826 East Telephone Road. Take 101 Freeway to Telephone Road, and market will be on the right side, at the drive-in.
ADMISSION	Admission $1 per person (children twelve and under are admitted free); free parking; outdoors, weather permitting.
FEATURES	Collectibles, books, new clothing, kitchenware, crafts, furniture, jewelry, new and used merchandise, porcelain, fresh produce, and toys. Averages 350 to a capacity of 550 vendors. Snacks and hot meals are served on the premises.
RATES	From $21 to $32 per 18'×20' space. Reservations are not required.
CONTACT	Terry Leach, Manager, 4826 East Telephone Road, Ventura, CA 93003.
PHONE	(805) 644-5043 or (805) 644-5061
FAX	(805) 644-8351

VENTURA: Ventura Flea Market and Swap Meet

WHEN   Seven times a year (call for dates), 9:00 A.M. to 3:00 P.M. In operation for over seventeen years.

WHERE   At the Ventura County Fairgrounds (Seaside Park).

ADMISSION   Admission $4 per person; ample free parking; outdoors, rain or shine.

FEATURES   A mix of antiques, garage-sale items and new merchandise (but no fresh produce or knives). Averages up to 800 vendors. Hot meals are available on the premises. Some 10,000 customers pass through the turnstiles daily.

RATES   From $30 to $50 per space per day. Reserve three weeks in advance for spaces in better locations.

CONTACT   R. G. Canning Attractions, P.O. Box 400, Maywood, CA 90270-0400.

PHONE   (323) 560-7469 (560-SHOW), ext. 13; office hours are Monday and Wednesday from 10:00 A.M. to 5:00 P.M.

FAX   (323) 560-5924

E-MAIL   rgc@rgcshows.com

WEB   www.rgcshows.com

VICTORVILLE: Victorville Fairgrounds Swap Meet

WHEN   Every weekend, 7:00 A.M. to 3:00 P.M. In operation since 1997.

WHERE   At 14800 Seventh Street.

ADMISSION   Admission $1 per person; free parking; outdoors, weather permitting.

FEATURES   Antiques and collectibles, books, new and vintage clothing, coins and stamps, kitchenware, crafts, furniture, jewelry, new merchandise, porcelain, fresh produce, and toys—"everything." Averages close to 350 vendors. Snacks and hot meals are served on the premises. No food concessions.

RATES $13 per 18'×20' space on Saturday and $10 on Sunday. Reservations are not required.

CONTACT   Greg Hahn, 14800 Seventh Street, Victorville, CA 92392.

PHONE   (800) 222-7467 (222-SHOP); weekends call (760) 955-1167.

VISALIA: Visalia Sales Yard

WHEN   Every Thursday and Sunday, 5:00 A.M. to 3:00 P.M. Family owned and operated since 1949.

WHERE   At 29660 Road 152.

ADMISSION   Free admission; free parking; outdoors, rain or shine.

FEATURES   Antiques and collectibles, books, new clothing, kitchenware, crafts, furniture, new and used merchandise, fresh produce, and toys—"you name it." Averages close to its capacity of 500 vendors. Snacks and hot meals are served on the premises.

RATES $8 per 10'×10' space per day; $10 reservation fee (spaces generally booked up on Thursday). Reservations are recommended.

CONTACT   Karen Green or Don Brumley, 29660 Road 152, Visalia, CA 93291.

PHONE   (209) 734-9092

      NFMA Member

YUCCA VALLEY: Sky Village Outdoor Marketplace

WHEN   Every weekend, 5:30 A.M. to 2:00 P.M. In operation since the 1970s.

WHERE   7028 Theatre Road.

ADMISSION   Free admission; ample free parking; outdoors, year-round.

FEATURES   The theme here is "junk to gems"—you can find anything from precious antiques to yard-sale fare. Averages up to 200 vendors. There is a café on the premises. A real, old-fashioned swap meet.

RATES $9 per space on Saturday and $8 on Sunday. Reservations are not required.

CONTACT   Bob Carr, P.O. Box 1808, Yucca Valley, CA 92286-1808.

PHONE   (760) 365-2104

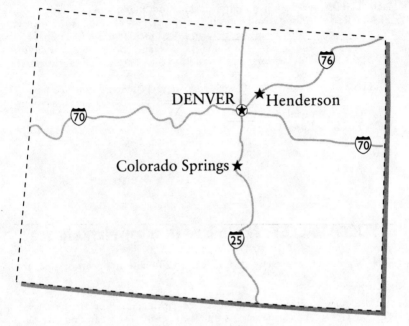

DENVER ★ Henderson

Colorado Springs ★

COLORADO

COLORADO SPRINGS: The Flea Market

WHEN	Every weekend, 7:00 A.M. to 4:00 P.M.; flea, farmers, and craft market open every Friday from June through September, 7:00 A.M. to 2:00 P.M. In operation for approximately twenty-five years.
WHERE	At 5225 East Platte Avenue (Highway 24), just west of Powers Boulevard. Take Highway 24 east approximately five miles from downtown Colorado Springs.
ADMISSION	Admission $1 per person; free parking for over 600 cars; outdoors, year-round.
FEATURES	Antiques and collectibles, books, new clothing, coins and stamps, kitchenware, crafts, furniture, jewelry, new and used merchandise, fresh produce, and toys. Averages 125 to a capacity of over 500 vendors. Snacks and hot meals are served on the premises. All-blacktop vending area, where "you'll find everything under the sun."
RATES	$16 per 20'×20' space daily for regular spots, $25 for prime spots; electricity is available at $5 per day. Reservations are not required (reserved spaces incur an added $3 charge).
CONTACT	Randy Cloud, Manager, P.O. Box 7229, Colorado Springs, CO 80933.
PHONE	(719) 380-8599

DENVER: Denver Collectors Fair

WHEN	One weekend a month from June through December (call for dates), Saturday 9:00 A.M. to 5:00 P.M. and Sunday 10:00 A.M. to 4:00 P.M. In operation since 1987.
WHERE	At the National Western Complex.
ADMISSION	Admission $1 per person (children under twelve are admitted free); ample free parking; indoors.
FEATURES	Just about anything that can be considered collectible. Averages 250 to 400 vendors. Food is served on the premises.
RATES	From $70 to $90 per 10'×10' space per event. Reservations are recommended.
CONTACT	Joan, 1153 Bergen Parkway M, PMB-475, Evergreen, CO 80439.
PHONE	(800) 333-3532 (333-FLEA) or (303) 526-5494
FAX	(303) 526-7339

NFMA Member

HENDERSON: Mile-High Flea Market

WHEN   Every Wednesday, Saturday, and Sunday, 7:00 A.M. to 5:00 P.M. In operation since 1986 at present location.

WHERE   At 7007 East 88th Avenue, at the junction of I-76, just north of Denver.

ADMISSION   Admission $1 per person on Wednesday, $2 on Saturday or Sunday; free for children under twelve; free parking for up to 5,000 cars; indoors year-round and outdoors, weather permitting.

FEATURES   Antiques and collectibles, books, new and vintage clothing, coins and stamps, kitchenware, crafts, furniture, jewelry, new merchandise, porcelain, fresh produce, toys, and used merchandise. Averages 1,000 to 1,800 vendors. Snacks and hot meals are served on the premises. Attracts over 40,000 buyers per weekend.

RATES $10 per space on Wednesday, and from $20 to $23 per space on Saturday or Sunday. Reservations are not required.

CONTACT   Andrew L. Hermes, Owner/General Manager, or Jim Hurrell, Marketing Director, 7007 East 88th Avenue, Henderson, CO 80640.

PHONE   (800) 861-9900 or (303) 289-4656

FAX   (303) 286-1922

E-MAIL   jim_hfm@msn.com

I-91

Coventry ★   ★ Mansfield

Farmington ★ ⊛ HARTFORD

I-395

New Milford
★

I-84

Woodbury
★

Wallingford ★

Niantic
★

I-95

CONNECTICUT

COVENTRY: Coventry Flea Market

WHEN	Every Sunday, 9:00 A.M. to 4:00 P.M. In operation since around 1990.
WHERE	At the junction of Routes 31 and 275.
ADMISSION	Free admission; free parking for up to 300 cars; indoors year-round and outdoors, weather permitting.
FEATURES	Antiques and collectibles, books, coins, vintage clothing, kitchenware, crafts, dolls, used furniture, glassware, jewelry, toys, used merchandise. Averages close to 80 vendors. Full snack bar on the premises.
RATES	From $10 per day for a 5'×10' space. Reserve two days in advance.
CONTACT	Joe or Rose Fowler, 110 Wall Street, Coventry, CT 06238.
PHONE	(860) 742-1993 or (860) 742-9362

FARMINGTON: Farmington Antiques Weekend

WHEN	In June and on Labor Day weekend (2000 dates: June 10–11, September 2–3; 2001: June 9–10, September 1–2), 10:00 A.M. to 5:00 P.M. In operation since 1980.
WHERE	At the Polo Grounds.
ADMISSION	$5 regular admission or $25 for early buyers (from 7:00 A.M.); ample free parking; outdoors, rain or shine.
FEATURES	Strictly upscale antiques—no crafts or reproductions allowed. Averages close to 600 vendors. Food is served on the premises. This is barely a flea market—highest booth rates in the country, very upscale merchandise—but it's one of the Northeast's leading antique shows and worth a visit if you're in the area.
RATES	From $275 per space per event. Reserve six months in advance—there is a waiting list.
CONTACT	Revival Promotions, Inc., P.O. Box 388, Grafton, MA 01519.
PHONE	(800) 677-7862 or (508) 839-9735; day of market call (860) 677-7862.
FAX	(508) 839-4635
WEB	www.farmington-antiques.com

MANSFIELD: Eastern Connecticut Flea Market

WHEN	Every Sunday from early spring through Thanksgiving, 9:00 A.M. to 3:00 P.M. In operation since the mid-1970s.
WHERE	At 228 Stafford Road, at the Mansfield Drive-in Theatre, at the intersection of Routes 31 and 32.
ADMISSION	Free admission; parking for more than 1,000 cars at 50¢ per car; outdoors, weather permitting.
FEATURES	Antiques and collectibles, books, new and vintage clothing, coins and stamps, kitchenware, crafts, used furniture, jewelry, new and used merchandise, porcelain, fresh produce, tools—"bargains galore!" Averages up to 200 vendors. Snacks and hot meals are served on the premises.
RATES	$20 per space per day. Reservations are not required.
CONTACT	Michael R. Jungden, 228 Stafford Road, Mansfield, CT 06250.
PHONE	(860) 456-2578
FAX	(860) 456-2578

NEW MILFORD: Elephant Trunk Flea Market

WHEN	Every Sunday, 6:00 A.M. to 2:30 P.M. In operation since 1977.
WHERE	At 490 Danbury Road (Route 7). Take exit 7 (Route 7 North) off I-84, and turn right at the end of the long exit ramp onto Route 7 North and follow five miles; the market will be on the left.
ADMISSION	Admission $1 per person; free parking for up to 1,200 cars; outdoors, weather permitting.
FEATURES	Antiques and collectibles, books, new and vintage clothing, coins and stamps, kitchenware, crafts, electronics, furniture, jewelry, new and used merchandise, plants, porcelain, fresh produce, and toys. Averages 100 to 300 vendors. Eight food vendors on the premises. This one's been around a while and is pretty big.
RATES	$25 per 20'×20' space per day. Reservations are not required.
CONTACT	Gregory H. Baecker, 23 Deerwood Lane, Woodbury, CT 06798.
PHONE	(860) 355-1448

NEW MILFORD: Maplewood Indoor Flea Market

WHEN	Every weekend, 8:30 A.M. to 4:00 P.M. In operation since 1991.
WHERE	On Danbury Road (Route 7), about four miles north of exit 7 off I-84 (on the left).
ADMISSION	Free admission; ample free parking; indoors, year-round.
FEATURES	New merchandise, antiques and collectibles, and used items. Averages 50 to 160 vendors. Food is served on the premises. Advertised as Connecticut's largest indoor flea market. There is a game room for kids.
RATES	From $30 to $90 per space per weekend. Reservations are recommended from November through March—call a week in advance.
CONTACT	Sandy or Keith, 458 Danbury Road, New Milford, CT 06776.
PHONE	(860) 350-0454
FAX	(203) 775-8171
WEB	www.fleamarkets.com

NFMA Member

NIANTIC: Between the Bridges Antiques and Collectibles Flea Market

WHEN	Daily except Wednesday, 10:00 A.M. to 5:00 P.M. In operation since 1992.
WHERE	At 65 Pennsylvania Avenue. Take exit 74 off I-95, then turn right and go three miles and market will be on the left, two blocks from the beach.
ADMISSION	Free admission; ample free parking; indoors, year-round.
FEATURES	Antiques, collectibles, and used furniture. Averages up to a capacity of 60 vendors. Food is served next door.
RATES	From $25 to $45 per six-day week. Reservations are required.
CONTACT	Diane or John Deer, 65 Pennsylvania Avenue, Niantic, CT 06357.
PHONE	(860) 691-0170

WALLINGFORD: Redwood Country Flea Market

WHEN	Every weekend plus Good Friday, Memorial Day, July Fourth, and Labor Day, 8:00 A.M. to 4:00 P.M. In operation for over twenty-six years.
WHERE	At 170 Hartford Turnpike. Take exit 13 off I-91 or exit 64 off Wilbur Cross Parkway.
ADMISSION	Free admission; free parking for 300 cars; outdoors year-round, weather permitting.
FEATURES	Antiques and collectibles such as baseball cards, books, bottles, new clothing, coins, comics, new furniture, jewelry, knives, fresh produce, and toys. Averages 75 to 85 vendors. Restaurant on premises. This one's crowded all four holidays.
RATES	Call for daily rates. Reservations are not required.
CONTACT	Ken Dubar or Steven Hugo, 12 Docker Drive, Wallingford, CT 06492-5200.
PHONE	(203) 269-5497 or (203) 269-3500

WOODBURY: Woodbury Antiques and Flea Market

WHEN	Every Saturday, 7:00 A.M. to 2:00 P.M. In operation since 1967.
WHERE	On Main Street South (Route 6). Take exit 15 off I-84 onto Route 6 and travel three and a half miles straight into Woodbury; the market will be on the right.
ADMISSION	Free admission; free parking; outdoors year-round, weather permitting.
FEATURES	A vast and ever-changing selection of antiques and collectibles, books, china, new and vintage clothing, coins and stamps, furniture, glassware, jewelry, memorabilia, a wide array of new merchandise. Averages 100 to a capacity of 150 vendors. Food vendors on the field offer hot dogs and burgers, grinders, fried dough, and ice cream. Widely promoted, with a strong presence of buyers and sellers; rated the state's best Saturday market by *Connecticut Magazine*.
RATES	$30 per 20'×20' space per day. Reservations are recommended.
CONTACT	Diane or Don Heavens, P.O. Box 184, Woodbury, CT 06798.

PHONE	(203) 263-2841
FAX	
E-MAIL	wdbyflea@woodburyfleamarket.com
WEB	www.woodburyfleamarket.com

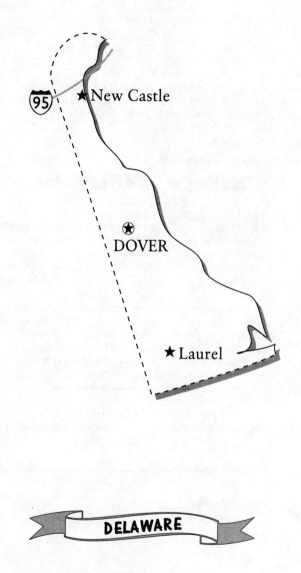

95 ★New Castle

⊛
DOVER

★Laurel

DELAWARE

DOVER: Spence's Auction and Flea Market

WHEN Every Tuesday and Friday, 8:00 A.M. to dusk (auction begins at 1:00 P.M.). In operation since 1933.
WHERE At 550 South New Street.
ADMISSION Free admission; ample free parking; indoors and outdoors, year-round.
FEATURES Antiques and collectibles, new and used merchandise. Averages up to 150 vendors. Food is served on the premises.
RATES $15 per space per day. Reservations are recommended.
CONTACT Scotty, 550 South New Street, Dover, DE 19901.
PHONE (302) 734-3441

LAUREL: Bargain Bill's Flea Market

WHEN Every Friday, 8:00 A.M. to 4:00 P.M., and every Saturday and Sunday, 6:00 A.M. to 5:00 P.M., In operation since 1978.
WHERE At junction of Dual 13 and Route 9, in western Delaware, fourteen miles north of Salisbury, Maryland, in the center of Delaware's eastern shore.
ADMISSION Free admission; free parking; indoors year-round and outdoors, weather permitting.
FEATURES Antiques and collectibles, books, new and vintage clothing, coins and stamps, crafts, furniture, jewelry, new and used merchandise, porcelain, fresh produce, and toys. Averages 200 to 400 vendors. Snacks and hot meals are served on the premises. Billed as the "shore's largest" and rated one of the nation's top-fifty flea markets by Good Housekeeping. Overnight camping, showers for indoor vendors.
RATES Indoors: $18.75 per 8'×10' space per day; outdoors: $10 for two tables per day. Reservations are not required.
CONTACT Leslie or Bill Brown, R. D. #4, Box 547, Laurel, DE 19956.
PHONE (302) 875-9958 or (302) 875-2478
FAX (302) 875-1830
E-MAIL fleamarket@magpage.com
WEB www.bwci.com/bbfmlg.htm or www.fleamarkets. com

NFMA Member

NEW CASTLE: New Castle Farmers Market

WHEN   Every Friday, Saturday, and Sunday, 10:00 A.M. to 6:00 P.M. In operation since 1956.

WHERE   At the intersection of Routes 13 and 273, within ten miles of the Maryland and Pennsylvania borders and five miles of the New Jersey border. Take exit 5A off I-95 and follow sign-posts to Route 13 South (market is across from the airport).

ADMISSION   Free admission; ample free parking; indoors year-round and outdoors, weather permitting.

FEATURES   Antiques and collectibles, fresh baked goods, vintage clothing, crafts, and fresh produce (only used items are sold at the flea market). Averages 100 to 175 vendors. Food is available on premises. An exceptionally clean market; many Pennsylvania Dutch merchants.

RATES   Outdoors: $12 per 20'×20' space on Friday, $16 on Saturday or Sunday; indoors: monthly leases only—call for rates. Reservations are not required; vendors are allowed in at 7:00 A.M.

CONTACT   Manager, 110 North Dupont Highway, New Castle, DE 19720.

PHONE   (302) 328-4102

FAX   (302) 328-9525

NFMA Member

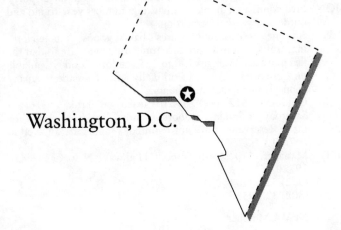

Washington, D.C.

DISTRICT OF COLUMBIA

WASHINGTON, D.C.: Flea Market at Eastern Market

WHEN   Every Sunday from March through Christmas (except the first Sunday in May), 10:00 A.M. to 5:00 P.M. (vendors may set up as early as 8:30 A.M.). In operation since 1984 under current management (Eastern Market was originally built in 1873, and the farmers market has been going on since the early 1800s; commercial vendors have been around since the turn of the century).

WHERE   Along Seventh Street, S.E. (one block from Pennsylvania Avenue on Capitol Hill). Use the Eastern Market stop on the Orange or Blue subway line.

ADMISSION   Free admission; street parking; indoors and outdoors, rain or shine.

FEATURES   Antiques and collectibles, books, new and vintage clothing, coins and stamps, kitchenware, crafts, furniture, household items, jewelry, new and used merchandise, porcelain, postcards, fresh produce, and toys. Emphasis is on collectibles and "attic oddities." Averages close to 150 vendors. Snacks and hot meals are served nearby. A real, old-fashioned neighborhood market in the middle of our nation's capital. International atmosphere with vendors from five continents. Aggressive advertising in the *Washington Post* and nationally circulated antiques journals.

RATES $30 per 100-square-foot space space per day (half-spaces are $20); tables are not provided. Prepaid reservations are required at least a week in advance.

CONTACT   Tom Rall, 1101 North Kentucky Street, Arlington, VA 22205.

PHONE   (703) 534-7612 or (202) 546-2698

FAX   (703) 534-0285

E-MAIL   marketflea@aol.com

WASHINGTON, D.C.: Georgetown Flea Market

WHEN   Every Sunday, 9:00 A.M. to 5:00 P.M. (call for additional dates); vendor setup begins at 6:00 A.M. In operation since 1973.

WHERE   Located in the parking facility of Hardy Middle School, on Wisconsin Avenue between S and T Streets N.W. (School's official address is 1819 Thirty-fifth Street, N.W.), across from the Georgetown Safeway supermarket.

ADMISSION   Free admission; parking nearby; outdoors year-round, weather permitting.

FEATURES   Antiques and collectibles of every description, books and prints, jewelry, used stuff ripe for recycling—just about anything goes here. Averages close to 100 vendors. Baked goods and farm fresh fruit and vegetables are sold on the premises. This one's good for antique hunters; known as the G-town flea, this market attracts beltway insiders and also has a literary element: Larry McMurtry based his novel *Cadillac Jack* on this market.

RATES   From $15 per 10'×4' space (small—no parking—drop off and load only); $25 per single space with parking; $45 per double space (for large trucks) or a single space on Furniture Row. Reservations are recommended—there's often a waiting list.

CONTACT   Michael Sussman, 2109 N Street, N.W., Washington, D.C. 20037.

PHONE   (202) 223-0289 (recording) or (202) 296-4989 (office)

FAX   (202) 223-0289

WEB   www.gflea.com or www.georgetownfleamarket.com

Celebrity Spottings: Georgetown Flea, Washington, D.C.

★ Madeleine Albright
★ Supreme Court Justice William Stephen Breyer
★ Cora Masters Barry (D.C.'s former first lady)
★ Larry McMurtry
★ Diane Keaton

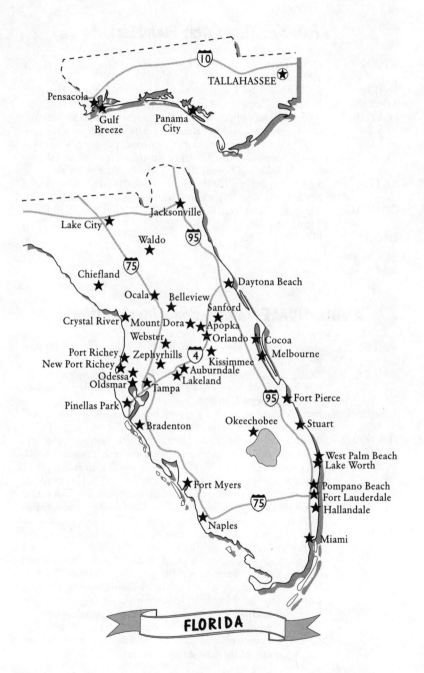

FLORIDA

APOPKA: Three Star Flea Market

WHEN	Every weekend, dawn to dusk. In operation since the early 1970s.
WHERE	At 2390 South Orange Blossom Trail (Highway 441).
ADMISSION	Free admission; ample free parking; outdoors, rain or shine.
FEATURES	Antiques and collectibles, books, new and vintage clothing, coins and stamps, kitchenware, crafts, used furniture, jewelry, new merchandise, porcelain, fresh produce, and other miscellaneous items. Averages up to a capacity of 60 vendors. Snacks and hot meals are served on the premises.
RATES	$10 per space per day includes tables (and clothes rack if needed). Reserve a week in advance.
CONTACT	Mary C. Markson, Owner, 2390 South Orange Blossom Trail, Apopka, FL 32703-1870.
PHONE	(407) 293-2722

AUBURNDALE: International Market World

WHEN	Every Friday, Saturday, and Sunday, 8:00 A.M. to 5:00 P.M. In operation since around 1980.
WHERE	At 1052 Highway 92 West, east of Lakeland (approximately one hour from both Orlando and Tampa), near the world-famous Cypress Gardens.
ADMISSION	Free admission; thirty acres of free parking; indoors, outdoors, and under cover, rain or shine.
FEATURES	Antiques and collectibles, clothing, crafts, furniture, jewelry, livestock, new and used merchandise, fresh produce, tools, toys—just about anything, including much that is unique or unusual. Averages 800 to a capacity of over 1,100 vendors. Snacks and hot meals are served on the premises. This is one of Florida's largest markets, billing itself as the "ultimate flea market and entertainment center." Special attractions include a zoo with exotic and native Florida wildlife, live entertainment, an airbrush artist, the Black Mountain Cloggers (dancers), an annual family circus, the annual Florida State Championship Bluegrass and Balloon Festival (third weekend in March), and Karaoke (with what is claimed to be Florida's largest selection of songs) on Saturday and Sunday, and many other special events all geared to wholesome family entertainment; the newest addition is a newly restored antique carousel (rides are $1 per person, many of them nostalgic seniors).

RATES	$10 per space on Friday, $17 on Saturday or Sunday, $40 per three-day weekend, or $155 per month. Reservations are not required.
CONTACT	Joe, Pat, or Roberta, or Barbara Hatch, 1052 Highway 92 West, Auburndale, FL 33823.
PHONE	(941) 665-0062
FAX	(941) 666-5726
E-MAIL	imw98@homtail.com
WEB	www.angelfire.com/biz/marketworld

BELLEVIEW: The Market of Marion

WHEN	Every weekend (plus every Friday from October through April), 8:00 A.M. to 4:00 P.M. In operation for over ten years.
WHERE	At 12888 Southeast U.S. Highway 441, three miles south of Belleview and thirteen miles south of Ocala, in Marion County.
ADMISSION	Free admission; free parking for more than 6,000 cars; indoors year-round and outdoors, weather permitting.
FEATURES	Antiques and collectibles, books, new clothing, kitchenware, crafts, new furniture, jewelry, new and used merchandise, porcelain, fresh produce, and toys. Averages 275 to 450 vendors. Snacks and hot meals are served on the premises. Marion Nature Park is nearby, with exotic and domestic animals.
RATES	May through October: $13 per space per day under cover, $5 outdoors; November through April: $15 per space under cover or $7 outdoors; $5 to $7 on Fridays, depending on location. Reservations are recommended.
CONTACT	Daniel or Brenda, 12888 Southeast U.S. Highway 441, Belleview, FL 34420.
PHONE	(352) 245-6766
FAX	(352) 245-8353

 NFMA Member

BRADENTON: Red Barn Flea Market

WHEN	Every Wednesday, Saturday, and Sunday, 8:00 A.M. to 4:00 P.M. Plaza area is open daily except Monday. In operation for over seventeen years.

WHERE   At 1707 First Street East (U.S. Route 41). Take exit 42 off I-75 onto State Route 64 to U.S. Route 41, then go left. Market will be about a mile down the road on the left.

ADMISSION   Free admission; free parking for up to 1,475 cars; indoors, outdoors, and under cover, year-round.

FEATURES   Antiques and collectibles, books, new clothing, coins and stamps, kitchenware, crafts, furniture, jewelry, new and used merchandise, porcelain, and toys, fresh produce, and seafood. Averages 450 to a capacity of more than 650 vendors. Snacks and hot meals are served on the premises. This large and diverse market publishes its own sixteen-page "where to find it" guide; in addition to the flea market there is a retail plaza with about twenty stores. Other services include a bike shop, stereo store, tackle shop, tropical fish store, etc.

RATES $18 per space per day outdoors or under cover; $25 per day indoors. Reservations are not required.

CONTACT   Lois Ploegstra, Vendor Manager, or Dan Shepard, 1707 First Street East, Bradenton, FL 34208.

PHONE   (800) 274-3532 (274-FLEA) or (941) 747-3794

FAX   (941) 747-6539

WEB   www.redbarnfleamarket.com

NFMA Member

CHIEFLAND: McCormack Flea Market

WHEN   Every Friday, Saturday, and Sunday, 7:30 A.M. to 4:00 P.M. In operation since 1984.

WHERE   On Highway 19 North (across from the Best Western motel).

ADMISSION   Free admission; free parking for up to 350 cars; indoors, year-round.

FEATURES   Antiques and collectibles, books, new clothing, kitchenware, crafts, used furniture, jewelry, new merchandise, porcelain, fresh produce, and toys. Averages 250 to 300 vendors. Two snack bars are located on the premises. RV park next door. Full hookups available at $12 per day, $60 per week, $165 per month; tent sites are $7.50 per day.

RATES $6 per space per day on Friday, $10 on Saturday, $8 on Sunday, or $22.50 for the three days (lower rates apply from April through October); R.V. hookups for vendors at booth sites available at $5 per night, $35 per week, or $150 per month. Reservations are not required except for booth spaces (call a week in advance).

CONTACT   Jack McCormack or Debbie Wilson, P.O. Box 1970, Chiefland, FL 32644-1970.
PHONE   (352) 493-1493
FAX   (352) 493-9907

NFMA Member

COCOA: Frontenac Flea Market

WHEN   Every Friday, Saturday, and Sunday, 8:00 A.M. to 4:00 P.M., and daily the week before Christmas Day. In operation since the late 1970s.
WHERE   At 5605 U.S. Highway 1, midway between Titusville and Cocoa; a half mile south of the Florida Power and Light plant, five miles from Spaceport U.S.A., and fifty miles from Orlando.
ADMISSION Free admission; free parking for up to 1,500 cars; indoors and outdoors, rain or shine.
FEATURES   Antiques and collectibles, auto accessories, books, new and vintage clothing, coins and stamps, kitchenware, crafts, electronics, furniture, jewelry, kitchen and household items, new merchandise, pets, plants, porcelain, fresh produce, sporting goods, and toys. Averages 400 to 500 vendors. Snacks and hot meals are served on the premises. On Brevard County's "space coast," near the Kennedy Space Center, local beaches, fishing areas, etc. This market publishes its own newspaper with map and vendor directory.
RATES $13 daily for an uncovered 10'×20' space; $17 for a covered 8'×10' space with one table; monthly rates are $75 per uncovered space and $95 per covered space; roll-up garage door enclosures and shed spaces are available on a monthly basis; electricity. Reservations are recommended; call on the preceding Thursday.
CONTACT   Ronnie Christian, Manager, P.O. Box 10, Sharpes, FL 32959.
PHONE   (407) 631-0241; office hours are Thursday, 9:00 A.M. to 5:00 P.M., Friday, 7:00 A.M. to 5:00 P.M., and weekends 6:30 A.M. to 5:00 P.M.
FAX   (407) 631-0246

CRYSTAL RIVER: Stokes Flea Market

WHEN	Every Wednesday and Thursday, 7:00 A.M. to 3:00 P.M. In operation since 1984.
WHERE	On Route 44 midway between Routes 19 and 491 on the Gulf Coast.
ADMISSION	Free admission; ample free parking; indoors and outdoors, year-round.
FEATURES	Antiques and collectibles, new and used merchandise, crafts, electronics, CDs and tapes. Averages 300 to 500 vendors. Restaurant on the premises. Overnight camping is available.
RATES	$5 per space per day outdoors, or $12 per day under cover. Reserve a week in advance.
CONTACT	Dinah Williams, P.O. Box 281, Crystal River, FL 34423-0281.
PHONE	(352) 746-7200 or (352) 746-6566

DAYTONA BEACH: Daytona Flea and Farmers Market

WHEN	Every Friday, Saturday, and Sunday, 8:00 A.M. to 5:00 P.M. In operation since the early 1980s.
WHERE	On I-95 and U.S. Highway 92, one mile west of the Speedway.
ADMISSION	Free admission; ample free parking; indoors and outdoors, rain or shine.
FEATURES	Antiques and collectibles, fresh produce (huge farmers market), and much more. Averages 600 to 1,000 vendors. Food is served at snack bars and at the Hop-a-longs, Harley's, and Fleamingo Restaurants on the premises. Over two million visitors annually, shopping on forty acres of selling space. Air-conditioned antique mall.
RATES	From $8 per 8'×10' space on Friday, $15 on Saturday or Sunday, including room for vehicle; call for monthly rates. Reservations are recommended.
CONTACT	Robin Ruenheck, P.O. Drawer 2140, Daytona Beach, FL 32115.
PHONE	(904) 253-3330
FAX	(904) 253-2347

FORT LAUDERDALE: Oakland Park Boulevard Flea Market

WHEN   Every Wednesday and Sunday, 10:00 A.M. to 7:00 P.M., and every Thursday, Friday, and Saturday, 10:00 A.M. to 9:00 P.M. In operation since 1971.

WHERE   At 3161 West Oakland Park Boulevard, a mile and a half west off I-95 (West Oakland Park Boulevard exit).

ADMISSION   Free admission; free parking for up to 700 cars; indoors, year-round.

FEATURES   A wide array of new merchandise, including baseball cards, books, clothing, kitchenware, crafts, electronics, furniture, health and beauty aids, jewelry, musical instruments, porcelain, and toys; fresh produce and seafood are also sold. Averages close to its capacity of 200 vendors. Snacks and hot meals are served on the premises. Claims to be Fort Lauderdale's first flea market with many long-term tenants (but don't look for antiques). Services include chiropractor, insurance agency, auto repair shop, etc.

RATES   From $600 per month (call for rates). Transient vendors are not accommodated.

CONTACT   Leonard Bennis, Manager, 3161 West Oakland Park Boulevard, Fort Lauderdale, FL 33311.

PHONE   (305) 949-7959 or (305) 733-4617

FORT LAUDERDALE: The Swap Shop of Fort Lauderdale

WHEN   Daily, 7:00 A.M. to 6:00 P.M. In operation since the early 1970s.

WHERE   At 3291 West Sunrise Boulevard (at 31st Avenue), between I-95 and the Florida Turnpike (at the Thunderbird Drive-in).

ADMISSION   Free admission; over fifty acres of parking at $1 per car on Saturday and Sunday (Monday through Friday free); indoors, outdoors, and under cover, rain or shine.

FEATURES   Antiques and collectibles, books, clothing, coins and stamps, kitchenware, crafts, electronics, furniture, jewelry, pet supplies, porcelain, fresh produce, and toys. Averages 1,500 to 2,000 vendors. Snacks and hot meals are served at over seventeen restaurants on the premises. Also known as the Sunrise Swap Shop or the Thunderbird Swap Shop, it's one of the South's largest indoor/outdoor flea markets. Thirteen-screen drive-in theater at night, playing first-run movies; free circus every day; auctions daily.

RATES   From $4 per 15'×20' space on Tuesday, Wednesday, or Friday; from $10 on Saturday, or from $15 on Sunday; free setup on Monday and Thursday; call for monthly rates. Broward County vendor's license and Florida sales tax number are required. Reservations are required for multiday rentals only.

CONTACT   Loana Leveritt, 3291 West Sunrise Boulevard, Fort Lauderdale, FL 33311.

PHONE   (954) 791-7927

FAX   (954) 792-7962

FORT MYERS: Fleamasters Flea Market

WHEN   Every Friday, Saturday, and Sunday, 8:00 A.M. to 4:00 P.M. In operation since 1985.

WHERE   At 4135 Anderson Avenue (State Road 82). From I-75 take State Road 82 (Dr. Martin Luther King, Jr. Blvd.) exit 23 west 1¾ miles to Fleamasters. Minutes from downtown Ft. Myers and Southwest Florida beaches.

ADMISSION Free admission; acres of free parking; indoors and outdoors, rain or shine.

FEATURES   Antiques and collectibles, books, new and vintage clothing, coins and stamps, kitchenware, crafts, furniture, jewelry, new merchandise, fresh produce, and toys. Averages 700 to a capacity of 1,200 vendors. Variety of restaurants and snack bars on the premises, serving everything from burritos to funnel cakes. "Southwest Florida's giant flea market."

RATES $20 per 10'×12' space per day, including two tables, or $53 per weekend; new vendors always welcome; call for monthly rates. Reservations are not accepted.

CONTACT   Manager, 4135 Dr. Martin Luther King, Jr. Blvd., Fort Myers, FL 33916.

PHONE   (941) 334-7001 (office hours are 9:00 A.M. to 5:00 P.M. Wednesday and Thursday, and 7:00 A.M. to 5:00 P.M. Friday, Saturday, and Sunday)

FAX   (941) 334-2087

E-MAIL   fleakeeper@aol.com

WEB   www.fleamall.com

FORT PIERCE: Biz-E-Flea Market

WHEN	Every weekend, 7:00 A.M. to whenever. In operation for over seventeen years.
WHERE	At 3252 North U.S. Route 1, between Vero Beach and Fort Pierce.
ADMISSION	Free admission; free parking for up to 1,000 cars; outdoors, rain or shine.
FEATURES	Antiques and collectibles, books, new and vintage clothing, kitchenware, crafts, furniture, jewelry, new merchandise, fresh produce, and toys. Averages 60 to 100 vendors. Snacks and hot meals are served on the premises. Family-type market with "bargains galore."
RATES	From $8 to $12 per 10'×10' space per day. Reservations are recommended.
CONTACT	Irma Partridge, 3252 North U.S. Route 1, Fort Pierce, FL 34951.
PHONE	(561) 466-3063

GULF BREEZE: The Flea Market

WHEN	Every weekend, plus selected holidays (call for dates), 9:00 A.M. to 5:00 P.M. In operation since 1993.
WHERE	At 5760 Gulf Breeze Parkway (Highway 98), fifteen miles east of Pensacola.
ADMISSION	Free admission; ample free parking; outdoors, year-round.
FEATURES	Antiques and collectibles, books, new and vintage clothing, coins and stamps, crafts, furniture, jewelry, new and used merchandise, porcelain, fresh produce, and toys. Averages 300 to 350 vendors. Snacks and hot meals are served on the premises. Visit sister markets in Prairieville, Louisiana (Greater Baton Rouge Flea Market), and Flea Market Mobile (Alabama). Bus tours welcome.
RATES	$15 per space per day or $25 per weekend. Reservations are recommended; transient vendors are welcome.
CONTACT	Audrey Thompson, 5760 Gulf Breeze Parkway, Gulf Breeze, FL 32561.
PHONE	(850) 934-1971 (office is open daily from 9:00 A.M. to 5:00 P.M.)

NFMA Member

HALLANDALE: Hollywood Dog Track Flea Market

WHEN   Every weekend, plus Fridays in winter, 8:00 A.M. to 3:00 P.M. In operation since 1991.

WHERE   At 831 North Federal Highway. Take I-95 to Pembroke Road, then head east to the intersection of Pembroke Road and Route 1.

ADMISSION   Admission 50¢ per person; parking at $1 per car includes admission for passengers; indoors and outdoors, weather permitting.

FEATURES   Antiques and collectibles, books, new and vintage clothing, kitchenware, crafts, furniture, jewelry, new and used merchandise, porcelain, fresh produce, and toys. Averages 200 to 600 vendors. Snacks and hot meals are served on the premises.

RATES   From $17 per space per day for used merchandise, or $55 per day for new merchandise; call for monthly rates. Reservations are not required for transient vendors.

CONTACT   Susan Adkins, or Sheila, 831 North Federal Highway, Hallandale, FL 33009.

PHONE   (954) 454-9400 or (954) 454-8666 (office; call Monday or Tuesday before noon)

FAX   (954) 454-8666

JACKSONVILLE: The Bargain House of Fleas

WHEN   Every weekend, 7:30 A.M. to 5:00 P.M., and every Wednesday, 6:00 A.M. to 2:00 P.M. In operation for over nineteen years.

WHERE   At 6016 Blanding Boulevard, three miles north of I-295.

ADMISSION   Free admission; free parking for up to 300 cars; indoors and outdoors, rain or shine.

FEATURES   Antiques and collectibles, books, new and vintage clothing, coins and stamps, kitchenware, crafts, used furniture, jewelry, new and used merchandise, novelty items, plants, porcelain, fresh produce, records, tapes, and toys; airbrush artist. Averages close to its capacity of 255 vendors. Snacks and hot meals are served on the premises. On a busy road in a residential district between two large naval bases.

RATES $7 per yard space, $14 under shed, or $15 indoors on Saturday; $6 in yard or $10 under shed on Wednesday. Reservations are recommended a week in advance.

CONTACT   Matthew Skenes, 6016 Blanding Boulevard, Jacksonville, FL
           32244.
PHONE   (904) 772-8008; for vendor reservations, call Yvonne
           Sowell, Wednesday through Sunday.

JACKSONVILLE: Beach Boulevard Flea Market

WHEN   Every weekend, 8:00 A.M. to 5:00 P.M. In operation since
           around 1996 under current management.
WHERE   At 11041 Beach Boulevard.
ADMISSION Free admission; ample free parking; outdoors under cover,
           year-round.
FEATURES   Variety of offerings, including antiques and collectibles, new
           and vintage clothing, crafts, furniture, jewelry, new and used
           merchandise, fresh produce, and toys. Averages close to 200
           vendors. Restaurant and four snack bars are on the premises.
RATES $10 per 3'×8' table per day. Reservations are recommended.
CONTACT   Charles Burchette, 11041 Beach Boulevard, Jacksonville, FL
           32246.
PHONE   (904) 645-5961

JACKSONVILLE: The Market Place
(Ramona Flea Market)

WHEN   Every weekend, 8:00 A.M. to 5:00 P.M. (vendors may arrive
           as early as 6:30 A.M.). In operation since August 1971.
WHERE   At 7059 Ramona Boulevard. Take the Lane Avenue exit off
           I-10 and go south to Ramona Boulevard, then west three
           blocks, and the market will be on the right.
ADMISSION Admission 50¢ per person; free for children under twelve;
           free parking for up to 3,000 cars; indoors and outdoors, rain
           or shine.
FEATURES   Antiques and collectibles, books, new and vintage clothing,
           kitchenware, crafts, furniture, jewelry, new and used mer-
           chandise, porcelain, fresh produce, and toys. Averages close
           to its capacity of 900 vendors. Snacks and hot meals are
           served on the premises.

RATES	Indoors: from $14.91 per 8'×8' space per day, or $116.45 per month, depending on location; outdoors: from $7.46 per space per 12'×30' space per day, or $58.22 per month. Reserve at least two weeks in advance.
CONTACT	Rick Waller, Manager, 7059 Ramona Boulevard, Jacksonville, FL 32205.
PHONE	(800) 583-3532 (583-FLEA) or (904) 786-1153 or (904) 786-3532 (786-FLEA)

KISSIMMEE: 192 Flea Market

WHEN	Daily, 9:00 A.M. to 6:00 P.M. In operation since the late 1980s.
WHERE	At 4301 West Vine Street (Irlo Bronson Memorial Highway/Route 192), near the Disney World complex. Accessible from I-4 or the Florida Turnpike.
ADMISSION	Free admission; free parking; indoors; year-round.
FEATURES	New merchandise, including collectibles (baseball cards, coins and stamps, Disneyana, etc.), clothing, cosmetics, crafts, electronics, gift items, housewares, jewelry, luggage, porcelain, fresh produce, and toys. Averages close to a capacity of 400 vendors. Food court on the premises. Discount items and bargains galore, but no antiques or used merchandise are available here.
RATES	From $18 per 10'×14' space per day, including one table. Reservations are not required.
CONTACT	Charlene Dean, 4301 West Vine Street, Kissimmee, FL 34746.
PHONE	(407) 396-4555
FAX	(407) 396-4518

KISSIMMEE: Osceola Flea and Farmers Market

WHEN	Every Friday, Saturday, and Sunday, 8:00 A.M. to 5:00 P.M. In operation since 1989.
WHERE	At 2801 East Irlo Bronson Memorial Highway (Route 192), southwest of Orlando. Take exit 244 off the Florida Turnpike, then turn left onto Route 192 and proceed two

and a half miles; market will be on the left. Or take the Route 192 exit off I-4 and go east about fifteen miles on Highway 192.

ADMISSION   Free admission; ten acres of free parking; outdoors and under cover, rain or shine.

FEATURES   Antiques and collectibles, books, clothing, coins and stamps, Disneyana and Florida souvenirs, kitchenware, crafts, dolls, fishing tackle, furniture, jewelry, pets, plants, porcelain, fresh produce, and tools. Averages 750 to 900 vendors. A full-service restaurant and three snack bars operate on the premises. Wheelchair and strollers are available for rental; call for tour bus incentives.

RATES $17.50 per day; extra tables are $3.75 each per day; electricity is available at $10 per day; call for monthly rates. Reservations are on a first-come, first-served basis.

CONTACT   Frank A. Buonauro, Jr., President, 2801 East Irlo Bronson Memorial Highway, Kissimmee, FL 34744.

PHONE   (407) 846-2811 or, within Orange County only, call (407) 238-1296; on market days call Pam White, general manager, at (407) 846-8314.

FAX   (407) 846-3392

 NFMA Member

LAKE CITY: Lake City Flea Market

WHEN   Every weekend, 7:00 A.M. to 4:00 P.M. In operation since 1978.

WHERE   At the fairgrounds on Branford Highway 247.

ADMISSION   Free admission; ample free parking; indoors and outdoors, year-round.

FEATURES   Anything and everything—new, used, collectible, "junque," whatever. Averages close to 200 vendors. Food is served on the premises.

RATES $9 per 10'×12' space per day. Reservations are required.

CONTACT   Ralph Tiner, 2640 East Montgomery, Lake City, FL 32055.

PHONE   (904) 752-1999

LAKE WORTH: Lake Worth High School Flea Market

WHEN   Every weekend, 4:00 A.M. to 3:00 P.M. In operation since 1987.

WHERE   At 1701 Lake Worth Road, in the school parking lot, under the I-95 overpass (between 6th Avenue and 10th Avenue exits) next to the Tri-Rail Station (for directions via Tri-Rail, call 800-TRI-RAIL). From the Florida Turnpike (I-95), take Exit 93 (Lake Worth exit), then go east five miles.

ADMISSION   Free admission; free parking for up to 2,000 cars; outdoors (under cover) year-round, rain or shine.

FEATURES   Antiques and collectibles, books, new and vintage clothing, coins and stamps, kitchenware, crafts, furniture, garage-sale items, glassware, jewelry, garage-sale items, fresh produce, and toys. Averages close to its capacity of 300 vendors. Several food trucks serve the market. A not-for-profit market with a family atmosphere; proceeds go to Lake Worth High School scholarships for needy students. Crowds swell to more than 3,000 shoppers on busy days. Heavy advertising on billboards (Florida Turnpike) and cable television (The Weather Channel).

RATES $10 for a single parking space per day; monthly rates are available. Reservations are on a first-come, first-served basis.

CONTACT   Betty or Ralph J. Milone, General Managers, P.O. Box 6592, Lake Worth, FL 33466-6592.

PHONE   (561) 439-1539

FAX   (561) 439-8742

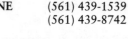

LAKELAND: Lakeland Farmers Market

WHEN   Every weekend, 7:00 A.M. to 3:00 P.M. In operation since 1970.

WHERE   At 2701 Swindell Road, at Memorial Boulevard and Swindell Road. One mile east of I-4 on Memorial Boulevard.

ADMISSION   Free admission; free parking for up to 2,000 cars; indoors and outdoors, rain or shine.

FEATURES   Antiques and collectibles, new and used merchandise, kitchenware, crafts, jewelry, and fresh produce. Averages 250 to a capacity of 300 vendors. Snacks and hot meals are served on the premises.

RATES $11 per space indoors on Saturday, $14 on Sunday; $7 per day outdoors. Reservations are suggested at least a week in advance.

CONTACT   Ann Edwards, Owner, or Jim Wilbanks, Manager, 2701
           Swindell Road, Lakeland, FL 33805.
PHONE   (941) 682-4809

    NFMA Member

MELBOURNE: Super Flea and Farmers Market

WHEN   Every Friday, Saturday, and Sunday, 8:00 A.M. to 4:00 P.M.
           In operation since 1986.
WHERE   At 4835 West Eau Gallie Boulevard, at the corner of I-95
           and West Eau Gallie Boulevard. Take exit 72 west off I-95.
ADMISSION Free admission; free parking for up to 1,500 cars; indoors,
           outdoors, and under cover, rain or shine.
FEATURES   Mostly new, discounted merchandise, plus antiques and col-
           lectibles, clothing, crafts, jewelry, garage-sale items, fresh
           produce, and a "gem mine," where customers do the pan-
           ning. Averages 250 to 300 vendors. Snacks and hot meals on
           the premises. A family-style market that calls itself
           "America's great outdoor mall."
RATES   From $7 to $26 per 8'×10' space per day, with one eight-
           foot table included; also have air-conditioned indoor spaces
           and 10'×15' spaces under sheds; monthly rates are available.
           Reservations are recommended for daily rentals.
CONTACT   Manager, 4835 West Eau Gallie Boulevard, Melbourne, FL
           32934.
PHONE   (407) 242-9124
FAX   (407) 242-1947
WEB   www.superfleamarket.com

MIAMI: Flagler Flea Market

WHEN   Every weekend, 8:00 A.M. to 4:00 P.M. In operation since 1984.
WHERE   At Northwest Seventh Street and 37th Avenue, at the Flagler
           Greyhound Track.
ADMISSION Admission 50¢; free for children under twelve; ample free
           parking; indoors year-round and outdoors, weather permit-
           ting.
FEATURES   Antiques and collectibles, new and vintage clothing, crafts,
           furniture, jewelry, fresh produce, and perfume. Averages
           525 to 550 vendors. Snack bar on premises.

RATES   From $12 to $30 per space per day. Reserve in advance if possible.
CONTACT   Armando R. Prats, P.O. Box 350940, Miami, FL 33135-0940.
PHONE   (305) 649-3000 or (305) 631-4505
FAX   (305) 631-4529

MIAMI: Opa Locka/Hialeah Flea Market

WHEN   Daily (flea market is mainly on weekends), 5:00 A.M. to 7:00 P.M. In operation since 1985.
WHERE   At 12705 Northwest 42nd Avenue. Take I-95 to the Northwest 103rd Street exit, and go west four miles to Northwest 42nd Avenue; then make a right and go north about a mile and half.
ADMISSION   Free admission; acres of parking at $1 per car on Saturday and Sunday (free during the week); indoors and outdoors, rain or shine.
FEATURES   Antiques and collectibles, books, new and vintage clothing, kitchenware, crafts, furniture, jewelry, new and used merchandise, porcelain, fresh produce, and toys. Averages 1,100 to 1,300 vendors. Snacks and hot meals are served on the premises.
RATES   From $35 per space per day. Reservations are not required.
CONTACT   Scott Miller, 12705 Northwest 42nd Avenue, Miami, FL 33054.
PHONE   (305) 688-0500 (ext. 25)

NFMA Member

MOUNT DORA: Florida Twin Markets

WHEN   Every weekend, 8:00 A.M. to 4:00 P.M. In operation since the mid-1980s.
WHERE   On Highway 441, half a mile north of Route 46.
ADMISSION   Free admission; 117 acres of free parking; indoors and outdoors, rain or shine.
FEATURES   Full spectrum of antiques and collectibles, new and used merchandise, and fresh produce and meats. Averages 400 to 600 vendors. Snacks and hot meals are served on the premises.

Florida Twin Markets consists of Renninger's Farmers and Flea Market and Renninger's Antique Center, open every weekend.

RATES $13.50 per space per day in the open air building; $7 per space per day outdoors. Reservations are not required.

CONTACT Bob Lynch, Manager, P.O. Box 1699, Mount Dora, FL 32757-1699.

PHONE (352) 383-8393

WEB www.renningers.com

NAPLES: Naples Drive-in and Flea Market

WHEN Every weekend year-round, plus every Friday from October through April, 7:00 A.M. to 3:00 P.M. In operation since the early 1980s.

WHERE At 7700 Davis Boulevard. Take exit 15 off I-75 and go south, then right at the first stoplight; the market will be three miles down the road on the left.

ADMISSION Free admission; free parking for up to 500 cars; outdoors, rain or shine.

FEATURES Antiques and collectibles, books, new and vintage clothing, coins and stamps, kitchenware, crafts, firearms, used furniture, jewelry, new and used merchandise, porcelain, fresh produce, and toys. Averages 100 to 200 vendors. Snacks and hot meals are served on the premises.

RATES $6 per space per day from June 1 through September 30, and $10 per day the rest of the year. Reservations are not required.

CONTACT Manager, 7700 Davis Boulevard, Naples, FL 33942-5311.

PHONE (941) 774-2900

FAX (941) 774-2900

NEW PORT RICHEY: Indoor Fleas

WHEN Every Friday, Saturday, and Sunday, 9:00 A.M. to 5:00 P.M. In operation since 1987.

WHERE At 3621 U.S. Highway 19.

ADMISSION   Free admission; ample free parking; indoors, year-round.
FEATURES   Antiques and collectibles, new and used merchandise. Averages 150 to 200 vendors. Food is served on the premises.
RATES $25 per 10'×12' space for three days or $150 per month. Reservations are not required.
CONTACT   Manager, 3621 U.S. Highway 19, New Port Richey, FL 34621.
PHONE   (727) 842-3665 on Thursday; ask for Marie
FAX   (727) 842-3665
E-MAIL   myway@gte.net

OCALA: I-75 Super Flea Market

WHEN   Every Friday, Saturday, and Sunday, 9:00 A.M. to 4:00 P.M. In operation since February 1998.
WHERE   At 4121 Northwest 44th Avenue (on I-75 between exists 70 and 71).
ADMISSION   Free admission; ample free parking; indoors and outdoors, year-round.
FEATURES   Averages up to its capacity of 1,200 vendors. Restaurant on the premises. Draws up to 25,000 a week.
RATES   From about $10 per day for an outdoor space. Reservations are recommended.
CONTACT   Sue Hogue or Patti Weingartner, P.O. Box 3656, Ocala, FL 34478.
PHONE   (352) 351-9220
FAX   (352) 401-1905

NFMA Member

OCALA: Ocala Drive-in Flea Market

WHEN   Every weekend, 7:00 A.M. to 4:00 P.M. In operation since 1979.
WHERE   At 4850 South Pine Avenue, three and a half miles south of Ocala on Route 301/27/441.
ADMISSION   Free admission; free parking for up to 1,000 cars; indoors and outdoors, rain or shine.
FEATURES   Antiques and collectibles, new and vintage clothing, kitchenware, crafts, jewelry, livestock, fresh produce, carpet sup-

plies, and auto tires. Averages 300 to 400 vendors. Snack bar on premises.

RATES $10.50 per roofed space per day; $8 per day for an exposed space. Reservations are not required.

CONTACT   Lou or Sheri Williams, 4850 South Pine Avenue, Ocala, FL 34480.

PHONE   (352) 629-1325

FAX   (352) 629-1325

ODESSA: Gunn Highway Flea Market

WHEN   Every weekend, 8:00 A.M. to 4:00 P.M. In operation since 1992.

WHERE   At the intersection of Gunn Highway and State Road 54.

ADMISSION   Free admission; free parking for up to 1,500 cars; indoors, outdoors, and under cover, rain or shine.

FEATURES   Antiques and collectibles, books, new and vintage clothing, coins and stamps, kitchenware, crafts, furniture, jewelry, new merchandise, porcelain, fresh produce, and toys—"a million new items and thousands of antiques." Averages up to several hundred vendors. Snacks and hot meals are served on the premises. Formerly known as Bargaineer Flea Market, now a division of Wagonwheel Flea Market out of Pinellas Park, Florida. Storage sheds available.

RATES   Under cover: $9 per day for one space, $15 for two, $20 for three; outdoors: $6 for one space, $11 for two, $15 for three. Reservations are not required.

CONTACT   Barbara Moore, Manager, 2317 Gunn Highway, Odessa, FL 33556.

PHONE   (813) 920-3181 (office hours are Wednesday through Sunday, 9:00 A.M. to 5:00 P.M.)

OKEECHOBEE: Market Place Flea Market

WHEN   Every weekend, 7:00 A.M. to 4:00 P.M. In operation since 1986.

WHERE   At 3600 Highway 441 South.

ADMISSION   Free admission; ample free parking; indoors, outdoors, and under cover, year-round.

FEATURES   A variety of new and used stuff. Averages 300 to 400 ven-

dors. There are five restaurants on the premises. Under new
management. Baby strollers are available.

RATES   From $15 per space per day; RVs are welcome. Reservations
               are required in winter only (call by September).

CONTACT   Mindy Schoppmeyer or Mary Porter, 3600 Highway 441
               South, Okeechobee, FL 34974.

PHONE   (941) 467-6639

OKEECHOBEE: Trading Post Flea Market

WHEN   Every weekend, plus Fridays, from October through April,
               8:00 A.M. to 3:00 P.M. In operation since the mid-1980s.

WHERE   At 3100 Highway 441 South, about two miles south of the
               center of Okeechobee. Look for the red and white roofs
               (next to K-Mart).

ADMISSION Free admission; free parking for up to 500 cars; indoors
               year-round and outdoors, weather permitting.

FEATURES   Antiques and collectibles, books, new and vintage clothing,
               coins and stamps, kitchenware, crafts, used furniture, jew-
               elry, new and used merchandise, pets and pet supplies,
               porcelain, fresh produce, and toys. Averages 170 to a capac-
               ity of 270 vendors. This is a clean and friendly market.

RATES   From $13 per 8'×10' space per day. Reservations are recom-
               mended ten days in advance during winter.

CONTACT   Jo Anne Award, Manager, 3100 Highway 441 South,
               Okeechobee, FL 34974.

PHONE   (941) 763-4114

FAX   (941) 763-9327

OLDSMAR: Oldsmar Flea Market

WHEN   Every Saturday and Sunday, 9:00 A.M. to 5:00 P.M. (gates
               open at 7:00 A.M.). In operation since November 1980.

WHERE   At 180 North Racetrack Road (at the intersection of
               Hillsborough Avenue).

ADMISSION Free admission; ample free parking; indoors, year-round.

FEATURES   Averages close to 800 vendors. Snacks and hot meals are
               served on the premises. The mightiest in the South. Free
               country and western band from noon to 4:00 P.M.

RATES	$10 per 8'×10' space per day outdoors; call for monthly rates indoors. Reservations are not required.
CONTACT	Babe Wright, Manager, P.O. Box 439, Oldsmar, FL 34677.
PHONE	(813) 855-2587 or (813) 855-5306
FAX	(813) 855-1263

ORLANDO: Central Florida Farmers Market

WHEN	Every weekend, 5:00 A.M. Until dusk. In operation for over sixteen years.
WHERE	At 4603 West Colonial Drive.
ADMISSION	Free admission; free parking; outdoors, year-round.
FEATURES	Antiques and collectibles, books, new and vintage clothing, coins and stamps, kitchenware, crafts, furniture, jewelry, new and used merchandise, pets, plants, porcelain, fresh produce, and toys. Averages 350 to 500 vendors. Snacks and hot meals are served on the premises.
RATES	$10 per 16'×20' space per day. Reservations are not required.
CONTACT	John Wild, 1552 Daly Street, Orlando, FL 32808.
PHONE	(407) 295-9448 or (407) 296-3868

PANAMA CITY: Fifteenth Street Flea Market

WHEN	Every Thursday through Sunday: Thursday, 9:00 A.M. to 3:00 P.M.; Friday, 9:00 A.M. to 4:00 P.M.; and Saturday and Sunday, 8:00 A.M. to 5:00 P.M. In operation since 1985.
WHERE	At 2233 East 15th Street. Take 15th Street exit off Highway 98 and market is across from the Bay County Fairground.
ADMISSION	Free admission; ample free parking; indoors year-round and outdoors, weather permitting.
FEATURES	Antiques and collectibles, books, new and vintage clothing, coins and stamps, kitchenware, crafts, furniture, jewelry, new and used merchandise, porcelain, fresh produce, and toys. Averages close to 300 vendors. Snacks are served on the premises.
RATES	$2 per table on Thursday or Friday; from $4 on Saturday or Sunday. Reserve three to four days in advance.

CONTACT   Leo Adkins, 2233 East 15th Street, Panama City, FL 32405.
PHONE   (850) 769-0137 or (850) 769-7401

PENSACOLA: T and W Flea Market

WHEN   Every weekend, 6:00 A.M. to whenever. In operation since 1979.
WHERE   At 1717 North T Street. Coming in on I-10, take exit 3 for Highway 29 South to W Street, then turn right; market is approximately four miles on the left.
ADMISSION Free admission; ample free parking; indoors and outdoors, rain or shine.
FEATURES   Variety of offerings including antiques and collectibles, new and used merchandise, produce, and poultry—"you name it, we have it." Averages up to 400 vendors. Snacks and hot meals are served on the premises. Well advertised on TV and radio and in newspapers. Tables have been booked every weekend for the past three years, according to the manager. Showers for overnight campers.
RATES   From $8 per table per day; $5 per night overnight charge. Reservations are required a week in advance.
CONTACT   Franklin "Red" Cotton, 1717 North T Street, Pensacola, FL 32505.
PHONE   (850) 433-4315

PINELLAS PARK: Mustang Flea Market

WHEN   Every Wednesday, Saturday, and Sunday, plus Thursday and Friday from May through September, 6:00 A.M. to 1:00 P.M. In operation since the 1970s.
WHERE   At 7301 Park Boulevard. Take exit 15 off I-275 and go west five miles and market will be on the right.
ADMISSION Free admission; free parking for up to 2,000 cars; outdoors, year-round.
FEATURES   Antiques and collectibles, books, new and vintage clothing, kitchenware, crafts, used furniture, jewelry, new and used merchandise, porcelain, fresh produce, and toys. Averages 200 to 350 vendors. Snacks and hot meals are served on the premises. Calls itself the "world's largest yard sale."

RATES $2.50 per 15'×15' space on Wednesday, Thursday, or Friday, and $6 per space on Saturday or Sunday. Reservations are not required.

CONTACT Betty Guinn, 7301 Park Boulevard, Pinellas Park, FL 34665.

PHONE   (727) 544-3066

PINELLAS PARK: Wagonwheel Flea Market

WHEN   Every weekend, 7:30 A.M. to 4:00 P.M. In operation since 1967.

WHERE   At 7801 Park Boulevard (74th Avenue); between Belcher and Starkey Road in Pinellas Park (midway between St. Petersburg and Clearwater). Take exit 15 West off I-275.

ADMISSION Free admission; parking for up to 6,000 cars at $1 per car (free tram from parking lot to various areas of the market); indoors, outdoors, and under cover, rain or shine.

FEATURES   Antiques and collectibles, books, new and vintage clothing, coins and stamps, kitchenware, crafts, furniture, jewelry, new merchandise, porcelain, fresh produce, and toys. Averages 1,200 to 1,800 vendors. Food is available from nineteen concessions, including the Wagonwheel Food Court, with seating for 300. "Twenty million customers can't be wrong!" On the site of the annual Pinellas County Fair, which runs for five days and nights annually in late March.

RATES $9.50 per day 10'×10' space under cover, or $6 per day in open air. Reserve a week in advance.

CONTACT   Misty Lynch, 7801 Park Boulevard, Pinellas Park, FL 34665.

PHONE   (727) 544-5319

FAX   (727) 541-4005

NFMA Member

POMPANO BEACH: Festival Flea Market Mall

WHEN   Every Tuesday through Friday, 9:30 A.M. to 5:00 P.M., and every weekend, 9:30 A.M. to 6:00 P.M. In operation for over five years.

WHERE   At 2900 West Sample Road, between Powerline and the exit 69 off Florida's Turnpike, two miles west of I-95.

ADMISSION Free admission; free parking; indoors, year-round.

FEATURES   Antiques and collectibles, books, brand-name discounted merchandise, crafts, electronics, jewelry, and toys; all new merchandise is guaranteed. Averages close to 850 vendors. International Food Court with everything from McDonald's to cappuccino bar. Combines flea market prices and merchandise with mall-like amenities, "where shop-a-holics unite"; there's a great variety of discount merchandise, as well as an eight-screen theater, state-of-the-art winner's arcade, and a hair salon.

RATES   Call for rates. Transient vendors are not accommodated.

CONTACT   Fran Morgan Folix, 2900 West Sample Road, Pompano Beach, FL 33073-3026.

PHONE   (800) 353-2627 (800-FLEA-MARKET) or (305) 979-4555

FAX   (305) 968-3980

WEB   www.festivalfleamarket.com

PORT RICHEY: U.S.A. Fleamarket

WHEN   Every Friday, Saturday, and Sunday, 8:00 A.M. to 4:00 P.M. In operation since the mid-1980s (formerly known as Fleamasters).

WHERE   At 11721 U.S. Highway 19, between State Roads 52 and 54 (access from Route 41 and I-75).

ADMISSION   Free admission; free parking for more than 5,000 cars; outdoors and under cover, year-round, rain or shine.

FEATURES   Antiques and collectibles, books, new and vintage clothing, coins and stamps, crafts, furniture, jewelry, new merchandise, porcelain, fresh produce, and toys. Averages 900 to a capacity of 1,100 vendors. Snacks and hot meals are served on the premises. An adventure in bargain shopping. Massive local advertising.

RATES   From $10 per 3'×8' aisle space to $13 per 10'×12' space on Friday or $16 on Saturday or Sunday; includes two tables; call for weekly or monthly rates; food concessions are three times monthly rate. Reservations are on a first-come, first-served basis.

CONTACT   Customer Service Office, 11721 U.S. Highway 19, Port Richey, FL 34668.

PHONE   (727) 862-3583

FAX   (727) 862-5724

SANFORD: Flea World

WHEN   Every Friday, Saturday, and Sunday, 8:00 A.M. to 6:00 P.M. In operation since May 1982.

WHERE   On Highway 17/92 between Sanford and Orlando, next to Fun World. Take exit 49 off Highway 4 and cross to 17/92 on Route 434, or take exit 50 off Highway 4 and cross to 17/92 on Lake Mary Boulevard.

ADMISSION   Free admission; free parking for up to 4,000 cars; indoors and outdoors, rain or shine.

FEATURES   Antiques and collectibles, books, new and vintage clothing, coins and stamps, kitchenware, crafts, furniture, jewelry, new and used merchandise, porcelain, fresh produce, and toys—everything from apples to zirconia. Averages close to 800 vendors. Snacks and hot meals are served on the premises. One of America's largest flea markets, on over 104 acres with an estimated 3 million shoppers annually. Free entertainment every Sunday; bingo twice daily on weekends; Fun World with go-kart tracks, miniature golf, bumper cars and boats, batting cages, nine midway rides, 350-game arcade, party facilities and more.

RATES   From $7 per 8'×10' space (includes a table and one electrical outlet) on Friday, or from $14 on Saturday and Sunday; annual leases are available for indoor spaces. Reservations are required except for "garage-sale" spaces, which are rented on a first-come, first-served basis.

CONTACT   Manager, Highway 17/92, Sanford, FL 32773.

PHONE   (407) 330-1792 (rental office is open Thursday through Sunday, 8:00 A.M. to 6:00 P.M.)

NFMA Member

STUART: B and A Flea Market

WHEN   Every weekend, 8:00 A.M. to 3:00 P.M. In operation since 1975.

WHERE   On U.S. Route 1 in Stuart. Take Stuart exit off the Florida Turnpike and follow signs to U.S. Route 1. Turn right and go to Luckhardt Street, then go left. Or, take exit 61 off I-95 and go east to Indian Street, then right to U.S. Route 1, then left, and market will be about a quarter of a mile down on the right.

ADMISSION   Free admission; ample parking at $1 per car (October through May); indoors and outdoors, year-round.

FEATURES   Antiques and collectibles, books, clothing, fashion and beauty supplies, furniture, kitchenware, crafts, jewelry, nautical specialties, fresh produce, and toys. Averages 400 to 600 vendors. Snacks and hot meals are served on the premises. A big market (one of the oldest on the so-called Treasure Coast) with a family atmosphere. There is a barber shop, pony rides, and a petting zoo on the premises.

RATES   From $20 per space per day under cover, or from $12 outdoors; tables are available at $2 per day; annual leases are available (call for rates). Reservations are required.

CONTACT   Mary Sue David, Manager, 2201 S.E. Indian Street, G-1, Stuart, FL 34997.

PHONE   (561) 288-4915; for reservations, call Arlene Rigsby at (561) 283-7015.

FAX   (561) 288-2140

NFMA Member

STUART: Lucky's Flea Market

WHEN   Every weekend, 8:00 A.M. to 3:00 P.M. In operation since 1970.

WHERE   At 1905 Southeast Luckhardt Street. Take exit 61 off I-95 and go east on Route 76 for two and a half miles to Indian Street; turn right, then travel one mile and turn left onto Route 1. The next traffic light will be Luckhardt Street; turn right, and market will be on the left.

ADMISSION Free admission; free parking for up to 600 cars; outdoors, rain or shine.

FEATURES Antiques and collectibles, books, cameras, new and vintage clothing, coins and stamps, kitchenware, crafts, used furniture, jewelry, new and used merchandise, plants, porcelain, fresh produce, sporting goods (including golf equipment), army-navy surplus, tools, and toys. Averages 150 to 300 vendors. Snacks and hot meals are served on the premises. A "true flea market," family owned and operated.

RATES   October through April: $13 per day per 12'×16' covered space with two tables, or $10 per day per 12'×36' space outdoors without tables. May through September: $11 per covered space per day, with two tables, or $8 per day outdoors without tables. Extra tables at $1 per day; electrical hookups are also available. Reserve a week to two weeks in advance (but walk-ins are welcome when space is available).

CONTACT   Greg or Alice Luckhardt, P.O. Box 1185, Stuart, FL 34995.

PHONE   (561) 288-4879 (office hours are Monday, Wednesday, and

Friday, 8:30 A.M. to 4:30 P.M.); day of market contact Jane Loihle at (561) 288-4879.

TALLAHASSEE: Flea Market Tallahassee

WHEN	Every weekend, 9:00 A.M. to 5:00 P.M. In operation since 1984.
WHERE	At 200 Capital Circle Southwest. From I-10, take exit 28 (from east) or 31 (from the West).
ADMISSION	Free admission; ample free parking; indoors and outdoors, year-round.
FEATURES	Average up to its capacity of 500 vendors. A variety of food and beverages are served. Up to 30,000 shoppers each weekend.
RATES	$24 per 8'×10' space or $30 per weekend. Reservations are not required.
CONTACT	Manager, 200 Capital Circle Southwest, Tallahassee, FL 32310.
PHONE	(850) 877-3811 (office hours are market hours plus Friday, 9:00 A.M. to 4:00 P.M. and Monday, 9:00 A.M. to noon)
FAX	(850) 656-3137

TALLAHASSEE: Uncle Bob's Flea Market

WHEN	Every weekend, 9:00 A.M. to 5:00 P.M. (a handful sell on Thursday and Friday).
WHERE	At 1501 Capital Circle Northwest.
ADMISSION	Free admission; ample free parking; outdoors, rain or shine.
FEATURES	Averages close to 50 vendors. Food is not served on the premises. This is a small market operating at a self-storage space. Under new management and growing.
RATES	$7 per table for one day or $10 for the weekend. Reservations are on a first-come, first-served basis.
CONTACT	Manager, 1501 Capital Circle Northwest, Tallahassee, FL 32303.
PHONE	(850) 576-2949

TAMPA: Big Top Flea Market

WHEN	Every weekend, 9:00 A.M. to 4:30 P.M. In operation since 1990.
WHERE	At State Road 582, five hundred yards east of exit 54 off I-75; market will be on the left. From I-4, take exit 7 (I-75 exit) to I-75, then head north on I-75 to exit 54.
ADMISSION	Free admission; ample free parking; indoors and outdoors, rain or shine.
FEATURES	Antiques and collectibles, books, new and vintage clothing, coins and stamps, kitchenware, crafts, furniture, household decor, jewelry (antique and costume), silver, new merchandise, porcelain, fresh produce, shoes, tools, and toys. Averages close to 400 vendors. Snacks and hot meals are served on the premises. Billed as Tampa's "cleanest, most modern flea market," with over 160,000 square feet of shopping area. Near Busch Gardens. Tour buses are welcome.
RATES	From $25 per 10'×12½' space per day indoors, or from $200 per month. Reserve a week in advance.
CONTACT	Ross Ozimek, 9250 East Fowler Avenue, Tampa, FL 33592.
PHONE	(813) 986-4004 Reservation office is open Wednesday through Friday, 8:30 A.M. to 5:00 P.M., and on market days from 7:00 A.M. to 5:00 P.M.
FAX	(813) 986-6296

TAMPA: Floriland Flea and Farmers Market

WHEN	Every weekend, 9:00 A.M. to 5:00 P.M. In operation since 1992.
WHERE	At 9309 North Florida Avenue, between Linebaugh Avenue and Busch Boulevard, right off I-275 (exit 33)—about two miles from Busch Gardens.
ADMISSION	Free admission; free parking for up to 2,500 cars; indoors, year-round.
FEATURES	Antiques and collectibles, books, new and vintage clothing, coins and stamps, kitchenware, crafts, furniture, jewelry, new and used merchandise, exotic plants and pets, porcelain, fresh produce, and toys. Averages 300 to 350 vendors. Full-service restaurant plus food concessions on the premises. Tampa's biggest and most comfortable flea market, with an antique center, live entertainment—a complete shopping extravaganza. Groups and tour buses are welcome.

RATES $27 per 10'×10' space per day, or $45 per weekend, or $173 per month. Reserve a week in advance.
CONTACT   Harold H. Holden, General Manager, 9309 North Florida Avenue, Tampa, FL 33612.
PHONE   (813) 932-4319
FAX   (813) 935-5558

TAMPA: Fun-Lan Swap Shop Flea Market

WHEN   Every Wednesday through Sunday (Sunday is biggest day), 6:00 A.M. to 2:00 P.M. In operation since 1979.
WHERE   At 2302 East Hillsboro Avenue, at the corner of 22nd Street, a mile east of Route 275.
ADMISSION   Free admission; ample free parking; outdoors and under cover, year-round.
FEATURES   Antiques and collectibles, new and used merchandise. Averages up to 450 vendors. Food is served on the premises. The Fun-Lan Drive-in Theatre has three screens.
RATES   From $1 per space per day on Wednesday and Friday, $3 on Thursday, and from $8 to $13 on Saturday and Sunday. Reservations are not required.
CONTACT   Lauren Duren, P.O. Box 11188, Tampa, FL 33680.
PHONE   (813) 237-0886 or (813) 234-2311 (recording for theater)
FAX   (813) 237-0886

WALDO: Waldo Farmers and Flea Market

WHEN   Every weekend, 7:30 A.M. to 4:30 P.M.; antique mall open daily. In operation since 1975.
WHERE   On Highway 301, one mile north of Waldo (fifteen minutes from Gainesville)—look for the big horse.
ADMISSION   Free admission; twenty acres of free parking; indoors year-round and outdoors, weather permitting.
FEATURES   Antiques and collectibles, books, new and vintage clothing, coins and stamps, kitchenware, crafts, furniture, jewelry, livestock, new merchandise, porcelain, fresh produce, and toys—everything from "bush hogs" (tractor-pulled grass cutters) to peanuts. Averages 700 to 1,000 vendors. Snacks and hot meals are served on the premises. Weekly atten-

dance averages 40,000 shoppers. Overnight parking allowed, and campers are welcome.

RATES From $5 per space per day. Reservations are recommended.

CONTACT Manager, 2373 Southwest Archer Road, Gainesville, FL 32608.

PHONE (352) 468-2255

FAX (352) 336-7474

 NFMA Member

WEBSTER: Sumter County Farmers Market

WHEN Every Monday, 8:00 A.M. to 3:00 P.M. (except when Christmas Day falls on a Monday). In operation since 1937.

WHERE On Highway 471, north of Highway 50; forty-five minutes south of Ocala, Florida; an hour north of Tampa, an hour west of Orlando, forty-five minutes north of Lakeland.

ADMISSION Free admission; free parking; indoors, outdoors, and under cover, rain or shine.

FEATURES Antiques and collectibles, crafts, fresh produce, plants, citrus trees and ornamental plants, new and vintage clothing, jewelry, new merchandise, furniture. Averages up to 1,700 vendors. Snacks and hot meals are served on the premises. Large wholesale area; market covers over forty acres.

RATES Under cover: $9 per space per day, including two tables (additional tables are available at $1 each); outdoor spaces: $7 per day. Every spot is permanently rented; line up at 7:00 A.M. Monday for cancellations.

CONTACT Larry Story, General Manager, P.O. Box 62, Webster, FL 33597.

PHONE (352) 793-2021 or (352) 793-3551

WEBSTER: Webster Westside Flea Market

WHEN Every Monday, 6:00 A.M. to whenever. In operation for several years.

WHERE At Route 478 and Northwest Third Street.

ADMISSION Free admission; acres of parking at $2 per car; indoors, and outdoors, year-round.

FEATURES Antiques and collectibles, books, new and used merchandise, fresh produce. Averages up to a capacity of 400 spaces under shed plus an additional 600 outdoor vendors. Two sit-down restaurants. Classic car show and swap meet on the first Sunday of every month from September through June. Camping and showers.

RATES $15 per 10'×10' space under shed per day; outside from $10 per space. Reservations are recommended.

CONTACT Manager, 516 Northeast Third, Webster, FL 33597.

PHONE (800) 438-8559 or (800) 832-7396 (voicemail); day of market call (352) 793-9877.

WEST PALM BEACH: Dr. Flea's International Flea Market

WHEN Every Thursday through Sunday, 10:00 A.M. to 6:00 P.M., and every Sunday 10:00 A.M. to 6:00 P.M. In operation since 1947.

WHERE At 1200 South Congress Avenue, a mile south of Palm Beach International Airport.

ADMISSION Free admission; free parking for up to 500 cars; indoors, year-round.

FEATURES Antiques and collectibles, books, new clothing, crafts, new furniture, jewelry, new and used merchandise, porcelain, fresh produce, Western wear, and toys. Averages 85 to 400 vendors. Snacks and hot meals are served on the premises.

RATES Call for monthly rental rates; some weekend spaces—call for availability. Reservations are not required.

CONTACT Dwight Hanners, 1200 South Congress Avenue, West Palm Beach, FL 33406.

PHONE (561) 965-1500

FAX (561) 965-0433

E-MAIL drflea@aol.com

WEB www.dr-fleas.com

 NFMA Member

ZEPHYRHILLS: Zephyrhills Flea Market

WHEN Every Friday, Saturday, and Sunday from September through May, 8:00 A.M. to 3:00 P.M. In operation since 1993.

WHERE 39336 Chancey Road, about a mile and a half east of route 301, on the south side of Zephyrhills.

ADMISSION Free admission; free parking for up to 3,000 cars; indoors, rain or shine.

FEATURES Antiques and collectibles, books, new clothing, coins and stamps, kitchenware, crafts, furniture, jewelry, hardware, new and used merchandise, porcelain, fresh produce, tools, and toys. Averages close to 300 vendors. Snacks and hot meals are served on the premises. A clean, friendly market.

RATES From $10 per space per day. Reservations are not required.

CONTACT Grace Strope or Jerry Zuppa, 39336 Chancey Road, Zephyrhills, FL 33540.

PHONE (813) 782-1483

FAX (813) 782-3800

 NFMA Member

From Collectors by Paul Griner

At the next table, another vendor had placed an old cigar box; it was lying open, filled with pens. Cloisonné crystal, a few silver and one gold, which gleamed beneath the others; she was mindful not to look. That was the cardinal rule of the market, not to display your interest, otherwise you spooked your prey—prices doubled or tripled, sometimes items suddenly weren't for sale, artificial scarcities were created and bidding could start; she would not allow herself to be the one to set it off. . . .

Lifting things, she said, "How much is this? And this? And this?" but did not listen to the vendor's replies. Canary-yellow Fiesta ware, a German beer stein, a glass cutter that felt heavy and surprisingly imbalanced in her palm. The pens were the fourth thing she handled. Some days she made the item she wanted the third thing, some days the fifth, and some days she wouldn't even ask, leaving whatever she wanted for another trip. On those occasions, when she returned, she'd offer half the asking price. . . .

"And this?"

He waited for her to look up and she was sure she knew why. Years before, she'd read that Arab traders, bargaining, watched your eyes, and once your pupils narrowed they were certain you had reached the price you were willing to pay and they would refuse to go any lower. Vendors throughout the various fairs seemed aware of that folklore; they were always watching her eyes.

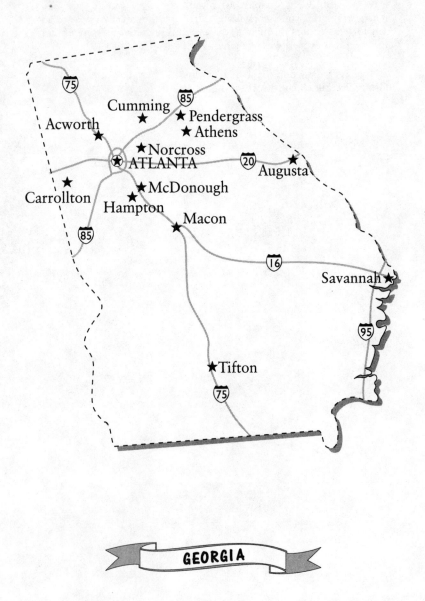

GEORGIA

ACWORTH: Lake Acworth Antiques and Flea Market

WHEN	Every weekend, 7:00 A.M. to 5:00 P.M. In operation since the mid-1970s.
WHERE	On Highway 41, at the intersection of Route 92. Take exit 121 off I-75, then follow Highway 92 to Cobb Parkway (Old Route 41), then make a right on Route 41 until Route 92 turns off to Dallas, and the market will be on the left.
ADMISSION	Free admission; parking available at $1 per car; indoors, outdoors, and under cover, rain or shine.
FEATURES	Antiques and collectibles, books, new and vintage clothing, crafts, furniture, jewelry, new and used merchandise, porcelain, fresh produce, and toys. Averages close to 400 vendors. Snacks and hot meals are served on the premises.
RATES	$5 per 10'×12' space per day. Reserve a week in advance.
CONTACT	Wendell Tummlin, 4375 Cobb Parkway N.W., Acworth, GA 30101.
PHONE	(770) 974-5896

ACWORTH: Yester-year Flea Market

WHEN	Every weekend, 8:00 A.M. to 5:00 P.M. In operation since 1975.
WHERE	At 4337 Highway 92, at the intersection with Route 41.
ADMISSION	Free admission; ample free parking; indoors year-round and outdoors, weather permitting.
FEATURES	Antiques and collectibles, books, new and vintage clothing, coins and stamps, kitchenware, crafts, furniture, jewelry, new and used merchandise, porcelain, fresh produce, and toys. Averages 275 to a capacity of 300 vendors. Snacks and hot meals are served on the premises. Door prizes each week.
RATES	Indoors: $60 per space per month; outdoors: $5 per 10'×10' space per day, covered: $10 per day. Reserve a week in advance for covered spaces.
CONTACT	Bill Abernathy, Owner, 4337 Acworth-Dallas Road, Acworth, GA 30101.
PHONE	(770) 974-6259

ATHENS: J and J Flea Market

WHEN   Every Friday, Saturday, and Sunday, 8:00 A.M. to 5:00 P.M.
                In operation since 1984.
WHERE   At 3000 Commerce Road (Highway 441), four miles north
                of Athens.
ADMISSION   Free admission; free parking for up to 3,000 cars; indoors
                and outdoors, rain or shine.
FEATURES   Antiques and collectibles, books, new and vintage clothing,
                kitchenware, crafts, used furniture, jewelry, livestock, new
                and used merchandise, porcelain, fresh produce, and toys.
                Averages close to 700 vendors. Great food at great prices
                on 125 acres of wooded land on a major tourist route near
                the University of Georgia, this market attracts as many as
                10,000 visitors a day.
RATES $8 per space per day indoors, $5 outdoors. Reservations are
                not required.
CONTACT   Jerry or Jimmy Farmer, 11661 Commerce Road, Athens, GA
                30607.
PHONE   (706) 613-2410

ATLANTA: Flea Market U.S.A.

WHEN   Daily except Tuesday and Wednesday: Thursday, 11:00 A.M.
                to 7:00 P.M., Friday, 11:00 A.M. to 9:00 P.M., Saturday, 10:00
                A.M. to 9:00 P.M., Sunday, noon to 7:00 P.M., and Monday,
                11:00 A.M. to 7:00 P.M. In operation for over seven years.
WHERE   At 1919 Metropolitan Parkway, S.W. (Highway 41/19),
                south of downtown Atlanta and north of the airport.
ADMISSION   Free admission; free parking for more than 1,000 cars;
                indoors, year-round.
FEATURES   Antiques and collectibles, books, electronics, kitchenware, new
                furniture, jewelry, and toys (mostly new merchandise, with
                very little secondhand merchandise). Averages up to a capacity
                of 450 vendors. Snacks and hot meals are served on the prem-
                ises. More like a discount mall than a flea market—but good
                for bargain hunters.
RATES   From $1 to $2 per square foot per month. Reserve a week in
                advance.
CONTACT   Kim, 1919 Metropolitan Parkway, S.W., Atlanta, GA 30315.
PHONE   (404) 763-3078 or (404) 901-2605 (beeper)

ATLANTA: Lakewood Antiques Market

WHEN   Second full weekend of each month: Friday and Saturday, 9:00
            A.M. to 6:00 P.M. and Sunday, 9:00 A.M. to 5:00 P.M. In opera-
            tion for over eighteen years.
WHERE   At 2000 Lakewood Way. Take exit 88 off I-75/85, to
            Highway 166 (south of the city) to Lakewood Freeway
            East.
ADMISSION   Admission $3 per person; free for children under twelve; free
            parking for up to 6,800 cars; indoors and outdoors, rain or
            shine.
FEATURES   Antiques and collectibles, architectural items, books, vintage
            clothing, crafts, garage-sale items, glassware, jewelry, porce-
            lain, and antique toys; no new merchandise. Averages 1,200
            to 1,500 vendors. Restaurant on the premises. Well publi-
            cized as the oldest flea market in Atlanta. Camping is avail-
            able on the grounds; showers are available for vendors;
            special motel rates available.
RATES $95 per 8'×10' space per weekend indoors, or $75 per
            10'×20' or 14'×15' space outdoors. Reservations are not
            required.
CONTACT   Ed Spivia, P.O. Box 6826, Atlanta, GA 30315.
PHONE   (404) 622-4488
FAX   (404) 627-2999

ATLANTA: Scott Antique Market

WHEN   Second weekend of every month: Friday and Saturday, 9:00
            A.M. to 6:00 P.M. and Sunday, 10:00 A.M. to 5:00 P.M. In
            operation since the mid-1980s.
WHERE   At the Atlanta Exposition Centers (north and south facili-
            ties), three miles east of Atlanta Airport. At exit 40
            (Jonesboro Road) off I-285.
ADMISSION   Admission $3 per person; free parking for up to 3,000 cars;
            indoors and outdoors, rain or shine.
FEATURES   Antiques and collectibles of all types. Averages close to its
            capacity of 2,400 vendors. Snacks and hot meals are served
            on the premises.
RATES $85 per 8'×10' space per weekend indoors, or $65 outdoors.
            Reservations are not required for outdoor spaces.
CONTACT   Don Scott, P.O. Box 60, Bremen, OH 43107.

PHONE   (740) 569-4112 or (740) 569-4912; day of market call (404) 361-2000

FAX   (740) 569-7595

AUGUSTA: South Augusta Flea Market

WHEN   Every weekend, 9:00 A.M. to 6:00 P.M. In operation since 1978.

WHERE   At 1562 Doug Bernard Parkway (formerly New Savannah Road). From I-20, take Bobby Jones Expressway (520) toward airport to end of road, then left, and market is a mile ahead on the right.

ADMISSION Free admission; seven acres of free parking; indoors and outdoors, rain or shine.

FEATURES   Antiques and collectibles, books, electronics, new and used merchandise—"everything." Averages close to 400 vendors. Three restaurants and four concession stands on the premises. Biggest market in the area.

RATES $5 per 12'×12' space; tables are available at $1 each. Spaces are assigned on a first-come, first-served basis.

CONTACT   Ronald Rhodes, 1562 Doug Bernard Parkway, Augusta, GA 30906.

PHONE   (706) 798-5500

CARROLLTON: West Georgia Flea Market

WHEN   Every weekend, 8:00 A.M. to 4:30 P.M. In operation since the early 1980s.

WHERE   At 3947 Highway 27 North. Take exit 3 (Bremen) off I-20 West and go south 2.4 miles, and market will be on the left.

ADMISSION Free admission; free parking for up to 3,000 cars; indoors, year-round.

FEATURES   Antiques and collectibles, books, new and vintage clothing, kitchenware, crafts, furniture, jewelry, livestock, new and used merchandise, porcelain, fresh produce, and toys. Averages 250 to a capacity of 500 vendors. Food concession on the premises serving full breakfast. RVs are welcome.

RATES   From $9 per 8' table per day. Reserve a week in advance.
CONTACT   Manager, 746 Kierbow Road, Carrollton, GA 30117.
PHONE   (770) 832-6551

CUMMING: Dixie 400 Flea Market

WHEN   Every weekend, 9:00 A.M. to 6:00 P.M. In operation since 1988.
WHERE   At 4755 Setting Down Circle, just off Highway 400, about
             eight miles north of town.
ADMISSION   Free admission; ample free parking; indoors and outdoors,
             year-round.
FEATURES   Just about everything (mostly used stuff). Averages close to
             90 vendors. Food is served on the premises.
RATES $5 per 6'×12' space per day outdoors or $10 per space
             indoors. Reservations are not required for outdoor spaces.
CONTACT   Manager, 4755 Setting Down Circle, Cumming, GA 30040.
PHONE   (770) 889-5895

HAMPTON: Sweeties Flea Market

WHEN   Every Friday, Saturday, and Sunday, 8:00 A.M. to 5:30 P.M.
             In operation since the early 1970s.
WHERE   At 2316 Highway 19/41, two miles south of the Atlanta
             Motor Speedway. Take exit 77 off I-75, then go straight out
             about twelve to fifteen miles, and market will be on the right.
ADMISSION   Free admission; free parking for up to 500 cars; outdoors,
             year-round.
FEATURES   Antiques and collectibles, books, new clothing, coins and
             stamps, kitchenware, crafts, used furniture, jewelry, new and
             used merchandise, fresh produce, and toys. Averages 75 to
             220 vendors. Hot meals are served on the premises.
RATES   From $10 to $25 per space per day, depending on size and
             location. Reserve a week in advance.
CONTACT   Pat or Jim Martin, P.O. Box 181, Hampton, GA 30228.
PHONE   (404) 946-4721
FAX   (770) 478-7727
E-MAIL   jmarti93995@aol.com

MCDONOUGH: Peachtree Peddlers Flea Market

WHEN   Every weekend: Saturday, 9:00 A.M. to 6:00 P.M. and Sunday, 10:00 A.M. to 6:00 P.M.; also, Fridays 11:00 A.M. to 7:00 P.M. from Thanksgiving through Christmas.

WHERE   On I-75 at exit 71 (Jonesboro Road), about a half hour's drive south of Atlanta.

ADMISSION Free admission; ample free parking; indoors and outdoors, year-round.

FEATURES   Wide variety of new, used, antique and collectible merchandise, local produce, crafts, and gift items. Averages close to 300 vendors. Peddlers Café and Grill is open six days a week. One of Georgia's largest indoor flea markets, located "in the heart of Georgia, on the friendly side of Atlanta," near various attractions.

RATES $60 per 10'×12' space indoors, $15 per 10'×20' outdoors (free setup on Thursday); tables are available at $1.50 per day.

CONTACT   Peggy Alexander, 155 Mill Road, McDonough, GA 30253.

PHONE   (888) 661-3532 (No1-FLEA) or (770) 914-2269

FAX   (770) 914-0911

E-MAIL   malexa3395@aol.com

WEB   www.smartfleamarkets.com/html/ shopping.html

  NFMA Member

MACON: Smiley's Flea Market and Yard Sale

WHEN   Every weekend, 7:00 A.M. to 5:00 P.M. In operation since 1985.

WHERE   At 6717 Hawkinsville Road (Highway 129 South), halfway between Macon and Warner Robins. Take exit 49 (northbound) or 49A (southbound) off I-75 in Macon, then go south four miles on Highway 247/129 and look for the big Smiley sign on the right.

ADMISSION Free admission; twenty acres of free parking (buses and RVs are accommodated); indoors and outdoors, rain or shine.

FEATURES   Antiques and collectibles, crafts, kitchenware, furniture, jewelry, new and used merchandise, military surplus (Robins AFB is just down the road), fresh produce, and toys. Averages 500 to 700 vendors. There are two concession stands on the premises. Part of the Smiley's "franchise" (with sister markets throughout the South) and billed as Georgia's "largest and finest," the market offers mostly discounted new merchandise and "junque"; the feel is humble and homey, but there's gems hiding in those piles.

RATES $11 per space for one day or $20 for two days within fenced area; call for monthly rates; electrical hookups are also available. Reservations are not required; call a week in advance for spaces within fenced area.

CONTACT   Terry Hudson, General Manager, or Ben Compen (Sr. or Jr.), 6717 Hawkinsville Road, Macon, GA 31216.

PHONE   (912) 788-3700 or (352) 331-2999

FAX   (912) 788-5344

 NFMA Member

NORCROSS: Pride of Dixie Antiques Market

WHEN   Fourth weekend of the month: Friday and Saturday, 9:00 A.M. to 6:00 P.M., and Sunday 11:00 A.M. to 5:00 P.M. In operation since 1992.

WHERE   At the North Atlanta Trade Center, 1700 Jeurgens Court. Take exit 36 (Indian Trail) off I-85, then go east on Indian Trail to Onbrook Parkway, then right on Jeurgens Court.

ADMISSION   Admission $4; ample free parking; indoors, year-round.

FEATURES   Antiques and collectibles. Averages close to 325 vendors. Food is served on the premises.

RATES $125 per 8'×10' for three days. Reservations are required.

CONTACT   Rhonda Perkins, 1700 Jeurgens Court, Norcross, GA 30093.

PHONE   (770) 279-9853

FAX   (770) 279-0019

PENDERGRASS: Pendergrass Flea Market

WHEN   Every weekend, 9:00 A.M. to 6:00 P.M. In operation since 1993.

WHERE   Two hundred yards from exit 50 off I-85 (near junction with Route 129).

ADMISSION   Free admission; free parking for up to 1,200 cars; indoors year-round and outdoors, weather permitting.

FEATURES   Antiques and collectibles, books, coins and stamps, kitchenware, crafts, furniture, livestock, and fresh produce, new and used merchandise, Oriental rugs, and toys. Averages 350 to a capacity of 650 vendors. Snacks and hot meals are served on the premises. There is a beauty shop and a health food store on the premises.

RATES $16 per 10'×10' space under cover per day, or $65 per 12'×20' lockable space per weekend. Reserve a week in advance.

CONTACT   Reed Smith, 5641 U.S. Highway 129N, Pendergrass, GA 30567.

PHONE   (706) 693-4466 or (770) 945-1900; day of market call Judy Pearson at (706) 693-4444.

FAX   (706) 693-4506

SAVANNAH: Keller's Flea Market

WHEN   Every weekend, 8:00 A.M. to 6:00 P.M. (Friday is vendor setup day, but buyers are welcome). In operation since 1987.

WHERE   At 5901 Ogeechee Road. Take exit 16 off I-95 and go a mile east; market is at the corner of U.S. Route 17 and Georgia Route 204.

ADMISSION   Free admission; free parking; indoors and outdoors, rain or shine.

FEATURES   Antiques and collectibles, new and vintage clothing, coins and stamps, kitchenware, crafts, furniture, jewelry, porcelain, new merchandise, and fresh produce. Averages up to a capacity of over 400 vendors. Janie Arkwright's Kitchens and Snack Bar serves "the world's best Bar-B-Q" (and much more). Billed as the largest flea market in the Coastal Empire. Hot showers on premises.

RATES   From $10 to $18 per 10'×10' space per day, includes one eight-foot table; extra tables are $2 per day; electricity hookup for RVs is $2 per day; display electricity is $1.50 minimum per day. Rentals are on a first-come, first-served basis; telephone reservations are not accepted.

CONTACT   Hubert or Cheri Keller, 5901 Ogeechee Road, Savannah, GA 31419.

PHONE   (912) 927-4848

FAX   (912) 925-2638

NFMA Member

TIFTON: New River Flea Market

WHEN   Every weekend, 6:00 A.M. until whenever. In operation since 1999.

WHERE   On Route 82 about a half mile past the fairgrounds, on the left.

ADMISSION   Free admission; ample free parking; indoors and outdoors, year-round.

FEATURES   Mix of new and used merchandise. Averages 50 to 120 vendors. American and Mexican food is served on the premises. A clean market, cool and shaded, in the heart of the lovely, rural Tift County in central Georgia. There is a garden center and petting zoo nearby.

RATES $5 per 4'×8' space per day. Reservations are not required.

CONTACT   Helen or Joe Barr, 44 Old Brookfield Road, Tifton, GA 31794.

PHONE   (912) 387-0016 or (912) 388-9313

FAX   (912) 388-9809

E-MAIL   louie@surfsouth.com

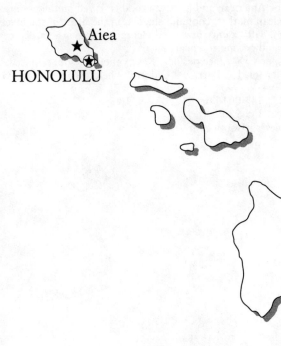

Aiea

HONOLULU

HAWAII

AIEA: Kam Super Swap Meet

WHEN Every Wednesday, Saturday, and Sunday, plus some holidays (call for dates), 5:30 A.M. to 1:00 P.M. In operation since the late 1980s.

WHERE At 98-850 Moanalua Road. Take Aiea exit off Moanalua/H-1 Freeway, and follow Moanalua Road to Kaonohi Street, then turn left, and market will be on the right as you're facing the ocean.

ADMISSION Admission 25¢ per person; free parking; outdoors, year-round.

FEATURES Antiques and collectibles, books, new and vintage clothing, kitchenware, crafts, furniture, jewelry, new and used merchandise, porcelain, fresh produce, plants, fruits, fish, and toys. Averages up to several hundred vendors. Snacks and hot meals are served on the premises.

RATES $6 per reserved space or $8 unreserved on Saturday or Sunday; $5 per reserved space or $7 per unreserved space on Wednesday. Reservations are not required.

CONTACT Manager, c/o Aloha Flea Market, 99-500 Salt Lake Blvd., Aiea, HI 96701-3756.

PHONE (808) 483-5933 (recorded message) or (808) 848-5555; for reservations, call (808) 483-5535.

FAX (808) 847-9270

HONOLULU: Aloha Flea Market

WHEN Every Wednesday, Saturday, and Sunday, 6:00 A.M. to 3:00 P.M. In operation since 1979.

WHERE At 9500 Salt Lake Boulevard, in the parking lot of the Aloha Stadium in Honolulu on the island of Oahu. Take Halawa Stadium exit off H-1 Freeway.

ADMISSION Admission 50¢ per person (children under twelve admitted free); free parking for up to several thousand cars; outdoors, rain or shine.

FEATURES Antiques and collectibles, books, new and vintage clothing, coins and stamps, kitchenware, crafts, furniture, jewelry, new and used merchandise, porcelain, fresh produce, toys, and a variety of Hawaiian novelties. Averages 500 to 1,000 vendors. Snacks and hot meals are served on the premises.

RATES From $10 to $42.75 per space per day, depending on size and location. Reservations are not required.

CONTACT   Edward Medeiros, 3478 Waialae Avenue, Honolulu, HI
            96816.
PHONE   (808) 732-9611 or (808) 486-1529
FAX   (808) 737-7764

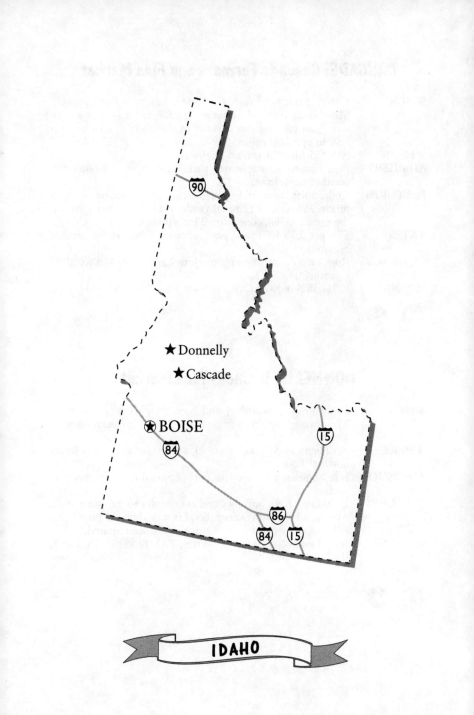

★ Donnelly

★ Cascade

★ BOISE

IDAHO

CASCADE: Cascade Farmers and Flea Market

WHEN	Every Friday, Saturday, and Sunday—plus holiday Mondays, from mid-May through Labor Day—plus a two-week run starting July Fourth weekend, 9:00 A.M. to 6:00 P.M. In operation since 1993.
WHERE	At 1455 Main Street, on Highway 55.
ADMISSION	Free admission; ample free parking; indoors and outdoors, weather permitting.
FEATURES	Collectibles, new and used merchandise, electronics, fresh produce. Averages 12 to 20 vendors. There is a snack bar on the premises. This one's small but atmospheric.
RATES	$25 per 20'×40' space per weekend. Reservations are not required.
CONTACT	Ron or Glenna Young or Jim Larsen, P.O. Box 399, Cascade, ID 83611.
PHONE	(208) 382-3600 or (208) 382-4894 or (208) 382-3049

DONNELLY: Donnelly Flea Market

WHEN	Every Friday, Saturday, and Sunday, plus holidays, from May through September; daylight to dusk. In operation since 1986.
WHERE	On Highway 55 (can't miss it), about two and a half hours north of Boise.
ADMISSION	Free admission; ample free parking; outdoors, weather permitting.
FEATURES	Everything from antiques and collectibles to yard-sale stuff. Averages 10 to 40 vendors. Food is served on the premises.
RATES	$10 per space per day. Reservations are not required.
CONTACT	Jerry Livingston or Sheri Gestrin, P.O. Box 399, Donnelly, ID 83615.
PHONE	(208) 325-8604

Pecatonica ★   Rockford ★   ★ Grayslake

Sycamore ★   St. Charles ★   Rosemont
                         ★   ★ Chicago
                    Melrose   ★ Alsip

🛡88   Sandwich ★

                         🛡80

            🛡39

                         🛡57

🛡74   Towanda ★
Peoria ★   ★ Bloomington

                              🛡74

            🛡72
SPRINGFIELD ✪

            ★ Pana

                    🛡70

                         🛡57

        ★
Belleville

Du Quoin ★

ILLINOIS

ALSIP: Tri-State Swap-O-Rama

WHEN	Every weekend, 7:00 A.M. to 4:00 P.M. In operation since the late 1970s.
WHERE	At 4350 West 129th. Take I-294 (Tri-State Tollway) to Cicero Avenue (Route 50), then go south to 131st, then east to the market.
ADMISSION	Admission 75¢; free parking for up to 3,500 cars; indoors year-round and outdoors, weather permitting.
FEATURES	All types of new and used merchandise, including baseball cards, books, bottles, new and vintage clothing, coins, comics, kitchenware, furniture, fresh produce, silver, stamps, and toys. Averages 650 to a capacity of 950 vendors. Hot meals are served on the premises. This market has recently been expanded and enlarged to accommodate more vendors and shoppers.
RATES	$20 per space per day indoors; $18 outdoors. Reservations are not required.
CONTACT	Jim Pierski or Albert Barrelli, 4600 West Lake Street, Melrose Park, IL 60160.
PHONE	(708) 344-7300 or (708) 271-8864

BELLEVILLE: Belleville Flea Market

WHEN	Third full weekend of every month, 8:00 A.M. to 4:00 P.M. In operation for over twenty-two years.
WHERE	At the Belle-Clair Exposition Center at the intersection of Routes 13 and 159 (Fairgrounds).
ADMISSION	Free admission; free parking for up to a thousand cars; indoors year-round and outdoors, rain or shine.
FEATURES	Antiques and collectibles, books, new and vintage clothing, coins and stamps, kitchenware, crafts, furniture, jewelry, porcelain, fresh produce, toys, and used merchandise. Averages 600 to 700 vendors. Snacks and hot meals are served on the premises. Biggest (and said to be the best) flea market in the area.
RATES	$13 per 10'×10' space per day outdoors; $15 per eight-foot table per day indoors. Reservations are required.
CONTACT	Betty Heinline, St. Clair County Fair Association, 200 South Belt East, Belleville, IL 62220.
PHONE	(618) 235-0666 or (618) 233-3377

BLOOMINGTON: Third Sunday Market

WHEN   Third Sunday of every month from May through November, 8:00 A.M. to 4:00 P.M. In operation since 1987.

WHERE   At the Interstate Center, exit 160B from I-55 and I-74 (Route 9 West).

ADMISSION   Admission $4.50 per person; ample free parking; indoors rain or shine and outdoors, weather permitting.

FEATURES   The focus is on antiques, collectibles, and crafts. Averages close to its capacity of 300 vendors. Food is served on the premises.

RATES $75 per 30'×30' space per day outdoors. Reservations are not required outdoors.

CONTACT   Manager, P.O. Box 396, Bloomington, IL 61702-0396.

PHONE   (309) 662-1978 or (309) 452-7926

CHICAGO: Ashland Avenue Swap-O-Rama

WHEN   Every Thursday, Saturday, and Sunday, 7:00 A.M. to 4:00 P.M. In operation since the 1980s.

WHERE   At 4100 South Ashland. Take I-94 (Dan Ryan Expressway) to Pershing Road, then west to Ashland, then south two blocks.

ADMISSION   Admission 50¢; free parking for up to 2,000 cars; indoors year-round and outdoors, weather permitting.

FEATURES   Baseball cards, books, bottles, new and vintage clothing, coins, comics, kitchenware, furniture, jewelry, knives, and fresh produce. Averages close to its capacity of 975 vendors. Hot and cold meals are served on the premises. This ethnically diverse market, which is part of the Chicago area's Swap-O-Rama chain, has absorbed many of the vendors from the historic Maxwell Street market. Other amenities include a barber shop, beauty parlor, lawyer's office, and photographer on the premises.

RATES   Indoors: $18 per space on Saturday, $20 on Sunday; outdoors: $18 per space per day. Reservations are not required.

CONTACT   Jim Pierski or Mike Campagna, 4600 West Lake Street, Melrose Park, IL 60160

PHONE   (708) 344-7300 or (773) 376-6993

CHICAGO: Maxwell Street Market

WHEN	Every Sunday, 7:00 A.M. to 3:00 P.M. In operation since the 1880s.
WHERE	On Canal Street between Taylor and 15th Streets.
ADMISSION	Free admission; parking at $3 per car; outdoors, year-round.
FEATURES	Everything from toilet paper to car engines—"a combination of Ace Hardware, Jewel Osco, and Wal-Mart." Averages close to 500 vendors. Food (including lots of Mexican) is served on the premises. This "teeming multicultural bazaar" is one of the oldest and most famously quirky in the country, drawing early-morning browsers and curiosity seekers from far and wide.
RATES	From $15 to $40 per space. Reservations are required.
CONTACT	Manager, 548 West Roosevelt Road, Chicago, IL 60607.
PHONE	(312) 922-3100
FAX	(312) 922-3169

DU QUOIN: Giant Flea Market

WHEN	Usually the first Sunday of every month (call for dates), 8:30 A.M. to 4:30 P.M. In operation for over twelve years.
WHERE	On the State Fairgrounds, on Route 51 on the south side of Du Quoin.
ADMISSION	Admission $1 per person; ample free parking; indoors, year-round.
FEATURES	Antiques and collectibles, books, new and vintage clothing, jewelry, new merchandise, and toys. Averages up to 125 vendors. Snacks and hot meals are served on the premises.
RATES	$13 per eight-foot table per day. Reserve two weeks in advance.
CONTACT	John Crouch, P.O. Box 9500, Springfield, IL 62791.
PHONE	(217) 529-6939

GRAYSLAKE: Lake County Antiques and Collectibles Show and Sale

WHEN   Second Sunday of every month, 8:00 A.M. to 3:00 P.M. In operation for over ten years.

WHERE   At the Lake County Fairgrounds, at the intersection of State Route 120 and U.S. Route 45, five miles west of I-94 (halfway between Chicago and Milwaukee).

ADMISSION   Admission $3 per person; early entry (6:00 A.M. to 8:00 A.M.) $10 per person; ample free parking; indoors year-round and outdoors, weather permitting.

FEATURES   Antiques and collectibles. Averages up to several hundred vendors. Snacks and hot meals are served on the premises. A diverse selection, excellent for good quality merchandise; four large indoor exhibit halls are restricted to antiques and collectibles; hundreds of vendors come from across the midwest.

RATES   Indoors: $90 per 8'×13' space or $75 per 10'×10' space, includes three tables; outdoors: $75 per 12'×20' space. Reservations are required for indoor spaces only.

CONTACT   Manager, c/o Lake County Promotions, P.O. Box 461, Grayslake, IL 60030.

PHONE   (847) 223-1433 or (847) 356-7499

FAX   (847) 356-1362

MELROSE PARK: Melrose Park Swap-O-Rama

WHEN   Every Friday, Saturday, and Sunday, 7:00 A.M. to 4:00 P.M. In operation since the mid-1980s.

WHERE   At 4600 West Lake Street. Take any major expressway to Mannheim Road (Route 45) to where it intersects with Lake Street (Route 20).

ADMISSION   Admission 50¢; free parking for up to 550 cars; indoors year-round and outdoors, weather permitting.

FEATURES   Wide range of new and used merchandise, fresh produce, and collectibles. Averages 375 to 420 vendors. Snacks and hot meals are served on the premises.

RATES   Indoors: $17 per space on Saturday, $19 on Sunday; outdoors: $11 on Saturday, $13 on Sunday. Reservations are not required.

CONTACT   Jim Pierski or Kathy Tyda, 4600 West Lake Street, Melrose
          Park, IL 60160.
PHONE   (708) 344-7300 or (708) 681-4335

PANA: Dutch Mill Flea Market

WHEN   Every Friday, Saturday, and Sunday, 9:00 A.M. to 4:30 P.M.
          In operation since the early 1990s.
WHERE   At the intersection of Routes 51 and 16 East in Pana (pro-
          nounced PAY-na).
ADMISSION Free admission; ample free parking; indoors and outdoors,
          rain or shine.
FEATURES Antiques and collectibles, Avon products, books, new and
          vintage clothing, kitchenware, crafts, furniture, jewelry,
          new and used merchandise, porcelain, fresh produce, tools,
          and toys. Averages up to a capacity of 68 indoor and 28
          outdoor vendors. Snack bar on premises; market is "known
          for its popcorn." This clean, family-run market claims to
          be the largest indoor market in Christian County.
RATES   Indoors: $10 per space per day includes three tables, or $25
          for three days; outdoors: $5 per space per day; monthly rates
          are also available. Reservations are not required.
CONTACT   Carl Sparling, Route 2, Box 268, Pana, IL 62557.
PHONE   (217) 562-4825 or (217) 423-4591

PECATONICA: The Pec Thing

WHEN   Two weekends a year, in May and September, 8:00 A.M. to
          5:00 P.M.—call for dates. In operation for over fifteen years.
WHERE   At the Winnebago County Fairgrounds, on Route 20
          between Freeport and Rockford. Turn north at the state
          police headquarters, to the sign on Seventh Street to the fair-
          grounds.
ADMISSION Admission $2 per person; free parking; indoors, outdoors,
          and under cover, rain or shine.
FEATURES Antiques and collectibles, new and vintage clothing, crafts,
          garage-sale items, jewelry, and much more. Averages up to a
          capacity of 500 vendors. Snacks and hot meals are served on
          the premises.

RATES   Inside: $50 per space per weekend; open shed: $35; outside space: $25; tables available at $7 each. Friday setup time is 2:00 P.M. to 9:00 P.M.; gates open for setup at 6:00 A.M. on market days. Reserve if possible; indoors booked from one show to the next; some outdoor space always available.

CONTACT   Winnebago County Fair Office, P.O. Box K, Pecatonica, IL 61063.

PHONE   (815) 239-1641

FAX   (815) 239-1653

WEB   www.winncountyfair.com

PEORIA: Giant Flea Market

WHEN   Usually the fourth Sunday of every month from April through September, and the fourth weekend from October through March, 8:30 A.M. to 4:30 P.M. In operation for over twenty-one years.

WHERE   At the Expo Gardens. Take University Street exit off I-74 and go north to Northmoor Road, then go left a quarter mile.

ADMISSION   Admission $1.25 per person; ample free parking; indoors, year-round.

FEATURES   Antiques and collectibles, books, new and vintage clothing, jewelry, new merchandise, and toys. Averages up to 100 vendors. Snacks and hot meals are served on the premises.

RATES $13 per eight-foot table for one day, or $20 for two days. Reserve two weeks in advance.

CONTACT   John Crouch, P.O. Box 9500, Springfield, IL 62791.

PHONE   (217) 529-6939

ROCKFORD: Sandy Hollow Indoor-Outdoor Flea Market

WHEN   Every weekend, 9:00 A.M. to 4:00 P.M. In operation for over twenty years.

WHERE   At Alpine and Sandy Hollow, one and a half blocks west of Alpine exit off Highway 20 on Sandy Hollow.

ADMISSION   Free admission; free parking for up to 1,500 cars; indoors year-round and outdoors, weather permitting.

FEATURES   Variety of offerings including antiques and collectibles, new and used merchandise, kitchenware, crafts, glassware, jewelry, fresh produce, and "junque." Averages 60 to 100 vendors. Hot meals available on premises.

RATES $25 per space per weekend, indoors or outdoors. Reservations are required one week in advance for indoor spaces only.

CONTACT   Albert or Carol Fritsch, 6350 Canyon Woods Drive, Rockford, IL 61109.

PHONE   (815) 397-6683 or (815) 874-3362; day of market contact Jane Henshell at (815) 874-6020.

ROSEMONT: Wolff's Flea Market

WHEN   Every Sunday from April through October, 7:00 A.M. to 3:00 P.M. In operation since 1991.

WHERE   At 6920 North Mannheim (between Higgins and Touhy, near O'Hare Airport), at the Rosemont Horizon. Take Lee Street exit off I-90 West (market is visible from exit), or take O'Hare Airport exit off I-90 East, then onto Mannheim North one mile to market.

ADMISSION   Admission $1 per person; 50 for seniors and children under twelve; free parking for up to 3,000 cars; outdoors, weather permitting.

FEATURES   Antiques and collectibles, books, new and vintage clothing, coins and stamps, computers, kitchenware, crafts, used furniture, porcelain, fresh produce, toys, and used merchandise (Beanie Babies were hot in 1999). Averages 250 to 500 vendors. Snacks and hot meals are served on the premises. One of the largest outdoor weekly markets in Chicagoland.

RATES $23 per space per day; call for monthly rates. Reservations are not required.

CONTACT   David and Donald Wolff, 970 Arkansas, Elk Grove Village, IL 60007.

PHONE   (847) 524-9590; day of market contact Don Wolff at (630) 833-7469.

FAX   (630) 833-4357

E-MAIL   dwolff517@aol.com

   NFMA Member

SAINT CHARLES: Kane County Antique and Flea Market

WHEN
First Sunday of each month, 7:00 A.M. to 4:00 P.M., and the preceding Saturday, noon to 5:00 P.M. In operation since 1967.

WHERE
On the Kane County Fairgrounds, at Route 64 and Randall Road, on the west side of Saint Charles (forty miles west of Chicago).

ADMISSION
Admission $5 per person; free for children under twelve; a hundred acres of free parking; indoors, outdoors, and under cover, rain or shine.

FEATURES
Antiques and collectibles, books, vintage clothing, crafts, "fancy junque," used furniture, jewelry, new and used merchandise, primitives, and toys. Averages 600 to 1,200 vendors. Snacks, sandwiches, and hot meals are served on the premises (including a country breakfast on Sunday). One of the country's largest and most diverse markets, drawing vendors from many states; billed as "best in the Midwest or anywhere," it has never canceled in more than thirty years.

RATES
Indoors: $125 per booth per weekend; open-sided shed: $105 per weekend; outdoors: $115 per 10'×20' space per weekend. Reservations are required for sheds and indoor spaces (when available); outdoor spaces are rented on a first-come, first-served basis.

CONTACT
Helen B. Robinson, P.O. Box 549, Saint Charles, IL 60174.

PHONE
(630) 377-2252 (office hours are Monday through Friday, 9:00 A.M. to 3:00 P.M.)

WEB
www2.pair.com/kaneflea

A Midwestern Flea Market Like No Other

The Kane County Flea Market has grown so much that even the most intrepid treasure-seekers face a major challenge in their assaults on the sprawling market. It's like visiting a Middle Eastern souk, a Babylon full of bargains, full of tumult and intrigue, that magically springs up the first weekend of every month. . . . The monthly monster of flea markets has been in business for more than twenty years under the reign of Helen Robinson, president. The dealers in antiques and collectibles here have become an institution at the market, cramming their wares into a variety of open-sided sheds marked "Swine," "Beef," Sheep," etc. Outdoors, as many as 1,000 nomadic merchants spread their goods on tables up and down dusty aisles linking the buildings and on blankets in outlying meadows.

—*Chicago Tribune*

Shoppers and sellers fill as many as 70,000 parking spaces on market days. On the fairgrounds, mixed patterns of auto, golf cart, and foot traffic are common sights. Golf carts are used only by market personnel, autos and trucks for large merchandise pickup, and good old-fashioned shoe leather for browsing the market.

The rigs the dealers drive reflect a cross-section of lifestyles—some arrive in fully loaded motor homes with all the comforts of home, including television, microwave oven, cellular phone and refrigerator, while others line up in a car pulling a rental trailer with a sleeping bag in the front seat.

"The quality and quantity of your merchandise is important here," said one dealer, "not the cost of your ride."

Since the "first come, first served" rule is in effect, dealers who want choice selling spots get lined up as early as midnight Thursday of the show weekend. (A city ordinance prohibits getting on line any earlier.) By the time Saturday morning rolls around, the smell of hot coffee and good deals fills the air.

Husband-and-wife teams are a common sight during the early hours—along with single dealers that many people know only by nicknames like Junkyard Bill, Chicken Charlie, Las Vegas Bernie, Dealer Dan, etc.

With several college professors setting up to sell at the market, Helen says, "Just about all the questions I have can be answered on the spot. I just walk into the booth and ask the expert."

Looking at an aerial photo of the market prompted one dealer to exclaim, "My gosh, it looks like an entire city from up there."

Adapted from *Queen Flea: The Inside Story of the Kane County Antique and Flea Market*, by Helen Robinson, as told to Jack Kelly.

SANDWICH: Sandwich Antiques Market

WHEN   On six Sundays from May through October, 8:00 A.M. to 4:00 P.M. (call for dates). In operation since 1988.
WHERE   On the fairgrounds on Route 34, sixty miles west of Chicago (call for precise directions).
ADMISSION   Admission $5 per person; acres of free parking; indoors and outdoors, rain or shine.
FEATURES   Antiques (including a selection of nineteenth-century furniture) and collectibles. Averages up to a capacity of 600 vendors. Snacks and hot meals are served on the premises. Said to rank among the best markets in Illinois. Furniture delivery service available.
RATES   Call for rates. Reservations are required a month in advance.
CONTACT   Robert C. Lawler, Manager, 1510 North Hoyne, Chicago, IL 60622-1804.
PHONE   (773) 227-4464 or (815) 786-3337
FAX   (773) 227-6322
E-MAIL   robert@antiquemarkets.com
WEB   www.antiquemarkets.com

SPRINGFIELD: Giant Flea Market

WHEN   Second Sunday of every month from September through December, and third Sunday from January through April, 8:30 A.M. to 4:30 P.M. In operation since the 1970s.
WHERE   At the State Fairgrounds. Take the Sangamon Avenue exit off I-55 and go one mile west.
ADMISSION   Admission $1 per person; ample free parking; indoors, regardless of weather.

FEATURES   Antiques and collectibles, books, new clothing, coins and stamps, jewelry, new merchandise, and toys. Averages up to 100 vendors. Snacks and hot meals are served on the premises.

RATES $13 per eight-foot table per day. Reserve two weeks in advance.

CONTACT   John Crouch, P.O. Box 9500, Springfield, IL 62791.

PHONE   (217) 529-6939

SYCAMORE: Sycamore Music Boosters' Antique, Craft, and Flea Market

WHEN   Annually on the Saturday and Sunday of the last full weekend before Halloween, 9:00 A.M. to 5:00 P.M. In operation since the early 1980s.

WHERE   At the Sycamore High School, sixty miles west of Chicago Route 64. Take Route 23 South to Spartan Trail Drive to the high school.

ADMISSION   Admission $2 per person; $1 for senior citizens and children 12 and under; ample free parking; indoors, rain or shine.

FEATURES   Antiques and collectibles, handmade clothing, crafts, jewelry, pumpkins, and holiday items. Averages close to its capacity of 155 vendors. Food is available at a cafeteria serving homemade pies and barbecue. Held in conjunction with the annual Sycamore Pumpkin Festival, which is said to be one of the largest events in Illinois; flea market attracts approximately 18,000 shoppers over the course of the weekend.

RATES $80 per 99'×12' space for the weekend. Reserve six months in advance.

CONTACT   Beverly A. Smith, Sycamore Music Boosters, P.O. Box 432, Sycamore, IL 60178.

PHONE   (815) 895-6750

TOWANDA: Towanda Antique Flea Market

WHEN   Every July Fourth, 9:00 A.M. to 5:00 P.M. In operation since the 1960s.

WHERE   In the town of Towanda; seven miles northeast of Bloomington. Take exit 171 off I-55.

ADMISSION   Free admission; free parking all over town; outdoors, rain or shine.

FEATURES   Antiques and collectibles, vintage clothing, coins and stamps, crafts, antique furniture, jewelry, primitives, and Indian artifacts. Averages up to 200 vendors. Snacks and hot meals are available in town. Billed as the biggest flea market in central Illinois on July 4, with accompanying festivities in town.

RATES $30 for a 12'×12' reserved space. Reserve three months in advance.

CONTACT   Mary Merritt, P.O. Box 97, Towanda, IL 61776.

PHONE   (309) 728-2810 or (309) 728-2384

Gary

80 90

Shipshewana

★ Cedar Lake

65

69

★ Muncie

Veedersburg
★
74

70

INDIANAPOLIS

Metamora ★ ★
74 Brookville

Nashville ★

Friendship ★
Canaan ★

65

64

INDIANA

BROOKVILLE: White's Farm Flea Market

WHEN   Every Wednesday, daybreak to noon. In operation since 1972.

WHERE   On Highway 152, three miles southeast of Brookville and four miles northwest of Cincinnati (seventy-five miles southeast of Indianapolis).

ADMISSION Free admission; free parking; indoors and outdoors, rain or shine.

FEATURES Good variety of new and used merchandise, including collectibles, new and vintage clothing, kitchenware, crafts, jewelry, knives, and fresh produce. Averages 300 to 400 vendors. Food available on premises. This is a true country market, where just about anything could turn up. Livestock auction at 1:00 P.M.

RATES $10 per 20'×24' space per day outdoors, or from $10 to $20 per 10'×13' space indoors. Reservations are not required.

CONTACT   Dave or Paula White, P.O. Box 53, Brookville, IN 47012.

PHONE   (765) 647-5360 or (765) 647-3574

FAX   (765) 647-6396

CANAAN: Canaan Fall Festival Flea Market

WHEN   At the annual Fall Festival, Friday, Saturday, and Sunday of the second weekend in September, Friday, 9:00 A.M. to 10:00 P.M.; Saturday, 9.00 A.M. to 10.00 P.M.; Sunday, 9:00 A.M. to 6:00 P.M. In operation since 1965.

WHERE   On the village square in Canaan. Pick up Chief White Eye Trail (Route 62) on the hilltop at Madison, and go ten miles from there on Route 62.

ADMISSION Free admission; free parking; outdoors, rain or shine.

FEATURES Antiques and collectibles, kitchenware, crafts, new furniture, jewelry, fresh produce, and much more. Averages up to a capacity of 150 vendors. Variety of food stands and "Fire Department fish sandwiches." Highlight event is the annual Pony Express mail-run relay from Canaan to Madison, beginning Saturday at 1:00 P.M. Many other events are associated with the festival, including Little Indian Papoose Contest, old-fashioned parade, balloon toss, egg toss, horseshoe pitching, frog jumping, and other contests; live entertainment, Chief White Eye Painting Contest; horse-drawn vehicles; kiddie rides; and museum tours.

RATES $30 per 20'×20' space for the three-day weekend; electricity is $5 extra. Reservations are required by August.

CONTACT   Gale Ferris, Sr., President, Canaan Restoration Council, 9713 North State Road 62, Canaan, IN 47224-9758.

PHONE   (812) 839-4770, or call Helyn Bishop, business manager, at (812) 839-3741.

CEDAR LAKE: Barn and Field Flea Market

WHEN   Every weekend, 9:00 A.M. to 5:00 P.M. during wintertime, otherwise dawn to 5:00 P.M. In operation since the 1970s.

WHERE   At 9600 West 151st Avenue, at the corner of Parrish Avenue, one mile east of Route 41.

ADMISSION   Free admission; ample free parking; indoors year-round and outdoors, weather permitting.

FEATURES   Antiques and collectibles, baseball cards, bottles, new and vintage clothing, coins, used furniture, jewelry, knives, dolls, antique firearms, clocks, and fresh produce; "70 percent antiques and collectibles, 30 percent new," according to the manager. Averages 30 to 250 vendors. Snack bar on premises. Farm atmosphere.

RATES $10 per space for one day or $15 for the weekend; electricity is available at a nominal charge. Reserve a week in advance if electricity is needed.

CONTACT   Larry or Pat Toomey, P.O. Box 411, Cedar Lake, IN 46303-0411.

PHONE   (219) 696-7368

CEDAR LAKE: Uncle John's Flea Market

WHEN   Every weekend, 8:00 A.M. to 4:00 P.M. In operation since the 1970s.

WHERE   At 15205 Wicker Avenue (State Route 41), eleven miles south of Route 30.

ADMISSION   Free admission; free parking for up to 500 cars; indoors year-round and outdoors, weather permitting.

FEATURES   Antiques and collectibles, books, new and vintage clothing, coins and stamps, kitchenware, crafts, furniture, jewelry, new and used merchandise, porcelain, fresh produce, toys—about three quarters used merchandise. Averages 100 to 250 vendors. Snacks and hot meals are served on the premises.

RATES   From $10 per space outdoors, depending on size and location; indoor spaces are rented on a monthly basis. Reservations are not required.

CONTACT   Kathy Antosch, 15205 Wicker Avenue, Cedar Lake, IN 46303-9367.

PHONE   (219) 696-7911

FAX   (219) 374-5605

FRIENDSHIP: Friendship Flea Market

WHEN   Two nine-day runs in June and September, usually in the middle of the month (call for dates), 9:00 A.M. to whenever. In operation since 1967.

WHERE   On Route 62, six miles west of Dillsboro (fifty miles west of Cincinnati). Take I-275 west to exit 16, then west on Highway 50 to Dillsboro, then west on Route 62, six miles to market.

ADMISSION Free admission; parking for up to 2,000 cars at $2 per car; indoors year-round and outdoors, weather permitting.

FEATURES Full spectrum of antiques and collectibles, coins and stamps, new and used merchandise, and fresh produce. Averages up to a capacity of 500 vendors. Snacks and hot meals are served on the premises. The market is located next door to the National Muzzle-Loading Rifle Association, whose members live in teepees and shoot the cap and ball rifle. Market draws over 100,000 shoppers per run.

RATES $20 per day or $150 for nine days, including electricity; outdoor spaces are 20'×20'; indoor spaces are 10'×10'. Reservations are required.

CONTACT   Tom Kerr or Jan Hopkins, 654 Wayskin Drive, Covington, KY 41015.

PHONE   (606) 341-1400 or (606) 356-7114; day of market call Tom Kerr at (812) 667-5645

FAX   (606) 363-8184

E-MAIL   friendflea@aol.com

GARY: Market City

WHEN   Every Friday, Saturday, and Sunday, 9:00 A.M. to 5:00 P.M. In operation since 1992.

WHERE   At 4121 Cleveland Street, at 41st Street.

ADMISSION   Free admission; free parking for up to 650 cars; indoors and outdoors, rain or shine.

FEATURES   Antiques and collectibles, books, new and vintage clothing, coins and stamps, electronics, kitchenware, crafts, furniture, glassware, jewelry, new and used merchandise, porcelain, fresh produce, tools, and toys. Averages 200 to a capacity of 275 vendors. Hot meals are served on the premises. Claims to be about 80 percent new merchandise (including close-out name-brand items).

RATES   From $6 per outdoor space per day. Reservations are not required for outdoor spaces.

CONTACT   Bill House, 126 South Main Street, Crown Point, IN 46307.

PHONE   (219) 887-3522

GARY: Village Flea Market

WHEN   Every Friday, Saturday, and Sunday, 9:00 A.M. to 5:00 P.M. In operation since the early 1980s.

WHERE   At 1845 West Ridge Road. Take Grant Street South exit off I-94. Go south on Grant about a mile and a half to Ridge Road, then right on Ridge Road and go one block.

ADMISSION   Free admission; free parking; indoors, year-round.

FEATURES   Antiques and collectibles, books, new and vintage clothing, kitchenware, crafts, furniture, hardware, jewelry, new and used merchandise, porcelain, and toys. Averages 70 to 80 vendors. Free coffee and donuts all day.

RATES $25 per 8'×10' space ($30 for a corner space) for three days, or $40 per 10'×13' wall space for three days. Reserve a week in advance.

CONTACT   Joseph D. Harkin, 5719 Hohman Avenue, Hammond, IN 46320.

PHONE   (219) 933-6622 or (219) 980-1111; market days call Cecelia Harkin at (219) 924-2960 or Shannon Gawlik at (219) 473-9173.

INDIANAPOLIS: Liberty Bell Flea Market

WHEN Every Friday, noon to 8:00 P.M.; Saturday, 10:00 A.M. to 7:00 P.M.; and Sunday, 10:00 A.M. to 6:00 P.M. In operation since 1975.

WHERE At 8949 East Washington Street. Take Post Road exit off I-70 on the east side of Indianapolis, then go south two miles on Post Road to the corner of Washington Street.

ADMISSION Free admission; free parking for up to 350 cars; indoors year-round and outdoors, from mid-April through late November, weather permitting.

FEATURES Antiques and collectibles, books, new and vintage clothing, coins and stamps, crafts, electronics, furniture, jewelry, new merchandise, porcelain, fresh produce, tools, and toys. Averages 150 to a capacity of 200 vendors. Snacks and hot meals are served on the premises.

RATES $45 per 12'×14' space indoors per weekend (lockable—renters may leave merchandise from week to week). Rentals are on a first-come, first-served basis.

CONTACT Noble Hall, 8949 East Washington Street, Indianapolis, IN 46219.

PHONE (317) 898-3180 or (317) 898-3181

INDIANAPOLIS: West Washington Flea Market

WHEN Every Friday, 1:00 P.M. to 8:00 P.M., and every Saturday and Sunday, 11:00 A.M. to 6:00 P.M. In operation since the 1960s.

WHERE At 6445 West Washington Street. Take Plainfield exit off I-465 and go a block and a half west on Washington Street; market will be on the left (look for a big liberty bell on building).

ADMISSION Free admission; free parking for up to 500 cars; indoors, year-round.

FEATURES Antiques and collectibles, books, clothing, kitchenware, crafts, jewelry, new and used merchandise, porcelain, fresh produce, and toys. Averages close to its capacity of 100 vendors. Snacks and hot meals are served on the premises.

RATES $48 per 12'×12' space per weekend. Reservations are recommended.

CONTACT Mirza Beg, 6445 West Washington Street, Indianapolis, IN 46241.

PHONE (317) 244-0941

METAMORA: Canal Days Flea Market

WHEN	First full weekend in October, 8:00 A.M. to 5:00 P.M. In operation since 1969.
WHERE	On Route 52, eight miles west of Brookville, Indiana, and about thirty-five miles west of Cincinnati, Ohio.
ADMISSION	Free admission; ample parking in pay lots nearby; outdoors, rain or shine.
FEATURES	Antiques and collectibles, books, new and vintage clothing, coins and stamps, crafts, furniture, holiday items, jewelry, new and used merchandise, porcelain, quilts, and toys. Averages close to 800 vendors. Snacks and hot meals are served on the premises.
RATES	$75 and up per space. Reserve up to a year in advance.
CONTACT	Al Rogers, Historic Metamora, Inc., P.O. Box 76, Metamora, IN 47030.
PHONE	(765) 647-2194 (office is open 9:00 A.M. to 2:00 P.M.)

MUNCIE: Greenwalt's Flea Market

WHEN	First or second weekend of every month, except June through August, Saturday, 9:00 A.M. to 5:00 P.M., and Sunday, 9:00 A.M. to 4:00 P.M.—call for dates. In operation since 1976.
WHERE	At the Delaware County Fairgrounds. Take I-69 to the Muncie/Franklin exit, then go approximately seven miles (road becomes McGalliard Avenue and Route 332) to Wheeling Avenue, then turn south and go seven blocks to the fairgrounds.
ADMISSION	Free admission; ample free parking; indoors, year-round.
FEATURES	Antiques and collectibles, coins, crafts, furniture, jewelry, knives, new merchandise, primitives, and toys. Averages close to 75 vendors. Hot meals are available on the premises. No alcoholic beverages allowed on the grounds (but smoking is permitted).
RATES	$35 per 10'×10' space per weekend; tables are available at $6 each. Reservations are required—there is usually a waiting list.
CONTACT	Mary Greenwalt, 604 North Kettner Drive, Muncie, IN 47304-9776.
PHONE	(765) 289-0194

NASHVILLE: Westward Ho! Flea Market

WHEN	Every weekend from April through October, plus Memorial Day, July 4, and Labor Day Mondays, 9:00 A.M. to 5:00 P.M.
WHERE	On State Rd. 46, four and a half miles east of Nashville, Indiana, in scenic Brown County.
ADMISSION	Free admission; ample free parking; outdoors and under cover, rain or shine.
FEATURES	Antiques, collectibles, crafts, new and used merchandise. Averages close to 100 vendors. Food concessions operate on the premises (home of the Great Tenderloin). Don't miss the live gospel music by John Baker.
RATES	Call for vendor rates.
CONTACT	Phyllis J. Thompson, P.O. Box 1167, Nashville, IN 47448.
PHONE	(812) 988-0750
E-MAIL	westwardhofm@hotmail.com
WEB	www.gnawboneindiana.com/westwardhofleamarket/

SHIPSHEWANA: Shipshewana Auction and Flea Market

WHEN	Every Tuesday and Wednesday from May through October: Tuesday, 7:00 A.M. to 5:00 P.M. and every Wednesday, 7:00 A.M. to 3:00 P.M. In operation since the 1940s.
WHERE	On Route 5, south of town.
ADMISSION	Free admission; ample parking at $2 per car; indoors and outdoors, rain or shine.
FEATURES	Antiques and collectibles, books, new and vintage clothing, kitchenware, crafts, new and used merchandise, fresh produce, and more. Averages up to several hundred vendors. Snacks and hot meals are served on the premises.
RATES	$30 per 20'×25' space for two days. Reservations are not required.
CONTACT	Manager, P.O. Box 185, Shipshewana, IN 46565.
PHONE	(219) 768-4129
FAX	(219) 768-7041
E-MAIL	shipsheauction@shipshenet.com

VEEDERSBURG: Janet's Flea Market and Antiques

WHEN	A few weekends a year, from May through October (call for dates), 8:00 A.M. to 6:00 P.M. (or until customers quit coming). In operation since 1977.
WHERE	At 305 Sugar Street.
ADMISSION	Free admission; ample free parking; outdoors, rain or shine.
FEATURES	Mostly antiques and collectibles. Averages 50 to 200 vendors. Food is served on the premises. Janet's antique store is open from April through October.
RATES	$50 per space per month for May, July, and September; $100 for 10 days in October. Reservations are required for October.
CONTACT	Janet or Harold Brown, 305 Sugar Street, Veedersburg, IN 47987-8217.
PHONE	(765) 294-2001

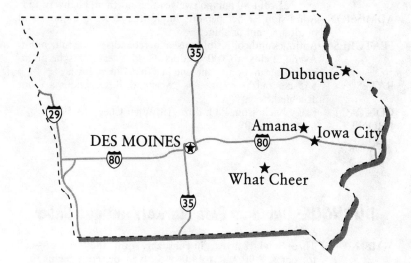

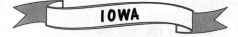

IOWA

AMANA: Collectors Paradise Flea Market

WHEN Two weekends a year, in June and October (call for dates), Saturday, 7:00 A.M. to 5:00 P.M., and Sunday, 7:00 A.M. to 4:00 P.M. In operation since 1991.

WHERE At the Amana Colonies Outdoor Convention Facility. Take exit 225 off I-80 and go twelve miles north on Highway 151.

ADMISSION Admission $1 per person; ample free parking; indoors and outdoors, rain or shine.

FEATURES Antiques and collectibles, used merchandise—the full gamut. Averages close to 100 vendors. Food is served on the premises. Sister market to the one in What Cheer, Iowa.

RATES $35 per outdoor space per weekend. Reservations are not accepted.

CONTACT Larry Nicholson, P.O. Box 413, What Cheer, IA 50268.

PHONE (515) 634-2109

DUBUQUE: Dubuque Flea Market/Antique Show

WHEN Three Sundays a year, in February, April, and October—call for dates, 8:00 A.M. to 4:00 P.M. (vendor setup begins 6:30 A.M.). In operation for over 35 years.

WHERE At the Dubuque County Fairgrounds, five miles west of town on Highway 20.

ADMISSION Admission $1 per person; free admission for children under twelve; free parking; indoors and outdoors, weather permitting.

FEATURES Antiques and collectibles, coins, stamps, kitchenware, and crafts. Averages up to 150 vendors. Food on premises, including hot dogs and burgers, fries, donuts, and rolls. "One man's junque is another man's treasure." In addition to the flea market, there are two arts and crafts shows at the fairgrounds twice a year on Sundays in April and November (in the middle of each month).

RATES Indoors: $14 per eight-foot space per day (wall space $16); eight-foot tables and chairs furnished free with space; Outdoors: $15 per 10'×20' space, no tables furnished. Reservations accepted for inside spaces only, with advance payment.

CONTACT Jerome F. Koppen, 260 Copper Kettle Lane, East Dubuque, IL 61025.

PHONE   (815) 747-7745; day of market call the fairgrounds at (815) 588-1406.
E-MAIL   jfk@netins.net

IOWA CITY: Sharpless Flea Market

WHEN   Second Sunday of every month, 8:00 A.M. to 4:00 P.M. (early birds can arrive as early as 5:30 A.M.). In operation since 1972.

WHERE   At 5049 Hoover Highway N.E. on I-80 at exit 249, the easternmost Iowa City exit.

ADMISSION   Admission $2 per person; "early bird" admission (before 8:00 A.M.) is $5 per person; free parking for more than 500 cars; indoors and outdoors, rain or shine.

FEATURES   Antiques and collectibles, new and vintage clothing, coins and stamps, furniture, jewelry, primitives, and toys. Averages close to 75 vendors. There is a restaurant and a popcorn stand on the premises.

RATES $20 per eight-foot table indoors (tables and chairs are provided) or $20 outdoors (no space limitation; chairs are provided, tables are extra). Reserve a week to a month in advance for indoor spaces; outdoors on a first-come, first-served basis.

CONTACT   Karen Dunlap, 5049 Hoover Highway N. E., Iowa City, IA 52240-8387.

PHONE   (319) 351-8888 or (319) 338-1714
FAX   (319) 643-7372

WHAT CHEER: Collectors Paradise Flea Market

WHEN   Three weekends a year (call for dates); 1999 dates: May 1–2, July 31–August 1, and October 3–4, Saturday, 7:00 A.M. to 5:00 P.M., and Sunday, 7:00 A.M. to 4:00 P.M. In operation since the 1970s.

WHERE   At the County Fairgrounds. Take exit 201 off I-80, and go south on Highway 21 for twenty miles.

ADMISSION   Admission $1 per person; early bird admission is $2 per person; ample free parking; indoors and outdoors, rain or shine.

FEATURES   Antiques and collectibles, used merchandise—the full gamut. Averages close to 500 vendors. Food is served on the premises. One of the bigger flea markets in the Midwest.

RATES $35 per outdoor space per weekend. Reservations are not required for outdoor spaces.

CONTACT   Larry Nicholson, P.O. Box 413, What Cheer, IA 50268.

PHONE   (515) 634-2109

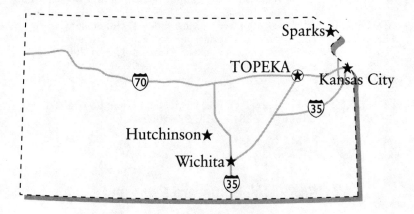

Sparks★

TOPEKA ★

Kansas City ★

70

35

Hutchinson★

Wichita★

35

KANSAS

HUTCHINSON: Mid-America Flea Market

WHEN	First Sunday of every month from October through June (call to confirm dates, which can vary), 9:00 A.M. to 4:00 P.M. In operation since 1969.
WHERE	At the Kansas State Fairgrounds at 20th and Main, in the Industrial Building.
ADMISSION	Admission 50¢; free parking; indoors, rain or shine.
FEATURES	This is only an antiques and collectibles flea market, with some miscellaneous items. Averages 150 to 200 vendors. Snacks and hot meals are served on the premises.
RATES	$17 per 10'×12' space. Reserve at least two weeks in advance.
CONTACT	Av Hardesty, P.O. Box 1585, Hutchinson, KS 67504-1585.
PHONE	(316) 663-5626 or (316) 665-9000

NFMA Member

KANSAS CITY: Boulevard Swap and Shop

WHEN	Every weekend, 6:00 A.M. to 1:00 P.M. In operation since 1975.
WHERE	At 1051 Merriam Lane, at the Boulevard Drive-in Theatre.
ADMISSION	Admission 50¢ per person; ample free parking; outdoors, weather permitting.
FEATURES	Basic variety of new and used merchandise. Averages close to 100 vendors. The drive-in's concession stand is open during market hours.
RATES	$5 and $7 per space per day. Reservations are not required.
CONTACT	Wes Neal, Manager, 1051 Merriam Lane, Kansas City, KS 66103.
PHONE	(913) 262-2414
FAX	(913) 262-2414

SPARKS: Sparks Flea Market

WHEN	First Sunday in May and three preceding days; three days in mid-July; Labor Day and the four preceding days; and a big five-day show in the fall (call for specific dates), daylight to dark. In operation for over sixteen years.
WHERE	At the K-7 Highway and 290th Road, twenty-three miles

west of St. Joseph, Missouri, and twenty-four miles north of Atchison, Kansas.

ADMISSION Free admission; five acres of free parking; indoors and outdoors, rain or shine.

FEATURES About 90 percent antiques and collectibles, plus vintage clothing, coins and stamps, kitchenware, antique furniture, jewelry, porcelain, fresh produce in season, toys, and used merchandise. Averages 400 to a capacity of 500 vendors. Restaurant with country cooking, plus many other food options, including the "best tenderloins in the state." Historical area is good for touring as well as flea market shopping. Church services in beautiful old Baptist church on Sundays.

RATES $45 per 20'×30' space outdoors or $55 per 10'×15' space indoors for entire show; electricity is available at $5 per day for outdoor spaces (provided free for indoor spaces); tables are available at $5 each per show. Reserve at least a month in advance.

CONTACT Ray Tackett, P.O. Box 223, Troy, KS 66087.

PHONE (785) 985-2411; day of market call (785) 442-5555.

WEB http://members.tripod.com/~sparks_flea_market/ index.htm

WICHITA: Mid-America Flea Market

WHEN One Sunday each month except July and August (call for dates, which vary from month to month; usually toward the end of the month), 9:00 A.M. to 4:00 P.M. In operation since 1978.

WHERE At the Kansas Coliseum, at I-135 and 85th Street North.

ADMISSION Admission $1 per person; ample free parking; indoors, year-round.

FEATURES Full spectrum of antiques and collectibles, such as baseball cards, books, vintage clothing, and toys. Averages 600 to 700 vendors. Snacks and hot meals are served on the premises.

RATES $17 per 8'×10' space. Reserve two to three weeks in advance.

CONTACT Av Hardesty, P.O. Box 1585, Hutchinson, KS 67504-1585.

PHONE (316) 663-5626 or (316) 775-2560

FAX

    NFMA Member

WICHITA: Village Flea Market

WHEN	Every Friday, Saturday, and Sunday, 9:00 A.M. to 5:30 P.M. In operation since mid-1970s.
WHERE	At 2301 South Meridian, at the corner of Pawnee, in the southwest part of Wichita, a mile and a half north of I-235 Bypass, and a mile and a half south of Route 54.
ADMISSION	Free admission; free parking for up to 1,000 cars; indoors year-round and outdoors, weather permitting.
FEATURES	Antiques and collectibles, books, new clothing, kitchenware, crafts, furniture, jewelry, new and used merchandise, and toys. Averages 100 to 150 vendors. Snacks and hot meals are served on the premises.
RATES	From $30 to $42 per space for all three days; tables are available at $4 for three days. Reservations are not required.
CONTACT	Dale Cooper, 2301 South Meridian, Wichita, KS 67213.
PHONE	(316) 942-8263

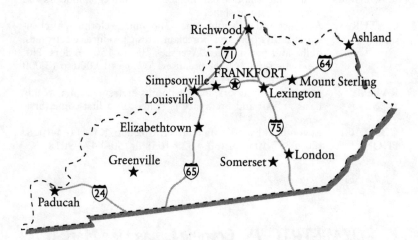

Richwood ★

Ashland ★

71

64

Simpsonville ★ FRANKFORT ★ ★ Mount Sterling

Louisville ★ Lexington

Elizabethtown ★

75

Greenville ★ Somerset ★ ★ London

65

Paducah ★ 24

KENTUCKY

ASHLAND: Hillbilly Flea Market

WHEN	Every Thursday through Sunday, 8:00 A.M. to 5:00 P.M. In operation since 1986.
WHERE	Located on Russell Road (Route 23) north of Ashland—in front of Armco Steel.
ADMISSION	Free admission; free parking for up to 450 cars; indoors and outdoors, rain or shine.
FEATURES	Antiques and collectibles, new and vintage clothing, kitchenware, crafts, jewelry, porcelain, fresh produce, electronics, dolls, and pet supplies. Averages 100 to 150 vendors. Hot meals are served on the premises. Averages 10,000 to 15,000 shoppers per weekend.
RATES	$6 per day outdoors; indoor booths are rented on a weekly basis at $40 and up. Space is rented on a first-come, first-served basis.
CONTACT	Elwood Gibbs, 100 Main Street, Greenup, KY 41144-1026.
PHONE	(800) 357-1058 or (606) 329-1058 or (606) 473-9018

ELIZABETHTOWN: Bowling Lanes Flea Market

WHEN	Every weekend, 8:00 A.M. to 5:00 P.M. In operation since the early 1980s.
WHERE	At 4547 North Dixie (U.S. 31 West), thirty-five miles south of Louisville on I-65, and eight miles south of Fort Knox.
ADMISSION	Free admission; free parking for up to 700 cars; indoors and outdoors, rain or shine.
FEATURES	Antiques and collectibles, books, new and vintage clothing, coins and stamps, kitchenware, crafts, furniture, jewelry, new and used merchandise, porcelain, fresh produce, and toys. Averages 100 to 150 vendors. Two snack bars on the premises; hot meals available. Billed as central Kentucky's largest flea market, attracting regular vendors and customers from across Kentucky and neighboring states—with a good variety of merchandise.
RATES	Indoors: $8 per 8'×8' space per day; outdoors: $7 per 11'×27' space. Reservations are on a first-come, first-served basis.
CONTACT	David or Dean Taylor, 4547 North Dixie, Elizabethtown, KY 42701.

| PHONE | (502) 737-5755 or (502) 737-7171 (bowling alley) |
| FAX | (502) 737-8300 |

GREENVILLE: Luke's Town and Country Flea Market

WHEN | Every Monday, 8:00 A.M. to dark, and every Tuesday, from daylight until noon. In operation since the late 1970s.

WHERE | On Highway 62 West.

ADMISSION | Free admission; limited free parking plus nearby lots at $1 per car; indoors year-round and outdoors, weather permitting.

FEATURES | Antiques and collectibles, books, new and vintage clothing, coins and stamps, kitchenware, crafts, cosmetics and perfumes, pets, furniture, jewelry, livestock, new merchandise, fresh produce, and toys. Averages 100 to 400 vendors. Snacks and hot meals, including homemade biscuits and cornbread are served on the premises. Mostly outdoors, with friendly family atmosphere. Tuesday is the big market day.

RATES | $2 per space on Monday (except holidays); $3 and up per space on Tuesday. Electrical hookups are available, and overnight parking is welcome. Reservations are recommended.

CONTACT | Wayne or Judy Rice, 2006 U.S. Highway 62 West, Greenville, KY 42345.

PHONE | (502) 338-4920 or (502) 338-6284

LEXINGTON: Lexington Flea Mall and Antique Center

WHEN | Every Friday, Saturday, and Sunday, 10:00 A.M. to 6:00 P.M.; indoor mall is open daily. In operation since 1999 (formerly operated across the street).

WHERE | At 1230 Eastland Center.

ADMISSION | Free admission; ample free parking; indoors and outdoors, year-round.

FEATURES | Averages close to 196 vendors. There is a café on the premises.

RATES | $10 per space per day outdoors (more indoors). Reservations are not required for outdoor spaces.

CONTACT   Manager, 1230 Eastland Center, Lexington, KY 40505.
PHONE   (606) 252-1076
FAX   (606) 252-1076

LONDON: Flea Land Flea Market

WHEN   Every weekend, 9:00 A.M. to 5:00 P.M. In operation since
           1990.
WHERE   On Barberville Road (Route 229) at 192 Bypass. Take exit
           38 (London) off I-75 North. Go right and proceed to sixth
           stoplight. Turn right again, and "you're looking right at it."
ADMISSION Free admission; ample free parking; indoors and outdoors,
           year-round.
FEATURES   "You name it" and it's here. Averages close to 500 vendors.
           Food is served on the premises.
RATES $12 per 10'×12' space outdoors per weekend or $38.50 per
           10'×15' space indoors. Reservations are recommended.
CONTACT   Manager, P.O. Box 862, London, KY 40741.
PHONE   (606) 864-3532 (864-FLEA)

LOUISVILLE: Derby Park Traders Circle Flea Market

WHEN   Every weekend, 9:00 A.M. to 5:00 P.M. In operation since the
           early 1980s.
WHERE   At 2900 South Seventh Street. Take 264 West to Taylor
           Boulevard, then right on Taylor, then at fifth light make a
           left onto Arcade; at the end of Arcade, take a left onto
           Seventh Street and look for entrance about an eighth of a
           mile on the right.
ADMISSION Free admission; six acres of free parking; indoors and out-
           doors, rain or shine.
FEATURES   Antiques and collectibles, new and vintage clothing, kitchen-
           ware, crafts, new merchandise, and fresh produce. Averages
           up to 150 vendors. Snacks and hot meals are served on the
           premises. Run by Parker Commercial Storage and Distri-
           bution, Inc. Camping and electric hookups available; hot
           shower facilities.
RATES   Indoors: from $25 per 6'×0' day; outdoors: $10 per day.
           Reservations are not required.

CONTACT	Manager, 2900 South Seventh Street, Louisville, KY 40216.
PHONE	(502) 636-3532 (636-FLEA) or (502) 636-5817 (reservation office hours are Monday through Friday, 9:00 A.M. to 5:00 P.M.)

NFMA Member

MOUNT STERLING: Mount Sterling October Court Days

WHEN	The third Monday of every October and the weekend preceding, 8:00 A.M. to dark. In operation since the end of the eighteenth century.
WHERE	On and around Main Street in the center of Mount Sterling, in Montgomery County, thirty miles east of Lexington and thirty miles west of Morehead. Take exit 110 off I-64.
ADMISSION	Free admission; ample street parking; indoors and outdoors, rain or shine.
FEATURES	Antiques and collectibles, new and vintage clothing, kitchenware, crafts, furniture, jewelry, new merchandise, fresh produce, and more. Averages 900 to 1,000 vendors. Many food vendors. The "granddaddy of all flea markets," begun in 1792 and currently attended by over 70,000 people annually.
RATES	From $125 per 20'×20' space outdoors for three days; rates for food vendors are higher; plus city license at $20. Reserve as far as possible ahead; spaces are booked up months in advance.
CONTACT	Roland Williams, 40 Broadway, Mount Sterling, KY 40353.
PHONE	(606) 498-8725
FAX	(606) 498-8727

PADUCAH: Traders Mall Flea Market

WHEN	Every weekend, 10:00 A.M. to 6:00 P.M. In operation since 1996.
WHERE	At 6900 Benton Road. Take exit 16 off I-24.
ADMISSION	Free admission; ample free parking; indoors and outdoors, year-round.
FEATURES	Everything from antiques to new merchandise. Averages up to a capacity of 300 vendors. There is a family-style restau-

rant on the premises. Claims to be Kentucky's largest indoor farmers market. Near Merv Griffin's Riverboat Casino (fifteen-minute drive to the west).

RATES From $25 per 10'×14' space per weekend. Reservations are not required.

CONTACT Manager, 6900 Benton Road, Paducah, KY 42003.

PHONE (502) 898-3144

RICHWOOD: Richwood Flea Market

WHEN Every weekend, 9:00 A.M. to 5:00 P.M.; every Tuesday, daybreak to whenever. In operation since the early 1980s.

WHERE At 10915 Dixie Highway (Route 25), fifteen minutes south of Cincinnati, Ohio. Take exit 175 off I-75.

ADMISSION Admission $1 per car; parking for over 4,000 cars; indoors and outdoors (Tuesday is outdoors only), rain or shine.

FEATURES Wide range of new and used merchandise, including antiques and collectibles, jewelry, knives, fresh produce, and antique and modern firearms. Averages close to 280 vendors. Snacks and hot meals are served on the premises. Tuesday farmers market starts at daybreak with over 200 vendors and as many as 10,000 customers in a weekend.

RATES $50 per weekend outdoors, or from $40 to $85 indoors; Tuesdays: $12 per day outdoors. Reservations are required for indoor setups only; call on Friday between 9:00 A.M. and 4:00 P.M.

CONTACT Mark Stallings, P.O. Box 153, Florence, KY 41022.

PHONE (606) 371-5800

FAX (606) 371-5680

E-MAIL richflea10@aol.com

WEB www.richwoodfleamarket.com

NFMA Member

SIMPSONVILLE: Shelby County Flea Market

WHEN Every weekend, 9:00 A.M. to 5:00 P.M. In operation since the early 1980s.

WHERE At the northeast corner of exit 28 off I-64, west of Lexington, Kentucky.

ADMISSION   Free admission; ten acres of free parking; indoors year-round and outdoors, weather permitting.

FEATURES   Antiques and collectibles, books, new and vintage clothing, kitchenware, crafts, furniture, jewelry, new and used merchandise, porcelain, and fresh produce. Averages 350 to 500 vendors. Snacks and hot meals are served on the premises.

RATES $35 per indoor space per weekend, $12 per 10'×20' outdoor space per day. Reservations are required for indoor spaces only (waiting list).

CONTACT   Dana Smith, P.O. Box 8, Simpsonville, KY 40067.

PHONE   (502) 722-8883

FAX   (502) 722-8881

SOMERSET: Lake Cumberland Flea Market

WHEN   Every weekend, 9:00 A.M. to 6:00 P.M. on Saturday and 10:00 A.M. to 6:00 P.M. on Sunday. In operation since 1993.

WHERE   95 Super Service Drive.

ADMISSION   Free admission; ten acres of free parking; indoors and outdoors, year-round.

FEATURES   Electronics, furniture, gifts, jewelry, novelties, and toys. Averages 80 to 120 vendors. There is a full-service restaurant on the premises.

RATES $34 per space per weekend ($38 for a front aisle). Reservations are not required.

CONTACT   C. V. Warner or Anna Gutting, 95 Super Service Drive, Somerset, KY 42501.

PHONE   (606) 678-0250

FAX   (606) 678-0250

NFMA Member

Arcadia

Greenwood

BATON ROUGE
Prairieville
New Orleans

LOUISIANA

ARCADIA: Bonnie and Clyde Trade Days

WHEN	The Friday, Saturday, and Sunday before the third Monday of every month, from daybreak to dark. In operation since 1990.
WHERE	On Highway 9 South. Take exit 69 off I-20, then go south for about three and a half miles (follow signs).
ADMISSION	Free admission; parking for several thousand cars at $3 per car; outdoors, year-round.
FEATURES	Antiques and collectibles, books, new clothing, kitchenware, crafts, furniture, pets, porcelain, fresh produce, and toys. Averages 200 to 325 vendors. Snacks and hot meals are served on the premises. "Washateria" (laundromat) on the premises; overnight RV parking for $14 per night, including water and electric hookups ($4 extra for sewage hookups).
RATES	$40 per regular lot per day, $80 per carport lot, $100 per pavilion lot. Reservations may be made up to two weeks in advance.
CONTACT	Ed Jones, Manager, P.O. Box 243, Arcadia, LA 71001.
PHONE	(888) 835-6112 or (318) 263-2437
FAX	(318) 263-9803
WEB	www.crafters.com

NFMA Member

BATON ROUGE: Deep South Flea Market

WHEN	Every Friday, Saturday, and Sunday, 10:00 A.M. to 6:00 P.M. In operation since the 1970s.
WHERE	At 5905 Florida Boulevard.
ADMISSION	Free admission; ample free parking; indoors, year-round.
FEATURES	Averages close to 60 vendors. Food is served on the premises.
RATES	$50 per 10'×10' for three days. Reservations are not required.
CONTACT	Billy Vallery, 5905 Florida Boulevard, Baton Rouge, LA 70806.
PHONE	(225) 923-0333 or (225) 923-0142

GREENWOOD: Greenwood Flea Market

WHEN	Every weekend, 9:00 A.M. to 6:00 P.M. In operation since the early 1980s.
WHERE	At 9249 Jefferson-Paige Road. Take exit 5 off I-20. Near Shreveport, Louisiana.
ADMISSION	Free admission; ample free parking; indoors and outdoors, rain or shine.
FEATURES	Antiques and collectibles, books, new clothing, coins and stamps, kitchenware, crafts, furniture, jewelry, new merchandise, porcelain, and toys. Averages 130 to a capacity of 150 vendors. Snacks and hot meals are served on the premises.
RATES	$27.50 per 10'×15' booth per weekend, or $110 per month. Reservations are not required for outdoor spaces.
CONTACT	Larry Millican, 9249 Jefferson-Paige Road, Greenwood, LA 71033.
PHONE	(318) 938-7201
FAX	(318) 938-5052

NEW ORLEANS: French Market Community Flea Market

WHEN	Daily (365 days a year), 7:00 A.M. to 7:00 P.M. In operation since the eighteenth century in its current location.
WHERE	At 1200 North Peters Street, where Elysian Fields meets the Mississippi River.
ADMISSION	Free admission; parking available nearby in the lot behind the flood wall or the lot on Decatur Street; outdoors, weather permitting.
FEATURES	Antiques and collectibles, books, new and vintage clothing, crafts, jewelry, new and used merchandise, fresh produce, and toys. Averages close to 250 vendors. Snacks and hot meals are served on the premises. Justly famous; weekends are the best but it's worth stopping by during the week if you're in the vicinity.
RATES	From $7 to $23 per 6'×8' space per weekday, or from $13 to $40 on Saturday or Sunday; city and state permits must be purchased prior to reservation. Reservations are not required.
CONTACT	Antoinette Guyton, c/o French Market Corporation, 1200 North Peters Street, New Orleans, LA 70117.

PHONE   (504) 596-3420 or (504) 596-3421
FAX   (504) 596-3427

 NFMA Member

NEW ORLEANS: Jefferson Flea Market

WHEN   Every Friday, Saturday, and Sunday, 10:00 A.M. to 6:00 P.M.
            In operation for over eighteen years.
WHERE   At 5501 Jefferson Highway, at the intersection of Clearview
            Park, off I-10.
ADMISSION   Free admission; free parking for up to 210 cars; indoors and
            under cover, year-round.
FEATURES   Antiques and collectibles, books, kitchenware, crafts, furni-
            ture, jewelry, new merchandise. Averages 100 to 120 ven-
            dors. Hot and cold meals are available on the premises.
RATES $15 per space (under cover) per day, table provided. Reserve
            a week in advance.
CONTACT   Jim Russell or Jerry Theddy, P.O. Box 23223, Harahan, LA
            70183.
PHONE   (504) 734-0087
FAX   (504) 734-0304

PRAIRIEVILLE: Greater Baton Rouge Flea Market

WHEN   Every weekend, 9:00 A.M. to 5:00 P.M. In operation since 1995.
WHERE   At 15545 Airline Highway (U.S. Highway 61), five miles
            south of Baton Rouge (between Baton Rouge and Gonzales).
ADMISSION   Free admission; ample free parking; indoors and under
            cover, year-round.
FEATURES   A variety of new and used items, antiques, and collectibles.
            Averages 200 to a capacity of 400 vendors. Food is served
            on the premises. A well-advertised, modern version of an
            old-fashioned flea market, with a family atmosphere; visit
            sister markets in Gulf Breeze, Florida, and Flea Market
            Mobile (Alabama). RVs are welcome.
RATES   From $20 per 8'×10' space per weekend. Reservations are
            recommended.
CONTACT   Keith Bryan or Steve Springer, 15545 Airline Highway (U.S.
            61), Prairieville, LA 70769.

PHONE	(225) 673-2682 or (334) 633-7533 (office is open daily)
FAX	(225) 673-9348
E-MAIL	kmbryan@eatel.net

NFMA Member

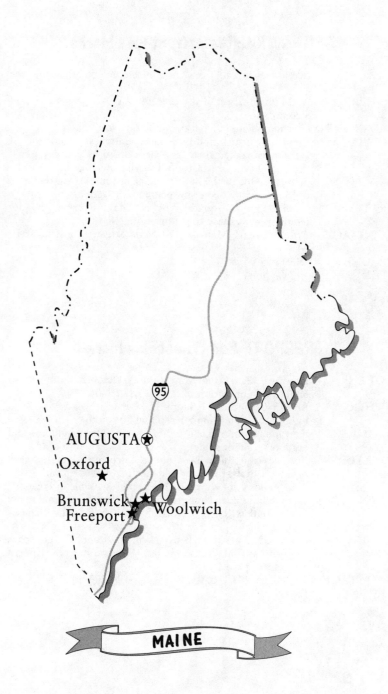

AUGUSTA⭐

Oxford ★

Brunswick ★★ Woolwich
Freeport ★

95

MAINE

BRUNSWICK: Waterfront Flea Market

WHEN	Every weekend, 8:00 A.M. to 5:00 P.M. In operation since the early 1990s.
WHERE	At 14 Main Street. Take Exit 24A off I-95 to get to Main Street.
ADMISSION	Free admission; free parking; indoors, year-round.
FEATURES	Everything from brand-new stuff to antiques—a good mix of collectibles, gadgets, etc. Averages up to its capacity of 70 vendors. There is a tasty, full-service lunch counter on the premises. One of the most popular flea markets in the State of Maine, with good atmosphere and selection.
RATES	From 11¢ per square foot per day. Reservations are required—call ahead to get on waiting list.
CONTACT	Arthur Young, Manager, 14 Main Street, Brunswick, ME 04011.
PHONE	(207) 729-0378
FAX	

FREEPORT: Red Wheel Flea Market

WHEN	Every weekend from May through October, 8:00 A.M. to 6:00 P.M. In operation since the early 1980s.
WHERE	At 275 U.S. Route 1 South. Take exit 17 off I-95 and go right onto Route 1, and market will be on the right.
ADMISSION	Free admission; free parking for up to 200 cars; indoors and outdoors, rain or shine.
FEATURES	Antiques and collectibles, books, kitchenware, crafts, used furniture, tools, toys, and old stuff. Averages up to 70 vendors. Food is not served on the premises. While in Freeport, visit the L. L. Bean store (open twenty-four hours) and many factory outlets. There's a nice antiques shop on the premises also.
RATES	Indoors: $25 per space per weekend; outdoors: $7; per space on Saturday and $10 on Sunday. Reservations are required for indoor space.
CONTACT	Ed Collett, 291 U.S. #1, Freeport, ME 04032.
PHONE	(207) 865-6492

OXFORD: Undercover Antique Mall and Flea Market

WHEN	Daily, 7:00 A.M. to 5:00 P.M. In operation since the 1970s.
WHERE	On Route 26, one half mile north of the Oxford Plains Speedway.
ADMISSION	Free admission; free parking for over 100 cars; indoors year-round and also outdoors, weather permitting.
FEATURES	Antiques and collectibles, books, coins and stamps, crafts, jewelry, porcelain, primitive reproductions, and toys. Averages 60 to 75 vendors. Snacks are served on the premises. Primarily an indoor antiques and collectibles market, but there are usually 20 to 30 outdoor vendors during summer months.
RATES	$5 per day outdoors and from $60 per month indoors. Reservations are recommended.
CONTACT	Bert Morin, 960 Main Street, Oxford, ME 04270.
PHONE	(207) 539-4149

WOOLWICH: Montsweag Flea Market

WHEN	Every weekend from early May through mid-October, plus every Wednesday and Friday from June through August, 6:30 A.M. to 4:00 P.M. (Wednesday is strictly antiques and collectibles). In operation since the mid-1970s.
WHERE	On Route 1 at the corner of Mountain Road in Woolwich, between Bath and Wiscasset.
ADMISSION	Free admission; three acres of free parking; outdoors, weather permitting.
FEATURES	Antiques and collectibles, crafts, used furniture, fresh produce, garage-sale items, glassware, jewelry, memorabilia, new and used merchandise, primitives, toys, and tools—a nice mix. Averages up to a capacity of 110 vendors. A snack bar on the premises serves breakfast and lunch and those wonderful ice-cream treats made from the famous Round Top Dairy of Damariscotta, Maine. (If you go to Wiscasset down the road, incidentally, don't miss the Sea Basket, on your left on Route 1. This is a fine example of a New England country flea market, with lots of old things for the "junktiquer" and a friendly atmosphere that is conducive to browsing.)
RATES	From $7 to $10 per table per day ($7 for two tables on Friday). Reserve as far in advance as possible; regulars have first refusal.

CONTACT   Norma Scopino or Gena Roupe, 6 Hunnewell Lane, Woolwich, ME 04579.

PHONE   (207) 443-2809 or (207) 443-3275

Rising Sun
North East
95
Baltimore
70
Bethesda
ANNAPOLIS

MARYLAND

BALTIMORE: North Point Drive-in Flea Market

WHEN	Every weekend, 7:00 A.M. to 2:00 P.M. In operation since the early 1990s.
WHERE	At 4001 North Point Boulevard.
ADMISSION	Admission 25 per person; ample free parking; indoors and outdoors, weather permitting.
FEATURES	"New, old, and junk" is the formula used to describe the mix of goods on display here. Averages up to 200 vendors. There is a snack bar on the premises.
RATES	$10 per space on Saturday, from $10 to $15 Sunday. Reservations are not required.
CONTACT	Manager, 7721 Old Battle Grove, Baltimore, MD 21222.
PHONE	(410) 477-1337

BALTIMORE: Patapsco Flea Market

WHEN	Every weekend, 9:00 A.M. indoors and 7:00 A.M. to 4:00 P.M. outdoors. In operation since the mid-1980s.
WHERE	At 1400 West Patapsco Avenue. Take I-95 to Route 295 West to Annapolis Road, then turn left onto Annapolis Road.
ADMISSION	Admission 25¢ per person; ample free parking; indoors year-round and outdoors, weather permitting.
FEATURES	Antiques and collectibles, books, new and vintage clothing, coins and stamps, kitchenware, crafts, new and used merchandise, porcelain, fresh produce, and toys. Averages up to a capacity of 1,500 vendors. Snacks and hot meals are served on the premises. Billed as Maryland's largest indoor-outdoor flea market. "When you want the best we'll make you forget the rest."
RATES	From $10 to $20 per table per day. Reserve a week in advance.
CONTACT	Bob Lomonico, 1400 West Patapsco Avenue, Baltimore, MD 21230.
PHONE	(410) 354-3041 or (410) 354-5262
FAX	(410) 254-3876

BETHESDA: Farmers Flea Market

WHEN	Every Sunday, from the first Sunday in March through the Sunday before Christmas, 8:00 A.M. to 5:00 P.M. In operation since 1973.
WHERE	At 7155 Wisconsin Avenue.
ADMISSION	Free admission; ample free parking; outdoors, weather permitting.
FEATURES	Antiques and collectibles such as books, bottles, vintage clothing, coins, kitchenware, jewelry, knives, silver, and stamps. Averages up to 50 vendors. Snacks and hot meals are served on the premises. Located in an affluent suburb of Washington, D.C. The members of the Montgomery County Farm Women's Co-op purchased the land and building back in 1930 to sell their produce directly to the public during the Great Depression. Occasionally there is live entertainment.
RATES	$20 for a 20'×20' space per day. Reservations are not required—just show up at 8:00 A.M.
CONTACT	James R. Bonfils, 4539 Alton Place N.W., Washington, D.C. 20814.
PHONE	(202) 966-3303

NORTH EAST: North East Auction Galleries Flea Market

WHEN	Every Tuesday, Thursday, Saturday, and Sunday, 7:00 A.M. to 5:00 P.M. In operation since 1971.
WHERE	At the junction of Route 40 and Mechanics Valley Road. Take exit 100 off I-95 to Route 40, then east to Mechanics Valley Road, and the market will be on the left at the traffic light.
ADMISSION	Free admission; eight acres of free parking; indoors and outdoors, rain or shine.
FEATURES	Antiques and collectibles, books, new and vintage clothing, coins and stamps, kitchenware, crafts, furniture, jewelry, livestock, new merchandise, porcelain, and fresh produce. Average 45 to 100 vendors. Snacks and hot meals are served on the premises.
RATES	Indoors: $15 per four-by-eight-foot table per day or $25 per weekend; outdoors: $10 per table per day. Reservations are recommended.

CONTACT   Robert C. Burkheimer, P.O. Box 551, North East, MD 21901.
PHONE   (800) 233-4169 or (410) 287-5588
FAX   (410) 287-287-2029
WEB   www.burkeimer.com

RISING SUN: Hunter's Sale Barn

WHEN   Every Monday, 3:00 P.M. to 9:00 P.M. In operation since 1965.
WHERE   On Route 276. Take exit 93 off I-95 (northbound or southbound), then take Route 275 to dead end, then right onto Route 276 and go two and a half miles; market will be on the right.
ADMISSION   Free admission; free parking for up to 1,500 cars; indoors year-round and outdoors, weather permitting.
FEATURES   Antiques and collectibles, crafts, furniture, jewelry, new merchandise, fresh produce, and toys. Averages 65 to 120 vendors. There is a full-service restaurant with home cooking, seating forty people. Family owned. There is an auction that happens at the same time as market.
RATES   From $15 per space per day. Reservations are recommended.
CONTACT   Norman, Carol, or Ronda Hunter, 2084 Tome Highway, Box 427, Rising Sun, MD 21911.
PHONE   (410) 658-6400

NFMA Member

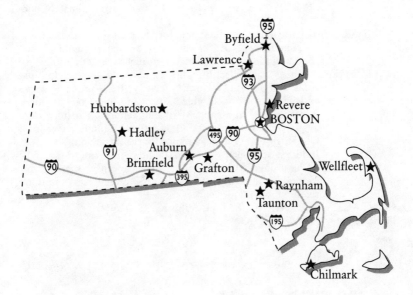

Byfield ★
Lawrence ★
95
93
Hubbardston ★
★ Hadley
★ Revere
BOSTON
Auburn
91
495 90
Brimfield
95
★ Grafton
90
395
★ Raynham
Taunton
Wellfleet ★
195
★ Chilmark

MASSACHUSETTS

AUBURN: Auburn Antique and Flea Market

WHEN Every Sunday year-round; every Saturday, April to November, 9:00 A.M. to 4:00 P.M. In operation since the 1970s.

WHERE At 733 Southbridge Street (Route 12). Take exit 10 off the Massachusetts Turnpike (I-90), or exit 8 off I-290, or exit 7 off I-395; then follow Route 12 south approximately one-half mile.

ADMISSION 50¢ for indoor market; free for children under twelve, free parking for up to 500 cars; indoors every Sunday, year-round; outdoors (only) every Saturday, weather permitting.

FEATURES Antiques and collectibles, books, new and vintage clothing, coins and stamps, furniture, jewelry, fresh produce, rocks and minerals, tools, videotapes, and new merchandise. Averages 100 to a capacity of 200 vendors. Hot meals are available on the premises. Only a twenty-minute drive from Old Sturbridge Village, a major tourist attraction.

RATES Indoors: $30 per 9'×9' space (Sunday only); outdoors: $10 on Saturdays, $15 on Sundays for a car-length space; eight-foot tables are available for rent at $3 each. Reservations are required for indoor spaces only.

CONTACT Manager, P.O. Box 33, Auburn, MA 01501.

PHONE (508) 832-2763

BRIMFIELD: J and J Promotions Antiques and Collectibles Shows

WHEN Three two-day shows a year, in May, July, and September: Friday, 6:00 A.M. to 5:00 P.M. and Saturday, 9:00 A.M. to 5:00 P.M. 1997 dates: May 14–15; July 9–10; September 17–18. In operation since 1959.

WHERE On Route 20, a quarter mile west of the stoplight at Brimfield Common, and six miles west of Old Sturbridge Village. From New York, take I-95 North to Hartford, then I-84 East to Sturbridge and Route 20, then west on 20 for approximately six miles.

ADMISSION Admission $5 per person on Friday, $3 on Saturday; several acres of parking at $5 per car; outdoors and under cover, rain or shine.

FEATURES Antiques and collectibles. Averages 600 to 800 vendors. Snacks and hot meals are served on the premises. The whole town explodes with antiques and collectibles on three summer weekends, and this market, one of several in the town, is its largest and the original "Brimfield."

RATES Call for rates. Reservations are required.
CONTACT Jill Reid Lukesh or Judith Reid Mathieu, P.O. Box 385, Route 20, Brimfield, MA 01010-0385.
PHONE (413) 245-3436 or (978) 597-8155
E-MAIL jnjbrimfld@hey.net
WEB www.jandj-brimfield.com

Celebrity Spottings: Brimfield, Massachusetts

★ Madonna
★ Barbra Streisand
★ Donna Karan
★ Whoopi Goldberg
★ Martha Stewart

★ Penny Marshall
★ Bill Cosby
★ Elton John
★ Ralph Lauren's minions

BYFIELD: Olde Byfield Antiques Flea Market

WHEN Every Sunday, 7:30 A.M. to 2:00 P.M.; a "state-of-the-art" indoor "international antique mart" is open daily, 10:00 A.M. to 5:00 P.M. In operation since 1995.
WHERE At exist 55 off I-95 in Byfield, two exits below Newburyport.
ADMISSION Admission 50¢ per person; ample free parking; indoors year-round and outdoors in summer, rain or shine.
FEATURES "Unique and unusual" antiques and collectibles, postcards, etc. Averages 150 to 200 vendors. Home-cooked food is served on the premises.
RATES $30 for one 10'×10' space, then $25 for each additional space. Reservations are recommended—there is a waiting list.
CONTACT Rick Hurst or Lynne, 12 Kent Way, Byfield, MA 01922.

PHONE   (978) 463-0655 or (781) 272-2899
FAX   (978) 463-0653
E-MAIL   rickhur@prodigy.net

CHILMARK: Community Church Flea Market

WHEN   Every Saturday (seasonal), 8:30 A.M. to 3:00 P.M. In opera-
            tion since 1967.
WHERE   At the Chilmark Community Church, at the Menemsha
            Crossroad.
ADMISSION   Free admission; roadside parking is available nearby; out-
            doors, weather permitting.
FEATURES   Antiques, collectibles, crafts, art, jewelry, furniture, and used
            merchandise. Averages 65 to 88 vendors. Snacks are served
            on the premises. This market has a country feel, and "gift
            shop" items and cheesy goods like factory seconds are dis-
            couraged.
RATES   From $20 to $40 per space per day. Reservations are recom-
            mended around the first of May—regular vendors return
            year after year.
CONTACT   Phyllis H. Conway, Box 16 RFD, 15 Moses West Road,
            Chilmark, MA 02535.
PHONE   (508) 645-5216
FAX   (508) 696-6374

GRAFTON: Grafton Flea Market

WHEN   Every Sunday from March through December (closed)
            January and February), plus holiday Mondays, 7:00 A.M. to
            5:00 P.M. In operation since 1970.
WHERE   Located on Route 140 by the Grafton-Upton town line.
            Take exit 21B (Upton) off Route 495, then go five miles to
            Route 140, then make a right turn and go one miles.
ADMISSION   Admission 50¢; free admission for children; free parking for
            up to 1,000 cars; indoors and outdoors, rain or shine.
FEATURES   Everything from antiques and collectibles to new and used
            merchandise, kitchenware, crafts, jewelry, and fresh pro-
            duce. Averages 250 to a capacity of 300 vendors. Snack food
            (hamburgers and hot dogs, grinders) served on the premises.

Unique pine grove atmosphere; attended by an average of 6,000 shoppers on good-weather days. "Come where the crowds are," with dealers from all over New England.

RATES $25 per space indoors per day; $20 outdoors; shaded or exposed spaces are available. Reserve a week in advance for indoor spaces; outdoor spaces are rented on a first-come, first-served basis.

CONTACT   Harry Peters, P.O. Box 206, Grafton, MA 01519.

PHONE   (508) 839-2217

HADLEY: Olde Hadley Flea Market

WHEN   Every Sunday from late April through the end of October, 6:00 A.M. to 4:00 P.M. In operation since 1980.

WHERE   At 45 Lawrence Plain Road (Route 47 South). Take exit 19 off Route 91 North, then go eastbound on Route 9 for one mile, then south on Route 47 for two miles. Off Route 91 South, take exit 20, then go one mile to Route 9, then eastbound one mile on Route 9, then south on Route 47 for two miles.

ADMISSION   Free admission; free parking for up to 500 cars; outdoors, weather permitting.

FEATURES   Antiques and collectibles, books, new and vintage clothing, coins and stamps, kitchenware, crafts, used furniture, jewelry, procelain, fresh produce, quilts, tools, and toys. Averages up to 200 vendors. Snacks and hot meals are served on the premises.

RATES $20 per 25'×25' space per day. Reservations are not required.

CONTACT   Raymond or Marion Szala, 45 Lawrence Plain Road, Hadley, MA 01035.

PHONE   (413) 586-0352

HUBBARDSTON: Rietta Ranch Flea Market

WHEN   Every Sunday from April through October, 6:00 A.M. to whenever. In operation since the 1960s.

WHERE   At 183 Gardner Road (Route 68).

ADMISSION	Free admission; free parking for more than 1,000 cars; indoors and outdoors, rain or shine.
FEATURES	Antiques and collectibles, books, new and vintage clothing, coins and stamps, kitchenware, crafts, furniture, jewelry, new and used merchandise, porcelain, fresh produce, and toys. Averages up to 500 vendors. There is a full-service restaurant on the premises. This market has a carnival atmosphere.
RATES	$15 per space per day, including one table. Reservations are not required.
CONTACT	Ronnie Levesque, P.O. Box 35, Hubbardston, MA 01452.
PHONE	(978) 632-0559

LAWRENCE: The Jolly Flea

WHEN	Every weekend, 10:00 A.M. to 5:00 P.M. In operation since 1997.
WHERE	At Plaza 114. Take exit 42B off I-495, and the market will be a quarter of a mile down on the left.
ADMISSION	Admission 50¢ per person; ample free parking; indoors, year-round.
FEATURES	New and used merchandise, clothing, electronics, crafts and gift items, jewelry, tools, and toys. Averages 150 to 200 vendors. Food is served on the premises. This new market offers good variety and plenty of bargains.
RATES	From $45 per 12'×10' space per weekend. Reservations are not required.
CONTACT	Manager, 73 Winthrop Avenue, Lawrence, MA 01843.
PHONE	(978) 682-2020
FAX	(978) 794-0003
E-MAIL	info@showpromotion.com
WEB	www.showpromotion.com

RAYNHAM: Raynham Flea Market

WHEN	Every Sunday, plus Saturdays from Thanksgiving to Christmas, 8:00 A.M. to 6:00 P.M. In operation since 1974.
WHERE	On South Street, at the intersection of Route 24 South, Route 44 West, and Route 495 South.

ADMISSION   Admission 50¢ per person until 10:00 A.M., $1 thereafter; 50¢ for seniors; children free; ten acres of free parking; indoors and outdoors, rain or shine.

FEATURES   Antiques and collectibles, books, new clothing, coins, comics, kitchenware, furniture, jewelry, knives, new merchandise, novelties, fresh produce, silver, sporting goods, stamps, and toys. Averages 500 to 800 vendors. Variety of food concessions.

RATES $30 inside, $20 outside. Reservations are recommended.

CONTACT   Manager, Judson and South Streets, Raynham, MA 02767.

PHONE   (508) 823-8923

FAX   (508) 824-2339

E-MAIL   raynhamflea@aol.com

WEB   www.raynhamflea.com

 NFMA Member

REVERE: Revere Swap 'N' Shop

WHEN   Every weekend from March through December, 7:00 A.M. to 4:00 P.M. In operation since 1968.

WHERE   At 565 Squire Road, just off the Northeast Expressway (I-95).

ADMISSION   Admission $1 per person on Sunday (free on Saturday); ample free parking; outdoors, weather permitting.

FEATURES   All types of stuff—new and used, collectible, junk—you name it. Averages up to 250 vendors. Food is served on the premises.

RATES   From $30 per 20'×20' space per day. Reservations are recommended (usually sold out on Sunday).

CONTACT   John Nerich, Manager, c/o Showcase Cinema, 565 Squire Road, Revere, MA 02151.

PHONE   (781) 289-7100

TAUNTON: Taunton Expo Flea Market

WHEN   Every weekend, plus holiday Mondays, 8:00 A.M. to 5:00 P.M. In operation since the mid-1980s.

WHERE   At the Taunton Expo Center on Route 44.

ADMISSION   Admission $1 per person; free for children under twelve; free parking for up to 8,000; indoors year-round and outdoors, weather permitting.

FEATURES	Antiques and collectibles, new and vintage clothing, coins and stamps, kitchenware, crafts, furniture, jewelry, new merchandise, porcelain, fresh produce, and toys. Averages up to 1,000 vendors. Several food concession stands on the premises. Average attendance is 12,000 shoppers per weekend.
RATES	Indoors: $250 per 10'×10' space per month; outdoors: $25 per 20'×20' space per weekend. Reservations are taken for monthly rentals.
CONTACT	Armand Gagne, P.O. Box 68, Taunton, MA 02780.
PHONE	(508) 880-3800
FAX	(508) 880-5100

WELLFLEET: Wellfleet Flea Market

WHEN	Every weekend and holiday Mondays from mid-April through October, plus every Wednesday and Thursday in July and August, 8:00 A.M. to 4:00 P.M. In operation since the early 1970s.
WHERE	On Route 6, on the Eastham-Wellfleet town line. After the Sagamore Bridge, stay on the Mid-Cape Highway and then go around the rotary in Orleans; take the second right off the rotary toward Provincetown, then go about four or five miles; market will be on your left.
ADMISSION	Admission $1 per carload except $2 per carload on Sunday from the last Sunday in June through Labor Day Sunday; parking for up to 1,700 cars (free with admission); outdoors, rain or shine.
FEATURES	Antiques and collectibles, books, new and vintage clothing, coins and stamps, kitchenware, crafts, furniture, jewelry, new, and used merchandise, porcelain, fresh produce, seafood (clams and oysters), toys, and other odds. Averages 75 to 230 vendors. Full snack bar on the premises. Cape Cod's biggest and best flea market. Playground.
RATES	$20 per space per day. Reservations are not required.
CONTACT	Eleanor Hazen, Wellfleet Drive-in, P.O. Box 811, Wellfleet, MA 02667.
PHONE	(508) 349-2520; day of market contact Eleanor Hazen at (508) 349-2270.
FAX	(508) 349-2902
E-MAIL	wftheatres@capecod.net
WEB	www.capecodaccess.com/wellfleetcinemas.html

★Copemish

Saginaw ★

Armada
★

Grand Rapids ★   LANSING
★   ★ Waterford

Mt. Clemens
★
Allegan ★   ★ Warren
Flat Rock
Paw Paw ★

MICHIGAN

ALLEGAN: Allegan Antique Market

WHEN   Last Sunday of every month from April through September, 7:30 A.M. to 4:00 P.M. In operation since 1978.

WHERE   At the Allegan County Fairgrounds. Take Allegan exit off 131 Expressway or Route 196 (exit 34) or exit 60 off Route 94.

ADMISSION   Admission $3 per person (group discounts are available); ample free parking; indoors and outdoors, rain or shine.

FEATURES   Antiques and collectibles, books, vintage clothing, furniture, glassware, jewelry, porcelain, toys, and wicker. Averages 300 to a capacity of 375 vendors. Hot meals are served by ten food concessions on the premises. Billed as western Michigan's finest antique market, located on the banks of the Kalamazoo River. Shady picnic areas with tables; camping on the fairgrounds on Saturday evening prior to market days.

RATES $60 per 12'×16' space indoors; $55 per 25'×25' space outdoors. Reservations are recommended.

CONTACT   Larry Wood, 2030 Blueberry Drive, N.W., Grand Rapids, MI 49504.

PHONE   (616) 453-8780 or (616) 735-3333

ARMADA: Armada Flea Market

WHEN   Every Sunday and Tuesday from April through October (season depends on weather), 6:00 A.M. to 3:00 P.M. In operation since 1960.

WHERE   At 25381 Ridge Road, a mile east of town.

ADMISSION   Free admission; ample free parking; outdoors, weather permitting.

FEATURES   Antiques and collectibles, new merchandise, fresh produce (and "some animals"). Averages 200 to 300 vendors. There is a snack bar on the premises.

RATES   From $10 per single space (room for one car) on Tuesday or $15 on Sunday. Reservations are on a first-come, first-served basis.

CONTACT   Manager, P.O. Box 525, Armada, MI 48005.

PHONE   (810) 784-9194 or (810) 784-9604

COPEMISH: Copemish Flea Market and Auction

WHEN	Every Friday, Saturday, and Sunday from May through October, 7:00 A.M. to dusk. In operation since the 1940s (under current management since 1994).
WHERE	At the intersection of Yates Road and M-115.
ADMISSION	Free admission; three acres of free parking; outdoors, rain or shine.
FEATURES	Antiques and collectibles, books, new and vintage clothing, coins and stamps, kitchenware, crafts, furniture, jewelry, new and used merchandise, porcelain, fresh produce, and toys. Averages up to 100 vendors. Restaurant on the premises open Wednesday through Sunday; food booths outdoors during market hours.
RATES	$10 for one space per day, $19 for two spaces, $27 for three spaces, $34 for four; electricity is available at $3 per day. Reservations are recommended, especially for holidays.
CONTACT	Jerry or Jason Dillingham or Jack Lardie, P.O. Box 116, Copemish, MI 49625.
PHONE	(616) 378-2430 or (616) 929-4317 or (616) 223-4359

FLAT ROCK: Flat Rock Historical Society Antique and Flea Market

WHEN	Twice a year, on the first Sundays in May and October, 8:00 A.M. to 4:00 P.M. In operation since the 1970s.
WHERE	At the Flat Rock Speedway, one mile south of town on Telegraph Road. Telegraph Road is three miles west of I-75.
ADMISSION	Free admission; free parking for up to 1,000 cars; outdoors, rain or shine.
FEATURES	Antiques and collectibles, vintage clothing (but no used clothing), kitchenware, crafts, jewelry, furniture, and toys. Averages up to 200 vendors. Snacks and sandwiches are served on the premises.
RATES	$25 per 20'×20' space per day. Reservations are not required.
CONTACT	Flat Rock Historical Society, P.O. Box 337, Flat Rock, MI 48134.
PHONE	(734) 782-5220

GRAND RAPIDS: Jack Loeks's Flea Market

WHEN	Every weekend from April through October, 6:00 A.M. to 3:00 P.M. In operation since the 1960s.
WHERE	At 1400 28th Street S.W., about three miles west of Route 131 (use 28th Street/Wyoming exit), in the parking lot behind Studio 28 movie theater.
ADMISSION	Admission 50¢ per person; free for children seventeen and under; ample free parking; outdoors, rain or shine.
FEATURES	Antiques and collectibles, books, new clothing, kitchenware, crafts, furniture, garage-sale items, jewelry, new and used merchandise, fresh produce, plants, toys. Averages up to 400 vendors. Snacks and hot meals are served on the premises.
RATES	$11 per 10'×20' space per day. Reservations are not required (must be made in person during market hours).
CONTACT	Bruce Johns, 1400 28th Street S.W., Grand Rapids, MI 49509.
PHONE	(616) 532-6301 or (616) 532-8218

MOUNT CLEMENS: Gibraltar Trade Center North

WHEN	Every Friday, noon to 9:00 P.M., every Saturday, 10:00A.M. to 9:00 P.M., and every Sunday, 10:00 A.M. to 6:00 P.M. In operation since 1990.
WHERE	At 237 North River Road. Take exit 237 (North River Road/Mount Clemens) off I-94, and market will be a half-mile down the road on the right.
ADMISSION	Admission $2 per carload; ample free parking; indoors year-round and outdoors from April through November, rain or shine.
FEATURES	Antiques and collectibles, books, new and vintage clothing, cosmetics, kitchenware, crafts, furniture, jewelry, new and used merchandise, marine supplies, and toys. Averages up to a capacity of 800 vendors. Snacks and hot meals are served on the premises. This large and well-advertised market boasts an average of 40,000 customers per weekend. Specialty shows for sports cards, antiques, arts and crafts, guns and knives are held weekly in a 50,000-square-foot show area.
RATES	From $78 per 6'×12' space per weekend. Reservations are recommended.
CONTACT	Manager, 237 North River Road, Mount Clemens, MI 48043.

PHONE	(810) 465-6440
FAX	(810) 465-0458
WEB	www.gibraltartrade.com

 NFMA Member

PAW PAW: Reits Flea Market

WHEN	Every Saturday, Sunday, and holiday Monday, 8:00 A.M. to 4:00 P.M. In operation since the 1960s.
WHERE	At 45146 Red Arrow Highway, five miles west of Paw Paw. Take exit 56 off I-94 twenty-five miles west of Kalamazoo) and go north to blinking light, then left on Red Arrow and proceed for one mile.
ADMISSION	Free admission; twenty acres of free parking; indoors year-round and outdoors from mid-April through October, rain or shine.
FEATURES	Wide range of new and used merchandise, including antiques and collectibles, fresh produce, plants—"something for everyone." Averages up to 500 vendors. Be sure to have a meal at Cathy's Kitchen on the premises; there's also a snack bar. A clean market located in Michigan's "fruit belt."
RATES	$10 per 22'×20' space per day. Reservations are not required.
CONTACT	Robert Hixenbaugh, 45146 Red Arrow Highway, Paw Paw, MI 49079.
PHONE	(616) 657-3428

SAGINAW: Giant Public Market

WHEN	Every Friday and Saturday, 10:00 A.M. to 7:00 P.M., and Sunday, 10:00 A.M. to 6:00 P.M. In operation since the mid-1980s.
WHERE	At 3435 Sheridan Avenue. Take exit 144/3 off I-75, then right to State, then left to Williamson, then right to market (about three miles down).
ADMISSION	Free admission; free parking for over 500 cars; indoors, year-round.
FEATURES	Antiques and collectibles, books, new and vintage clothing, coins and stamps, kitchenware, crafts, used furniture, jew-

elry, new merchandise, porcelain, fresh produce, and toys. Averages 80 to 100 vendors. Snacks and hot meals are served on the premises. Market is well-stocked, and there are many larger vendors who use ten or more selling spaces (1,000 square feet or more) each.

RATES $15 per 100-square-foot space per day; $36 per three-day weekend. Reservations are not required.

CONTACT Robert Reiss, 3435 Sheridan Avenue, Bridgeport, MI 48601.

PHONE (517) 754-9090

TRUFANT: Trufant Auction and Flea Market

WHEN Every Thursday from April through October, dawn to 4:00 P.M. Auction starts at 10:00 A.M. In operation since 1954.

WHERE At 303 North C Street, just two blocks from downtown Trufant, in Montcalm County, approximately thirty-five miles northeast of Grand Rapids.

ADMISSION Free admission; ample free parking; outdoors, rain or shine.

FEATURES Antiques and collectibles, books, new clothing, coins and stamps, kitchenware, crafts, furniture, jewelry, new and used merchandise, porcelain, fresh produce, and toys. Averages 250 to 300 vendors. Lunch-wagon-type food (burger, fries, etc.) is served on the premises. Family owned and operated for more than four decades.

RATES $8 per twenty feet of frontage per day. Reservations are available on a monthly basis only.

CONTACT Maurice Petersen, 13670 Dickerson Lake Road, Trufant, MI 49347.

PHONE (616) 984-2160 or (616) 984-2573 (Mike Petersen)

WARREN: Country Fair Antique Flea Market

WHEN Every Friday, 4:00 P.M. to 9:00 P.M., and every Saturday and Sunday, 10:00 A.M. to 6:00 P.M. In operation since the late 1970s.

WHERE At 20900 Dequindre Boulevard. Take I-75 to 8 Mile Road exit, then go eight miles to Dequindre Boulevard.

ADMISSION Free admission; ample free parking; indoors, year-round.

FEATURES Variety of offerings, including antiques and collectibles and new and used merchandise. Averages 200 to 300 vendors. Snacks and hot meals are served on the premises.

RATES From $56 per 5'×10' space for three days. Reservations are recommended.

CONTACT Joe Sherman, 20900 Dequindre Boulevard, Warren, MI 48091.

PHONE (810) 757-3740 or (810) 757-3741

WATERFORD: Dixieland Flea Market

WHEN Every Friday, 4:00 P.M. to 9:00 P.M., and every Saturday and Sunday, 10:00 A.M. to 6:00 P.M. In operation since 1976.

WHERE At 2045 Dixie Highway (Highway 10), at the corner of Telegraph Road (Highway 24), a few miles northwest of Detroit (south of Pontiac).

ADMISSION Free admission; free parking for up to 800 cars; indoors year-round and outdoors, weather permitting.

FEATURES Antiques and collectibles, books, new and vintage clothing, kitchenware, crafts, furniture, jewelry, new and used merchandise, porcelain, and toys. Averages 180 to its capacity of 250 vendors. Snacks and hot meals are served on the premises. We wear a smile.

RATES Indoors: $45 per 5'×10' space per weekend, or $80 per 10'×12' space; outdoors: $28 per space per weekend. Reservations are not required.

CONTACT Barbara Kernen, 2045 Dixie Highway, Waterford, MI 48328.

PHONE (248) 338-3220

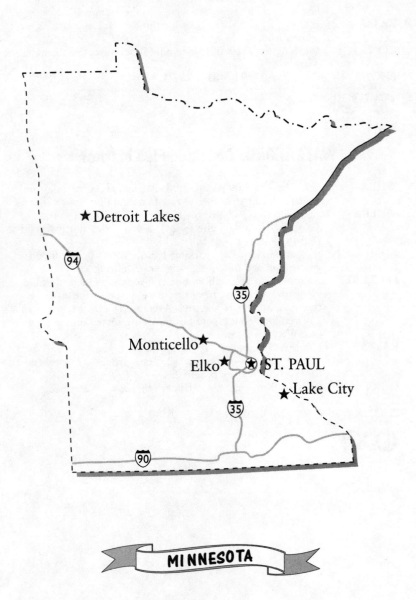

★Detroit Lakes

94

35

Monticello★
Elko★ ★ ST. PAUL
Lake City★

35

90

MINNESOTA

DETROIT LAKES: Shady Hollow Flea Market

WHEN	Every Sunday from Memorial Day through Labor Day, all day. In operation since 1970.
WHERE	On Highway 59.
ADMISSION	Free admission; ample free parking; indoors and outdoors, rain or shine.
FEATURES	Antiques and collectibles, crafts, used merchandise, and fresh produce and flowers. Averages 75 to 125 vendors. Food is served on the premises (and it's tasty). This is a fine market in lake country, with green grass (in season) and friendly people.
RATES	From $15 per space per day. Reservations are not required.
CONTACT	Ardis R. Hanson, 1760 East Shore Drive, Detroit Lakes, MN 56501.
PHONE	(218) 847-9488 or (218) 847-5706

ELKO: Traders Market

WHEN	Two three-day events (Saturday through Monday) annually around July 4 and Labor Day, 8:00 A.M. to 5:00 P.M. on Saturday and 9:00 A.M. to 5:00 P.M. on Sunday and Monday. In operation since 1983.
WHERE	From the Twin Cities (Minneapolis and St. Paul), take 35W or 35E south to I-35 and County Road 2 (exit 76, Elko-New Market), and market is right there.
ADMISSION	Admission $3.50 per person; ample free parking; indoors and outdoors, rain or shine.
FEATURES	Antiques and collectibles are the focus. Averages close to 300 vendors. Food is served on the premises.
RATES	$65 per 15'×25' space for three days outdoors or $95 per 8'×12' indoors. Reservations are required.
CONTACT	Patty or Al, 1008 Main Street, Hopkins, MN 55343.
PHONE	(612) 461-2400
FAX	(612) 869-5379

LAKE CITY: Eighty-five-Mile Garage Sale

WHEN	First full weekend in May, all day; Lake City also has a Friday-night street market from Memorial Day through Labor Day (5:30 P.M. to 8:30 P.M.) with vendors and other attractions. In operation since 1991.
WHERE	Along Highway 61 (Minnesota) and Highway 35 (Wisconsin) around Lake Pepin.
ADMISSION	Free admission; ample free parking; outdoors, rain or shine.
FEATURES	Averages 300 to 400 vendors. Food is served by various charities (including Kiwanis pancake breakfast). Thirteen communities join to create a flea market fair that encircles the lake with food, used items, crafts, and entertainment. Johnny Appleseed Days festival happens on the first full weekend in October (Lake City grows a quarter of the state's apples) with antiques and collectibles market, with over 5,000 visitors.
RATES	Most people are selling out of their driveways (i.e., no transient vendors); call for rates for Friday-night market.
CONTACT	Lake City Chamber of Commerce, P.O. Box 150, Lake City, MN 55041.
PHONE	(651) 345-4123
FAX	(651) 345-4195
E-MAIL	lcchamber@mr.net
WEB	www.lakecity.org

MONTICELLO: Osowski's Flea Market

WHEN	Every weekend, 9:00 A.M. to 5:00 P.M. In operation since the 1970s.
WHERE	On Orchard Road.
ADMISSION	Free admission; ample free parking; indoors year-round and outdoors, weather permitting.
FEATURES	Selection includes antiques and collectibles, garage-sale items, new and used merchandise, and fresh produce. Averages 250 to 500 vendors. Snacks are served on the premises. Also known as the Orchard Fun Market.
RATES	$10 per space per day. Reservations are on a first-come, first-served basis.
CONTACT	Manager, 1479 127th Street N.E., Monticello, MN 55362.
PHONE	(612) 295-2121

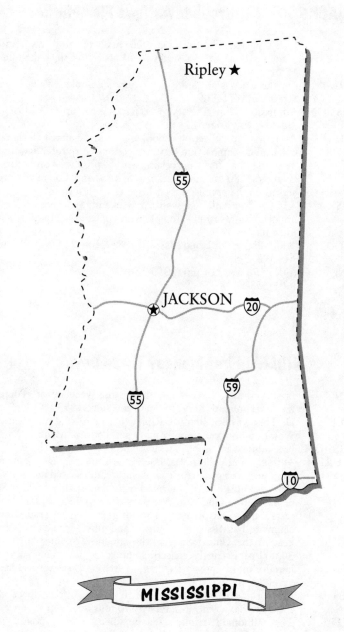

Ripley ★

55

JACKSON   20

59

55

10

MISSISSIPPI

JACKSON: Fairgrounds Antique Flea Market

WHEN	Every weekend: Saturday, 8:00 A.M. to 5:00 P.M. and Sunday, 10:00 A.M. to 5:00 P.M. In operation since the mid-1980s.
WHERE	On the Mississippi State Fairgrounds complex. Take High Street exit off I-55.
ADMISSION	Admission $1 per person; free parking for up to 500 cars; indoors, year-round.
FEATURES	Antiques and collectibles, books, new and vintage clothing, coins and stamps, kitchenware, crafts, furniture, jewelry, new merchandise, porcelain, fresh produce, and toys. Averages 180 to 200 vendors. Snacks and hot meals are served on the premises.
RATES	$35 per booth along a wall per weekend; $45 per booth on an aisle. Reservations are not required; call on Mondays for information.
CONTACT	Frank Barnett or Doug McCurley, P.O. Box 23579, Jackson, MS 39225-3579.
PHONE	(601) 353-5327 or (601) 353-5367
FAX	(601)353-5367

RIPLEY: First Monday Trade Days

WHEN	First Monday of every month and the weekend preceding, from daybreak to dark. In operation since 1893.
WHERE	On Highway 15, south of Ripley, between New Albany and Walnut (approximately 75 miles southeast of Memphis).
ADMISSION	Free admission; ample parking; outdoors, rain or shine.
FEATURES	Antiques and collectibles, books, new and vintage clothing, coins and stamps, crafts, new furniture, household items, jewelry, all kinds of new and used merchandise, livestock, fresh produce, toys, and pets. Averages close to 500 vendors. Full restaurant on the premises. The "original" Ripley Trade Days claims to be Mississippi's largest and among the oldest markets in the United States, with an average attendance of 30,000 per event. Free electrical hookups, RV dump station, laundry room, shower facilities, church services every Sunday at 6:00 A.M.
RATES	$25 for first 18'×18' space, $22.50 each additional space for the three-day event. Reserve two to four weeks in advance.
CONTACT	The Windham family (Wayne, Betty, Jerry, Keith, or Marcy), 10590 Highway 15 South, Ripley, MS 38663.

PHONE	(601) 837-7442 or (601) 837-4051; for vendor reservations call (800) 474-7459 (4-RIPLEY).
FAX	(601) 837-7080
E-MAIL	hww@dixie-net.com
WEB	www.firstmonday.com

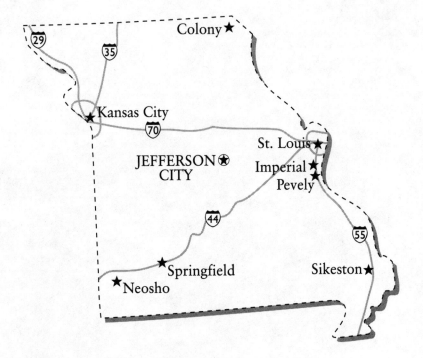

Colony ★

MISSOURI

COLONY: Colony #1 Flea Market

WHEN	First weekend of every month from March through November, all day. In operation since around 1980.
WHERE	On Route V off Route K, a mile and a half northwest of town.
ADMISSION	Free admission; free parking for up to 800 cars; outdoors, rain or shine.
FEATURES	Antiques and collectibles, books, new clothing, coins and stamps, kitchenware, crafts, furniture, new and used merchandise, porcelain, fresh produce, and toys. Averages close to 200 vendors. Snacks and hot meals are served on the premises. Auctions every Friday at 7:00 P.M. and every Saturday at 7:00 P.M.; shower house on grounds.
RATES	$12 per 20'×30' space per weekend; electricity is available at $6 per day. Reservations are not required.
CONTACT	Danny or Dawnetta White, R.R. 1, Box 64A, Rutledge, MO 63563.
PHONE	(660) 434-5504

IMPERIAL: Barnhart Flea Market

WHEN	Every weekend, 6:00 A.M. to 5:00 P.M. In operation since 1986.
WHERE	At 6850 Highway 61/67. Take I-55 to Barnhart Antonio exit, then go east to Highway 61/67, approximately one quarter mile.
ADMISSION	Free admission; ample parking; indoors and outdoors, year-round.
FEATURES	Antiques and collectibles, new and used. Averages up to 150 vendors. There is a concession stand on the premises (lunch delivery is available). There are camping facilities close by.
RATES	Inside: $12 per 5'×10' space per day; outside: $10 per 20'×20' space per day. Reservations are not required for outdoor space.
CONTACT	Manager, 6850 Highway 61/67, Imperial, MO 63052.
PHONE	(314) 464-5503
FAX	(314) 464-5503

KANSAS CITY: Kansas City Flea Market

WHEN	Selected weekends from July through December (call for dates), 8:00 A.M. to 4:00 P.M. In operation since 1986.
WHERE	At 1775 Universal Street, at the North Kansas City Market Center.
ADMISSION	Admission $2 per person; free for children under twelve; free parking for up to 3,500 cars; indoors, rain or shine.
FEATURES	The mix is about 70 percent old, 30 percent new; merchandise includes antiques and collectibles, Beanie Babies, kitchenware, crafts, used furniture, jewelry, "junque," toys, and used merchandise. Averages 250 to 400 vendors. Snacks are available on the premises. Claims to be the largest market in a 300-mile radius.
RATES	From $58 per 10'×10' space per weekend. Reservations are recommended.
CONTACT	Joan, 1153 Bergen Parkway M, PMB-475, Evergreen, CO 80439.
PHONE	(800) 333-3532 (333-FLEA) or (303) 526-5494
FAX	(303) 526-7339

NEOSHO: South Elwood Flea Market

WHEN	Every weekend plus Memorial Day and Labor Day, all day. In operation since 1988.
WHERE	At 17895 Kentucky Road (Highway 59), four miles east of Neosho.
ADMISSION	Free admission; ample free parking; outdoors, year-round, weather permitting.
FEATURES	Antiques and collectibles, used goods, tools, and fresh produce in season. Averages 50 to 100 vendors. Food is not served on the premises.
RATES	$5 per 16'×20' per day. Reservations are not required.
CONTACT	Manager, 17895 Kentucky Road (Highway 59), Neosho, MO 64850.
PHONE	(417) 451-5140

PEVELY: Big Pevely Flea Market

WHEN	Every Saturday and Sunday (sellers set up Friday), 7:00 A.M. to 5:00 P.M. In operation since at least the early 1960s.
WHERE	At Exit 180 off I-55, thirty miles south of St. Louis.
ADMISSION	Free admission; free parking; indoors and outdoors, rain or shine.
FEATURES	Averages up to a capacity of 750 vendors. Burgers and country breakfast are served on the premises. Under new management; said to be one of the larger markets in Missouri.
RATES	$12 per open-air space per day, $17 outdoors under cover, or $18 indoors. Reservations are not required.
CONTACT	Lee or Charlie, P.O. Box 419, Pevely, MO 63070.
PHONE	(636) 479-5400
FAX	(636) 479-7680
E-MAIL	pevelyfleamkt@jen1.com

NFMA Member

ST. LOUIS: Frison Flea Market

WHEN	Every Friday, Saturday, and Sunday, 9:00 A.M. to 5:00 P.M. In operation since 1982.
WHERE	At 7025 Saint Charles Rock Road.
ADMISSION	Free admission; two and a half acres of free parking; indoors and outdoors, weather permitting.
FEATHERS	Variety of offerings, including antiques and collectibles, new and used merchandise, coins and stamps, kitchenware, crafts, jewelry, and fresh produce. Averages up to a capacity of 350 vendors. Snacks and hot meals are served on the premises. There is also a tattoo salon, and jewelry and appliance repair.
RATES	$15 per 10'x10' space per day; winter rates are $5 cheaper per day; storage and table included for long-term vendors (out-of-town vendors have first preference). Reservations are not required; out-of-town vendors have priority.
CONTACT	Jack Frison, 7025 St. Charles Rock Road, St. Louis, MO 63133.
PHONE	(314) 727-0460 or (314) 608-6000 (mobile phone) or (314) 582-0446 (pager)
FAX	(314) 727-0460

NFMA Member

SIKESTON: Tradewinds Trading Post and Auction

WHEN	Every Friday, Saturday, and Sunday, from dawn to dusk. In operation since 1971.
WHERE	At 875 West Malone Avenue, on Old Highway 60 (known as West Malone in west part of town).
ADMISSION	Free admission; free parking; indoors and outdoors, rain or shine.
FEATURES	"Anything that's legal," including antiques, collectibles, crafts, furniture, and fresh produce. Averages up to 250 vendors. Hot meals are available on the premises.
RATES	$7 per space per day, $5 on Sunday. Reservations are on a first-come, first-served basis.
CONTACT	Don or Kim Byrd, 875 West Malone Avenue, Sikeston, MO 63801-2558.
PHONE	(573) 471-3965 or (573) 471-8419 (leave message on machine)

SPRINGFIELD: I-44 Swap Meet

WHEN	Every weekend from mid-March through mid-December, from daybreak to dark. In operation since 1984.
WHERE	At 2600 block of East Kearney, half a mile north on Neergard; or at the 82-mile marker of I-44.
ADMISSION	Admission $1 per carload; parking at $1 per car; outdoors, rain or shine.
FEATURES	Variety of offerings, including antiques and collectibles, new and used merchandise, native crafts, fresh produce, furniture. Averages 200 to 400 vendors. Food is available from four chuck wagons on the premises. This market is said to attract an average of 10,000 to 15,000 buyers a weekend.
RATES	$6 per space on Saturday, $8 on Sunday. Reservations are not required.
CONTACT	Bob or Butch, 2743 West Kearney, Springfield, MO 65803.
PHONE	(417) 864-4340
FAX	(417) 864-6508

MONTANA

See Appendix for Brief Listings

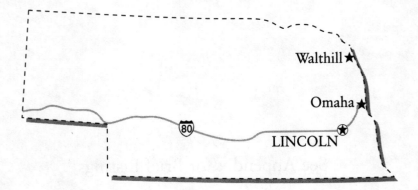

LINCOLN: Pershing Auditorium Monthly IndoorFlea Market

WHEN	Several events every year (seven in 1999), generally in the middle of the month (call for dates), 10:00 A.M. to 5:00 P.M. In operation since the 1970s.
WHERE	At 226 Centennial Mall South, four blocks north of the State Capitol Building in downtown Lincoln.
ADMISSION	Admission 75¢; street parking; indoors.
FEATURES	Full spectrum of antiques, collectibles, new and used merchandise. Averages 50 to 70 vendors. Snacks and hot meals are served on the premises.
RATES	$45 per weekend for three tables (8'×13'); $62 for five tables (8'×21'); $70 for seven tables (8'×29'). Reservations are required.
CONTACT	Derek Andersen, P.O. Box 81126, Lincoln, NE 68501.
PHONE	(402) 441-7500
FAX	(402) 441-7913
E-MAIL	andersen@inetnebr.com
WEB	www.interline.ci.lincoln.ne.us (click on "Pershing Auditorium")

OMAHA: Blue Ribbon Flea Market and Antique Mall

WHEN	Daily except Christmas, Thanksgiving, and Easter, 9:00 A.M. to 6:00 P.M. (open Friday evenings until 8:00 P.M.). In operation since 1993.
WHERE	At 6606 Grover Street. Take 72nd Street exit off I-80 and go one block north to Grover Street, then go right six blocks.
ADMISSION	Free admission; ample free parking; indoors, year-round.
FEATURES	Antiques and collectibles, books, vintage clothing, kitchenware, crafts, furniture, jewelry, new and used merchandise, porcelain, and toys. Averages close to its capacity of 200 vendors. Snacks are served on the premises.
RATES	Monthly rentals only $42 per 5'×5' space or $75 per 5'×10' space. Reservations are not required.
CONTACT	George LaPole, 6606 Grover Street, Omaha, NE 68106.
PHONE	(402) 397-6811

WALTHILL: Flea Market and Hillbilly Auction

WHEN   The first full weekend of every month except November through January (call for dates), all day. In operation since 1993.

WHERE   On I-75, sixty miles north of Decatur.

ADMISSION   Free admission; ample free parking; indoors and outdoors, weather permitting.

FEATURES   Collectible and used stuff, plus animals (coon dogs), sporting equipment, and more. Averages 50 to 100 vendors. Food is served on the premises. Auctions are held on Saturday and Sunday at 1:00 P.M.

RATES $10 per 30'×30' space per weekend; long-term leases are also available (call for rates). Reservations are not required.

CONTACT   Don Nottleman, R. R. #1, Walthill, NE 68067.

PHONE   (402) 846-9150 or (402) 349-9320.

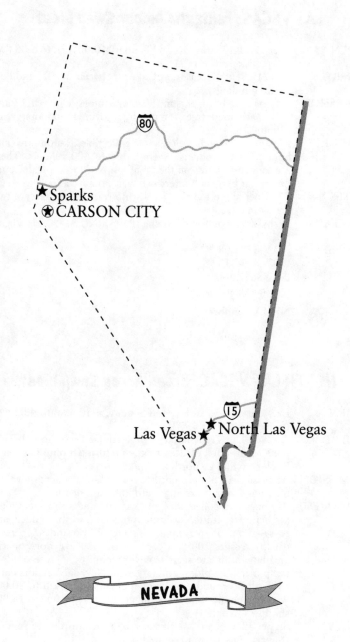

Sparks

CARSON CITY

Las Vegas North Las Vegas

NEVADA

LAS VEGAS: Fantastic Indoor Swap Meet

WHEN	Every Friday, Saturday, and Sunday, 10:00 A.M. to 6:00 P.M. In operation since 1991.
WHERE	At 1717 South Decatur, at Oakey (between the IRS and Post Office buildings).
ADMISSION	Admission $1 per person (50¢ for seniors; children 12 and under admitted free); ample free parking; indoors, year-round.
FEATURES	Mostly new merchandise, some collectibles, automotive and home design products. Averages up to 600 vendors. There are four restaurants on the premises. Not for "upscale" antiquers, but bargain hunters will want to have a look.
RATES	$375 per space for four weeks (no transients). Reserve two weeks in advance.
CONTACT	Berny Krebs or Kandi Roche, P.O. Box 26179, Las Vegas, NV 89126.
PHONE	(702) 877-0087
FAX	(702) 877-3102
E-MAIL	fism8888@aol.com
WEB	www.fantasticswap.com

NFMA Member

NORTH LAS VEGAS: Broad Acres Swap Meet

WHEN	Every Friday, Saturday, and Sunday, 6:30 A.M. to 4:00 P.M. In operation since 1977.
WHERE	At 2960 Las Vegas Boulevard North (at Pecos Street). Take Lake Mead Boulevard East exit and turn left onto Las Vegas Boulevard and go north one mile.
ADMISSION	Admission $1 per person; free for children under twelve; fifteen acres of free parking; outdoors, rain or shine.
FEATURES	Antiques and collectibles, books, new and vintage clothing, kitchenware, crafts, furniture, porcelain, fresh produce, and toys—about 55 percent new merchandise and 45 percent used. Averages 700 to a capacity of 1,200 vendors. Snacks and hot meals are served on the premises. A true outdoor swap meet, the oldest and largest in Nevada. Vendors come from all over, and crowds of shoppers can swell to 20,000 weekly (summer is low season and attracts 10,000 to 14,000 shoppers weekly).
RATES	$8 per 12'×25' space on Friday, $15 on Saturday or Sunday. Reservations are not required.

CONTACT Jake Bowman, P.O. Box 3059, North Las Vegas, NV 89030.
PHONE (702) 642-3777

 NFMA Member

SPARKS/RENO: El Rancho Swap Meet

WHEN   Every weekend, 6:00 A.M. to 3:00 P.M. In operation since
            1940.
WHERE   At the theater, 555 El Rancho Drive.
ADMISSION   Admission 50¢ per person; ample free parking; outdoors,
            year-round.
FEATURES   New, used clothing, shoes, appliances, garage-sale stuff.
            Averages 150 to 200 vendors. Food is served on the prem-
            ises.
RATES $15 per space per day. Reservations are not required.
CONTACT   Lance, Manager, 555 El Rancho Drive, Reno, NV 89431.
PHONE   (702) 331-3227 or (702) 358-6920
FAX   (702) 358-2833
WEB   www.centurytheaters.com

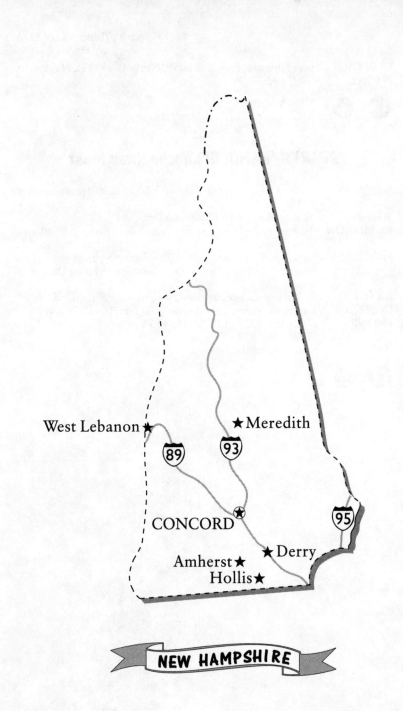

West Lebanon ★

★ Meredith

89

93

★ CONCORD

★ Derry

Amherst ★
Hollis ★

95

NEW HAMPSHIRE

AMHERST: Amherst Outdoor Antique Market

WHEN
The last Sunday of every month from April through October, 6:00 A.M. to 3:00 P.M. In operation since 1960.

WHERE
At 157 Hollis Road (Route 122 South). Take exit 8 off Route 3 (Everett Turnpike, Nashua Bypass), then take Route 101A to Route 122; go left at 122, and market will be on your right, about midway between 101-A and Route 130.

ADMISSION
Free admission; ample parking at $5 per car; outdoors, weather permitting.

FEATURES
Variety of offerings, including antiques and collectibles and new and used merchandise. Averages up to 500 vendors. Good food available. This market is part of the Amherst Outdoor Antique Auto Show—for dealers, collectors, and browsers.

RATES
Call for rates. Reservations are recommended—expect a waiting list.

CONTACT
Werner or Elna Carlson, 51R Dudley Street, Arlington, MA 02476-4504.

PHONE
(603) 673-2093 or (781) 641-0600 or (781) 729-6233

FAX
(781) 641-0647

DERRY: Grandview Flea Market

WHEN
Every weekend, 7:00 A.M. to 3:30 P.M. In operation since 1969.

WHERE
At the junction of Route 28 and 28 Bypass. Take exit 4 off Route 93 to Route 102, Derry Circle (rotary). Take Route 28 Bypass half a mile; market is on left across from Clam Haven, at the lights.

ADMISSION
Admission 50¢ per adult on Sunday, free on Saturday and during January and February; free for children under twelve; free parking for over 1,000 cars; indoors and outdoors, weather permitting.

FEATURES
Antiques and collectibles, electronics, furniture, jewelry, knives, new and used merchandise, groceries, and fresh produce. Averages 100 to 400 vendors. Snacks and hot meals are served on the premises. As many as 5,000 shoppers on summer Sundays. Statues (one is a life-size representation of a pink polka-dotted elephant) are placed throughout the grounds. Classic car shows are held monthly; driving range and pony rides nearby (seasonal).

RATES
Outdoors: $20 per space per day ($35 for both days); $1.50

table rental; indoor transient: $20 per space with three tables; indoor permanent: 20¢ per square foot when available. Reservations are not required for outdoors spaces.

CONTACT   Martin or Kathi Taylor, 34 South Main Street, Derry, NH 03038.

PHONE   (603) 432-2326 (weekends only)

HOLLIS: Brad and Donna's Silver Lake Flea Market and Antique Fair

WHEN   Every Sunday from April through October, 5:30 A.M. to 4:00 P.M. In operation since 1968.

WHERE   On Route 122, at 447 Silver Lake Road.

ADMISSION   Free admission; ample free parking; outdoors, weather permitting.

FEATURES   Runs from antiques and collectibles to typical flea. Averages 100 to 150 vendors. There are three food concessions on the premises. Right across the street from the Hollis Flea Market (see separate listing), shoppers can do both in one pass.

RATES   From around $15 per space. Reservations are recommended.

CONTACT   Bradford Tukey, P.O. Box 100, Hollis, NH 03049.

PHONE   (603) 465-7677

FAX   (603) 465-9898

E-MAIL   bhtukey@aol.com

NFMA Member

HOLLIS: Hollis Flea Market

WHEN   Every Sunday from the first Sunday in April through the second Sunday in November, 7:00 A.M. to 4:00 P.M. In operation since the 1960s.

WHERE   At 436 Silver Lake Road.

ADMISSION   Free admission; parking is available at $1 per car; outdoors, weather permitting.

FEATURES   Antiques and collectibles, books, new and vintage clothing, coins and stamps, kitchenware, crafts, furniture, jewelry, new and used merchandise, porcelain, fresh produce, and toys. Averages up to 200 vendors. Snacks and hot meals are served on the premises. A well-known and well-attended market.

RATES $18 per 14'×20' space per day. Reserve a week in advance.
CONTACT   Gil or Alice Prieto, 436 Silver Lake Road, Hollis, NH
             03049.
PHONE   (603) 882-6134 or (603) 465-7813
FAX   (603) 882-0927
E-MAIL   hollisflea@aol.com

MEREDITH: Burlwood Antique Center

WHEN   Daily, May through October, 10:00 A.M. to 5:00 P.M. In
             operation since 1984.
WHERE   At the intersection of Routes 104 and 3. Take exit 23 off
             Route 93, then nine miles east on Route 104.
ADMISSION   Free admission; free parking for over 100 cars; indoors,
             year-round.
FEATURES   Antiques and collectibles only; one floor of the building is
             devoted to antique furniture. Averages up to 170 vendors.
             Food is not available on the premises. In the heart of the
             lakes region of New Hampshire; good for upscale antiquers.
RATES $18 per day per linear foot for built-in booths; no transients.
             Reserve a year in advance.
CONTACT   Nancy J. Lindsey, 900 Bunker Hill Road, South Tamworth,
             NH 03883.
PHONE   (603) 279-6387

WEST LEBANON: Colonial Antique Markets

WHEN   Daily (except Thanksgiving, Christmas), 9:00 A.M. to 5:30
             P.M. In operation since the mid-1970s.
WHERE   On Airport Road (Route 12-A). Take exit 20 off I-89 (near
             the Vermont border) and look for the back of the building
             on Airport Road, then drive around to front, and office is the
             second door.
ADMISSION   Free admission; free parking for up to 70 cars; indoors year-
             round and outdoors on Sundays, weather permitting.
FEATURES   Antiques and collectibles, books, bottles, vintage clothing,
             coins and stamps, crafts, dolls, used furniture, estate jewelry,
             postcards, tools, and toys. Averages 50 to 60 vendors. Hot
             meals are served on Sundays; snacks are available all week.

An antique mall with a real outdoor flea market on Sundays, with low prices and good turnover.

RATES Indoors: $27.50 per space per week; outdoors: $12 per day (Sundays only). Reservations are not required.

CONTACT The Andersons, 5 Airport Road, Suite 23, Colonial Plaza, West Lebanon, NH 03784.

PHONE (603) 298-8132 or (603) 298-7712 or (802) 875-2252

East Rutherford

80

★Belvidere

78

★Neshanic Station

Flemington
★East Brunswick

Lambertville★
Englishtown★
★Collingwood Park

TRENTON⊛
Lakewood

New Egypt
Palmyra★
★Columbus

95
★
Berlin
Manahawkin★

Absecon★

Dorchester
★

NEW JERSEY

ABSECON: L'Erario's Flea Market

WHEN   Every weekend, 7:00 A.M. to whenever. In operation since around 1970.
WHERE   At the intersection of Jim Leeds and Pitney Roads in Absecon Highlands. Call for further directions.
ADMISSION Free admission; free parking; outdoors, weather permitting.
FEATURES Antiques and collectibles, new and vintage clothing, furniture. Averages 50 to 75 vendors. A restaurant, a deli, and an ice-cream parlor are on the premises, as well as a video shop and baseball card shop.
RATES $15 per space on Saturday, $18 on Sunday. Reservations are not required.
CONTACT   Joseph L'Erario, P.O. Box 572, Absecon, NJ 08201.
PHONE   (609) 652-0540

Just Like in the Movies

Under the headline, "It Lays Nest Eggs," the *New York Times* reported in 1993 that an extremely rare statuette of the Maltese falcon—originally used as a prop in the 1941 Humphrey Bogart classic—turned up at a flea market in New Jersey. Ara Chekmayana, a fifty-three-year-old film editor from Maspeth, Queens, identified a Warner Brothers code number on its base and bought it for $8. Chekmayana took it to Christie's East for an estimate: $30,000 to $50,000. Chekmayana's dream, to finance his own independent film, had come true.

BELVIDERE: Five Acres Flea Market

WHEN   Every weekend, plus holidays, 7:00 A.M. to 4:00 P.M. In operation since 1969.
WHERE   On Route 46. Take exit 12 on Route 80, then south for

seven miles to traffic light, then left, and market will be 1,000 feet ahead on the right.

ADMISSION   Free admission; free parking; outdoors year-round, weather permitting; there is also a newly renovated indoor antique center.

FEATURES   Antiques and collectibles, books, new clothing, kitchenware, crafts, furniture, jewelry, new merchandise, fresh produce. Averages 50 to 100 vendors. Hot dog cart on the premises. Bar and game room on the premises.

RATES $10 per space on Saturday, $15 on Sunday. Reservations are not required.

CONTACT   Totsy Phillips, P.O. Box 295, Belvidere, NJ 07823-0295.
PHONE   (908) 475-2572

BERLIN: Berlin Farmers Market

WHEN   Every weekend, 8:00 A.M. to 4:00 P.M. In operation since 1942 (three generations).

WHERE   At 41 Clementon Road. Take Walt Whitman Bridge to Route 42 southbound to the Blackwood/Clementon exit, then onto Route 534 East for 6.2 miles. Or take the Tacony-Palmyra Bridge to Route 73 southbound, to Berlin Circle, then take second right onto Milfor.

ADMISSION   Free admission; free parking for up to 1,500 cars; indoors year-round and outdoors, weather permitting.

FEATURES   Antiques and collectibles, books, new and vintage clothing, coins and stamps, kitchenware, crafts, fresh produce, furniture, jewelry, and toys. Also, butcher shop, barbershop, Western wear, household items, electronics. Averages 100 to 600 vendors. Snacks and hot meals are served on the premises, which includes a clam bar. Candy and health foods also available. One of the oldest and largest markets on the East Coast. Indoors there are over 80 stores with "mall merchandise at flea market prices"; outdoors, flea and farmers market stuff.

RATES   For sale of strictly used merchandise: $15 for one day or $20 for two days; for new merchandise: $25 for one day or $35 for two days. Reserve a week in advance if possible.

CONTACT   Stan Giberson, Jr., 41 Clementon Road, Berlin, NJ 08009.
PHONE   (609) 767-1284 or (609) 767-1246
FAX   (609) 767-8435
WEB   bfmmkt@cyberenet.net

    NFMA Member

COLLINGWOOD PARK/FARMINGDALE:
Collingwood Auction and Flea Market

WHEN	Every Friday, Saturday, 9:00 A.M. to 5:00 P.M., and every Sunday, 9:00 A.M. to 5:00 P.M. In operation since 1957.
WHERE	On State Highways 33 and 34, half mile west of the Collingwood traffic circle, four miles south of Colts Neck on Highway 34 and seven miles east of Freehold on Highway 33; from Garden State Parkway, take exit 100A (southbound) or 100B (northbound).
ADMISSION	Free admission; free parking for up to 2,500 cars; indoors and outdoors, rain or shine.
FEATURES	Antiques and collectibles, books, new and vintage clothing, coins and stamps, kitchenware, crafts, furniture, jewelry, new and used merchandise, porcelain, fresh produce, and toys. Averages 400 to a capacity of 600 vendors. Snacks and hot meals are served on the premises. Antique and shrubbery auctions are held on Wednesday through Saturday nights.
RATES	From $2 per space on Friday, $6 on Saturday, and $9 on Sunday. Reservations are recommended; call on Friday.
CONTACT	Roland Schneider or Henry, 1350 State Highway 33, Farmingdale, NJ 07727.
PHONE	(732) 938-7941 or (732) 919-9821
FAX	(732) 938-4652

NFMA Member

COLUMBUS: Columbus Farmers Market

WHEN	Every Thursday, Saturday, and Sunday, 7:30 A.M. to 3:00 P.M. Indoor shops are open Thursday and Saturday, 8:00 A.M. to 8:00 P.M.; Friday, 10:00 A.M. to 8:00 P.M.; and Sunday, 8:00 A.M. to 5:00 P.M. In operation since 1929.
WHERE	At 2919 Route 206 South, close to Route 295.
ADMISSION	Free admission; ample free parking; indoors and outdoors, year-round.
FEATURES	Antiques and collectibles, books, new and vintage clothing, coins and stamps, kitchenware, crafts, furniture, jewelry, musical instruments, new merchandise, porcelain, fresh produce, tools, and toys. Averages 500 to a capacity of 1,500 vendors. Also includes a bakery, restaurants. Bills itself as the Delaware Valley's Largest Flea Market. Shoe repair and locksmith also available.
RATES	$30 per space on Thursday, $10 on Saturday; $11 for the

sale of used items and $30 for the sale of new items on Sunday. Reservations are recommended.

CONTACT   Columbus Shopping Center, Inc., 2919 Route 206 South, Columbus, NJ 08054.

PHONE   (609) 267-0400

DORCHESTER: Campbell's Flea Market

WHEN   Every weekend from March through December, 7:00 A.M. to 4:00 P.M. In operation since the late 1960s.

WHERE   On Route 47 at Morristown Causeway, three miles south of the end of Route 55 in Cumberland County, at first traffic light.

ADMISSION   Free admission; ample free parking; indoors year-round and outdoors, weather permitting.

FEATURES   Antiques and collectibles, books, vintage clothing, kitchenware, crafts, jewelry, fresh produce, and toys. Averages 25 to 100 vendors. Deli sandwiches and an ice-cream parlor on the premises. Country store—rural setting with shaded outdoor tables, located by the historic Maurice River.

RATES $10 per table per day ($5 in May). Reservations are not required.

CONTACT   Stewart or Terrie Campbell, 3890 Route 47, Dorchester, NJ 08316.

PHONE   (609) 785-2222

EAST BRUNSWICK: Route 18 Market

WHEN   Every Friday, 11:00 A.M. to 9:00 P.M.; Saturday, 10:00 A.M. to 9:00 P.M.; and Sunday, 11:00 A.M. to 6:00 P.M. In operation since 1978.

WHERE   At 290 Route 18. Take exit 9 off the New Jersey Turnpike, then take Route 18 South to third traffic light; just past light, take jug-handle turn onto Route 18 North; market is on the right after you come back through the intersection.

ADMISSION   Free admission; ample free (paved) parking; indoors, year-round.

FEATURES   Discount merchandise (cosmetics, electronics, etc.) as well as antiques and collectibles, crafts, jewelry, and used merchandise. Averages close to 150 vendors. Prepared food and discount grocery items are sold on the premises. This "multimerchandise" market was voted the best flea market in central New Jersey for 1998 by the *Home News Tribune*; there are discount shops as well as flea market vendors. Tailor, nail salon, jewelry repair also available.

RATES   Daily, weekly, and monthly rates available on request. Reservations are recommended.

CONTACT   Barbara Passwaters or Bruce Berkowitz, 290 Route 18, East Brunswick, NJ 08816.

PHONE   (732) 254-5080

FAX   (732) 254-1761

EAST RUTHERFORD: Meadowlands Marketplace

WHEN   Every Thursday and Saturday, plus Memorial Day, July Fourth, and Labor Day (Saturdays only January through March), 9:00 A.M. to 5:00 P.M. In operation since the early 1990s.

WHERE   At Giants Stadium parking lot 17, on Route 3 West. From I-80, take Route 46 East to Route 3 East to the Sports Complex. From New York City, use the George Washington Bridge to the New Jersey Turnpike South, take exit 16W to the Sports Complex.

ADMISSION   Free admission; ample parking for up to 20,000 cars; outdoors, rain or shine.

FEATURES   Automotive accessories, books, electronics, clothing, kitchenware, crafts, new furniture, jewelry, new merchandise, plants, porcelain, fresh produce, sporting goods, and toys. Averages 600 to 800 vendors. Snacks and hot meals, including American and ethnic fast food, are served on the premises. One of the largest outdoor flea markets in northern New Jersey, with a very diverse assortment of vendors. Special bus trip packages with money-saving coupons for groups and organizations.

RATES $40 per space (equal to four parking spaces) on Thursday and $100 on Saturday; monthly rates available; tables not supplied. Reservations are not required.

CONTACT   Bob Brumale or Larry Fishman, Meadowlands Sports Complex, East Rutherford, NJ 07073.

PHONE   (201) 935-5474

FAX	(201) 935-5495
E-MAIL	solonpond@aol.com
WEB	www.fleamarketsusa.com

ENGLISHTOWN: Englishtown Auction

WHEN	Every weekend: Saturday, 7:00 A.M. to 4:00 P.M. and Sunday, 9:00 A.M. to 4:00 P.M. In operation since 1929.
WHERE	At 90 Wilson Avenue. Take exit 9 off New Jersey Turnpike onto Route 18 South for six miles, then turn right at Englishtown sign and travel six more miles.
ADMISSION	Free admission; free parking; indoors and outdoors, rain or shine.
FEATURES	Antiques and collectibles, books, new clothing, kitchenware, crafts, electronics, furniture, jewelry, leather goods, new and used merchandise, porcelain, fresh produce (plus bakery and butcher shop), school, and offices. Averages up to a capacity of 1,500 vendors. Three food courts available.
RATES	From $5 per table per day. Reservations are not required.
CONTACT	Carla, Manager, 90 Wilson Avenue, Englishtown, NJ 07726.
PHONE	(732) 446-9644
FAX	(732) 446-1220
WEB	www.englishtownauction.com

NFMA Member

FLEMINGTON: Flemington Fair Flea Market

WHEN	Every Wednesday from April through November, 7:00 A.M. to 3:00 P.M.; annual Easter and Halloween festivals—call for dates. In operation for over nineteen years.
WHERE	At the Flemington Fairgrounds on Highway 31, one and a quarter miles north of the Flemington Circle; can be reached off Route 78 or Route 202.
ADMISSION	Free admission; ample free parking; indoors and outdoors, rain or shine (unless the rain is super hard).
FEATURES	Antiques and collectibles, books, new and vintage clothing, coins and stamps, kitchenware, crafts, dolls, furniture, jewelry, new merchandise, porcelain, fresh produce, and flowers and plants. Averages up to 150 vendors. Grocery items are

available. In a beautiful country setting "filled with trees and perfect for a picnic." The fairgrounds have been in operation for over 142 years.

RATES $6 per 8'×20' space per day; tables are available at $2 each; indoor rentals are $500 per season. Reservations are not required.

CONTACT   Melissa L. Yerkes, 25 Kuhl Road, Flemington, NJ 08822.

PHONE   (908) 782-7326; day of market call fair office at (908) 782-2413 to check on local weather.

LAKEWOOD: Route 70 Flea Market

WHEN   Every weekend, 7:00 A.M. to 4:00 P.M., plus "yard sale" every Friday, 8:00 A.M. to 2:00 P.M. In operation since the 1970s.

WHERE   At 117 Route 70, between the Garden State Parkway and Route 9.

ADMISSION   Free admission; free parking for up to 1,000 cars; indoors and outdoors, rain or shine.

FEATURES   Antiques and collectibles, books, new and vintage clothing, coins and stamps, kitchenware, crafts, furniture, jewelry, livestock, new and used merchandise, porcelain, fresh produce, and toys. Averages close to 1,000 vendors. Snacks and hot meals are served on the premises. A true open-air flea market.

RATES $7 per day for one twenty-four-square-foot space includes table; Friday rate is $4 per table. Reservations are required.

CONTACT   Yvonne Weintraub or Mike Gingrich, 117 Route 70, Lakewood, NJ 08701.

PHONE   (908) 370-1837

FAX   (732) 840-5684

LAMBERTVILLE: Lambertville Antique Market

WHEN   Indoor antiques shops are open every Wednesday, 8:00 A.M. to 4:00 P.M., Thursday and Friday, 10:00 A.M. to 4:00 P.M., and Saturday and Sunday, 8:00 A.M. to 4:00 P.M.; outdoor antique market is open every Wednesday, Saturday, and Sunday from 6:00 A.M. on. In operation since 1971.

WHERE   On Route 29, a mile and a half south of Lambertville. From Philadelphia, take I-95 North to Lambertville exit onto Route 29 approximately ten miles, and market will be on the right. From New York, take Route 287 to Route 202 South to Lambertville exit.

ADMISSION   Free admission; free parking for up to 350 cars; indoors year-round and outdoors, weather permitting.

FEATURES   Antiques and collectibles only (no new merchandise): books, vintage clothing and furniture, glassware, antique jewelry, toys, and much more. Average 60 to 120 vendors. Restaurant serving "homestyle" cooking on the premises. Upscale market more for antiquers than junktiquers. Three buildings contain six antiques shops plus over sixty showcases for quality merchandise.

RATES   Indoor pavilion: $12 per space on Wednesday, $32 on Saturday, $48 on Sunday; outdoors: $22 per space on Saturday, $40 on Sunday (covered booths are $42 on Sunday). Reserve two to three weeks in advance (outdoor spaces do not require reservations except on Sunday).

CONTACT   Tom or Heidi Cekoric or Robert Errhalt, 1864 River Road, Lambertville, NJ 08530.

PHONE   (609) 397-0456

WEB   www.lambertville.com

MANAHAWKIN: Manahawkin Flea Market

WHEN   Every Friday, Saturday, and Sunday, 8:00 A.M. to 5:00 P.M. In operation since 1978.

WHERE   At 629 East Bay Avenue. Take exit 63 off the Garden State Parkway and follow signs to Manahawkin Business District until Bay Avenue.

ADMISSION   Free admission; free parking for up to 250 cars; indoors and outdoors, rain or shine.

FEATURES   Antiques and collectibles, new and vintage clothing, coins and stamps, kitchenware, crafts, jewelry, porcelain, new merchandise, furniture, and fresh produce. Averages 50 to 100 vendors. Snacks and hot meals are served on the premises.

RATES $20 per space per day on Saturday and Sunday; $5 on Friday. Reservations are not required.

CONTACT   Warren or Jill Petrucci, P.O. Box 885, Manahawkin, NJ 08050.
PHONE   (609) 597-1017
FAX   (609) 597-1017

MOUNT LAUREL: William Spencer's Antique Show and Sale

WHEN   Second Sunday of every month from March through December, 9:00 A.M. to 5:00 P.M. There are also crafts shows, usually the fourth Saturday of every month (call for dates). In operation since the 1950s.
WHERE   At 118 Creek Road, one mile from Rancocas Woods exit (exit 43) off I-295.
ADMISSION Free admission; free parking for up to 400 cars; outdoors, weather permitting (rain date is following Sunday; no rain dates for December shows).
FEATURES   Antiques and collectibles only. Averages close to 100 vendors. Snacks and hot meals are served on the premises. This is an upscale event that is borderline flea market/antique show.
RATES $50 per day (based on annual contract). Transient vendors are not accommodated.
CONTACT   Isabel Michaski, 118 Creek Road, Rancocas Woods, NJ 08054.
PHONE   (856) 235-1830
FAX   (856) 235-8552

NESHANIC STATION: Neshanic Flea Market

WHEN   Every Sunday from March through Christmas, 7:00 A.M. to 2:00 P.M. In operation since the late 1960s.
WHERE   At 100 Elm Street.
ADMISSION Free admission; two acres of parking at 50¢ per car; outdoors, weather permitting.
FEATURES   Antiques and collectibles, books, new clothing, kitchenware, crafts, used furniture, jewelry, fresh produce, toys, and used merchandise. Averages up to several hundred vendors. Snacks (including but not limited to hot dogs, pork roll sandwiches, eggs and bacon) are served on the premises.

Beautiful setting, friendly people, good selection of merchandise.

RATES $12 per space per day; tables are not supplied. Reservations are not required—just show up between 6:00 A.M. and 7:00 A.M. on Sunday morning.

CONTACT   Mary Weiss, 100 Elm Street, Neshanic Station, NJ 08853.

PHONE   (908) 369-3660

NEW EGYPT: New Egypt Auction and Farmers Market

WHEN   Every Wednesday and Sunday, 7:00 A.M. to noon (call for auction dates). In operation since 1949.

WHERE   On Route 537, a mile east of Route 528 (between Routes 528 and 539, six miles west of the Six Flags Great Adventure theme park and about seven miles from Fort Dix/Maguire AFB).

ADMISSION   Free admission; ample free parking; indoors year-round and outdoors, weather permitting.

FEATURES   Antiques and collectibles, books, clothing, coins and stamps, kitchenware, crafts, electronics, furniture, household items, jewelry, porcelain, fresh produce, sporting goods and exercise equipment, automotive supplies, sewing materials, and tools. Averages 30 to 100 vendors. Snacks and hot meals are served on the premises. Unpaved, low-key, and friendly. You'll find a machine shop, recycling and salvage depot, etc.—not just another shopping mall but a unique "flea market village."

RATES $6 per space on Wednesday, $7 on Sunday. Reservations are not required.

CONTACT   Les Heller, 150 Evergreen Road, New Egypt, NJ 08533-1208.

PHONE   (609) 758-2082; in New Jersey, call (800) 660-2582

E-MAIL   swanneck@erols.com

PALMYRA: Tacony-Palmyra Flea Market

WHEN   Every weekend, 4:00 A.M. to 3:00 P.M. In operation since around 1970.

WHERE	On Route 73 South.
ADMISSION	Free admission; free parking for up to 850 cars; outdoors, rain or shine, year-round.
FEATURES	Antiques and collectibles, books, new clothing, coins and stamps, kitchenware, crafts, furniture, jewelry, new merchandise, porcelain, and fresh produce. Averages 275 to 425 vendors. Snacks and hot meals are served on the premises.
RATES	$25 per 18'×18' space per day. Reservations are not required.
CONTACT	Manager, P.O. Box 64, Palmyra, NJ 08065.
PHONE	(609) 829-3000 or (609) 829-3001

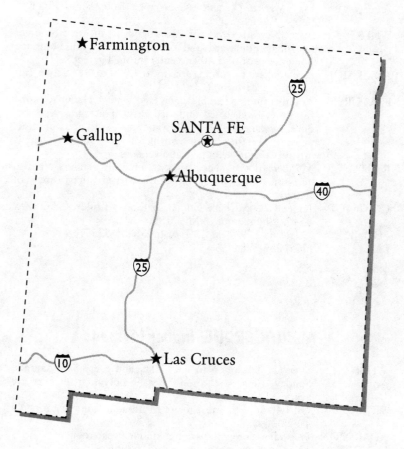

★Farmington

★Gallup

SANTA FE
★

★Albuquerque

NEW MEXICO

★Las Cruces

ALBUQUERQUE: Fairgrounds Flea Market

WHEN Every weekend except in September, 7:00 A.M. to 5:00 P.M. In operation "forever."

WHERE At the New Mexico State Fairgrounds, at the intersection of Louisiana Boulevard and Central. Take South Louisiana Boulevard exit off I-40 and enter through gate 9.

ADMISSION Free admission; parking for up to 1,000 cars at $2 per car; outdoors, year-round.

FEATURES Antiques and collectibles, new and vintage clothing, crafts, furniture, jewelry, new and used merchandise, and fresh produce. Averages 700 to 1,200 vendors. Snacks and hot meals are served on the premises. Stroller, wagon, and table rentals are available for shoppers and vendors.

RATES $12 per 10'×10' space per day; monthly vendors are also accommodated (call for rates). Reservations are not required.

CONTACT James Fahl, Michelle Gomez, or Bobby Childers, P.O. Box 8546, Albuquerque, NM 87198.

PHONE (505) 265-1791 (ext. 215) or (505) 255-8255

FAX (505) 266-7784

ALBUQUERQUE: Indoor Mercado

WHEN Every Friday, noon to 6:00 P.M., and every Saturday and Sunday, 10:00 A.M. to 6:00 P.M. In operation for over five years.

WHERE Off I-40 at 12th Street (close to Albuquerque's historic Old Town).

ADMISSION Free admission; free parking; indoors, year-round.

FEATURES Most of the booths sell new stuff, but there is also a smattering of antiques and collectibles, Southwest arts and crafts, vintage clothing, and jewelry. Averages up to 100 vendors. Food is available on the premises.

RATES From $10 per 10'×10' space per day or $220 per 10'×10' space per month. Reservations are required.

CONTACT Manager, 2035 12th Street, Albuquerque, NM 87104.

PHONE (505) 243-8111

ALBUQUERQUE: Star Flea Market

WHEN	Every weekend, 6:00 A.M. to whenever. In operation since 1974.
WHERE	At 543 Coors Boulevard Southwest.
ADMISSION	Free admission; ample free parking; outdoors, weather permitting.
FEATURES	New, used, collectible—whatever. Averages close to 150 vendors. Food is served on the premises.
RATES	$6 per space per day. Reservations are recommended.
CONTACT	Joe Rue, Manager, 139 Old Coors Road, Albuquerque, NM 87105.
PHONE	(505) 831-3106
FAX	(505) 836-1628

FARMINGTON: Farmington Flea Market

WHEN	Every Friday, Saturday, and Sunday, from dawn to dusk. In operation for over twenty-seven years.
WHERE	On Highway 550 between Farmington and Aztec.
ADMISSION	Free admission; acres of free parking; outdoors, rain or shine.
FEATURES	All types of new and used merchandise, furniture, household items—"everything." Averages 65 to 160 vendors. Snacks and hot meals are served on the premises. No charge for overnight parking.
RATES	$4 per space on Friday or Sunday, and $8 on Saturday. Reserve a week in advance if possible.
CONTACT	Cathey Wright, 7701 East Main Street, Farmington, NM 87401.
PHONE	(505) 325-3129

GALLUP: Gallup Flea Market

WHEN	Daily except Sunday (Saturday is the big day), 8:00 A.M. to dark. In operation since 1978.
WHERE	On Old Route 666. Take I-40 exit 26 (Sheetrock).
ADMISSION	Free admission; ample free parking; outdoors, year-round.

FEATURES	Antiques and collectibles, native American crafts and fine art (including jewelry, rugs, pottery, kachina dolls), new and used merchandise, toys. Averages up to 350 vendors. Food (including Navajo foods) are served served on the premises. In the heart of "Indian Country."
RATES	$10 per ten-foot frontage on Saturday, or $4 per space Monday through Friday. Reservations are recommended.
CONTACT	Vi Fenley, P.O. Box 1888, Gallup, NM 87305.
PHONE	(505) 722-7328

LAS CRUCES: Big Daddy's Marketplace

WHEN	Every weekend, 6:30 A.M. to 4:00 P.M. In operation since 1981.
WHERE	At 7320 North Main Street, out by Oñate High School.
ADMISSION	Free admission; ample free parking; outdoors and under cover, year-round.
FEATURES	New and used merchandise and fresh produce. Averages 300 to a capacity of 400 vendors. Two Mexican restaurants and one with international cuisine. A real old-time flea market, clean and well run.
RATES	$6 per space outdoors, $8 under shed. Reservations are not required.
CONTACT	Manager, P.O. Box 1954, Las Cruces, NM 88004.
PHONE	(505) 382-9404

SANTA FE: Trader Jack's Flea Market

WHEN	Every Friday, Saturday, and Sunday, 7:00 A.M. to 7:00 P.M. In operation since the 1980s in its present location.
WHERE	On Flea Market Road, just off Taos Highway (north of Santa Fe), by the Opera grounds.
ADMISSION	Free admission; free parking; outdoors, weather permitting.
FEATURES	Antiques and collectibles, Native American and Mexican crafts, new and vintage clothing, furniture, jewelry, new and used merchandise, and fresh produce. Averages 12 to 100 vendors. Mexican food and refreshments (including a cappuccino bar!) are available on the premises. This is a funky

but interesting market in a lovely part of New Mexico, amid the Sangre de Cristo Mountains.

RATES $5 per space on Friday, $10 per day on Saturday or Sunday. Advance reservations are not accepted—registration is in person on market days only.

CONTACT   Manager (mailing address not available).

PHONE   No phone number—just go up there.

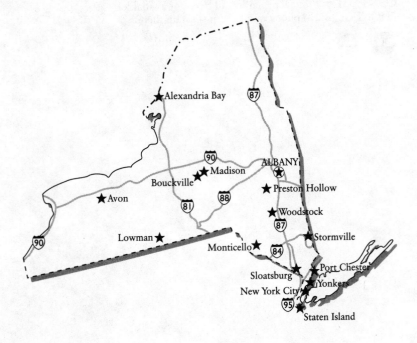

★ Alexandria Bay

87

90
★ Madison
Bouckville

ALBANY
★
★ Preston Hollow

88

81
★ Avon

★ Woodstock
87

Lowman ★
★ Stormville

Monticello ★
84

Sloatsburg
Port Chester
★ Yonkers
New York City ★
95
★ Staten Island

NEW YORK

ALEXANDRIA BAY: Ameri/Can Market

WHEN	Every Friday, Saturday, and Sunday, and holidays from Memorial Day to Labor Day, 10:00 A.M. to 6:00 P.M.
WHERE	On Route 12.
ADMISSION	Free admission; ample free parking; indoors and outdoors, rain or shine.
FEATURES	Mostly used, collectible, and "junque." Averages 30 to 65 vendors. Snack bar. Minigolf, arcade, kiddie rides, etc.
RATES	$10 per 10'×10' space per day. Reservations are not required.
CONTACT	Manager, P.O. Box 2169, Liverpool, NY 13088.
PHONE	(315) 482-2016
FAX	(315) 482-2016
E-MAIL	americanflea@yahoo.com
WEB	www.thousandisland.com/fleamarket/

AVON: East Avon Flea Market

WHEN	Every Sunday from mid-May through mid-October, 6:00 A.M. to 4:00 P.M. In operation since the 1970s.
WHERE	At 1520 Rochester Road (Route 15), south of Rochester, just north of Routes 5 and 20.
ADMISSION	Free admission; free parking for up to 1,700 cars; outdoors, rain or shine.
FEATURES	Antiques and collectibles, books, new and vintage clothing, coins and stamps, kitchenware, crafts, jewelry, new and used merchandise, porcelain, fresh produce, and toys. Averages up to 350 vendors. Snacks and hot meals are served on the premises. Attracts as many as 6,000 shoppers on busy days.
RATES	$20 per space per day. Reservations are not required; vendors may show up between 6:00 A.M. and 8:30 A.M. on day of market.
CONTACT	Manager, 1520 Rochester Road, Avon, NY 14414.
PHONE	(716) 226-8320 or (716) 271-5195

NFMA Member

BOUCKVILLE: Bouckville Antique Pavilion

WHEN	Every Sunday, May through October—plus special shows (Wednesday through Sunday) over the fourth full weekend in June and the third weekend in August, 6:00 A.M. to 4:00 P.M. In operation since 1984.
WHERE	In the center of Bouckville, on Route 20 (25 miles west of Utica, 35 miles east of Syracuse, and 98 miles west of Albany).
ADMISSION	Free admission; acres of free parking; indoors and outdoors, rain or shine.
FEATURES	Antiques and collectibles such as baseball cards, books, coins, comics, used furniture, antique jewelry, porcelain, stamps, and toys. No new merchandise. Averages 60 to 80 vendors. Snacks and hot meals are served on the premises. The August show is one of the largest in the Northeast; the June events include a tractor pull and pre-1943 auto show.
RATES	From $15 to $20 per space on Sunday; call for rates for the June and August events. Reservations are not required.
CONTACT	Steve or Lynda Bono, R. D. #1, Box 111, Bouckville, NY 13310.
PHONE	(315) 893-7483

LOWMAN: Lowman Flea Market

WHEN	Every weekend, 8:00 A.M. to 4:00 P.M. In operation since at least the 1960s.
WHERE	On Route 17.
ADMISSION	Free admission; ample free parking; indoors and outdoors, year-round.
FEATURES	Antiques and collectibles, household items, new merchandise, and crafts. Averages close to 100 vendors. There is a concession stand on the premises.
RATES	$10 per 15'×20' space per day. Reservations are not required.
CONTACT	Jim Stage, P.O. Box 26, Lowman, NY 14861.
PHONE	(607) 734-3670

MADISON: Country Walk Antiques Flea Market

WHEN	Three five-day events, in June, August, and September (call for dates), 8:00 A.M. to 4:00 P.M. In operation since 1992.
WHERE	On Route 20 between Madison and Bouckville.
ADMISSION	Free admission; ample free parking; outdoors, weather permitting.
FEATURES	Antiques and collectibles, plus crafts in the September event. Averages up to 250 vendors. Food is served on the premises.
RATES	$90 for five days ($50 for September); tent space available; free showers for vendors. Reservations are required.
CONTACT	Manager, 7029 Route 20, Madison, NY 13402.
PHONE	(315) 893-7621

MONTICELLO: The Flea Market at Monticello Raceway

WHEN	Every weekend plus holidays from July through Labor Day, 9:00 A.M. to 5:00 P.M. In operation since 1976.
WHERE	At the Monticello Raceway, on Route 17B in Sullivan County. Take exit 104 off Route 17.
ADMISSION	Free admission; free parking for up to 1,000 cars; outdoors, weather permitting.
FEATURES	Mainstay of this market is "upscale" new merchandise at discount prices—but don't expect to find antiques and collectibles. Averages up to 100 vendors. Snacks and hot meals are served on the premises. Located in the heart of the Catskill Mountains region of upstate New York. Live harness racing at the Raceway (next door) on Sundays.
RATES	From $25 to $40 per space per day. Reservations are not required; space is always available—management on-site from 8:00 A.M. every market day.
CONTACT	Alan Finchley, Manager, 42 Ohio Avenue, Long Beach, NY 11561.
PHONE	(914) 796-1000
FAX	(516) 897-3765

MONTICELLO: Village of Monticello Street Fair

WHEN	One Saturday a month from May through September (call for dates), 9:00 A.M. to 5:00 P.M. In operation since 1998.
WHERE	On Broadway (Route 42) between Liberty and Bank Streets. Take Route 17 (I-86 exits 104, 105, 106).
ADMISSION	Free admission; ample free parking; outdoors, weather permitting.
FEATURES	Anything and everything. Averages up to 300 vendors. Food is served on the premises. An average of 20,000 shoppers turn out for this event. Rides and games are available for the children.
RATES	$60 per space per weekend; vendors may park overnight. Reservations are recommended.
CONTACT	Alan Finchley, Catskill Shows, Inc., 42 Ohio Avenue, Long Beach, NY 11561.
PHONE	(516) 897-3765
FAX	(516) 897-1800

NEW YORK CITY: The Annex Antiques Fair and Flea Market ("The Annex")

WHEN	Every weekend, sunrise to sunset. In operation since 1976.
WHERE	On Avenue of the Americas (Sixth Avenue) between 24th and 27th Streets, in three different parking lots.
ADMISSION	Admission $1 per person on lot between 25th and 26th Streets; others are free; limited street and garage parking; public transportation is recommended; outdoors, weather permitting.
FEATURES	Saturday's market has everything imaginable in antiques, collectibles, and interesting secondhand stuff; on Sunday there is also new merchandise. Averages 300 to a capacity of 600 vendors. The Annex is Manhattan's largest and most comprehensive weekly collectibles market, located in a bustling commercial district of Manhattan. Under the same management is The Garage, on 25th Street, between Sixth and Seventh Avenues on 25th Street (see separate listing).
RATES	From $50 to $150 per 9'×12' space; all vendors must prominently display a New York State certificate of authority to collect sales tax. Reserve as far in advance as possible; rental fees are payable one week in advance.

CONTACT   Michael Santulli or Alan Boss, P.O. Box 7010, New York, NY 10023.

PHONE   (212) 243-5343; day of market call Dan at (212) 243-7922

FAX   (212) 463-7099

E-MAIL   info@metropolitanevents.com

NEW YORK CITY: The Annex at Columbus Circle

WHEN   Daily from April through Christmas, 11:00 A.M. to 7:00 P.M. In operation since 1995.

WHERE   At 10 Columbus Circle on the Coliseum Plaza, on the west side of Columbus Circle at 59th Street (southwest corner of Central Park).

ADMISSION   Free admission; paid parking on premises; outdoors, rain or shine.

FEATURES   Antiques and collectibles, accessories, books, new and vintage clothing, crafts, jewelry, new and used merchandise. Averages 40 to 70 vendors. Food kiosks serve snacks at the market; many restaurants are nearby.

RATES $50 per six-foot table per day; monthly rates are available for food and merchandise kiosks. Reserve a week in advance.

CONTACT   Michael Santulli (Manager) or Alan Boss, P.O. Box 7010, New York, NY 10023.

PHONE   (212) 243-5343 or (212) 463-0200

FAX   (212) 463-7099

E-MAIL   info@metropolitanevents.com

Score One for the Luddites

The author and a friend recently completed a forty-three-mile bicycle tour through all five boroughs of New York City on vintage bikes that had already survived at least one New York City winter chained to outdoor signposts. The total price paid for the two bikes, a Schwinn and a Raleigh, was $120.

NEW YORK CITY: The Annex at South Street Seaport

WHEN	Every Thursday, Friday, and Saturday, 11:30 A.M. to 7:00 P.M. In operation since April 1999.
WHERE	On Burlington Slip at the corner of South Street in lower Manhattan.
ADMISSION	Free admission; street parking only; public transportation is recommended; outdoors, rain or shine.
FEATURES	Antiques and collectibles, crafts, and fine art. Averages 70 to 80 vendors. Food is served on the premises. Seaport Museum and shopping at the South Street Seaport, a major tourist area.
RATES	$85 per space per day. Reserve a week in advance.
CONTACT	Michael Santulli (Manager) or Alan Boss, P.O. Box 7010, New York, NY 10116.
PHONE	(212) 534-3212 or (212) 463-0200
FAX	(212) 463-7099
E-MAIL	info@metropolitanevents.com

NEW YORK CITY: Eastside Antique, Flea, and Farmers Market at P.S. 183

WHEN	Every Saturday, 6:00 A.M. to 6:00 P.M. In operation since the 1970s.
WHERE	At Public School 183-M, 419 East 66th Street, between First and York Avenues (alternate entrance through schoolyard on 67th Street), a block away from Cornell Medical Center on the Upper East Side of Manhattan.
ADMISSION	Free admission; metered street parking; public transportation is recommended; indoors, rain or shine, and outdoors, weather permitting.
FEATURES	Antiques and collectibles, books, new and vintage clothing, coins and stamps, cosmetics, costume jewelry, new and used merchandise, plants, porcelain, prints, and fresh produce. Averages 150 to 200 vendors. Snacks are served on the premises. Under new management since 1997.
RATES	$45 per space per day indoors, or from $23 to $90 outdoors. Reserve a week in advance.
CONTACT	Margaret Lerner, Greenflea, Inc., 162 West 72nd Street, #4RR, New York, NY 10023.
PHONE	(212) 721-0900 (office hours are Monday through Wednesday, 11:00 A.M. to 2:00 P.M.); day of market call the school at (212) 734-3578.
FAX	(212) 721-6394
E-MAIL	greenflea@aol.com

NEW YORK CITY: The Garage

WHEN	Every weekend, 8:00 A.M. to 5:00 P.M. In operation since 1993.
WHERE	At 112 West 25th Street, between Avenue of the Americas (Sixth Avenue) and Seventh Avenue—just 200 feet from the world-famous outdoor Annex Antiques Fair and Flea Market.
ADMISSION	Free admission; parking is available on third floor of garage (about $5 per car) or nearby (public transportation is recommended); indoors, year-round.
FEATURES	Antiques and collectibles, books and ephemera, vintage clothing, crafts, used furniture, jewelry, Oriental rugs, porcelain, and toys. Averages 100 to 150 vendors. Snacks are served on the premises. The Garage is a good complement to

its sister market, the outdoor Annex, a block away on Sixth Avenue.

RATES $75 to $150 per 11'×12' space; vendors must have New York State sales tax license. Reserve at least a week in advance.

CONTACT Michael Santulli (Manager) or Alan Boss, P.O. Box 7010, New York, NY 10023.

PHONE (212) 647-0707 or (212) 463-0200

FAX (212) 463-7099

NEW YORK CITY: I.S. 44 Flea Market/Greenflea

WHEN Every Sunday except Easter, 10:00 A.M. to 5:00 P.M. In operation since the early 1980s.

WHERE At the schoolyard on 77th Street and Columbus Avenue, across the street from the American Museum of Natural History on Manhattan's Upper West Side, a block from Central Park.

ADMISSION Free admission; street parking (public transportation recommended); indoors year-round and outdoors, weather permitting.

FEATURES Antiques and collectibles, baskets, books, new and vintage clothing, international crafts, furniture, jewelry, new and used merchandise, plants, porcelain, fresh produce, and toys (balance is about 40 percent old, 60 percent new merchandise). Averages 225 to a capacity of 350 vendors. Snacks are served on the premises, and there are many restaurants and food shops nearby. Proceeds from market benefit the students of I.S. 44, P.S. 87, and the district.

RATES From $23 to $125 per space per day, depending on size and location. Reservations are required—call for information.

CONTACT Judith Gehrke, Greenflea, Inc., 162 West 72nd Street, #4RR, New York, NY 10023.

PHONE (212) 721-0900 Monday through Wednesday, 11:00 A.M. to 2:00 P.M.; on Saturday, call (212) 734-3578; on Sunday, call (212) 877-7371.

FAX (212) 721-6934

E-MAIL greenflea@aol.com

NEW YORK CITY: SoHo Antiques and Flea Market

WHEN   Every weekend, 9:00 A.M. to 5:00 P.M. In operation since 1991.

WHERE   At 465 Broadway (corner of Grand Street, one block north of Canal Street). Use IRT local subway (#6 train) to either the Spring Street or the Canal Street stop.

ADMISSION   Free admission; metered street parking and garages nearby; public transportation is recommended; outdoors year-round, weather permitting.

FEATURES   Antiques and collectibles, architectural objects, books, vintage clothing, coins and stamps, kitchenware, crafts, fine and decorative arts, folk art, furniture, glassware, jewelry, memorabilia, textiles, and toys. Averages 65 to 90 vendors. Snacks and hot meals are available in the neighborhood. A premier opportunity for unusual treasures—justly described as a must-stop on New York's weekend flea market trail. Located in Manhattan's artsy SoHo district, with many interesting galleries, shops, restaurants, and museums nearby.

RATES   From $70 to $120 per space per day depending on size and location. Reservations are recommended.

CONTACT   Ted Brachfeld, Manager, P.O. Box 337, Garden City, NY 11530.

PHONE   (212) 682-2000

PORT CHESTER: Empire State Flea Market/Mall/ Jewelry Exchange

WHEN   Every Friday, noon to 8:00 P.M.; Saturday and Sunday, 10:00 A.M. to 6:00 P.M.; and daily with extended hours from Thanksgiving through Christmas. In operation since 1976.

WHERE   In Caldor Shopping Center, 515 Boston Post Road (Route 1). Take exit 21 off I-95; or take exit 11 off I-287. The market is located fifteen miles from the Tappan Zee Bridge, twenty-five miles from the George Washington Bridge, on the New York–Connecticut border.

ADMISSION   Free admission; free parking for up to 1,900 cars; indoors, year-round.

FEATURES   Home of Westchester County's only fine jewelry exchange, plus about 100 vendors selling only new merchandise at discount prices; don't expect to find antiques. Averages close to its capacity of 300 vendors. Snacks and hot meals are served on the premises. Billed as New York State's original indoor new merchandise market, with some 5,000 shoppers each market day.

RATES   Monthly rentals only, average $500 per space per month. Reservations are not accepted—there is a waiting list.

CONTACT   Alan Finchley, 515 Boston Post Road, Port Chester, NY 10573.

PHONE   (914) 939-1800 or, outside of New York State, call (800) 220-7467 (220-SHOP); or call Alan Finchley at (914) 892-3765.

FAX   (914) 939-5046

NFMA Member

PRESTON HOLLOW: Preston Hollow Antique and Flea Market

WHEN   Every Sunday; antique market is open daily except Thursday, plus holidays, 9:00 A.M. to 4:00 P.M. In operation since about 1990.

WHERE   At the intersection of Routes 145 and 81, where Albany, Greene, and Schoharie Counties meet; call for further directions.

[ADMISSION   Free admission; free parking for up to 300 cars; outdoors, rain or shine.

FEATURES   Antiques and collectibles, books, new clothing, crafts, furniture, jewelry, new merchandise, and porcelain. Averages close to 50 vendors. Snacks and hot meals are served on the premises.

RATES $20 per 20'×20' space per day. Reservations are recommended a week in advance, but vendors are welcome on day of market.

CONTACT   Dorothy Como, R. D. #1, Box 88, Preston Hollow, NY 12469.

PHONE   (518) 239-4251

SLOATSBURG: New York Merchant Village

WHEN   Every week from May through October, hours vary seasonally—call ahead. In operation since 1999.

WHERE	On the New York State Thruway (I-87) at the Sloatsburg rest area (just north of exit 15).
ADMISSION	Free admission; ample free parking; outdoors and under cover, rain or shine.
FEATURES	Upscale new merchandise at discount prices (no used merchandise or antiques). Averages up to 40 vendors. Food court nearby. Attracts a high volume of motorists and tour buses (considering it is located at a rest stop on the highway).
RATES	From $500 per month; no transient vendors. Reservations are required.
CONTACT	Alan Finchley, 42 Ohio Avenue, Long Beach, NY 11561.
PHONE	(914) 397-9840
FAX	(516) 897-1800

STATEN ISLAND: Yankee Peddler Day

WHEN	The first Sunday in May, June, and October, and the second Sunday in September, 10:00 A.M. to 5:00 P.M. In operation since 1969.
WHERE	At Historic Richmond Town. Take the Staten Island Ferry to the S74 bus to Richmond Road and Court Place; by car, turn left out of the ferry terminal onto Bay Street and go about two miles, then turn right on Vanderbilt Avenue; at the fourth light, bear left onto Richmond Road; about four miles on, turn left onto Saint Patrick's Place. Follow signs from there.
ADMISSION	Admission $1 per person (50¢ for children); free parking; outdoors, with rain date.
FEATURES	Antiques and collectibles, crafts, vintage clothing, used furniture, porcelain, jewelry, and more. Averages close to its capacity of 150 vendors. Snacks and hot meals are served on the premises.
RATES	$40 per 10'×19' space (one parking space). Reservations are required two weeks in advance, prepaid.
CONTACT	Angela Russo or Judith McMillen, c/o Education Department, Staten Island Historical Society, 441 Clarke Avenue, Staten Island, NY 10306.
PHONE	(718) 351-1611 (ext. 280 or 281)
FAX	(718) 351-6057

STORMVILLE: Stormville Airport Antique Show and Flea Market

WHEN	Seven Sundays per year in April, May, July, August, September, October, and November (call for dates), dawn to dusk. In operation since 1970.
WHERE	At the Stormville Airport on Route 216 (between Routes 52 and 55) in Dutchess County.
ADMISSION	Free admission; free parking for approximately 3,000 cars; outdoors, rain or shine.
FEATURES	Antiques and collectibles, books, new and vintage clothing, coins and stamps, kitchenware, crafts, furniture, jewelry, new merchandise, porcelain, and toys. Averages close to 600 vendors. Snacks and hot meals are served on the premises. Fun for the whole family (but no pets). Lodging nearby.
RATES	$60 per day if prepaid; $75 on weekend of market; vendors may set up on the preceding Saturday. Reservations are not required.
CONTACT	Pat Carnahan, P.O. Box 125, Stormville, NY 12582.
PHONE	(914) 221-6561
FAX	(914) 226-4766

NFMA Member

WOODSTOCK: Mower's Saturday Market

WHEN	Every Saturday, 8:00 A.M. to 6:00 P.M. In operation since 1978.
WHERE	On Maple Lane, one block from the Village Green.
ADMISSION	Free admission; ample free parking; outdoors, weather permitting.
FEATURES	An old-fashioned open-air market with "everything from antiques to zebras, from zithers to artwork." Averages 35 to 50 vendors. Food is available at the market.
RATES	$18 per 10'×10' space. Reserve a week in advance.
CONTACT	John Mower, P.O. Box 556, Woodstock, NY 12498.
PHONE	(914) 679-6744
FAX	(914) 679-9674
E-MAIL	fleamarket@ulster.net
WEB	www.uslter.net/~fleamarket

YONKERS: Yonkers Raceway Market

WHEN	From the last Sunday in March through the last Sunday before Christmas, 9:00 A.M. to 4:00 P.M. In operation since the 1970s.
WHERE	At the Yonkers Raceway. Take exit 2 (northbound) or exit 4 (southbound) off the New York State Throughway (I-87).
ADMISSION	Admission $1 per person or $2 per carload; parking for up to 8,500 cars at $2 per car; outdoors, rain or shine.
FEATURES	A variety of new and used merchandise, including books, clothing, collectibles (baseball cards, comics, etc.), furniture, jewelry, fresh produce, and toys. Averages 350 to 450 vendors. Snacks and hot meals are served on the premises. Market is right next to the racetrack (for easy access to simulcast betting).
RATES	$40 per Sunday per reserved space or $50 unreserved.
CONTACT	Marty McGrath, Yonkers Raceway, Yonkers, NY 10704.
PHONE	(914) 963-3898 or (914) 968-4200 (ext. 216)

Winston-Salem
Deep Gap ★
Hickory
Morgantown ★
Dallas ★
Fletcher
Murphy
Monroe
Charlotte
Kannapolis
Salisbury
Thomasville
Greensboro
★ RALEIGH
Fuquay-
Varina
★ Goldsboro
★ Fayetteville
★ Wilmington

NORTH CAROLINA

CHARLOTTE: Metrolina Expo

WHEN	First Saturday of every month, and the Thursday and Friday preceding, 8:00 A.M. to 5:00 P.M., and Sunday, 9:00 A.M. to 5:00 P.M.; there are also "antique spectaculars" in March, June, and November (call for dates). In operation for over twenty-seven years.
WHERE	At 7100 North Statesville Road. Take exit 16-A (Sunset Road) off I-77 and follow signs to Fairgrounds.
ADMISSION	Admission $3 per person; free parking for up to 20,000 cars; indoors year-round and outdoors, weather permitting.
FEATURES	Antiques and collectibles, books, vintage clothing, crafts, used and antique furniture, and toys. Averages 1,500 to 5,000 vendors. Hot and cold food and refreshments are served on the premises. This one is good and big. Camping and other facilities available.
RATES	Call for rates. Reserve at least three weeks in advance.
CONTACT	Manager, P.O. Box 26652, Charlotte, NC 28221.
PHONE	(800) 824-3770 or (704) 596-4643
WEB	www.metrolinaexpo.com

DALLAS: I-85 Flea Market

WHEN	Every weekend, 8:00 A.M. to 4:00 P.M. In operation since 1984.
WHERE	At 3867 Dallas-High Shoals Highway. From I-85 in Gastonia (approximately twenty-five miles south of Charlotte and sixty miles north of Spartanburg, South Carolina), head north on Route 321 for three miles to Cherryville exit, then turn right at traffic light.
ADMISSION	Free admission; free parking; indoors and outdoors, rain or shine.
FEATURES	Antiques and collectibles, cosmetics, new clothing, coins and stamps, crafts, electronics, furniture, fine and costume jewelry, silver, livestock, new and used merchandise, Oriental rugs, pets, fresh produce, tools, toys, and wicker. Average 400 to a capacity of 600 vendors. Snacks and hot sandwiches are served on the premises.
RATES	Indoors: $20 per 12'×12' space per day or $125 per month, includes two tables with own door and parking space. Outdoors: $12 per day or $80 per month for covered shed with two tables; $8 per day or $40 per month for open space

with two tables. Reserve two weeks in advance for indoor spaces.

CONTACT David Stewart, P.O. Box 402, Dallas, NC 28034.
PHONE (704) 922-1416 or (704) 992-1416 (recorded message); digital pager: (704) 834-8093
FAX (704) 922-4525
E-MAIL davidstewart321@prodigy.net

DEEP GAP: Wildcat Flea Market

WHEN Every Friday, Saturday, Sunday, and holidays from May through October: Friday, 9:00 A.M. to 4:30 P.M., and Saturday and Sunday, 7:00 A.M. to 6:00 P.M. In operation since 1973.

WHERE At 8156 U.S. Highway 421 South, one half mile from the Blue Ridge Parkway entrance, eight miles east of Boone.

ADMISSION Free admission; ample free parking; indoors rain or shine and outdoors, weather permitting.

FEATURES Antiques and collectibles, books, kitchenware, mountain crafts, furniture, gift items, glassware, jewelry, musical instruments and recordings, new merchandise, novelties, porcelain, fresh produce, and toys. Averages up to 60 vendors. Restaurant on the premises. Tour buses are welcome. "North Carolina's most outstanding" auction every Saturday (and some Tuesdays) at 6:00 P.M., year-round, featuring estate merchandise and other items.

RATES Outdoors: $5 per 8'×10' space under cover on Saturday or Sunday, free on Friday; indoors: $100 per 10'×10' space per month inside main building or from $60 per space in warehouse area. Reservations are recommended.

CONTACT Elaine, Jack, or Kevin Richardson, 8156 U.S. Highway 421 South, Deep Gap, NC 28618.

PHONE (828) 264-7757; for information on the auction call Col. Elbert Graybeal at (336) 246-7209.

FAYETTEVILLE: Great American Marketplace

WHEN	Every Friday, Saturday, and Sunday, 9:00 A.M. to 6:00 P.M. In operation since 1992.
WHERE	At 4909 Raeford Road.
ADMISSION	Free admission; ample free parking; indoors and outdoors, year-round.
FEATURES	Find a wide selection of new and used products at low prices. Averages close to 200 vendors. Food is served on the premises. There is a friendly atmosphere and courteous staff.
RATES	From $5 per table outdoors. Reservations are required.
CONTACT	Manager, 4909 Raeford Road, Fayetteville, NC 28304.
PHONE	(910) 423-4440

FAYETTEVILLE: U.S. Flea Market Mall

WHEN	Every Friday, Saturday 10:00 A.M. to 8:00 P.M., and Sunday, 10:00 A.M. to 7:00 P.M. In operation since the late 1980s.
WHERE	At 504 North McPherson Church Road. Take I-95 to Business 95 (301) to Owen Drive to McPherson Church Road.
ADMISSION	Free admission; free parking for up to 800 cars; indoors, year-round.
FEATURES	Antiques and collectibles, books, new and vintage clothing, coins and stamps, kitchenware, crafts, electronics, ethnic crafts, furniture, jewelry, new and used merchandise, pets, porcelain, sporting goods, tools and automotive parts. Averages close to 285 vendors. Snacks and hot meals are served on the premises. Ninety-five percent new merchandise.
RATES	$20 per 10'×10' space per day or $50 for three days; monthly rates also available. Reservations are not required.
CONTACT	Manager, P.O. Box 35065, Fayetteville, NC 28303.
PHONE	(910) 868-5011

FLETCHER: Smiley's Flea Market and Antique Mall

WHEN   Friday, Saturday, and Sunday, daylight to 5:00 P.M.; antiques mall (with over 60 dealers) is open daily, 10:00 A.M. to 5:00 P.M. In operation since 1984.

WHERE   On Route 25, halfway between Asheville and Hendersonville. Take exit 13 off I-26, then go north on Highway 25 (back toward Asheville) for about a half mile, and the market will be on the right.

ADMISSION Free admission; free parking for up to 3,000 cars; buses and motor homes also accommodated; indoors, outdoors, and under cover, rain or shine.

FEATURES Huge variety—everything from "peanuts to bulldozers," with huge quantities of antiques and collectibles, new and vintage clothing, crafts, electronics, furniture, jewelry, kitchenware, new and used merchandise, musical equipment, porcelain, fresh produce, and toys. Averages 450 to a capacity of 700 vendors. Snacks (including good funnel cakes) and hot meals are served on the premises. This sprawling market has good action year-round.

RATES   Indoors: from $11 per space per day depending on size (some "shoppes" are rented on a monthly basis, starting at $149 per month); outdoors: $7 per table/space. Reservations are not required for outdoor spaces.

CONTACT Wade McAbee, Manager, or Ben Campen (Sr. or Jr.), P.O. Box 458, Fletcher, NC 28732.

PHONE   (828) 684-3532 (684-FLEA) or (352) 331-2999

FAX   (828) 684-5651

NFMA Member

FUQUAY-VARINA: Fuquay Flea Market

WHEN   Every weekend, 8:00 A.M. to 5:00 P.M. In operation since the early 1980s.

WHERE   On Highway 55 East. From Raleigh, take Route 401 South to Highway 55E, then left on 55E a quarter mile and market will be on the left.

ADMISSION Free admission; free parking for up to 350 cars; indoors, year-round.

FEATURES Antiques and collectibles, books, new and vintage clothing, kitchenware, crafts, furniture, jewelry, fresh produce, and toys. Averages 130 to a capacity of 150 vendors. Snacks are available on the premises.

RATES   From $14 per 12½'×15' space per day. Reserve a week in advance.
CONTACT   Bill Alexander, P.O. Box 607, Fuquay-Varina, NC 27526.
PHONE   (919) 552-4143

GOLDSBORO: Goldsboro Flea Market

WHEN   Every weekend: Saturday, 8:00 A.M. to 5:00 P.M. and Sunday, 10:00 A.M. to 5:00 P.M. In operation for over five years.
WHERE   At 2102 Wayne Memorial Drive (right behind the Days Inn). Take the Wayne Memorial Drive exit off I-70 Bypass.
ADMISSION   Free admission; free parking for up to 350 cars; indoors and outdoors, rain or shine.
FEATURES   Antiques and collectibles, books, new clothing, kitchenware, crafts, new and vintage clothing, new furniture, jewelry, new and used merchandise, porcelain, fresh produce, and toys. Averages 200 to 300 vendors. Snacks and hot meals are served on the premises. Where the customers send their friends. On the route to North Carolina's Crystal Coast; draws as many as 10,000 shoppers every weekend.
RATES   Indoors: $20 per 10'×12' space per day or $32 for two days; outdoors: $10 per space; some spaces include pegboard and shelf; electricity and tables are $1 each per day when available. Reservations are not required.
CONTACT   Keith Hartzog, 2102 Wayne Memorial Drive, Goldsboro, NC 27530.
PHONE   (800) 282-3532 (800-282-FLEA) or (919) 736-4422

GREENSBORO: Super Flea Flea Market

WHEN   Generally the second Sunday of every month from June through December: Saturday, 8:00 A.M. to 5:00 P.M. and Sunday, 10:00 A.M. to 5:00 P.M. In operation since 1976.
WHERE   At the Greensboro Coliseum; follow signs posted on all roads into Greensboro.
ADMISSION   Admission $2 per person; parking for up to 5,200 cars at $3 per car; indoors, year-round.

FEATURES	Antiques and collectibles, books, new and vintage clothing, coins and stamps, kitchenware, crafts, furniture, jewelry, new and used merchandise, porcelain, and toys. Averages close to its capacity of 300 vendors. Snacks are served on the premises.
RATES	$70 per 8'×10' space per weekend, includes a table and two chairs; extra tables are available at $8 each; electricity is available at $25 per weekend. Reserve two weeks in advance.
CONTACT	William D. Smith, 703 Simpson Street, Greensboro, NC 27401.
PHONE	(336) 373-8515
WEB	www.superflea.com

HICKORY: Springs Road Flea Market

WHEN	Every weekend, 8:00 A.M. to 4:00 P.M. In operation since 1984.
WHERE	At 3451 Springs Road, near St. Stephen's High School.
ADMISSION	Free admission; ample free parking; indoors, outdoors, and under cover, year-round.
FEATURES	Antiques and collectibles, books, new clothing, kitchenware, crafts, jewelry, new and used merchandise, porcelain, fresh produce, and toys. Averages up to 200 vendors. Hot meals are served on the premises.
RATES	Call for rates (about $5 to $10 per space per day). Reservations are recommended; waiting list for indoor spaces.
CONTACT	Rumley Enterprises, 3451 Springs Road Northeast, Hickory, NC 28601.
PHONE	(828) 256-7669

KANNAPOLIS: Koco's Flea Mall

WHEN	Every Friday, Saturday, and Sunday, 10:00 A.M. to 6:00 P.M. (8–6 on Sat.) In operation since 1994 under current management.
WHERE	At 485 South Cannon Boulevard.
ADMISSION	Free admission; ample free parking; indoors, year-round.
FEATURES	Crafts, clothing, cosmetics, tools. Averages to 70 vendors.

Food is served on the premises. Over 50,000 square feet of selling space. Twenty-four-hour security.

RATES $8 per table per day. Reservations are not required in summer months.

CONTACT Manager, 485 South Cannon Boulevard, Kannapolis, NC 28083.

PHONE (704) 938-9100

MONROE: Sweet Union Flea Market

WHEN Every weekend, 8:00 A.M. to 5:00 P.M. In operation since around 1970.

WHERE At 402 Highway 74 West.

ADMISSION Free admission; ample free parking; indoors and outdoors, year-round.

FEATURES Everything from antiques and collectibles to new and used general merchandise to "junque." Averages close to 300 vendors. Food is served on the premises.

RATES From $10 per 10'×10' space outdoors per day. Reservations are on a first-come, first-served basis.

CONTACT Manager, 402 Highway 74 West, Monroe, NC 28110.

PHONE (704) 283-7985

MORGANTON: Jamestown Flea Market

WHEN Every weekend, 7:00 A.M. to 5:00 P.M. In operation since 1985.

WHERE On Jamestown Road. Take exit 100 off I-40 and travel one mile toward town.

ADMISSION Free admission; free parking; indoors, outdoors, and under cover, rain or shine.

FEATURES Antiques and collectibles, automotive supplies, books, new and vintage clothing, coins and stamps, kitchenware, crafts, furniture, hardware, jewelry, new and used merchandise, porcelain, fresh produce, and toys. Averages 300 to a capacity of 400 vendors. Snacks and hot meals are served on the premises. Vendors overnight OK.

RATES Indoors: $10 per space per day; outdoors: $5 exposed or $6 under shed; tables are provided; electricity is provided for most spaces. Reservations are recommended.

CONTACT P. W. Patton, P.O. Drawer 764, Morganton, NC 28655.

PHONE   (828) 584-4038 (office hours are Thursday afternoon and all day Friday)

MURPHY: Decker's Flea Market

WHEN   Every weekend year-round, plus Fridays from April through October, 7:00 A.M. to 3:00 P.M. In operation since 1981.

WHERE   At the junction of Routes 19 and 129 (Blairsville Highway), in the mountains of western North Carolina, two hours north of Atlanta (take I-75), or two hours west of Asheville, North Carolina (take Highway 74), or two hours east of Chattanooga, Tennessee (take Highway 74).

ADMISSION   Free admission; free parking for up to 250 cars; indoors and outdoors, year-round.

FEATURES   Antiques and collectibles, books, new and vintage clothing, kitchenware, crafts, used furniture, jewelry, livestock, new and used merchandise, porcelain, fresh produce, and toys. Averages 65 to 990 vendors. Snacks (including funnel cakes) and hot meals are served on the premises.

RATES $5 and up per space per day; tables are provided. Reserve a week in advance.

CONTACT   Jerry or Chad Decker, P.O. Box 453, Murphy, NC 28906.

PHONE   (828) 837-5753 or (828) 837-0786

RALEIGH: Fairgrounds Flea Market

WHEN   Every weekend (except October), 9:00 A.M. to 5:00 P.M. In operation since 1971.

WHERE   On the North Carolina State Fairgrounds, located at the intersection of Blueridge Road and Hillsborough Street.

ADMISSION   Free admission; ample free parking; indoors and outdoors, rain or shine.

FEATURES   Large selection of antiques and collectibles, crafts, furniture, new and used merchandise—a good mix. Averages 300 to 700 vendors. Food is available on the premises. The oldest, the biggest, and the best in town.

RATES $16 per 10'×20' space per day. Reservations are recommended.

CONTACT   Joan Long, P.O. Box 33517, Raleigh, NC 27636.

PHONE	(919) 829-3533
FAX	(919) 829-3533
WEB	www.mail.agr.state.nc.us

RALEIGH: Raleigh Flea Market Mall

WHEN Every weekend, 9:00 A.M. to 5:00 P.M. In operation since 1987.

WHERE At 1924 Capital Boulevard. Take the Capital Boulevard exit off the Raleigh Beltline (I-440), going toward downtown Raleigh, then go left at the third stoplight.

ADMISSION Free admission; eleven acres of free parking; indoors year-round and outdoors, weather permitting.

FEATURES Antiques and collectibles, books, new and vintage clothing, crafts, furniture, jewelry, new and used merchandise, fresh produce—"everything from A to Z." Averages 150 to 175 vendors. Snacks and hot meals are served on the premises. Includes 100,000 square feet of indoor space plus a large outdoor vending area with shaded spaces.

RATES $10 per outdoor space per day. Waiting list on indoor spaces; outdoor spaces are on a first-come, first-served basis.

CONTACT Doug Brown, 1924 Capital Boulevard, Raleigh, NC 27604.

PHONE (919) 839-0038 or (919) 856-0021

FAX (919) 856-0021

RALEIGH: Watson's Flea Market

WHEN Every weekend, 8:00 A.M. to 5:00 P.M. (outdoor space is open from dawn to dusk). In operation since 1981.

WHERE At 1436 Rock Quarry Road.

ADMISSION Free admission; ample free parking; indoors and outdoors, rain or shine.

FEATURES General merchandise—old and new, with a good measure of garage-sale stuff. Averages 140 to 250 vendors. Food is served on the premises.

RATES $5 per 10'×20' space outdoors; indoor space is rented by the square foot (call for rates). Reservations are not required.

CONTACT   Ebern or Ingrid Watson, 1436 Rock Quarry Road, Raleigh,
               NC 27611.
PHONE   (919) 832-6232
FAX   (919) 832-1637
E-MAIL   ewatson@intrstar.com

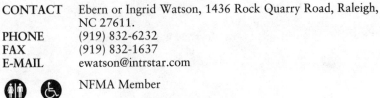

               NFMA Member

SALISBURY: Webb Road Flea Market

WHEN   Every weekend, 8:00 A.M. to 5:00 P.M. In operation since the
               late 1980s.
WHERE   At 905 Webb Road, four miles south of Salisbury. Take exit
               70 off I-85.
ADMISSION   Free admission; free parking for over 1,000 cars; indoors,
               outdoors, and under cover, rain or shine.
FEATURES   Antiques and collectibles, new and vintage clothing, kitchen-
               ware, crafts, furniture, jewelry, new merchandise, porcelain,
               and fresh produce. Averages up to a capacity of more than 800
               vendors. There is a snack bar and other concessions on the
               premises. This large, well-promoted market has an average
               daily attendance of about 10,000 customers. Security on prem-
               ises. Video game room; restrooms have baby-changing area.
RATES   Indoors: $60 per 10'×10' space for four weeks, includes one
               table; when available, indoor spaces are $10 per day.
               Outdoors: from $5 to $9 per space under cover. Electricity is
               available at a small fee; showers are available for vendors.
               Reservations are recommended.
CONTACT   John Nash, Jr., 905 Webb Road, Salisbury, NC 28146-
               8536.
PHONE   (704) 857-6660

THOMASVILLE: Eleven Acres Flea Market

WHEN   Every Saturday and Sunday, 5:00 A.M. to 3:00 P.M. In opera-
               tion since 1985.
WHERE   At 825 Julian Avenue. Take exit 103 off I-85 to Highway
               109 north to Julian Avenue, and market will be on the right
               (one-quarter mile from I-85).
ADMISSION   Free admission; free parking for up to 500 cars; indoors,
               outdoors, and under cover, rain or shine.

FEATURES	Antiques and collectibles, books, new and vintage clothing, kitchenware, crafts, electronics, furniture, jewelry, livestock, new and used merchandise, porcelain, fresh produce. Averages 175 to a capacity of 300 vendors. Snacks and hot meals are served on the premises.
RATES	$10 per table per day outdoors (free on Fridays), or $20 per table indoors. Reservations are on a first-come, first-served basis; some spaces are rented by the month.
CONTACT	Andrew Pope or Tarra Gasque, 9 College Street, Thomasville, NC 27360-4105.
PHONE	(336) 472-0244 or (336) 476-9566
FAX	(336) 472-6249
E-MAIL	apope3333@aol.com

WILMINGTON: Starway Flea Market

WHEN	Every Friday, 7:30 A.M. to 4:00 P.M.; every Saturday, 6:00 A.M. to 4:00 P.M.; and every Sunday, 7:30 A.M. to 4:00 P.M. In operation since the early 1970s.
WHERE	At 2346 Carolina Beach Road (Route 421), twelve miles from the beach at the old drive-in movie theater.
ADMISSION	Free admission; parking for up to 1,000 cars (50¢ per car on Saturday only); indoors year-round and outdoors, weather permitting.
FEATURES	Antiques and collectibles, books, new and vintage clothing, coins and stamps, kitchenware, crafts, furniture, jewelry, new and used merchandise, porcelain, fresh produce, toys, and vehicles (boats, cars, etc.). Averages 150 to 200 vendors. Snacks and hot meals are served on the premises. Billed as the largest and oldest indoor/outdoor flea market in the Cape Fear region, with fifteen acres of selling space; lots of room for special events such as circuses and boat and car shows; over 5,000 people come through the gates on an average weekend.
RATES	From $5 per 10'×10' space on Friday or Sunday outdoors, $10 on Saturday. Reserve a week in advance (for inside building only).
CONTACT	Manager, 2346 Carolina Beach Road, Wilmington, NC 28401.
PHONE	(910) 763-5520

WINSTON-SALEM: Cook's Flea Market

WHEN	Every weekend, 8:00 A.M. to 5:00 P.M. In operation for over five years.
WHERE	At 5721 University Parkway. Take Highway 52 North to University Parkway, then left at stoplight and go to to Robinwood Lane (second stoplight) and go left to market (behind Shoney's).
ADMISSION	Free admission; free parking; indoors, year-round.
FEATURES	Antiques and collectibles, books, clothing, kitchenware, crafts, furniture, jewelry, new and used merchandise, fresh produce, tools, and toys. Averages up to 400 vendors. Snacks and hot meals are served on the premises.
RATES	$34 per 10'×10' space per weekend; tables are available at $2 per day; electricity is available at $4 per weekend. Reserve two weeks in advance.
CONTACT	Cathie or Jack Hooks or Jane Hargett, 5721 University Parkway, Winston-Salem, NC 27105.
PHONE	(336) 661-0999 or (336) 661-0610
WEB	www.cooksplaza.com

  NFMA Member

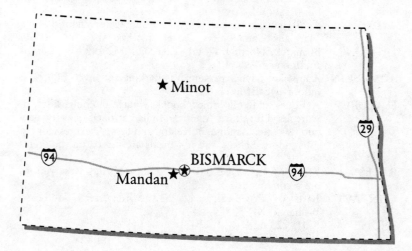

★ Minot

BISMARCK

Mandan ★ ✪

NORTH DAKOTA

MANDAN: Dakota Midwest Antique Show Flea Market

WHEN   First weekend of every month (except January): Saturday, 9:00 A.M. to 5:00 P.M., and Sunday, 10:00 A.M. to 4:00 P.M. In operation for over eight years.

WHERE   At 901 Division Street, just off the Sunset Interchange, at the Mandan Community Center (across the river from Bismarck, North Dakota). Take exit 152 off I-94 and go south one mile.

ADMISSION Admission $1 per person; free parking for up to 300 cars; indoors, year-round.

FEATURES   Antiques and collectibles, books, vintage clothing, kitchenware, used furniture, American Indian artifacts, jewelry, new and used merchandise, porcelain, and toys. Averages close to 70 vendors. Snacks and hot meals are served on the premises.

RATES $15 per 8' space per day or $20 per weekend. Reservations are recommended.

CONTACT   Barb or Bruce Skogen, 2512 93rd Street Southeast, Bismarck, ND 58504.

PHONE   (701) 223-6185

E-MAIL   bskogen@btigate.com

MINOT: Magic City Flea Market

WHEN   About fourteen weekends a year in all months but January, 9:00 A.M. to 4:00 P.M.—call for dates; a couple shows a year specially feature antiques, coins, and baseball cards; three shows are devoted to arts and crafts. In operation since 1977.

WHERE   On Business Highway 2, on the North Dakota State Fairgrounds.

ADMISSION Admission $1; ample free parking; indoors year-round, with outdoor spaces available June through September, rain or shine.

FEATURES   Mainly antiques and collectibles, such as baseball cards, books, coins, and stamps, crafts, used furniture, jewelry, silver, and toys. Averages 120 to 150 vendors. Food is served on premises. One of the largest markets in the area, heavily advertised and in a prime location.

RATES $10 per day for wall space or corner space, all other indoor spaces $8; tables are available at $3 per day. All outdoor spaces $12 per 10'×20' per space per day (available June through September). Reservations accepted with advance payment.

CONTACT Richard W. Timboe, P.O. Box 1672, Minot, ND 58702.
PHONE (701) 852-1289 or (701) 838-1150

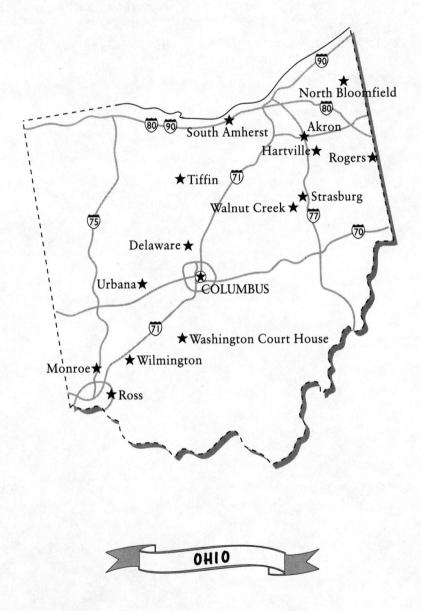

North Bloomfield ★

South Amherst ★

Akron ★

Hartville ★

Rogers ★

★ Tiffin

★ Strasburg

Walnut Creek ★

Delaware ★

COLUMBUS ★

Urbana ★

★ Washington Court House

★ Wilmington

Monroe ★

★ Ross

OHIO

AKRON: Akron Antique Market

WHEN	Four weekends a year (call for dates), 9:00 A.M. to 4:00 P.M. In operation since 1994.
WHERE	At the Summit County Fairgrounds, State Route 91 at East Howe Road.
ADMISSION	Admission $3 per person; ample parking at $1 per car; indoors, rain or shine.
FEATURES	Antiques and vintage collectibles. Averages close to 230 vendors. Food is served on the premises.
RATES	$50 per 10'×10' space per event. Reservations are recommended.
CONTACT	Manager, Luck Pro, Inc., P.O. Box 5473, Akron, OH 44334.
PHONE	(216) 867-6724

COLUMBUS: Amos Flea Market

WHEN	Every Friday, Saturday, and Sunday, 10:00 A.M. to 7:00 P.M. In operation since around 1980.
WHERE	At 3454 Cleveland Avenue.
ADMISSION	Free admission; free parking; indoors, year-round.
FEATURES	Standard mix of collectibles, new and used merchandise. Averages 150 to 200 vendors.
RATES	$36 per 8'×9' space per day or $36 per week. Reservations are not required.
CONTACT	Manager, P.O. Box 44503, Columbus, OH 43204.
PHONE	(614) 262-0044

COLUMBUS: South Drive-in Theatre Flea Market

WHEN	Every Wednesday, Saturday, and Sunday from April through October, 7:00 A.M. to 2:00 P.M. In operation since 1975.
WHERE	At 3050 South High Street, a mile north of I-270.
ADMISSION	Admission 50¢ per carload; parking for up to 1,000 cars is free with admission; outdoors, weather permitting.
FEATURES	Antiques and collectibles, new and vintage clothing, crafts, furniture, jewelry, yard-sale items, and used merchandise. Averages 150 to 300 vendors. Snacks are served on the premises.

RATES $5 per space on Saturday or Sunday, $1 on Wednesday. Reservations are not required.

CONTACT Skip Yassenoff, Rainbow Enterprises, 865 King Avenue, Columbus, OH 43212.

PHONE (614) 298-7122

FAX (614) 291-3134

E-MAIL 76026.517@compuserve.com

WEB www.fleamarkets.com

 NFMA Member

COLUMBUS: Westland Flea Market

WHEN Every Friday, Saturday, and Sunday, 10:00 A.M. to 7:00 P.M. In operation since 1993.

WHERE On West Broad Street, four stoplights east of I-270.

ADMISSION Free admission; free parking for up to 400 cars; indoors, and outdoors, rain or shine.

FEATURES Antiques and collectibles, clothing, crafts, jewelry, and yard-sale items. Averages 100 to 150 vendors. There is a snack bar on the premises.

RATES From $8 per space per weekend. Reservations are not required.

CONTACT Skip Yassenoff, Rainbow Enterprises, 865 King Avenue, Columbus, OH 43212.

PHONE (614) 298-7122

FAX (614) 291-3134

E-MAIL 76026.517@compuserve.com

WEB www.fleamarkets.com

NFMA Member

DELAWARE: Kingman Drive-in Flea Market

WHEN Every Sunday from April through October, 7:00 A.M. to 2:00 P.M. In operation since 1985.

WHERE On Route 23, two miles south of Delaware.

ADMISSION Admission 50¢ per carload; parking for up to 700 cars is included in admission price; outdoors, weather permitting.

FEATURES Yard-sale items and collectibles of various descriptions. Averages 150 to 300 vendors.

RATES $6 per space per day. Reservations are not required.

CONTACT   Skip Yassenoff, Rainbow Enterprises, 865 King Avenue, Columbus, OH 43212.
PHONE   (614) 298-7122
FAX   (614) 291-3134
E-MAIL   76026.517@compuserve.com
WEB   www.fleamarkets.com

HARTVILLE: Hartville Flea Market

WHEN   Every Monday and Thursday, 7:00 A.M. to 4:00 P.M. In operation since 1939.
WHERE   At 788 Edison Street N.W. (Route 619). Take I-77 south of Akron to Route 619, then east about six miles to Hartville.
ADMISSION Free admission; ample parking at $1 per car; indoors year-round and outdoors, weather permitting.
FEATURES Antiques and collectibles, coins and stamps, toys, fresh produce, new and vintage clothing, furniture—"just about anything." Averages 800 to 1,000 vendors. Food is served on the premises. One of Ohio's oldest and biggest flea markets.
RATES   From $3 to $8 per space. Reserve a week in advance.
CONTACT   Marion Coblentz, 788 Edison Street, Hartville, OH 44632.
PHONE   (330) 877-9860; day of market call Bruce Blanke at (330) 877-8577.
FAX   (330) 877-8961
E-MAIL   mcoblentz@hotmail.com
WEB   www.hartvillefleamarket.com

 NFMA Member

MONROE: Turtle Creek Flea Market

WHEN   Every weekend, 9:00 A.M. to 5:00 P.M. In operation since 1981.
WHERE   At 320 North Garver Road. Take exit 29 off of I-75; market is one block west of the exit.
ADMISSION Free admission; ample free parking; indoors and outdoors, year-round.
FEATURES Antiques and collectibles, books, new and vintage clothing, coins and stamps, kitchenware, crafts, furniture, jewelry, new and used merchandise, porcelain, fresh produce, and toys. Averages up to 400 vendors. Food is available on the premises.

RATES	$35 per 10'×13' space indoors, $11 to $15 outdoors. Reserve for indoor spaces.
CONTACT	Manager, 320 North Garver Road, Monroe, OH 45050.
PHONE	(513) 539-4497
WEB	www.fleamarkets.com

NFMA Member

NORTH BLOOMFIELD: Bloomfield Flea Market

WHEN	Every Thursday, 8:00 A.M. to 3:00 P.M. In operation since the 1940s.
WHERE	On Highway 87, a little less than a mile west of North Bloomfield.
ADMISSION	Free admission; ample free parking; indoors and outdoors, rain or shine.
FEATURES	Full spectrum of antiques, collectibles, new and used merchandise, fresh produce, and fresh and cured meats. Averages 100 to 200 vendors. There is an abundance of concessions, including cheese deli, two sausage stands, elephant ears, cotton candy made on the premises. Grounds are available for concerts, auto shows, and other events.
RATES	$10 per booth per day indoors, $9 outdoors. Reservations are recommended.
CONTACT	Jo or Bill Herman, P.O. Box 51, Kinsman, OH 44428-0051.
PHONE	(330) 876-7233

ROGERS: Rogers Community Auction and Open-Air Market

WHEN	Every Friday, 7:00 A.M. to whenever. In operation since 1955.
WHERE	On State Route 154, eight miles.
ADMISSION	Free admission; ample free parking; indoors and outdoors, year-round.
FEATURES	Antiques and collectibles, books, fresh produce, new and used merchandise, etc. Averages close to 1,300 vendors. Food is served on the premises. This event attracts up to 40,000 shoppers every Friday.
RATES	From $12 per 15'×30' space outdoors. Reservations are not required.

CONTACT   Jim, Ken, or Bill Baer, 45625 S.R. 154, Rogers, OH 44455.
PHONE   (330) 227-3233

 NFMA Member

ROSS: Stricker's Grove Flea Market

WHEN   Every Thursday, 8:00 A.M. to 1:00 P.M. In operation since
           1977.
WHERE   On Route 128, a mile from Ross in a western suburb of
           Cincinnati, ten miles from the Indiana border.
ADMISSION Free admission; twenty-six acres of free parking; indoors from
           October through April and outdoors, weather permitting.
FEATURES   Antiques and collectibles, books, household items, and furni-
           ture. Averages 32 to 100 vendors. Snacks and hot meals are
           served on the premises.
RATES $11 per space includes two tables. Reservations are recom-
           mended for indoor spaces (from October through April).
CONTACT   Gladys Jordan, 9468 Reading Road, Cincinnati, OH 45215.
PHONE   (513) 733-5885

SOUTH AMHERST: Johnnie's Flea Market

WHEN   Every Wednesday, Saturday, and Sunday from May through
           October, 8:00 A.M. to 5:00 P.M. In operation since 1987.
WHERE   On Route 113, a mile west of Route 58.
ADMISSION Free admission; free parking; indoors and outdoors, rain or
           shine.
FEATURES   Antiques and collectibles, books, new and vintage clothing,
           kitchenware, crafts, dolls, furniture, jewelry, new and used
           merchandise, plants, porcelain, fresh produce, tools, toys, and
           much more. Averages 100 to 200 vendors. Snacks and hot
           meals are served on the premises. Under new management.
RATES $7 per space per day. Waiting list for indoor spaces; outdoor
           setups are on a first-come, first-served basis.
CONTACT   John Mayfield, 46585 Telegraph Road, Amherst, OH
           44001.
PHONE   (440) 986-5681

STRASBURG: Garver Store Flea Market

WHEN	Every Sunday, 8:00 A.M. to 5:00 P.M. In operation since 1979.
WHERE	On Wooster Avenue (State Routes 250 and 21) in downtown Strasburg, "between the stoplights." Take exit 87 off I-77.
ADMISSION	Free admission; ample free parking; indoors year-round and outdoors, weather permitting.
FEATURES	Antiques and collectibles, books, new and vintage clothing, kitchenware, crafts, furniture, jewelry, glassware, new and used merchandise, porcelain, and toys (including Beanie Babies)—"anything you can imagine." Averages 190 to a capacity of 200 vendors. Visit the lunch counter for good food and conversation. Make a day of it.
RATES	Summer: $10 per booth downstairs, $9 upstairs; winter: $12 per space downstairs, $10 upstairs. Reserve a week in advance.
CONTACT	Vic or Winnie Gessner, 211 Second Street Northwest, Strasburg, OH 44680.
PHONE	(330) 878-5664
FAX	(330) 878-5664
E-MAIL	garverflea@tusco.net
WEB	www.americanantiquities.com/garver.html

TIFFIN: Tiffin Flea Market

WHEN	Eight weekends annually from May through October (call for dates), 9:00 A.M. to 4:00 P.M. In operation since 1978.
WHERE	At the Seneca County Fairgrounds off State Routes 224 and 53, on Hopewell Avenue. Signs are posted.
ADMISSION	Free admission; free parking for up to 1,000 cars; indoors and outdoors, rain or shine.
FEATURES	Variety of offerings, including antiques and collectibles, clothing, crafts, new and used merchandise, fresh produce, tools, and more. Averages up to 200 vendors. Snacks and hot meals are served on the premises; Sunday barbecues and dinners available. One of the largest flea markets in northwestern Ohio, sponsored by the Seneca County Junior Fair Foundation, with proceeds going to Junior Fair youth—4-H, Scouts, Future Farmers of America, etc. Camping, showers; market is advertised on radio, TV, and in ninety Ohio newspapers.
RATES	$8 per day for a 10'×10' space inside or a 15'×15' space

outside; tables are $5 each per weekend. Reservations are required for indoor spaces; outdoor spaces are on a first-come, first-served basis.

CONTACT   Don Ziegler, 6627 South Township Road 173, Bloomville, OH 44818.
PHONE   (419) 983-5084
E-MAIL   Fleamarket@tiffinohio.com
WEB   www.tiffinohio.com/fleamarket

URBANA: Urbana Antique Show and Flea Market

WHEN   First full weekend of each month except August, summer hours: Saturdays, 9:00 A.M. to 5:00 P.M.; Sundays, 9:00 A.M. to 4:00 P.M.; winter hours are 9:00 A.M. to 4:00 P.M. both days. In operation since 1971.
WHERE   On the fairgrounds in Urbana. From downtown Urbana at Monument Square, go toward Springfield, Ohio, on Route 68; go south several blocks to Park Avenue and turn left on Park Avenue to fairgrounds.
ADMISSION Admission 50¢ per person; free for children under twelve; ample free parking; indoors and outdoors, rain or shine.
FEATURES   A wide range of new and used merchandise, collectibles, garage-sale items, etc.; fresh produce in season. Averages 150 to 350 vendors. Snacks and hot meals are served on the premises. Sponsored by the Champaign County Agricultural Society. This busy antiques and collectibles market has been growing for over two decades.
RATES   Indoors: from $22 to $35 per weekend for three tables; outdoors: $11 per day or $20 per weekend for thirty-foot frontage. Reservations are required for indoor spaces only; for outdoor spaces, just show up and pick a spot.
CONTACT   Elizabeth or Steve Goddard, 934 Amherst Drive, Urbana, OH 43078.
PHONE   (937) 653-6013 (Elizabeth) or (937) 788-2058 (Steve)

WALNUT CREEK: Holmes County's Amish Flea Market

WHEN	Every Thursday through Saturday from April through mid-December, 9:00 A.M. to 5:00 P.M. in operation since 1990.
WHERE	On S.R. 39, three miles east of Berlin and thirty-five miles south of Canton, in the heart of Amish Country. Take exit 83 off I-77 and travel west on S.R. 39 for twenty minutes.
ADMISSION	Free admission; ample parking at $1 per car; indoors year-round and outdoors, weather permitting.
FEATURES	Antiques and collectibles, crafts, furniture, gifts, jewelry, fresh produce, tools, and much more. Averages 95 to 130 vendors. There is a cafeteria that serves Amish-style food. You'll find friendly faces, food, entertainment, and much more at this market.
RATES	$6 per 10'×20' space per weekend outdoors or $35 per 10'×10' space indoors. Outdoor spaces are rented on a first-come, first-served basis; there is a waiting list for indoor spaces.
CONTACT	Ben Mast or Mary Ann Schrock, P.O. Box 172, Walnut Creek, OH 44687.
PHONE	(330) 893-2836
FAX	(330) 893-3523
E-MAIL	amishflea@valkyrie.net
WEB	www.fleamarkets.com/amish/index.html

NFMA Member

WASHINGTON COURT HOUSE: Washington Court House Flea Market

WHEN	Monthly except July, 9:00 A.M. to 3:00 P.M.—call for dates. In operation since the 1950s.
WHERE	On the Fayette County Fairgrounds, at 213 Fairview Avenue, on the southwest edge of town between Routes 22 and 62.
ADMISSION	Free admission; free parking for up to 2,000 cars; indoors year-round and outdoors, weather permitting.
FEATURES	Antiques and collectibles, books, crafts, jewelry, knives, new and used merchandise, and toys. Averages 100 to 200 vendors. Snacks and hot meals are served on the premises.
RATES	Indoors: $20 per table per weekend; outdoors: $20 per 20' space per weekend. Reservations are not required.

CONTACT   Janeann Bloomer, Fayette County Fair Board, P.O. Box 1017, Washington C.H., OH 43160.

PHONE   (740) 335-5856 during business hours or (740) 335-5345 evenings, until 10:00 P.M.

FAX   (740) 335-6940

WILMINGTON: Caesar Creek Flea Market

WHEN   Every weekend, 9:00 A.M. to 5:00 P.M. In operation since the late 1970s.

WHERE   At 7763 State Route 73 West, between Wilmington and Waynesville. From Dayton, south about 20 miles on I-75 to Route 73, then east on 73 to the market; from Cincinnati, north on I-71 to exit 45, then left on Route 73 and go about one-half mile to the market.

ADMISSION   Admission 50¢ per person or $1 per carload; ample free parking; indoors year-round and outdoors, weather permitting.

FEATURES   Antiques and collectibles, crafts, dolls, jewelry, pet supplies, and more. Averages close to 300 vendors. Seven snack bars are located on the premises; specialty is "broasted" chicken. This market attracts 15,000 customers per weekend. Wheelchair service and stroller rental are available.

RATES   From $36 per 10'×12' space per weekend indoors and $14 outdoors (under cover). Reservations are recommended; call a week or two in advance for indoor spaces.

CONTACT   Linda Burke or Lisa Dawson, 111 West First Street, Suite 848, Dayton, OH 45402.

PHONE   (937) 382-1669

FAX   (937) 383-2724

E-MAIL   turtle848@aol.com

WEB   www.caesarcreek.com

NFMA Member

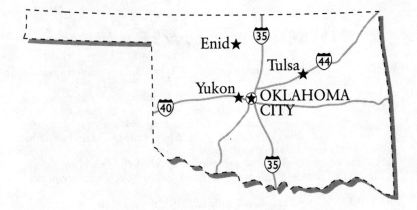

OKLAHOMA

ENID: Enid Flea Market

WHEN	Every Friday, Saturday, and Sunday, 9:00 A.M. to 6:00 P.M. In operation since 1986.
WHERE	At 1821 South Van Buren (Highway 81). From the intersection of routes 412/60 and Highway 81, go south nine blocks and market will be on the left.
ADMISSION	Free admission; three acres of free parking; indoors year-round and outdoors, weather permitting.
FEATURES	Antiques and collectibles, books, new and vintage clothing, kitchenware, crafts, farm equipment, furniture, jewelry, new and used merchandise, porcelain, fresh produce, and toys. Averages 30 to a capacity of 100 vendors. Snacks are served on the premises. Auction every Tuesday at 7:00 P.M.
RATES	$10 per 12'×14' space per day or $85 per month. (Vendors may also set up in parking lot for $7 per space per day). Reservations are not required.
CONTACT	Cody Smith, Owner, or Kim Groom, Manager, or Chreyl Pitts, Assistant Manager, 1821 South Van Buren, Enid, OK 73703.
PHONE	(580) 237-5352 or (580) 233-7653 for Tuesday auctions

OKLAHOMA CITY: AMC Flea Market

WHEN	Every weekend, 9:00 A.M. to 6:00 P.M. In operation since the mid-1980s.
WHERE	At 1001 North Pennsylvania Avenue. From westbound I-40, take Virginia exit, then one block north, then one block west, then north ten blocks to the corner of Northwest Tenth and Pennsylvania. From eastbound I-40, take Pennsylvania exit to Northwest Tenth.
ADMISSION	Free admission; free parking for up to 800 cars; indoors and outdoors, rain or shine.
FEATURES	Variety of offerings, including antiques and collectibles, furniture, new and vintage clothing, jewelry, books, grocery items, boots and shoes, kitchenware, and crafts. Averages 300 to 400 vendors. Four restaurants serving American, German, and Chinese food. A clean and safe shopping environment with 135,000 square feet of selling space.
RATES	Indoors: $44 per 8'×12' space per weekend or $158 per month; outdoors: $7 per 10'×24' space per day. Market is

open to vendors on Monday and Friday, 9:00 A.M. to 5:00 P.M. Reservations are not required.
CONTACT   Nick Adams, P.O. Box 76179, Oklahoma City, OK 73107.
PHONE   (405) 232-5061

OKLAHOMA CITY: Mary's Ole Time Swap Meet

WHEN   Every weekend, from daylight to dark. In operation since the early 1960s.
WHERE   At 7905 Northeast 23rd Street, off I-35 or I-40.
ADMISSION Free admission; thirty acres of free parking; indoors and outdoors, rain or shine.
FEATURES   Antiques and collectibles, books, vintage clothing, kitchenware, crafts, furniture, jewelry, livestock, new merchandise, and fresh produce. Averages 200 to 500 vendors. Snacks and hot meals are served on the premises.
RATES $5 per space per day. Reservations are not required.
CONTACT   Dennis Sisemore, 7905 Northeast 23rd Street, Oklahoma City, OK 73141.
PHONE   (405) 427-0051

TULSA: Great American Flea Market and Antique Mall

WHEN   Every Friday through Sunday, 10:00 A.M. to 6:00 P.M. (mall is open daily). In operation since 1989.
WHERE   At 9216-9236 East Admiral.
ADMISSION Free admission; free parking for up to 800 cars; indoors and outdoors, rain or shine.
FEATURES   Antiques and collectibles, vintage clothing, coins and stamps, kitchenware, crafts, furniture, jewelry, and fresh produce. Averages close to 225 vendors. Hot and cold meals are served on the premises.
RATES $33 per 8'×10' space for three days. Reservations are recommended a week in advance.
CONTACT   Ty Hogan, 6019 South 66th East Avenue, Tulsa, OK 74145.
PHONE   (918) 492-3476

FAX   (918) 492-3477
E-MAIL   lilprisca@aol.com

NFMA Member

TULSA: Tulsa Flea Market

WHEN   Every Saturday (except for four Saturdays in late September and early October), 8:00 A.M. to 5:00 P.M. In operation since 1972.

WHERE   On the state fairgrounds. Take Yale exit off freeway, to 21st Street.

ADMISSION Free admission; ample free parking; indoors, year-round.

FEATURES   Antiques and collectibles, books, new and vintage clothing, coins and stamps, kitchenware, crafts, used furniture, jewelry, new merchandise, porcelain, plants, primitives, fresh produce, quilts, records, and toys. Averages close to 235 vendors. Snacks are available on the premises. Specializes in antiques, collectibles, and primitives.

RATES $25 per 10'×12' space per day; tables are available at $3 each. Reserve four or five weeks in advance.

CONTACT   Patsy Larry, P.O. Box 4511, Tulsa, OK 74159.

PHONE   (918) 744-1386 (office hours are Wednesday through Friday, 8:00 A.M. to noon)

YUKON/OKLAHOMA CITY: Route 66 Traders Market

WHEN   Every Friday, Saturday, and Sunday from March through November: Friday noon to 6:00 P.M., and Saturday and Sunday, 9:00 A.M. to 6:00 P.M. In operation since June 1999.

WHERE   At 3201 North Richland Road, off Route 66; take exit 132 off I-40 (west of Oklahoma City) and go north a half mile, then a east a mile.

ADMISSION Free admission; ample free parking; outdoors and under cover, rain or shine.

FEATURES   Antiques and collectibles, new and used merchandise, clothing, produce, plants, and souvenirs. Averages up to a capacity of 200 vendors. Food is served on the premises. Auctions on Sunday afternoons.

RATES	$8.50 per 10'×20' space outdoors, or $15 per day for a covered space. Reserve the prior Sunday.
CONTACT	Jerald Ashby, Marilyn Ashby, or Cheri Ashby Gardner, 3201 North Richland Road, Yukon, OK 73099.
PHONE	(405) 752-1752 or (405) 530-3366 or (405) 202-2707 (mobile phone)
FAX	(405) 752-9229
E-MAIL	jashby@telepath.com

   NFMA Member

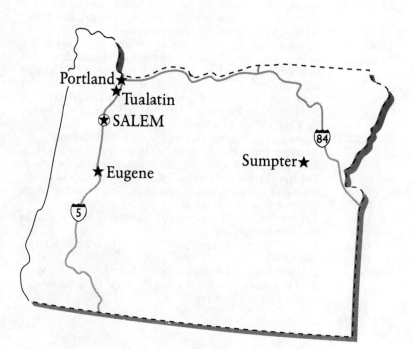

Portland ★
★ Tualatin
✪ SALEM

84

Sumpter ★

★ Eugene

5

OREGON

EUGENE: Picc-a-dilly Flea Market

WHEN Sundays, year-round but not every Sunday (twenty shows in 1996, in all months but July and August—call for dates), 10:00 A.M. to 4:00 P.M. In operation since 1970.

WHERE At the Lane County Fairgrounds (all the way in the back). From northwest (99 North): 99 becomes Seventh Street. Go right on Garfield, left on 13th. From west (on West 11th): go right on Garfield, left on 13th. From south: take University of Oregon exit off I-5 to Jefferson, right on 11th, then left on Monroe. From east: I-105 becomes Jefferson, then go right on West 11th, left on Monroe.

ADMISSION Admission $1.50; free parking for 2,500 cars; indoors.

FEATURES Antiques and collectibles, including baseball cards, bottles, new and vintage clothing, kitchenware, crafts, porcelain, and fresh produce. Averages up to 400 vendors. Snacks and hot meals are served on the premises. Said to be the oldest and largest market in the area.

RATES $17 per 8'×2½' table per day. Reservations are required as far as possible in advance.

CONTACT Peggy Ward or Suzanne Jackson, P.O. Box 2364, Eugene, OR 97402.

PHONE (541) 683-5589, Monday through Saturday, 9:00 A.M. to 4:00 P.M. during week prior to each market day (answering machine on all other days)

PORTLAND: America's Largest Antique and Collectible Sale

WHEN Three weekend events in March, July, and October (call for dates): Saturday, 8:00 A.M. to 7:00 P.M., and Sunday, 9:00 A.M. to 5:00 P.M. In operation since 1981.

WHERE At the Portland Expo Center. Take Expo Center exit (306-B) off I-5 and follow signposts.

ADMISSION Admission $5 per person; parking for up to 3,000 cars available at $3 per car; indoors, year-round.

FEATURES Antiques and collectibles, books, vintage clothing, crafts, antique jewelry, porcelain, and antique toys. Averages 750 to 900 vendors. Snacks and hot meals are served on the premises. Upscale merchandise and lots of it—this one's a true antiques-collectibles blowout.

RATES $140 per 10'×10' space outdoors per weekend. Reserve as far as possible in advance; July event sells out two months in advance and the other two events sell out as far as two years in advance.

CONTACT   Palmer, Wirfs and Associates, 4001 Northeast Halsey, Portland, OR 97232.

PHONE   (503) 282-0877 (office hours are Monday through Friday, 9:00 A.M. to 4:30 P.M.)

FAX   (503) 282-0877

E-MAIL   cpalmer@transport.com

WEB   www.palmerwirfs.com

PORTLAND: #1 Flea Market

WHEN   Every weekend, 9:00 A.M. to 5:00 P.M. In operation since the early 1990s.

WHERE   At 17420 Southeast Division Street. Take 181st Street exit off I-85 East, then go south two miles and turn right onto Division Street.

ADMISSION   Admission 50¢ per person, 25¢ for senior citizens, and free for children under twelve, free parking for up to 200 cars; indoors and outdoors, rain or shine.

FEATURES   Antiques and collectibles, books, new clothing, kitchenware, crafts, furniture, vintage jewelry, new and used merchandise, and toys. Averages 250 to 300 vendors. Snacks and hot meals are served at a complete deli on the premises.

RATES $10 per table per day. Reservations are recommended in winter (tables are rented on a first-come, first-served basis in summer).

CONTACT   Lee Richardson, 17119 Southeast Division Street, Portland, OR 97236.

PHONE   (503) 761-4646

PORTLAND: Saturday Market

WHEN   Every weekend from May through Christmas, Saturday, 10:00 A.M. to 5:00 P.M. and Sunday, 11:00 A.M. to 4:30 P.M. In operation since 1974.

WHERE	At 108 West Burnside, beneath the Burnside Bridge on the west side of the Willamette River, in the Old Town section of Portland.
ADMISSION	Free admission; parking nearby on light-rail line; outdoors (about a third of the market is covered by a bridge), rain or shine.
FEATURES	This market specializes in handmade crafts by local artists. Averages 230 to 275 vendors. There is an international food court with two dozen booths. Everyone in town knows about this one, from the hippies to the yuppies. Credit and debit cards are accepted.
RATES	From $25 per space on Saturday and from $15 on Sunday. This is a juried event; vendors must apply in advance.
CONTACT	Paul Verhoeven, Executive Director, 108 West Burnside or Lize Posner, Portland, OR 97209.
PHONE	(503) 222-6072
FAX	(503) 222-0254
E-MAIL	info@saturdaymarket.org
WEB	www.saturdaymarket.org

SUMPTER: Sumpter Valley Country Fair

WHEN	Every Memorial Day, Fourth of July, Labor Day (usually the weekend plus Monday), 8:00 A.M. to 5:00 P.M. In operation since 1987.
WHERE	Off Highway 7—follow the canary-yellow signs in town (in northeast Oregon).
ADMISSION	Free admission; free parking for more than 300; outdoors, rain or shine.
FEATURES	Antiques and collectibles, books, coins, clothing, kitchenware, crafts, furniture, jewelry, new and used merchandise, primitives, toys, and lots more (something for everyone). Averages up to 150 vendors. Snacks and hot meals are served on the premises.
RATES	$2.25 per foot of frontage per event. Reservations are recommended; advance payment is required.
CONTACT	Nancy or Leland Myers, Sumpter Valley Community Association, P.O. Box 213, Sumpter, OR 97877-0213.
PHONE	(541) 894-2264
FAX	(541) 894-2329
E-MAIL	leemyers@triax.com

TUALATIN: Sandy Barr's Flea Mart

WHEN	Every weekend, 8:00 A.M. to 5:00 P.M. (vendors arrive at 7:00 A.M. In operation since around 1970 (in current location since 1999).
WHERE	At 17942 Southwest McEwan Road; take exit 290 off I-5.
ADMISSION	Admission $1 per person; 50¢ for children under twelve, ample free parking; indoors, year-round.
FEATURES	Antiques and collectibles, books, new and vintage clothing, coins and stamps, kitchenware, crafts, used furniture, jewelry, new merchandise, porcelain, fresh produce, and toys. Averages 250 to 350 vendors. There is a restaurant on the premises. The market has moved, but many of the same vendors can be found in the new location.
RATES	From $25 per table per weekend. Reservations are not required.
CONTACT	Sandy Barr, 17942 Southwest McEwan Road, Tualatin, OR 97062.
PHONE	(503) 639-3395
FAX	(503) 639-9896
E-MAIL	gpfandy@aol.com
WEB	www.angelfire.com/biz2/sandybarrsfleamart

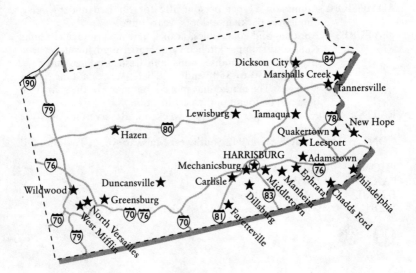

Dickson City ★
Marshalls Creek ★
★ Tannersville
84

90

79

Lewisburg ★   Tamaqua ★
78
New Hope ★
Quakertown ★
★ Leesport
80
★ Hazen

76

HARRISBURG ★
Mechanicsburg ★   ★ Adamstown
Duncansville ★   Carlisle ★   ★ ★   76   Philadelphia ★
Wildwood ★   Middletown   Manheim   Ephrata   Chadds Ford
★ Greensburg   83
North Versailles   Dillsburg
West Mifflin   81
70   Fayetteville
70   76
70
79

PENNSYLVANIA

ADAMSTOWN: Renninger's #1 Antique Market

WHEN   Every Sunday, 7:30 A.M. to 4:00 P.M. In operation for over thirty-six years.

WHERE   On Route 272, a half mile north of exit 21 off the Pennsylvania Turnpike.

ADMISSION   Free admission; free parking for up to 800 cars; indoors and outdoors, rain or shine.

FEATURES   Full spectrum of antiques and collectibles—a very big selection with something for everyone. Averages 450 to close to 750 vendors. Snacks and hot meals are served on the premises. Justly famous. For Renninger's Extravaganza events, see listing under Kutztown, PA.

RATES $15 per outdoor space per day. Reservations are not required.

CONTACT   Brian Block, 2500 North Reading Road, Denver, PA 17517.

PHONE   (717) 336-2177

ADAMSTOWN: Shupp's Grove

WHEN   Every weekend from April through October, plus three "extravaganza" weekends annually, in April, June, and September (the Friday, Saturday, and Sunday after the fourth Thursday of the month), 7:00 A.M. to 5:00 P.M. In operation since 1962.

WHERE   At 1686 Dry Tavern Road. Take exit 21 off Pennsylvania Turnpike, then right on Route 272 North, then right on Route 897 South, and market will be three-quarters of a mile ahead on the left.

ADMISSION   Free admission; several acres of free parking; outdoors, weather permitting.

FEATURES   Antiques, art, and collectibles. Averages close to 250 vendors. Snacks and hot meals are served on the premises. (Hint: while in the area, stop at Friar Tuck's Deli in the thick of the woods for delicious homemade soups, sandwiches, pies, and cakes). The first outdoor antique market in beautiful Lancaster County, a favorite with antiquers nationwide.

RATES $15 per space per day; $99 for three days during "extravaganza" weekends. Reservations are not required except during "extravaganza" weekends.

CONTACT   Marilyn or Carl Gehman, P.O. Box 892, Adamstown, PA 19501.

PHONE	(717) 484-4115
E-MAIL	shupps@redrose.net
WEB	www.shuppsgrove.com

CARLISLE: Spring and Autumn Antique and Collectible Shows

WHEN	Generally the third Friday, Saturday, and Sunday in May and September, 7:00 A.M. on. In operation since 1991.
WHERE	At the Carlisle Fairgrounds. From Pennsylvania Turnpike, take exit for Route 11 South, then go to Clay Street.
ADMISSION	$4 per person for admission after 10:00 A.M. Friday; $10 for "early bird" admission (7:00 A.M.); children under twelve are admitted free; ample free parking; indoors, outdoors, and under cover, rain or shine.
FEATURES	High-quality antiques and collectibles: furniture, jewelry, glassware, vintage clothing, military memorabilia, books, and prints. Averages 650 to 790 vendors. There is a large food court on the premises. Good variety of upscale merchandise.
RATES	$65 per 10'×30' space outdoors, $175 per 10'×15' space indoors, $145 per 13'×15' space under a tent. Reservations are not required.
CONTACT	Carlisle Event Hotline, 1000 Bryn Mawr Road, Carlisle, PA 17013-1588.
PHONE	(717) 243-7855
FAX	(717) 243-0255
E-MAIL	cpc@epix.net
WEB	www.antiquesatcarlisle.com

CHADDS FORD: Pennsbury–Chadds Ford Antique Mall

WHEN	Lower level open Saturday and Sunday, and upper level open daily except Tuesday and Wednesday, 10:00 A.M. to 5:00 P.M. In operation for over twenty-five years.
WHERE	At 640 East Baltimore Pike (Route 1), between Longwood Gardens and the Brandywine River Museum.

ADMISSION   Free admission; free parking for up to 250 cars; indoors, year-round.

FEATURES   Antiques and collectibles, books, coins and stamps, ephemera, crafts, oak and Victorian furniture, jewelry, porcelain, military items, Oriental rugs, antique tools, and toys—generally upscale items. Averages close to 150 vendors. Snacks are available on the premises; 22,000 square feet of display area.

RATES   Monthly rentals only, from $145 for an 8'×10' space. Reserve two months in advance.

CONTACT   Alfred Delduco, 640 East Baltimore Pike, West Chester, PA 19317.

PHONE   (610) 388-6546 or (610) 388-1620

DICKSON CITY: Circle Drive-in Theatre Flea Fair

WHEN   Every Sunday from March through December, 7:00 A.M. to 4:00 P.M. In operation since the mid-1970s.

WHERE   At 12 Salem Avenue, on the Scranton-Carbondale Highway (Route 6).

ADMISSION   Free admission; limited parking at 50¢ per car; outdoors, rain or shine.

FEATURES   Antiques and collectibles, books, new and vintage clothing, coins and stamps, kitchenware, crafts, fish and fresh produce, furniture, jewelry, new merchandise, and toys. Averages up to 500 vendors. There is a "modern" refreshment stand on the premises. Advertised as the largest flea market in northeastern Pennsylvania, with thousands of buyers.

RATES $15 per 18'×18' space per day, plus a $5 Dickson City Boro selling permit. Reservations are on a first-come, first-served basis.

CONTACT   Michael J. Delfino, 12 Salem Avenue, Carbondale, PA 18407-1903.

PHONE   (570) 876-1400 or (570) 282-1131
FAX   (570) 282-7299
E-MAIL   mdelfino@epix.net

   NFMA Member

DILLSBURG: Haar's Flea Market

WHEN Every Sunday, 7:00 A.M. to 4:00 P.M. and Tuesday and Friday evenings, 5:30 P.M. to 9:00 P.M. In operation since the late 1980s.

WHERE At 185 Logan Road, right off Route 15 a mile north of town. Twelve miles south of Harrisburg along Route 15 (to Ore Bank Road, then turn left to market).

ADMISSION Free admission; free parking for up to 300 cars; indoors year-round and outdoors, weather permitting.

FEATURES Antiques and collectibles, books, kitchenware, crafts, furniture, jewelry, new and used merchandise, fresh produce, and toys—"something for everyone." Averages close to 40 vendors. Snacks and hot meals are served on the premises.

RATES $10 per 7'×12' space day indoors, or $5 outdoors (Sunday only). Reserve a week in advance.

CONTACT Elwood Haar, 185 Logan Road, Dillsburg, PA 17019.

PHONE (717) 432-3011 or (717) 432-4381

DUNCANSVILLE: Duncansville Antique Depot Flea Market

When Every weekend, 9:00 a.m. to 5:00 p.m. A new market (in operation since 1994).

Where At the intersection of Routes 22 and 764, thirty minutes north of Bedford and the Pennsylvania Turnpike (use Highway 220); from Pittsburgh: take Route 22 East.

Admission Free admission; free parking for up to 800 cars; indoors year-round and outdoors, weather permitting.

Features Antiques and collectibles, books, new clothing, coins and stamps, kitchenware, crafts, furniture, jewelry, new and used merchandise, porcelain, fresh produce, and toys. Averages 180 to 220 vendors. There is a restaurant on the premises. Draws upward of 5,000 shoppers each weekend. Auction, craft show, and antique gallery—call for further information.

Rates $30 per space per weekend indoors, $12 outdoors; tables are provided; electricity is available at no additional charge. Reservations are accepted if prepaid; otherwise spaces are rented on a first-come, first-served basis.

Contact Tom George or Bonni Lindberg, P.O. Box 111, Duncansville, PA 16635.

Phone	(814) 696-4000
Fax	(814) 696-4185

EPHRATA: Green Dragon Farmers Market and Auction

WHEN	Every Friday, 9:00 A.M. to 10:00 P.M. In operation since the 1920s.
WHERE	At 955 North State Street (spur of Route 272), between Route 322 and the Pennsylvania Turnpike (use exit 21, Lancaster-Reading Interchange exit); look for the dragon and sign.
ADMISSION	Free admission; thirty-five acres of free parking; indoors and outdoors, rain or shine.
FEATURES	Antiques and collectibles, books, new and vintage clothing, coins and stamps, kitchenware, crafts, meats and furniture, jewelry, livestock, new merchandise, porcelain, fresh produce and baked goods. Averages 250 to a capacity of 400 vendors. Snacks and hot meals are served on the premises. The dragon comes alive every Friday as the rooster crows early morn. Auction sales every Friday, with livestock, hay and straw, dry goods, etc.
RATES	$15 per 10'×20' space per day or $25 per 20'×20' space. Reserve a week in advance.
CONTACT	Larry L. Loose, 955 North State Street, Ephrata, PA 17522.
PHONE	(717) 738-1117

FAYETTEVILLE: Fayetteville Antique Mall

WHEN	Daily except Thanksgiving, Christmas, and New Year's Days, 9:00 A.M. to 5:00 P.M. In operation since the early 1980s.
WHERE	At 3625-53 Lincoln Way East, eighteen miles west of Gettysburg, or four miles east of Chambersburg, on Route 30. Take exit 6 off I-81 and go east four miles on Route 30.
ADMISSION	Free admission; free parking for up to 200 cars; indoors and outdoors, rain or shine.
FEATURES	Antiques and collectibles, books, cast iron, vintage clothing, kitchenware, furniture, glassware, jewelry, primitives, fresh produce, tools, toys, and used merchandise. Averages close to

280 indoor vendors. Snacks and hot meals are served on the premises.

RATES $7 per space outdoors under cover per day (call for monthly indoor rates). Reservations are not required for outdoor setups.

CONTACT L. L. Dymond, Jr., 3625-53 Lincoln Way East, Fayetteville, PA 17222.

PHONE (717) 352-8485

FAX (717) 352-9223

GREENSBURG: Greengate Flea Market

WHEN Every Sunday (outdoors from April through September and indoors October through March), 7:00 A.M. to 3:00 P.M. In operation since 1991 (indoor market open since 1997).

WHERE At the Green Gate Mall on Route 30, approximately seven miles from exit 7 off the Pennsylvania Turnpike.

ADMISSION Free admission; free parking for up to 5,000 cars; indoors and outdoors, rain or shine.

FEATURES Antiques and collectibles; books; new clothing; kitchenware; crafts; fashion accessories; furniture; jewelry; factory, new, and used merchandise; porcelain; fresh produce; and toys. Averages 100 to 125 vendors. Two food concessions serve hot meals and homemade baked goods.

RATES $10 per ten-foot space per day, $15 per twenty-one-foot space. Reservations are accepted, but walk-ins OK too—just show up after 6:00 A.M.

CONTACT Carol Craig, 214 Kenneth Street, Greensburg, PA 15601.

PHONE (724) 837-6881

E-MAIL ccraig6801@aol.com

HAZEN: Warsaw Township Volunteer Fire Company Flea Market

WHEN First Sunday of every month and the Saturday preceding, from May through October, all day. In operation since 1974.

WHERE Right in front of the Fire Hall on Route 28, between Hazen and Sugar Hill; take exit 14 off I-80.

ADMISSION Free admission; parking at $1 per car; outdoors, rain or shine.

FEATURES Antiques and collectibles, new and used merchandise, crafts, clothing, and tools. Averages close to 450 vendors. Food is served on the premises; there is a chicken barbecue on Sunday. The market is sponsored by the Warsaw Township Volunteer Fire Company.

RATES $15 per space per day. Reservations are recommended.

CONTACT Clyde Lindemuth, R.D. #5, Box 156B, Brookville, PA 15825.

PHONE (814) 328-2536 or (814) 328-2528 (Fire Hall)

KUTZTOWN: Renninger's #2 Antique Market

WHEN Every Saturday, plus three two-day extravaganza events per year, usually in late April, late June, and late September (call for dates), 8:00 A.M. to 4:00 P.M. In operation since the mid-1970s.

WHERE At 740 Noble Street, off Route 222, a mile south of the middle of Kutztown, between Reading and Allentown.

ADMISSION Free admission (except during extravaganzas); ample free parking; indoors and outdoors, year-round.

FEATURES Antiques and collectibles, books, new and vintage clothing, kitchenware, crafts, used furniture, jewelry—you name it. Averages close to 250 vendors. There is a Pennsylvania Dutch market on the premises. The justly famous extravaganzas are true antiques and collectibles blowouts, drawing buyers and sellers from almost every state in the Union.

RATES $10 per 10'×25' space per day in the pavilion, or $8 per 18'×25' space per day outdoors (extravaganza booths are from $100 to $180 per space per event). Reservations are recommended for extravaganza events.

CONTACT Renninger's Promotions, 27 Bensinger Drive, Schuykill Haven, PA 19501.

PHONE (570) 385-0104 (Monday through Thursday) or (610) 683-6848 (Friday and Saturday); for extravaganzas, call (570) 336-2177 (Monday through Friday) or (610) 683-6848 (Saturday)

FAX (570) 385-0605

WEB www.renningers.com

LEESPORT: Leesport Farmers Market

WHEN   Every Wednesday year-round, plus the first Sunday of every month from April through the first Sunday of December, 7:00 A.M. to 3:00 P.M.; farmers market open every Wednesday year-round, 9:00 A.M. to 8:00 P.M. In operation since 1947.

WHERE   One block east of Route 61 at the north end of Leesport, ten miles north of Reading and eight miles south of Hamburg.

ADMISSION   Free admission; acres of free parking; indoors and outdoors, rain or shine.

FEATURES   Antiques and collectibles, books, new and vintage clothing, coins and stamps, kitchenware, crafts, fabrics, furniture, garden supplies, health and beauty aids, household items, jewelry, new merchandise, porcelain, and toys. Averages 200 to 500 vendors. Snacks and hot meals are served on the premises. Livestock auction every Wednesday at 1:00 P.M.; craft fairs on selected weekends throughout the year, including Easter, springtime, midsummer, harvest time, and Christmas—call for specific dates. Banquet hall with seating capacity of 800 available for private functions.

RATES $10 per 12'×35' unsheltered space per day; $10 per eight-foot table in a ten-foot-wide unsheltered space; from $20 per space for all indoor and sheltered spaces. Reservations are not required.

CONTACT   Daniel "Woody" Weist, P.O. Box 747, Leesport, PA 19533.
PHONE   (610) 926-1307

LEWISBURG: Route 15 Flea Market Center

WHEN   Every Wednesday through Saturday, 10:00 A.M. to 6:00 P.M., and Sunday, 8:00 A.M. to 5:00 P.M. In operation since 1989.

WHERE   On Route 15, two miles north of Lewisburg. Take exit 30-A off I-80 and drive four miles south (next to the Silver Moon Antique Mall and Route 15 Furniture Outlet).

ADMISSION   Free admission; free parking for up to a thousand cars; indoors and outdoors, year-round, rain or shine.

FEATURES   Antiques and collectibles, books and magazines, new and bargain-priced clothing and furniture, coins and stamps, kitchenware, crafts, electronics, jewelry, new and used merchandise, all kinds of fresh produce, flowers, tools, and toys. Averages 600 to a capacity of 1,000 vendors. Silver Moon Restaurant and banquet facilities on the premises. A family-owned and -operated facility in a rural valley near the

Susquehanna River, with "something for everyone, and always a warm welcome" Silver Moon Antique Mall next door has 150 vendors. Bingo every Wednesday night; special shows and auctions (call for dates).

RATES	$30 per space per day. Reservations are required in winter months.
CONTACT	Sandy Keister, Manager, P.O. Box 73, West Milton, PA 17886.
PHONE	(570) 568-8080 or (570) 568-0452
FAX	(570) 568-8580
E-MAIL	sandart@rt15fleamarket.com
WEB	www.rt15fleamarket.com

 NFMA Member

MANHEIM: Root's Country Market and Auction

WHEN	Every Tuesday, 9:00 A.M. to 9:00 P.M. In operation since 1925.
WHERE	At 705 Graystone Road, in Lancaster County.
ADMISSION	Free admission; ample free parking; indoors and outdoors, year-round.
FEATURES	Antiques and collectibles, household goods, and other used items. Averages 200 to 250 vendors. A variety of delicatessen items—meats, cheeses, baked goods—are served on the premises.
RATES	Inquire for rates. Reserve by the preceding Monday.
CONTACT	Thomas Longenecker, 705 Graystone Road, Manheim, PA 17545.
PHONE	(717) 898-7811
FAX	(717) 898-7432
E-MAIL	toml@rootsmarket.com
WEB	www.rootsmarket.com

NFMA Member

MARSHALLS CREEK: R & J Flea World

WHEN	Every weekend plus holidays, 9:00 A.M. to 5:00 P.M. In operation since 1985.
WHERE	Take exit 52 off I-80.
ADMISSION	Free admission; ample free parking; indoors and outdoors, rain or shine.

FEATURES	New and used, clothing, furniture, and reproductions. Averages 500 to 675 vendors. Food is served on the premises. Daily attendance averages 20,000 on a good day.
RATES	From $25 per space per day. Reservations are recommended around the holidays.
CONTACT	Joseph or Ruth Tiburzi, P.O. Box 1221, Marshalls Creek, PA 18335.
PHONE	(570) 223-0690
FAX	(570) 223-1604
E-MAIL	rtiburzi@noln.com

NFMA Member

MECHANICSBURG: Silver Springs Flea Market

WHEN	Every Sunday, 7:00 A.M. to 3:00 P.M. In operation since 1968.
WHERE	At 6416 Carlisle Pike, on Route 11 midway between Harrisburg and Carlisle.
ADMISSION	Free admission; ample free parking; indoors and outdoors, rain or shine.
FEATURES	Full spectrum of antiques, collectibles, new and used merchandise, fresh produce, postcards. Averages 500 to 1,000 vendors. Snacks and hot meals are served on the premises. Claims to be the biggest in Pennsylvania.
RATES	$10 per 12'×20' space per day outside; inside spaces are rented by the month: from $40 for a 3'×8' table. Reservations are not required for outdoor spaces.
CONTACT	Anna Smith, 6414 Carlisle Pike, Mechanicsburg, PA 17055.
PHONE	(717) 766-7215 or (717) 766-9027

MIDDLETOWN: Saturday's Market

WHEN	Every Saturday, 5:30 A.M. to 6:00 P.M. In operation since 1983.
WHERE	At 3751 East Harrisburg Pike (Route 230), between Middletown and Elizabethtown. Just off Route 283, exit Toll House Road, left on 230, then one mile.
ADMISSION	Free admission; acres of free parking; indoors and outdoors, rain or shine.
FEATURES	The "total" farmers and flea market, with antiques and col-

lectibles, new and vintage clothing, jewelry, crafts, fresh produce, and new merchandise. Averages 300 to 500 vendors. More than fifteen different food concessions on the premises. Billed as Pennsylvania's largest indoor market.

RATES Indoors: From $50 per month, depending on size; outdoors: $11 per day for one space, $20 for two spaces, $30 for three spaces. Reservations are not required.

CONTACT Rod or Joanne Rose, 3751 East Harrisburg Pike, Middletown, PA 17057.

PHONE (717) 944-2555 (office is open Monday, Thursday, Friday, and Saturday)

FAX (717) 944-3232

E-MAIL rod@saturdaysmarket.com

WEB www.saturdaysmarket.com/

 NFMA Member

NEW HOPE: Rice's Market

WHEN Every Tuesday morning, 6:00 A.M. to 1:00 P.M. In operation since the 1890s.

WHERE At 6326 Greenhill Road.

ADMISSION Free admission; more than ten acres of parking at $1 per car; indoors year-round and outdoors, weather permitting.

FEATURES Antiques and collectibles, books, coins and stamps, kitchenware, crafts, furniture, jewelry, new and used merchandise, porcelain, fresh produce, and toys. Averages up to 1,000 vendors. Snacks and hot meals are served on the premises.

RATES $20 per space per day or $80 per month. Reservations are recommended.

CONTACT Chuck Kane or John Blanche, 6326 Greenhill Road, New Hope, PA 18938.

PHONE (215) 297-5993

FAX (215) 297-8722

E-MAIL ricesmkt@aol.com

WEB www.ricesmarket.com

 NFMA Member

NEWRY: Leighty's 29-Acre Flea Market

WHEN Every weekend, 8:00 A.M. to 5:00 P.M. In operation for over twenty years.

WHERE   On Old Route 220, near Altoona.
ADMISSION   Free admission; ample free parking; indoors and outdoors, year-round.
FEATURES   Antiques and collectibles, books, new and vintage clothing, kitchenware, crafts, furniture, garage-sale items, new and used merchandise—"all sorts of stuff." Averages 40 to 260 vendors. Snacks and hot meals are served on the premises; giant farmers market (40,000 square feet). Golf range, sport shop, camping.
RATES   From $10 per 11'×28' space per day. Reservations are not required for outdoor spaces.
CONTACT   Roger Azzarello, Manager, P.O. Box 307, Newry, PA 16665.
PHONE   (814) 695-5052 or (814) 695-5151; day of market contact Heidi at (814) 696-7018
FAX   (814) 696-8543
WEB   sacbudi@aol.com

NORTH VERSAILLES: Pittsburgh Super Flea Market

WHEN   Every weekend, 9:00 A.M. to 5:00 P.M. In operation since 1989.
WHERE   At the New Eastland Mall and Marketplace, 833 East Pittsburgh-McKeesport Boulevard, just off Lincoln Highway (Route 30) less than five miles east of Pittsburgh (between Forest Hills and McKeesport).
ADMISSION   Free admission; free parking for over 5,000 cars and buses; indoors and outdoors, rain or shine.
FEATURES   Antiques and collectibles, books, new and vintage clothing, coins and stamps, kitchenware, crafts, furniture, jewelry, new and used merchandise, porcelain, fresh produce, and toys. Averages close to 300 vendors. Snacks and hot meals are served on the premises. Everything "from A to Z."
RATES   Indoors: from $10 per day for a table per day, or $15 per 10'×12' space for one day or $25 per weekend; outdoors: from $10 per day. Reservations are not required.
CONTACT   Ed Williams, General Manager, 833 East Pittsburgh-McKeesport Boulevard, North Versailles, PA 15137.
PHONE   (412) 673-3532 (673-FLEA); office hours are Monday through Friday, 9:00 A.M. to 5:00 P.M.
FAX   (412) 673-4015
E-MAIL   ppns0010@aol.com

NFMA Member

PHILADELPHIA: Quaker City Flea Market

WHEN   Every weekend, 8:00 A.M. to 4:00 P.M. In operation since
            1972.
WHERE   At Tacony and Comly Streets. Take the Bridge Street exit (to
            Northeast Philadelphia) off I-95.
ADMISSION   Free admission; free parking for up to 200 cars; indoors
            year-round and outdoors, weather permitting.
FEATURE   Antiques and collectibles, books, new and vintage cloth-
            ing, coins and stamps, kitchenware, crafts, used furniture,
            jewelry, some new merchandise, toys, and produce.
            Averages 140 to a capacity of 200 vendors. Food is served
            on the premises. Billed as the oldest flea market in
            Philadelphia.
RATES   Indoors from $50 per week; outdoors, $20 per day for used
            items, $25 per day for new items. Reservations are not
            required for outdoor spaces.
CONTACT   Jim or Joan Aiello, 5001 Comly Street, Philadelphia, PA
            19135.
PHONE   (215) 744-2022
FAX   (215) 535-0395

QUAKERTOWN: Quakertown Flea and
Farmers Market

WHEN   Every Friday and Saturday, 9:00 A.M. to 9:00 P.M., and every
            Sunday, 10:00 A.M. to 5:00 P.M. In operation since 1932.
WHERE   On Station Road, just east of Route 309.
ADMISSION   Free admission; ample free parking; indoors and outdoors,
            rain or shine.
FEATURES   Antiques and collectibles (though not particularly upscale),
            crafts, jewelry, new and used merchandise. Averages 200 to
            a capacity of 325 vendors. There are dozens of food estab-
            lishments on the premises, with meats, vegetables, etc.; try
            the soft pretzels. The quality of the stuff is variable, but the
            atmosphere is full of regional flavor; just don't expect fancy
            antiques.
RATES   From $10 per outdoor space per day. Reservations are either
            prepaid four weeks in advance or on a first-come, first-
            served basis.
CONTACT   John R. Chism, 201 Stations Road, Quakertown, PA 18951.
PHONE   (215) 536-4115

FAX	(215) 536-9019
E-MAIL	jchiz@prodigy.net

 NFMA Member

TAMAQUA: Hometown Farmers Market

WHEN	Every Wednesday, 8:00 A.M. to 8:00 P.M. In operation since 1951.
WHERE	On Route 54 (west of Route 309), about two miles north of town.
ADMISSION	Free admission; ten acres of free parking; indoors and outdoors, rain or shine.
FEATURES	Antiques and collectibles, new merchandise, household items, and fresh produce. Averages 250 to a capacity of 450 vendors. There is a restaurant and ten snack stands on the premises. This clean, well-lit market has a "hometown" feel and a healthy bustle.
RATES	$25 per space per week. Reservations are not required.
CONTACT	Robert or Andrea Dunn, R.D. #1, Box 1371, New Ringgold, PA 17960.
PHONE	(570) 668-2630
FAX	(570) 668-3833

 NFMA Member

TANNERSVILLE: Pocono Peddlers Village

WHEN	Every Friday through Monday, 9:00 A.M. to 5:00 P.M. In operation since 1988.
WHERE	On Route 611.
ADMISSION	Free admission; ample free parking; indoors and outdoors, year-round.
FEATURES	Antiques, crafts, collectibles. Averages close to 80 vendors. Food is not served on the premises.
RATES	$5 per space per day outdoors, or from $140 per space per month indoors. Reservations are not required.
CONTACT	Ralph Reifinger, Rouse 611, Tannersville, PA 18372.
PHONE	(717) 629-6366

WEST MIFFLIN: Woodland Flea Market

WHEN	Every weekend from March through December (closed January and February), plus Memorial Day, July Fourth, and Labor Day, 6:00 A.M. to 2:00 P.M. In operation since 1963.
WHERE	At 526 Thompson Run Road, in the Woodland Drive-in Theater, two miles from Kennywood Park and two miles from the Allegheny County Airport; seven miles from downtown Pittsburgh.
ADMISSION	Free admission; ample free parking; indoors year-round and outdoors, weather permitting.
FEATURES	Antiques and collectibles, new and used merchandise, and fresh produce. Averages 300 to 500 vendors. Snacks, baked goods, and hot meals are served on the premises.
RATES	$10 per day for one space or $15 for two spaces; garage rentals are available at $100 per month. Reservations are not required.
CONTACT	Bob or Nancy, 526 Thompson Run Road, West Mifflin, PA 15122.
PHONE	(412) 462-4370
FAX	(412) 462-4334
E-MAIL	morerum@ol.com

WILDWOOD: Wildwood Peddlers Fair

WHEN	Every Sunday, 6:00 A.M. to 4:00 P.M. In operation for over twenty-six years.
WHERE	At 2330 Wildwood Road. From Pittsburgh, take Route 8 South to Wildwood Road (Yellow Belt); market is next to North Park.
ADMISSION	Free admission; parking available at $1 per car; indoors year-round and outdoors, weather permitting.
FEATURES	Antiques and collectibles, books, new and vintage clothing, coins and stamps, kitchenware, crafts, furniture, jewelry, new merchandise, and toys. Averages 350 to 500 vendors. Snacks and hot meals are served on the premises; fish, poultry, and fresh produce are also available.
RATES	$12 per 14'x22' space outdoors per day (call for monthly indoor rates). Reservations are not required.
CONTACT	Manager, 2330 Wildwood Road, Wildwood, PA 15091.
PHONE	(412) 487-2200

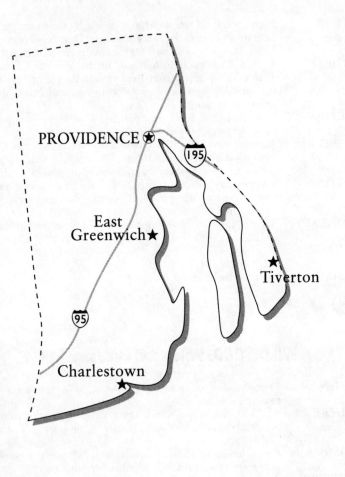

PROVIDENCE ★

East
Greenwich ★

Tiverton ★

Charlestown ★

RHODE ISLAND

CHARLESTOWN: General Stanton Flea Market

WHEN
Every weekend plus holiday Mondays from April through November, 7:00 A.M. to 4:00 P.M. In operation for over twenty-nine years.

WHERE
At 4115 A and B Old Post Road (entrance off Route 1), a mile north of the junction with Route 2. From Connecticut, take exit 92 off I-95, then go three miles to Route 78, to Route 1, then left (northbound) twelve miles. From Hartford, take Route 2 East to 78.

ADMISSION
Free admission; parking for up to 3,000 cars at $1 per car; outdoors, seasonally.

FEATURES
Antiques and collectibles, books, new and vintage clothing, coins and stamps, kitchenware, crafts, used furniture, jewelry, fresh produce, and toys. Averages up to a capacity of over 200 vendors. Snacks and hot meals are served on the premises. Near the beaches in a historical tourist and resort area between Mystic, Connecticut, and Newport, Rhode Island. On the grounds of the historic General Stanton Inn, with fine food, drink, and lodging.

RATES
$15 per 15'×20' space on Saturday and from $25 to $35 per space on Sunday. Reservations are not required.

CONTACT
Angelo or Janice Falcone, P.O. Box 222, Charlestown, RI 02813.

PHONE
(401) 364-8888

FAX
(401) 364-3333

EAST GREENWICH: Rocky Hill Flea Market

WHEN
Every Sunday, from the first Sunday in April through the last Sunday in November, 5:00 A.M. to 2:30 P.M. In operation since the 1960s.

WHERE
On the Rocky Hill Fairgrounds, 1408 Division Road. Take exit 8A (North or South) off I-95, then right at the stoplight.

ADMISSION
Free admission; acres of parking at $1 per car; outdoors, rain or shine.

FEATURES
Antiques and collectibles, new and vintage clothing, kitchenware, crafts, jewelry, porcelain, new merchandise, and fresh produce in season. Averages up to 380 vendors. Snacks and hot meals are served on the premises.

RATES
$17 per 20'×25' space per day. Reservations are recommended.

CONTACT   Gary Hamilton, 12 Lockwood Street, West Warwick, RI
            02893.
PHONE   (401) 884-4114

TIVERTON: Route 177 Flea Market

WHEN   Every weekend plus holiday Mondays, 8:00 A.M. to 5:00
            P.M. In operation since the 1960s.
WHERE   At 1560 Bulgar Marsh Road. From Boston, take Route 24 to
            Route 81 South, then left at only traffic light.
ADMISSION   Free admission; free parking for up to 300'cars; indoors
            year-round and outdoors, weather permitting.
FEATURES   Antiques and collectibles, books, new and vintage clothing,
            coins and stamps, kitchenware, crafts, furniture, jewelry,
            new and used merchandise, porcelain, fresh produce, and
            toys. Averages 35 to 70 vendors. Hot meals are served on the
            premises. One of the oldest flea markets in the area.
RATES $5 per space on Saturdays and holidays, $15 on Sundays.
            Reservations are not required.
CONTACT   Tom Ouellette, 1560 Bulgar Marsh Road, Tiverton, RI 02878.
PHONE   (401) 625-5954 or (401) 624-9354

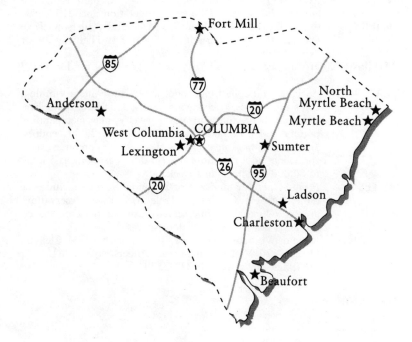

Fort Mill

85

77

20

North
Myrtle Beach

Anderson

Myrtle Beach

West Columbia COLUMBIA

Lexington

Sumter

26

95

20

Ladson

Charleston

Beaufort

SOUTH CAROLINA

ANDERSON: Anderson Jockey Lot and Farmers Market

WHEN	Every weekend: Saturday, 7:00 A.M. to 6:00 P.M., and Sunday, 9:00 A.M. to 6:00 P.M. In operation since 1974.
WHERE	On Highway 29 between Greenville and Anderson. Take exit 32 off I-85 North onto Highway 8 to Highway 29, or exit 34 off I-85 South to Highway 29.
ADMISSION	Free admission; acres of free parking; indoors, outdoors, and under cover, rain or shine.
FEATURES	Antiques and collectibles, books, new and vintage clothing, coins and stamps, kitchenware, crafts, dolls, electronics, livestock, fresh produce, furniture, jewelry, new merchandise, pottery and porcelain. Averages 1,500 to 2,000 vendors. Snacks and hot meals are served on the premises. This sprawling indoor-outdoor market draws as many as 50,000 to 60,000 customers in a weekend.
RATES	From $6 per day outdoors or $10 indoors; rates include one table, with extra tables available at $3 each. Reservations are on a first-come, first-served basis for outdoor spaces; there is a waiting list for indoor spaces.
CONTACT	Ronald Whitman, Manager, or W. Richard McClellion, Owner, 120 West Whitner Street, Anderson, SC 29621.
PHONE	(864) 224-2027 or (864) 224-2279

 NFMA Member

BEAUFORT: Laurel Bay Flea Market

WHEN	Every Saturday, dawn to dusk. In operation since 1994.
WHERE	On Highway 116. Take Highway 21 to Highway 116 (turn at Marine Corps Air Station stoplight), then go three miles. Follow signs from Route 170 to "Laurel Bay." Twenty miles from Hilton Head.
ADMISSION	Free admission; free parking for up to 250 cars; outdoors, weather permitting.
FEATURES	Antiques and collectibles, books, new and vintage clothing, coins and stamps, kitchenware, crafts, used furniture, jewelry, new and used merchandise, porcelain, fresh produce, and toys. Averages 50 to 125 vendors. Food is not served.
RATES	$5 per 8'×3' table per day. Reservations are not required.

CONTACT   Kathleen or Thomas McTeer, P.O. Box 1653, Beaufort, SC
           29901.
PHONE   (803) 521-9794

CHARLESTON: Low Country Flea Market and Collectibles Shows

WHEN   Third full weekend of each month (but the second full
            weekend in February and November, plus a big Christmas
            festival held in late November), Saturday, 9:00 A.M. to
            6:00 P.M., and Sunday 10:00 A.M. to 5:00 P.M. In operation
            since the late 1970s.
WHERE   At the Gaillard Auditorium, 77 Calhoun Street (between Bay
            Street and Meeting Street).
ADMISSION   Admission $2 per person; free for children; ample parking at
            $1 to $2 per car; indoors, year-round.
FEATURES   Antiques and collectibles, books and prints, crafts and jew-
            elry; mainly antique items such as furniture, silver, toys,
            quilts, and primitives. Averages 25 to 79 vendors. Snacks
            and hot meals are served on the premises. Caters to antiques
            dealers, decorators, and the like, as well as general collec-
            tors. "A fun place to be!"
RATES $85 per 10'×10' space for the weekend (includes one table
            and two chairs). Reserve at least two weeks in advance.
CONTACT   The Nelson Garretts or Donna Kidd, 605 Johnnie Dodds
            Boulevard, Mount Pleasant, SC 29464.
PHONE   (843) 884-7204 or (843) 577-7400 (auditorium) or (843)
            722-9286 or (843) 849-1949
FAX   (843) 849-1949

FORT MILL: Pineville Flea Market

WHEN   Every Friday, Saturday, and Sunday, 8:00 A.M. to 5:00 P.M.
            (Friday 8:00 A.M. to 4:00 P.M.). In operation since 1995.
WHERE   At 3674 Highway 51, five miles from Fort Mill, near the North
            Carolina border; between Caro Winds and the Pineville.
ADMISSION   Free admission; ample free parking; outdoors and under
            cover, year-round.

FEATURES   Mix of new, used, collectible, and "junque." Averages up to 400 vendors. Food is served on the premises.

RATES   From $5 per space outdoors (call for rates, which vary depending on location). Reservations are required.

CONTACT   Manager, 3674 Highway 51, Fort Mill, SC 29715.

PHONE   (800) 527-4117 or (803) 957-6570

WEB   www.charlotte.com

LADSON: Coastal Carolina Flea Market

WHEN   Every weekend, 8:00 A.M. to 5:00 P.M. In operation since 1981.

WHERE   On Highway 78 (another entrance on College Park Road). Take exit 203 off I-26, and there is an entrance about a block from the interstate.

ADMISSION   Free admission; fifteen acres of free parking; indoors year-round and outdoors, rain or shine.

FEATURES   Antiques and collectibles, books, clothing, kitchenware, furniture, jewelry, new and used merchandise, pets, sporting goods and collectibles, fresh produce, woodcrafts. Averages close to 800 vendors. Restaurant and three food concessions on the premises. Billed as the Low Country's largest.

RATES   Indoors: $12 per 10'×10' space with one eight-foot table per day; outdoors: $6 per day. Reserve two weeks in advance for indoor spaces (there is sometimes a waiting list); outdoor spaces are on a first-come, first-served basis.

CONTACT   Michael W. Masterson, P.O. Box 510, Highway 78, Ladson, SC 29456.

PHONE   (843) 797-0540 (office is open Wednesday through Sunday)

FAX   (843) 797-0541

NFMA Member

LEXINGTON: Barnyard Flea Market

WHEN   Every Friday, Saturday, and Sunday, all day. In operation since 1988.

WHERE   On Route 1 between Lexington and Columbia.

ADMISSION   Free admission; ample free parking; indoors, outdoors, and under cover, year-round.

FEATURES   Antiques and collectibles, books, new and vintage clothing, crafts, jewelry, new and used merchandise, and fresh produce. Averages close to 500 vendors. Food is available on the premises.

RATES From $5 per table outdoors or from $10 per 10'×10' space indoors. Reservations are required.

CONTACT Dick Stewart, 4414 August Road, Lexington, SC 29072.

PHONE (800) 628-7496 or (803) 957-6570

MYRTLE BEACH: Big Deals Bazaar and Flea Market

WHEN Every weekend during winter, and daily (except Tuesday) during spring and summer (call to confirm), 8:00 A.M. to 7:00 P.M. on Saturday and 10:00 A.M. to 5:00 P.M. on Sunday (weekdays, 9:00 A.M. to 5:00 P.M.). In operation since March 1999.

WHERE At 4761 Highway 501, six miles west of town.

ADMISSION Free admission; free parking for up to 650 cars; indoors and outdoors, rain or shine.

FEATURES Everything from collectibles and household items to new merchandise. Averages 150 to 200 vendors. Food is served on the premises.

RATES From $150 per space per month. Reservations are recommended.

CONTACT Jan Watts or Wilma Lewis, 4761 Highway 501, Myrtle Beach, SC 29575.

PHONE (800) 244-3325 (BIG-DEAL) or (843) 236-7474

FAX (843) 236-9078

WEB www.mbflea.com

NFMA Member

MYRTLE BEACH: Myrtle Beach Flea Market

WHEN Daily from June through Labor Day, and every Thursday through Sunday the rest of the year, 10:00 A.M. to 4:00 P.M. In operation since 1994.

WHERE On Highway (Business) 17, near the heart of Myrtle Beach.

ADMISSION Free admission; ample free parking; indoors, year-round.

FEATURES A variety of new and used merchandise. Averages close to its capacity of more than 300 vendors. Food is served on the premises. Offers "shopping and fun rolled into one" and is heavily promoted on TV, billboards, etc. Owned by American Park 'n' Swap, an experienced flea market "franchise" company with half a dozen other markets. ATM machine, hourly prize drawings.

RATES
Daily rates from $15 per 10'×10' space in summer; monthly rates from $110 to $235 per month; includes electricity and security; tables at $2 per day or $30 per month. Reservations are recommended.

CONTACT
Judy Mode, General Manager, 3820 South Kings Highway, Myrtle Beach, SC 29577.

PHONE
(843) 477-1550

FAX
(843) 238-2555

E-MAIL
ppn0010@aol.com

NFMA Member

NORTH MYRTLE BEACH: North Myrtle Beach Flea Market

WHEN
Every Friday, Saturday, and Sunday, 9:00 A.M. to 4:00 P.M. In operation since the early 1980s.

WHERE
At the intersection of Highways 17 and 9.

ADMISSION
Free admission; free parking for up to 500 cars; indoors, year-round.

FEATURES
Antiques and collectibles, books, new and vintage clothing, coins and stamps, kitchenware, crafts, furniture, jewelry, new merchandise, porcelain, fresh produce, shoes, old and new tools, toys, "hubcaps, etc., etc." Averages close to its capacity of 350 vendors. Hot meals are served on the premises. Located one mile from the Atlantic Ocean in a tourist area that has as many as 450,000 visitors per week.

RATES
$10 per 8'×10' space per day. Reserve a week in advance.

CONTACT
Jesse Medlock, P.O. Box 3467, North Myrtle Beach, SC 29582.

PHONE
(843) 249-4701

SUMTER: The Market at Shaw

WHEN
Every Friday, 9:00 A.M. to 6:00 P.M.; every Saturday, 7:00 A.M. to 7:00 P.M.; and every Sunday, 1:30 P.M. to 6:00 P.M. In operation since 1990.

WHERE	On Highway 378 East, across from Shaw AFB (approximately thirty miles east of Columbia). Take exit 135 west off I-95 and then go approximately twenty-three miles on Highway 378.
ADMISSION	Free admission; eighteen acres of free parking, mostly paved; outdoors and under cover, rain or shine.
FEATURES	Antiques and collectibles, books, new and vintage clothing, coins and stamps, kitchenware, crafts, furniture, jewelry, new and used merchandise, porcelain, fresh produce, and toys. Averages 80 to 135 vendors. Snacks and hot meals are served on the premises. All-steel building.
RATES	$5 per table on Friday, Saturday, or Sunday. Reserve a week to two weeks in advance.
CONTACT	Mr. Weir or Mr. Firmbach, 4666 Broad Street Extension, Sumter, SC 29154.
PHONE	(803) 494-5500 or (803) 494-2635. Day of market contact Bob Kimber at (803) 494-5500.

WEST COLUMBIA: U.S. #1 Metro Flea Market

WHEN	Every Friday, 8:00 A.M. to 5:00 P.M.; every Saturday, 6:00 A.M. to 6:00 P.M.; and every Sunday, 9:00 A.M. to 6:00 P.M.; wholesale market every Wednesday, 7:00 A.M. to noon. In operation for over fifteen years.
WHERE	At 3500 Augusta Road. Take exit 111-A off I-26, then go one and a half miles, or take exit 58 off I-20 and then go three and a half miles.
ADMISSION	Free admission; ten acres of free parking; indoors and outdoors, rain or shine.
FEATURES	Collectibles (including such items as baseball cards, bottles, coins, comics, jewelry, and toys), books, new and vintage clothing, kitchenware, used furniture, new merchandise, porcelain, and fresh produce. Averages 800 to a capacity of 900 vendors. Snacks and hot meals are served on the premises. Just a few miles from the State Capitol.
RATES	$12 per space per day indoors, $8 outdoors. Reservations are recommended.
CONTACT	Richard J. Hook, P.O. Box 1457, Lexington, SC 29071.
PHONE	(803) 796-9294

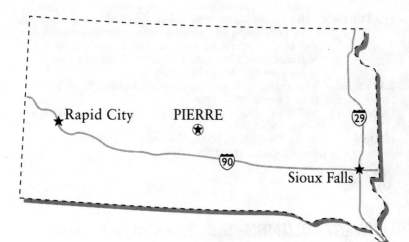

Rapid City   PIERRE ⊛   90   Sioux Falls   29

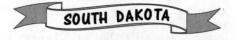

SOUTH DAKOTA

RAPID CITY: Black Hills Flea Market

WHEN   Every weekend from May through September, 7:00 A.M. to dusk. In operation for over twenty-one years.

WHERE   At 5500 Mount Rushmore Road, at the city limits of Rapid City. Take exit 57 off I-90 onto the I-90 Loop then to Mount Rushmore Road (Route 16 West, the main highway to Mount Rushmore National Memorial).

ADMISSION Free admission; ample free parking; indoors and outdoors, rain or shine.

FEATURES Variety of offerings, including antiques and collectibles, crafts, new and used merchandise, fresh produce in season, saddles and tack, and home-baked goodies—"something for everyone. Anything from plants to collectible bits of Americana gleaned from cereal boxes of years ago." Averages up to 150 vendors. Snacks and hot meals are served on the premises. Reputed to be a well-kept market with many regular dealers plus others passing through from various parts of the country on the flea market circuit. "The faces of Presidents Washington, Jefferson, Lincoln, and Roosevelt are an inspiration to us all." Several campgrounds nearby.

RATES $4 per day "tailgate," including one table; indoor booths $13 to $16 per day, including tables; indoors arts and crafts section $11 per day, including one table; additional tables available at $2 each per day. Reservations are required a week in advance.

CONTACT   Deborah Cooley or Robert Jeffrey, 5500 Mount Rushmore Road, Rapid City, SD 57701.

PHONE   (605) 343-6477 or (605) 348-1981 or (605) 399-2699

SIOUX FALLS: Benson's Flea Market

WHEN   One weekend a month except June, July, and August (generally first weekend of the month—call for dates): Saturday, 9:00 A.M. to 5:00 P.M. and Sunday 11:00 A.M. to 4:00 P.M. In operation since the 1960s.

WHERE   On the Lyons Fairgrounds in Expo Building W.H.

ADMISSION Admission $1 per person; free parking; indoors.

FEATURES Antiques and collectibles, baseball cards, books, bottles, coins, comics, crafts, furniture, household items, jewelry, and more. Averages up to 250 vendors. Snacks and hot meals are served on the premises.

RATES	$30 per eight-foot table per weekend, or $95 per booth with four tables. Reserve a month in advance.
CONTACT	Ed or Bonnie Benson, Head Fleas, P.O. Box 236, Sioux Falls, SD 57101.
PHONE	(605) 334-1312

CHATTANOOGA: East Ridge Flea Market

WHEN	Every weekend plus Christmas week, 9:00 A.M. to 6:00 P.M. In operation since 1993.
WHERE	At 6725 Ringold Road.
ADMISSION	Free admission; ample free parking; indoors and outdoors, year-round.
FEATURES	Full spectrum of antiques and collectibles, used merchandise, etc. Averages 130 to 150 vendors. Three restaurants on the premises. RV park across the street.
RATES	$23 per 10'×10' space per day, or $18 per day based on monthly commitment. Reservations are not required.
CONTACT	Ginger Long, Manager, 6725 Ringold Road, Chattanooga, TN 37412.
PHONE	(423) 894-3960

CLARKSVILLE: Clarksville Gigantic Flea Market

WHEN	Third weekend of every month, plus a Thanksgiving extravaganza (call for dates), Friday, 3:00 P.M. to 7:00 P.M., Saturday 9:00 A.M. to 7:00 P.M., and Sunday, 11:00 A.M. to 5:00 P.M. In operation since 1994.
WHERE	At 1600 Fort Campbell Boulevard (the Two Rivers Mall).
ADMISSION	Free admission; ample free parking; indoors, rain or shine.
FEATURES	Antiques and collectibles, designer clothing, tools, and quality new and used merchandise. Averages 300 to a capacity 350 vendors. Food is served on the premises. This market attracts over 25,000 visitors per event and draws vendors from a dozen states.
RATES	$95 per space per event. Reserve a month in advance.
CONTACT	Michael or Richard Epperson, Sale-a-Rama Promotions, 254 Seville Street, Suite 3, Florence, AL 35360.
PHONE	(800) 672-8988 or (256) 764-6400
FAX	(256) 764-6481

CROSSVILLE: Crossville Flea Market

WHEN
Every weekend plus Labor Day and Memorial Day Mondays and the Friday after Thanksgiving, 7:00 A.M. to 3:00 P.M. In operation since 1970.

WHERE
On Highway 70 North, midway between Knoxville and Nashville. Take exit 317 off I-40 onto Highway 127, then go right onto Highway 70 North and market will be a mile and a half down on the right.

ADMISSION
Free admission; free parking for up to 12,000 cars; indoors, outdoors, and under cover, rain or shine.

FEATURES
Antiques and collectibles, books, new and vintage clothing, coins and stamps, kitchenware, crafts, furniture, jewelry, livestock, new and used merchandise, porcelain, fresh produce, and toys. Averages 300 to a capacity of 450 vendors. Concession stands operate on the premises. Billed as the largest weekly open-air market in the state—"where a flea market is still a flea market." Member of the Tennessee Flea Market Association.

RATES
Saturday: $6 per 12'×14' space ($8 under shed), includes two tables; Sunday: $4 per space ($5 under shed) with free tables. Reservations are not required (but most reserve at least a day in advance).

CONTACT
Lois Wilbanks, Owner, or Mary Brown, P.O. Box 3037, Crossville, TN 38557.

PHONE
(931) 484-9970 or (931) 456-9073

FAX
(931) 707-1339

NFMA Member

KNOXVILLE: Esau's Antique and Collectible Market

WHEN
Third weekend of every month (plus an extravaganza in October), Friday, 9:00 A.M. to 7:00 P.M., and Saturday, 9:00 A.M. to 5:00 P.M. In operation since the mid-1970s.

WHERE
At Chilhowee Park, Take exit 392 (Rutledge Pike exit) off I-40 East through Knoxville.

ADMISSION
Admission $3 per person, good for both days; twenty acres of free parking; indoors and outdoors, rain or shine.

FEATURES
Antiques and collectibles, books, new and vintage clothing, coins and stamps, crafts, jewelry, new merchandise, pottery, and porcelain. Averages 300 to a capacity of 350 vendors. Snacks and hot meals are served on the premises. A member of the Tennessee Flea Market Association. "Bring your truck."

RATES	$70 per space per weekend indoors, $40 outdoors; Tennessee sales tax number required (or a sales tax certificate may be purchased from the market). Reserve a month in advance.
CONTACT	Salina Garrett or Cindy Crabtree, P.O. Box 50096, Knoxville, TN 37950.
PHONE	(800) 588-3728 or (423) 588-1233
FAX	(423) 588-6938
E-MAIL	esauinc@aol.com

LEBANON: Parkland Flea Market

WHEN	Every weekend from March through Christmas, 7:00 A.M. to 5:00 P.M. In operation since 1977.
WHERE	On Highway 231, six miles south of exit 238 off I-40 (across from Cedars of Lebanon State Park), between Lebanon and Murfreesboro; thirty miles from Nashville.
ADMISSION	Free admission; free parking for up to 400 cars; indoors and outdoors, rain or shine.
FEATURES	Antiques and collectibles, books, new clothing, crafts, new furniture, jewelry, livestock, new merchandise, fresh produce, and toys. Averages close to 300 vendors. Snacks and hot meals are served on the premises. Attracts some 8,000 customers each week. Close to state park and campgrounds.
RATES	$10 per 12'×12' space per day, with two tables included. Reserve two weeks in advance.
CONTACT	E. Gwynn Lanius, President, 403 Cambridge Road, Lebanon, TN 37087-4207.
PHONE	(615) 444-1279; day of market call (615) 449-6050

MEMPHIS: Memphis "Big One" Flea Market

WHEN	The third weekend of each month except September, 9:00 A.M. to 6:00 P.M. In operation since 1971.
WHERE	On the Mid-South Fairgrounds, at Central Avenue and East Parkway in midtown Memphis.
ADMISSION	Free admission; free parking for up to 5,000 cars; indoors year-round and outdoors, weather permitting.
FEATURES	Antiques and collectibles, new and vintage clothing, coins

and stamps, crafts, porcelain, furniture, jewelry. Averages 600 to 700 vendors. Snack bar on premises. The big one.

RATES	From $70 for the weekend; tables are $5 each. Reservations are recommended.
CONTACT	Mike Hardage, 955 Early Maxwell, Memphis, TN 38104-5932.
PHONE	(901) 276-3532 (276-FLEA); office hours are weekdays, 9:30 A.M. to 4:30 P.M.
FAX	(901) 276-0701
E-MAIL	ppns0010@aol.com

NFMA Member

NASHVILLE: Tennessee State Fairgrounds Flea Market

WHEN	Fourth weekend of every month: Saturday, 6:00 A.M. to 6:00 P.M. and Sunday, 7:00 A.M. to 4:00 P.M. In operation since 1967.
WHERE	On the State Fairgrounds at Wedgewood Avenue and Nolensville Road. Take exit 81 (Wedgewood) off I-65.
ADMISSION	Free admission; parking for up to 4,000 cars at $2 per car; indoors, outdoors, and under cover, rain or shine.
FEATURES	Antiques and collectibles, books, new and vintage clothing, coins and stamps, kitchenware, crafts, furniture, jewelry, new and used merchandise, porcelain, and toys. Averages 1,000 to 1,200 vendors. Snacks and hot meals are served on the premises. Big and long established, this fairgrounds market is a browser's delight.
RATES	Average $75 per space per weekend indoors, and $60 outdoors/under sheds. Reserve a month in advance.
CONTACT	Debbie Gregoire, P.O. Box 40208, Nashville, TN 37204.
PHONE	(615) 862-5016
FAX	(615) 862-5015
WEB	www.nashvile.org/tsf

NFMA Member

SEVIERVILLE: Great Smokies Craft Fair and Flea Market

WHEN	Every Friday, 10:00 A.M. to 6:00 P.M.; and every Saturday and Sunday, 9:00 A.M. to 6:00 P.M. In operation since 1990.
WHERE	At 220 Dumplin Valley Road West. Take exit 407 off I-40 and go right on Dumplin Valley Road.
ADMISSION	Free admission; free parking; indoors, outdoors, and under cover, rain or shine.
FEATURES	Antiques and collectibles, clothing, crafts, factory-direct items of all kinds, furniture, tools, and toys. Averages 230 to 300 vendors. Food court on premises. Tour buses welcome.
RATES	$55 per 10'×20' space indoors for three days, or $12 per 10'×12' space per day outdoors. Reserve a week in advance for outdoor spaces; waiting list for indoor spaces.
CONTACT	Manager, 220 Dumplin Valley Road West, Kodak, TN 37764.
PHONE	(423) 932-3532 (932-FLEA)

NFMA Member

SWEETWATER: Fleas Unlimited

WHEN	Every weekend, 8:00 A.M. to 5:00 P.M. In operation since 1991.
WHERE	Near exit 60 off I-75; at the junction of Highway 68.
ADMISSION	Free admission; free parking; indoors and outdoors, weather permitting.
FEATURES	Antiques and collectibles, books, new and vintage clothing, coins and stamps, kitchenware, crafts, furniture, jewelry, porcelain, fresh produce, and toys. Averages 300 to 350 vendors. Snacks and hot meals are served on the premises. Fleas Unlimited has a reputation as a "trader's paradise."
RATES	From $20 per space per day. Reservations are recommended.
CONTACT	Rhonda Busby or Whittney Burnette, 121 Country Road 308, Sweetwater, TN 37874.
PHONE	(423) 337-3532 (337-FLEA)
FAX	(423) 337-4694

TRENTON: First Monday Flea Market

WHEN	First Monday of every month and the preceding Saturday and Sunday (special dates in May, October, and November); from daybreak to dark. In operation for over a hundred years.
WHERE	On the Gibson County Fairgrounds, just off Business Route 45 West, on "Manufacturers Row."
ADMISSION	Free admission; ample free parking; indoors, outdoors, and under cover, year-round.
FEATURES	Antiques and collectibles, books, new clothing, kitchenware, crafts, furniture, jewelry, livestock, new and used merchandise, fresh produce, and toys. Averages 150 to a capacity of 300 vendors. Snacks and hot meals are served from concessions on the fairgrounds.
RATES	$12 per 20'×20' space per day outdoors, $20 for two days, $25 for three days; electricity is available at $4 per day/overnight. Reservations are not required.
CONTACT	Sonny Shanklin, 185 Shanklin Road, Trenton, TN 38382.
PHONE	(901) 855-2981 or (901) 692-4060

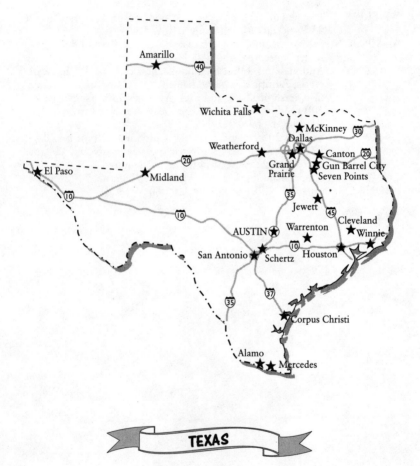

TEXAS

ALAMO: All-Valley Flea Market

WHEN   Every weekend, from daybreak to dark. In operation since the 1960s.

WHERE   At the northwest corner of Cesar Chavez and Expressway 83, between Alamo and San Juan.

ADMISSION   Admission 25¢ per person; parking for more than 500 cars (free with admission); indoors year-round and outdoors, weather permitting.

FEATURES   Antiques and collectibles, books, new and vintage clothing, coins and stamps, kitchenware, crafts, furniture, jewelry, livestock, new and used merchandise, porcelain, fresh produce, and toys. Averages 600 to a capacity of more than 1,000 vendors. Food is available on the premises. Billed as the largest flea market south of Dallas–Fort Worth, with as many as 30,000 shoppers on winter weekends or 15,000 on summer weekends. Forty RV hookups, showers, and other amenities await the weary traveler.

RATES $12.50 per space per day. Reserve a week in advance for covered spaces.

CONTACT   David Villegas, 501 North Bridge Street, #528, Hidalgo, TX 78557.

PHONE   (956) 781-1911

FAX   (956) 787-8071

AMARILLO: Old ICX Flea Market

WHEN   Every Friday, Saturday, and Sunday, 9:00 A.M. to 6:00 P.M. In operation since the late 1980s.

WHERE   At 513 South Ross Street. Take Ross Street exit off I-40 and go north on Ross past two sets of stoplights, and market will be on the right.

ADMISSION   Free admission; free parking for up to 200 cars; indoors and outdoors, rain or shine.

FEATURES   Full spectrum of antiques and collectibles, jewelry, new and used merchandise, and fresh produce. Averages 70 to a capacity of 100 vendors. Snacks and hot meals are served on the premises. Strong on collectibles such as baseball cards, coins, and toys, including a Star Trek booth.

RATES $21 per 10'×10' space for three days; $31 per 10'×15' space. Reservations are not required.

CONTACT   Shirley Roberts, 513 South Ross Street, Amarillo, TX 79104.

PHONE   (806) 373-3215, Monday through Thursday, 9:00 A.M. to
               3:00 P.M.

AMARILLO: T-Anchor Flea Market

WHEN   Every weekend (except Christmas), 9:00 A.M. to 5:00 P.M. In
               operation since 1978.
WHERE   At 1401 Ross Street (off I-40), across from Burger King.
ADMISSION   Free admission; free parking; indoors year-round, and out-
               doors, in summertime.
FEATURES   Antiques and collectibles, books, new and vintage clothing,
               coins and stamps, kitchenware, crafts, furniture, jewelry,
               new and used merchandise, fresh produce, and toys.
               Averages close to 165 vendors. Food is available on the
               premises.
RATES   Indoors: from $20 per 10'×10' space per weekend; outdoors:
               $8.25 per 10'×20' space per day. Reservations are on a first-
               come, first-served basis.
CONTACT   Claudia Blythe, P.O. Box 31182, Amarillo, TX 79120.
PHONE   (806) 373-0430 (every day except Tuesday and Wednesday)

AUSTIN: Austin Country Flea Mart

WHEN   Every Saturday and Sunday, 10:00 A.M. to 6:00 P.M. In oper-
               ation since 1984.
WHERE   At 9500 Highway 290 East. Take Highway 290 East toward
               Houston for five miles from I-35.
ADMISSION   Free admission; free parking; indoors and outdoors, rain or
               shine.
FEATURES   A bit of everything, including antiques and collectibles, new
               and used merchandise, gold, shoes, and fine foods. Averages
               up to a capacity of 550 vendors. Variety of food concessions
               on the premises.
RATES $35 per weekend. Reservations are recommended.
CONTACT   Buzz Cook, 9500 Highway 290 East, Austin, TX 78724.
PHONE   (512) 928-2795

               NFMA Member

AUSTIN: City Wide Garage Sale

WHEN   Fourteen weekends a year (call for dates), Saturday, 10:00
           A.M. to 6:00 P.M. and Sunday, 11:00 A.M. to 5:00 P.M. In
           operation since 1977.
WHERE   At the City Coliseum.
ADMISSION Admission $3.50 per person (children under twelve are
           admitted free); ample free parking; indoors, year-round.
FEATURES   Mainly antiques and collectibles. Averages 120 to 135 ven-
           dors. There is a concession stand on the premises. Billed as
           "Austin's antiques and collectibles marketplace."
RATES $100 per 8'×10' weekend. Reserve a month in advance.
CONTACT   Christopher Dwyer, 512 East Riverside Drive, #104, Austin,
           TX 78704.
PHONE   (512) 441-2828 or (877) 840-3829
FAX   (512) 441-1918
E-MAIL   citywide@onr.com
WEB   www.cwgs.com

CANTON: First Monday Trade Days

WHEN   The Thursday, Friday, Saturday, and Sunday preceding the
           first Monday of every month, dawn to dusk. In operation-
           since 1873 (probably even earlier).
WHERE   Entrances on Highway 19 and F.M. 859 in Canton, just off
           I-20 fifty-five miles east of Dallas); 35 miles west of Tyler
           (use Highway 64).
ADMISSION Free admission; parking for up to half a million visitors at $3
           per car; indoors, outdoors, and under cover, rain or shine.
FEATURES   A virtually unlimited range of items, from antiques and col-
           lectibles to new and vintage clothing (including Western
           wear), coins and stamps, kitchenware, crafts, electronics,
           antique firearms, new and used merchandise of all descrip-
           tion—a huge selection. Averages 1,500 to 3,000 vendors. A
           wide variety of snacks, deli items, and hot meals are sold on
           the premises. This is a world-famous flea market and defi-
           nitely one of the biggest and best in the country, with all
           sorts of interesting stuff (and people); there are many special
           events such as Texas State Bluegrass Festivals (April and
           June), auto swap meets (March, April, May, September, and
           October), RV rallies, Christmas bazaar, trade shows, ban-
           quets, etc. First-aid-facilities, information centers, shower
           facilities, local lodging (book well in advance!) and RV facil-

ities available (Canton is a haven for RV owners); fishing, golf, tennis and other recreational facilities; there is a special newsprint guide published for each event.

RATES $50 per 12'×20' space. For reserved areas call a month ahead (as early the second Wednesday after the First Monday).

CONTACT City of Canton, P.O. Box 245, Canton, TX 75103.

PHONE (903) 567-6556

FAX (903) 567-1753

E-MAIL cityhall@vzinet.com

WEB www.firstmondaycanton.com

CANTON: Old Mill Marketplace

WHEN The Friday, Saturday, and Sunday preceding the first Monday of every month, 8:00 A.M. to 5:00 P.M. In operation since 1994.

WHERE On Highway 64, two blocks east of the courthouse.

ADMISSION Free admission; ample parking at $3 per car and from $6 for RVs; indoors and outdoors, rain or shine.

FEATURES Collectibles, crafts, and more. Averages 800 to 1,000 vendors. Food is served on the premises. Part of the First Monday festivities, this outfit runs alongside the city's massive event (see separate listing) and contributes to the excitement.

RATES From $45 per space per day. Reserve several months in advance.

CONTACT Debbie Davis, Route 5, Box 605, Canton, TX 75103.

PHONE (903) 567-5445

FAX (903)567-5562

E-MAIL oldmill@flash.net

WEB www.oldmillmarketplace.com

NFMA Member

CLEVELAND: Olde Security Square

WHEN Every weekend, 10:00 A.M. to 6:00 P.M. In operation since the mid-1980s.

WHERE On Highway 105, between Cleveland and Conroe.

ADMISSION Free admission; five acres of free parking; indoors and outdoors, rain or shine.

FEATURES   Antiques and collectibles, books, new and vintage clothing, coins and stamps, kitchenware, crafts, antique firearms, furniture, jewelry, new merchandise, porcelain, fresh produce, toys. Averages 200 to 300 vendors. Snacks and hot meals are served on the premises. Family-oriented market with "some of everything." Growing fast with plenty of room for expansion. RV hookups.

RATES   From $10 per 4'×8' table per day outdoors. Reservations are required; long waiting list on indoor spaces.

CONTACT   Manager, 20024 Highway 105, Cleveland, TX 77327.

PHONE   (281) 592-6017

CORPUS CHRISTI: Corpus Christi Trade Center

WHEN   Every Friday, Saturday, and Sunday, 9:00 A.M. to 7:00 P.M. In operation since 1983.

WHERE   At 2833 South Padre Island Drive, on the south end of that street (between Kostoryz and Ayers).

ADMISSION   Free admission; free parking for up to 500 cars; indoors, year-round.

FEATURES   Antiques and collectibles, books, new and vintage clothing, coins and stamps, kitchenware, crafts, furniture, jewelry, new merchandise, plants, porcelain, fresh produce, and toys. Averages 150 to 200 vendors. There is a snack bar on the premises. Veterinarian; sewing machine and television repair; custom made boots; door prizes.

RATES   From $55 per 8'×12' space per weekend. Reservations are recommended.

CONTACT   Manager, 2833 South Padre Island Drive, Corpus Christi, TX 78415.

PHONE   (512) 854-4943

FAX   (512) 854-9663

DALLAS: Bargain City Bazaar

WHEN   Every Friday, Saturday, and Sunday, 10:00 A.M. to 7:00 P.M. In operation since around 1980.

WHERE   At 735 North Westmoreland, one mile south of I-30.

ADMISSION   Free admission; free parking for up to 700 cars; indoors, year-round.

FEATURES	Collectibles, furniture, jewelry, toys, new clothing, and fresh produce. Averages up to a capacity of 150 vendors. Snacks and hot meals are served on the premises. Offers 100,000 square feet of selling space.
RATES	$25 per six-foot table per day; call for availability. Reservations are recommended.
CONTACT	Rod Lehr and Brady Bryant, 735 North Westmoreland, Dallas, TX 75211.
PHONE	(214) 330-8111

EL PASO: Ascarate Flea Market

WHEN	Every weekend, 5:00 A.M. to 6:00 P.M. In operation since the early 1970s.
WHERE	At 6701 Delta Drive, at the Ascarate Drive-in Theater.
ADMISSION	Free admission; free parking for up to 600 cars; outdoors, weather permitting.
FEATURES	Antiques and collectibles, new and vintage clothing, coins and stamps, kitchenware, crafts, furniture, jewelry, new and used merchandise, porcelain, fresh produce, and toys. Averages 300 to 350 vendors. Snacks and hot meals are served on the premises.
RATES	$14 per 18'×24' space on Saturday, $10 on Sunday. Reservations are not required.
CONTACT	Artemio Juarez, 6701 Delta Drive, El Paso, TX 79905.
PHONE	(915) 779-2303
FAX	(915) 778-8265

GRAND PRAIRIE: Traders Village

WHEN	Every weekend, 8:00 A.M. to dusk. In operation since 1973.
WHERE	At 2602 Mayfield Road, just off Highway 360, a mile north of I-20, or five miles south of Six Flags Over Texas theme park.
ADMISSION	Free admission; parking for up to 8,000 cars at $2 per car; indoors, outdoors, and under cover, rain or shine.
FEATURES	Antiques and collectibles, crafts, electronics, auto accessories (and automobiles, sometimes!), Western riding tack and saddles, sporting goods, haircuts, plants, new and vin-

tage clothing, fresh produce, livestock, imports, and office equipment. Averages 1,600 to a capacity of 2,000 vendors. Food offerings include pizza by the slice, hot links, smoked turkey, southern fried chicken and catfish, Mexican food, funnel cakes, and hot dogs. A major operation, in the heart of the Dallas–Fort Worth area; over 27 million people have visited this market. There is a large RV park nearby with extensive facilities; Antique Auto Swap Meet is held on the second weekend in June; National Championship Indian Pow-Wow, weekend after Labor Day; prairie dog chili cookoff; antique tractor show.

RATES	$20 per day for an open lot or a kiosk; $25 per day for a covered lot; monthly rental only in enclosed buildings. Reserve a week in advance.
CONTACT	Allan Hughes, 2602 Mayfield Road, Grand Prairie, TX 75052.
PHONE	(972) 647-2331 or (972) 647-8205
FAX	(972) 647-8585
WEB	www.tradersvillage.com

 NFMA Member

GUN BARREL CITY: Gun Barrel Flea Market

WHEN	Every weekend, 8:00 A.M. to 5:00 P.M. In operation since the early 1970s.
WHERE	At 1307 West Main Street in Gun Barrel City (near Cedar Creek Lake). From Dallas, take I-175 to Mabank, then right at stoplight, then three miles, then right again, then two miles to light. Wal-Mart will be on right, market on left.
ADMISSION	Free admission; free parking for more than 150 cars; indoors year-round and outdoors, weather permitting.
FEATURES	Antiques and collectibles, books, new and vintage clothing, coins and stamps, kitchenware, crafts, furniture, jewelry, livestock, new and used merchandise, odds and ends, porcelain, fresh produce, and toys. Averages 50 to 80 vendors. Snacks and hot meals are served on the premises. RV hookups.
RATES	From $8 per 16'×32' space per weekend. Reservations are not required.
CONTACT	Lorene Bowles, Owner, or Bonnie Ellis, Manager, 1307 West Main Street, Gun Barrel City, TX 75147-8021.
PHONE	(903) 887-1000 or (903) 887-1972

HOUSTON: The Houston Flea Market (aka The Original Common Market)

WHEN	Every weekend, 8:00 A.M. to 6:00 P.M. In operation since 1968.
WHERE	6116 Southwest Freeway (Route 59). Take the Fountainview exit off 59 South, or the Chimney Rock exit off 59 North, then U-turn under the freeway.
ADMISSION	Free admission; seven acres of parking at $1 per car; indoors and outdoors, rain or shine.
FEATURES	Antiques and collectibles, appliances, books, new and vintage clothing, kitchenware, crafts, electronics, furniture, jewelry, new and used merchandise, pets, porcelain, fresh produce, toys, and Western wear. Averages 275 to 350 vendors. Snacks and hot meals are served on the premises. Billed as Houston's original flea market with large weekend crowds. Special events pavilion.
RATES	$18 per 10'×20' space on Saturday and $29 on Sunday. Reservations are recommended no later than the Friday preceding market day.
CONTACT	Manager, P.O. Box 573007, Houston, TX 77257-3007.
PHONE	(713) 782-0391
FAX	(713) 781-0642

 NFMA Member

HOUSTON: Traders Village

WHEN	Every weekend, 7:00 A.M. to 6:00 P.M. In operation since 1989.
WHERE	At 7979 North Eldridge Road, three-tenths of a mile south of Highway 290 (Northwest Freeway) or eight miles north of I-10 (Katy Freeway).
ADMISSION	Free admission; ample parking at $2 per car; indoors, outdoors, and under cover, rain or shine.
FEATURES	Antiques, collectibles, new and used merchandise, clothing, jewelry, fresh produce, plants, office equipment, auto accessories, sporting goods. Averages 600 to a capacity of 800 vendors. Snacks and hot meals are served on the premises, including concessions run by Traders Village. This is a fast-growing offshoot of the original location in Grand Prairie. "Free enterprise at its best." Stroller and wagon rental, first-

aid facilities, ATM machine, kiddie rides, and full-service RV park on the premises.

RATES $20 per day for an open lot, or $41 per weekend for a reserved space. Reserve up to five days in advance.

CONTACT   George Esparza, 7979 North Eldridge Road, Houston, TX 77041.

PHONE   (281) 890-5500

FAX   (281) 890-6568

E-MAIL   tvh@flash.net

WEB   www.tradersvillage.com

NFMA Member

HOUSTON: Trading Fair II

WHEN   Every Friday, Saturday, and Sunday, 10:00 A.M. to 6:00 P.M. In operation since 1974.

WHERE   At 5512 South Loop East. From Astrodome, use 610 Loop East (toward the Galveston Freeway) for four miles, exit at Crestmont at which point the market is highly visible.

ADMISSION   Free admission; ample free parking; indoors, year-round.

FEATURES   All types of antiques and collectibles, jewelry, crafts, new merchandise, and toys. Averages up to 450 vendors. Snacks and hot meals are served on the premises. Wide selection, good value, and they're expanding to five acres outdoors.

RATES $50 per 10'×10' space per weekend. Reservations are recommended.

CONTACT   W. S. Henkle, 5515 South Loop East, Houston, TX 77033.

PHONE   (713) 731-1111

FAX   (713) 731-1121

WEB   www.houstonenjoy.com

JEWETT: Flea Market of Jewett

WHEN   Second Saturday of each month and the Friday preceding and Sunday following, plus extra markets on the third weekends in November and December, all day. In operation since 1977.

WHERE   On Highway 79.

ADMISSION   Free admission; ample free parking; outdoors, rain or shine.

FEATURES	Antiques and collectibles, new and used merchandise, household items, "junque"—you name it. Averages close to 150 vendors. Food is served on the premises.
RATES	$18 per 12'×25' space per weekend. Reservations are required.
CONTACT	Dana Sullivan, Manager, P.O. Box 762, Centerville, TX 75833.
PHONE	(903) 536-7689
E-MAIL	jfmarket@risecom.net

McKINNEY: Third Monday Trade Day

WHEN	Every Friday, Saturday, and Sunday before the third Monday, 9:00 A.M. to 4:00 P.M. In operation since 1966.
WHERE	On Highway 380 West, two miles west of U.S. 75.
ADMISSION	Free admission; parking for up to 2,000 cars at $2 per car; outdoors, year-round.
FEATURES	Everything from new and used to collectible and antique. Averages close to 400 vendors. Food is served on the premises.
RATES	$35 per 12'×24' space per weekend. Reservations are recommended.
CONTACT	Manager, 4550 West University Drive, McKinney, TX 75070.
PHONE	(972) 542-7174
FAX	(972) 562-5466
E-MAIL	darrell@tmtd.com
WEB	www.tmtd.com

MERCEDES: Mercedes Flea Market

WHEN	Every weekend, 6:00 A.M. to 6:00 P.M. In operation since 1968.
WHERE	At the two-mile marker on Expressway 83, just west of town.
ADMISSION	Admission 25 per person; free parking for up to 400 cars; indoors and outdoors, rain or shine.
FEATURES	Antiques and collectibles, books, new and vintage clothing, coins and stamps, kitchenware, crafts, furniture, jewelry,

livestock, new and used merchandise, fresh produce, and toys. Averages close to 500 vendors. Snacks and hot meals are served on the premises. Billed as one of the oldest markets in the Rio Grande Valley, with an average total of 10,000 customers per weekend.

RATES $6 per shaded space on Saturday, $9 on Sunday; $4.50 per outdoor space on Saturday, $8 on Sunday. Reserve a week in advance.

CONTACT   Sylvia Villegas, Manager, 21 East Coma, Suite 115, Hidalgo, TX 78557.

PHONE   (956) 781-1911 weekend (956) 565-2751

FAX   (956) 787-8071

MIDLAND: Rankin Highway Flea Market

WHEN   Every weekend, 7:30 A.M. to 6:00 P.M, in summer, and 8:00 A.M. to 5:00 P.M. in winter. In operation since the 1980s.

WHERE   At 2840 Rankin Highway.

ADMISSION Free admission; limited free parking; indoors year-round and outdoors, weather permitting (some outdoor vendors will stay open in inclement weather).

FEATURES   Antiques and collectibles, new and vintage clothing, kitchenware, crafts, furniture, jewelry, new merchandise, and fresh produce. Averages 60 to 70 vendors. There is a snack bar on the premises.

RATES   Call for rates (100 indoor ministorage spaces are rented on a monthly basis). Reservations are not required.

CONTACT   Joseph or Joyce Romine, 2840 Rankin Highway, Midland, TX 79706.

PHONE   (915) 684-5060

SAN ANTONIO: Eisenhauer Road Flea Market

WHEN   Every day: Monday through Friday, noon to 7:00 P.M.; weekends, 9:00 A.M. to 7:00 P.M. In operation since the late 1970s.

WHERE   At 3903 Eisenhauer Road. Go west on Eisenhauer Road from 410 Loop or IH-35, down one mile on right.

ADMISSION	Free admission; ten acres of free parking; indoors daily, outdoors on weekends only.
FEATURES	Wide range of new and used merchandise, collectibles, jewelry, and fresh produce. Averages 200 to 300 vendors. Snacks and hot meals (including barbecue) are served on the premises. Two and a half acres under roof, air conditioned.
RATES	$15 per table outdoors on Saturday or Sunday, or $25 per week for an indoor table. Reservations are not required.
CONTACT	Pat Walker, 3903 Eisenhauer Road, San Antonio, TX 78218.
PHONE	(210) 653-7592
FAX	(210) 657-1692

SAN ANTONIO: Flea Mart San Antonio

WHEN	Every weekend, 10:00 A.M. to 6:00 P.M. In operation since 1987.
WHERE	At 12280 Highway 16 South, a mile and a half south of Loop 410.
ADMISSION	Admission $1 per person; parking for up to 2,000 cars at $1 per car; outdoors and under cover, rain or shine.
FEATURES	New and used merchandise and fresh produce. Averages 750 to a capacity of 950 vendors. Snacks and hot meals are served on the premises.
RATES	$40 per space per weekend. Reservations are not required.
CONTACT	Tom Browning, 12280 Highway 16 South, San Antonio, TX 78224-3028.
PHONE	(210) 624-2666

NFMA Member

SAN ANTONIO: Northwest Center Flea Market

WHEN	Every weekend, 8:00 A.M. to 5:00 P.M. In operation since the mid-1970s.
WHERE	At 3600 Fredericksburg Road.
ADMISSION	Free admission; free parking for up to 1,000 cars; indoors year-round and outdoors, weather permitting.
FEATURES	Antiques and collectibles, books, new and vintage clothing, kitchenware, crafts, furniture, jewelry, new and used merchandise, porcelain, fresh produce, and toys. Averages close

to 180 vendors. Snacks and hot meals are served on the premises. For the unusual.

RATES   From $14 per space per day (indoors or outdoors). Reservations are not required.

CONTACT   Jim Markwell, 3600 Fredericksburg Road, Suite 126, San Antonio, TX 78201.

PHONE   (210) 736-6655 or (210) 736-6677

SCHERTZ: Bussey's Flea Market

WHEN   Every weekend, 7:00 A.M. to 6:00 P.M. In operation for over sixteen years.

WHERE   At 18738 IH-35 North. Take exit 175 or 177 off I-35 north of San Antonio.

ADMISSION Free admission; parking for up to 1,500 cars at $1 per car; outdoors, rain or shine.

FEATURES Antiques and collectibles, books, new and vintage clothing, coins and stamps, kitchenware, crafts, furniture, jewelry, new and used merchandise, Mexican imports, fresh produce, and toys. Averages close to 500 vendors. Hot meals are available on the premises. Attracts as many as 5,000 shoppers on Saturdays and more than 13,000 on Sunday. ATM on the premises.

RATES $12 per space on Saturday, from $15 to $20 on Sundays. Reservations are required.

CONTACT   Harold J. Smith, 18738 IH-35 North, Schertz, TX 78154.

PHONE   (210) 651-6830

  NFMA Member

SEVEN POINTS: Big Daddy's Traders Market

WHEN   Every weekend, 8:00 A.M. to 6:00 P.M. In operation since 1990.

WHERE   On Highway 274, a mile-south of town (sixty miles east of Dallas and twenty miles south of Canton), near Cedar Creek Lake. Take Route 175 from Dallas east to Route 274 south at Kemp.

ADMISSION Free admission; four acres of free parking; mostly indoors (a few vendors outdoors), rain or shine.

FEATURES	Antiques and collectibles, books, new clothing, crafts, golf carts, jewelry, new and used merchandise, fresh produce, and toys. Averages 75 to 100 vendors. Snacks and hot meals are served on the premises. A heavily advertised market with about 50 percent new merchandise.
RATES	Indoors: $110 per 10'×20' space per month; under roof: $22 per weekend; outdoors: $10 per weekend. Reservations are recommended.
CONTACT	Jim Shafer, Manager, or Larry Hart, Owner, P.O. Box 43718, Seven Points, TX 75143.
PHONE	(903) 432-4911 or (903) 778-2887
FAX	(903) 778-2887
E-MAIL	shartlhart@aol.com

NFMA Member

WARRENTON: Bar W Antiques and Collectibles

WHEN	Twice a year, in April and September, daylight to dusk. In operation since 1996.
WHERE	Along the sides of Highway 237—stretching about three-quarters of a mile.
ADMISSION	Free admission; ample free parking; outdoors, rain or shine.
FEATURES	A variety of antiques, collectibles, and used merchandise. Averages 75 to 175 vendors. Food is served on the premises. Camping facilities are nearby.
RATES	Rates vary depending on location (spaces are 12'×20'). Reservations are recommended.
CONTACT	Roy Wied, Manager, P.O. Box 33, Warrenton, TX 78961.
PHONE	(409) 278-3447

WEATHERFORD: Crowder's First Monday Trade Grounds

WHEN	Every Friday, Saturday, and Sunday preceding the first Monday of every month, 7:00 A.M. to 7:00 P.M. In operation since 1892.
WHERE	At 405 Santa Fe Drive in downtown Weatherford, twenty-five miles west of Fort Worth. Take exit 409 off I-20 onto Clear Lake Road, which becomes Santa Fe Drive.

ADMISSION	Free admission; street parking nearby at $3 per car; outdoors, rain or shine.
FEATURES	Antiques and collectibles, books, new and vintage clothing, coins and stamps, kitchenware, crafts, furniture, jewelry, new merchandise, and fresh produce. Averages close to 200 vendors. Snacks and hot meals are served on the premises. An old-time, fun market with animals, antiques, and everything in between, located on five acres right next to the city's much larger Trade Days operation. Racetrack nearby.
RATES	$30 per 12'×25' space per weekend; plus $16 for electricity hookup; different rates for food vendors. Reservations are recommended; drop-ins are welcome if space is available.
CONTACT	Barbara Crowder, P.O. Box 1504, Weatherford, TX 76086.
PHONE	(817) 596-8586

WICHITA FALLS: Holliday Street Flea Market

WHEN	Every weekend, 7:00 A.M. to whenever. In operation for over thirty-two years.
WHERE	At 2820 Holliday Street, about three blocks west of Highway 287, in the south-central part of town near the Bank of Holliday Creek.
ADMISSION	Free admission; free parking for up to 1,000 cars; indoors and outdoors, rain or shine.
FEATURES	Antiques and collectibles, army surplus, books, new and vintage clothing, kitchenware, crafts, furniture, jewelry, fresh produce, toys, and used merchandise. Averages 150 to 210 vendors. Snacks and hot meals are served on the premises.
RATES	Under sheds; $10 per 12'×12' space per day; outdoors: $7 per 12'×30' space; electricity is available at an extra charge (some spaces require long extension cables for electrical hookup). Shed spaces by reservation; outdoor spaces on a first-come, first-served basis; seventy-five lockable booths are rented on a monthly basis. Vendors may arrive on Friday morning after 8:00 A.M.
CONTACT	Jim or Vivian Parish, 2820 Holliday Street, Wichita Falls, TX 76301.
PHONE	(940) 767-9038 or call Keith Parish at (940) 767-1712.

WINNIE: Larry's Old Time Trade Days

WHEN   Weekend following first Monday of every month, 7:00 A.M. to 7:00 P.M. In operation since 1992.

WHERE   At I-10 at Highway 1663; use exit 829, about twenty miles west of Beaumont.

ADMISSION   Admission $2 per carload; ample parking; indoors and outdoors, year-round.

FEATURES   Antiques and collectibles, new and used merchandise. There is also an antique pavilion. Averages 500 to 700 vendors. Twenty-five food concessions. Holiday Inn Express in the front parking lot.

RATES $30 per space 20'×20' per weekend. Reservations are not required.

CONTACT   Larry Tinkel, 14902 Highway 1663, Winnie, TX 77665.

PHONE   (409) 892-4000 or (409) 296-3300

FAX   (409) 296-3301

UTAH

See Appendix for Brief Listings

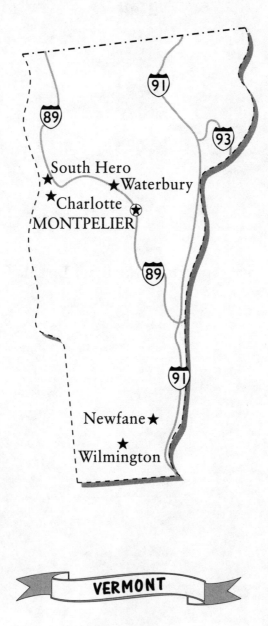

CHARLOTTE: Charlotte Flea Market

WHEN   Every weekend, from April through October, 6:00 A.M. to 6:00 P.M. In operation since around 1970.

WHERE   On Route 7, ten miles south of Burlington and ten miles north of Vergennes.

ADMISSION   Free admission; five acres of free parking; outdoors, rain or shine.

FEATURES   Antiques and collectibles, books, new and vintage clothing, coins and stamps, kitchenware, crafts, furniture, household items, jewelry, new and used merchandise, porcelain, and toys. Averages up to 100 vendors. Snacks and hot meals are served on the premises. Located in the lovely Champlain Valley.

RATES $10 per space per day, including three eight-foot tables. Reservations are not required.

CONTACT   Larry Lavalette, P.O. Box 415, Shelburne, VT 05482-0415.

PHONE   (802) 425-2844

NEWFANE: The Original Newfane Flea Market

WHEN   Every Sunday from mid-April through mid-November, daylight to whenever. In operation since 1967.

WHERE   On Route 30, thirteen miles north of Brattleboro, Vermont. Take exit 2 off I-91 and pick up Route 30 North.

ADMISSION   Free admission; five acres of free parking; outdoors, weather permitting.

FEATURES   Antiques and collectibles, books, new and vintage clothing, coins and stamps, kitchenware, crafts, furniture, jewelry, new and used merchandise, porcelain, fresh produce, and toys—"anything legal." Averages close to 100 vendors. "Simply delicious" snacks and hot meals are served on the premises. Vendors from all over the East Coast come to sell here; visit the large general store, too.

RATES $20 per van or car-length space per day; Saturday night camping is OK. Reservations are not required; just show up.

CONTACT   Bill or Mark Morse, P.O. Box 5, Newfane, VT 05345.

PHONE   (802) 365-4000 or (802) 365-7710 or (802) 365-7771 (on Sunday)

SOUTH HERO: South Hero Flea Market

WHEN	Every weekend plus holidays from Memorial Day through September, 8:00 A.M. to 4:00 P.M. In operation since around 1990.
WHERE	On Route 2.
ADMISSION	Free admission; ample free parking; indoors and outdoors, in summertime.
FEATURES	Collectibles, yard-sale items, and other used merchandise. Averages up to 50 vendors. Food is not served on the premises. A bit off the beaten path, but situated in a very scenic part of Lake Champlain. Ownership changed hands in 1999, and there may be some changes afoot.
RATES	From $7 per space per day outdoors; call for indoor rates. Reservations are not required.
CONTACT	Charles Langlois, 21 Curtis Street Avenue, Burlington, VT 05401.
PHONE	(802) 864-5091

WATERBURY: Waterbury Flea Market

WHEN	Every weekend and holidays from May through October, all day. In operation since the early 1970s.
WHERE	On Route 2, right off I-89 on the field by the two silos.
ADMISSION	Free admission; ample free parking; outdoors, weather permitting.
FEATURES	Antiques and collectibles, books, new and vintage clothing, crafts, furniture, household items, jewelry, new and used merchandise, fresh produce, and toys. Averages up to 75 vendors. Snacks are available on the premises. A good one, so long as the weather is friendly, and it sure is pretty in Waterbury.
RATES	$12 per 25'×25' space per day. Reservations are not required.
CONTACT	Reginald Erwin, 71 North Main Street, Waterbury, VT 05676.
PHONE	(802) 244-5916
FAX	(802) 244-1574

WILMINGTON: Wilmington Antique and Flea Market

WHEN	Every weekend plus holiday Mondays from mid-May through mid-October, all day. In operation since 1983.
WHERE	At the junction of Routes 100 and 9 East. Take exit 2 west off I-91 and go twenty-two miles west on Route 9; from Albany, take Route 7 East fifty miles to Bennington, and then go east on Route 9.
ADMISSION	Free admission; free parking for up to 200 cars; outdoors, weather permitting.
FEATURES	Antiques and collectibles, books, new and vintage clothing, coins and stamps, kitchenware, crafts, furniture, jewelry, new merchandise, porcelain, fresh produce, and toys. Averages up to 90 vendors. Caterer on the premises. Choice location with heavy east-west travel through southern Vermont. Bus groups welcome.
RATES	$15 per space per day. Reservations are not required.
CONTACT	The Gores, P.O. Box 22, Wilmington, VT 05363-0022.
PHONE	(802) 464-3345

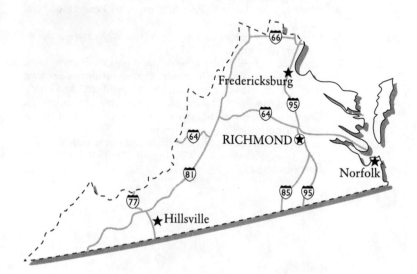

VIRGINIA

FREDERICKSBURG: Manor Mart Flea Market

WHEN	Every weekend, 7:00 A.M. to 4:00 P.M. In operation since 1983.
WHERE	On U.S. Highway 1, three miles south of Fredericksburg. Take the Massaponax exit off I-95 and go south two miles.
ADMISSION	Free admission; free parking for up to 250 cars; indoors year-round and outdoors, weather permitting.
FEATURES	Antiques and collectibles, books, new clothing, kitchenware, crafts, dolls, furniture, jewelry, NASCAR items, new and used merchandise, porcelain, fresh produce and grocery items, and toys. Averages up to 100 vendors. Snacks are available on the premises.
RATES	Indoors: $12 per space per day (includes table and shelf); outdoors: $10 for sixteen feet of frontage. Reservations are not required (space is always available).
CONTACT	Nick Dommisse, 10307 Bedford Court, Fredericksburg, VA 22408-2580.
PHONE	(540) 898-4685

HILLSVILLE: VFW Flea Market

WHEN	Annually, on Labor Day and the preceding Friday, Saturday, and Sunday, 8:00 A.M. to 6:00 P.M. In operation for over thirty-one years.
WHERE	At the VFW Complex, 701 West Stuart Drive, one mile off I-77 exit 14 (Hillsville exit) on Route 221.
ADMISSION	Admission $1 per person; free admission for children under 12; parking at $3 per car or $10 per RV; indoors and outdoors, rain or shine.
FEATURES	Antiques and collectibles, new and vintage clothing, crafts, jewelry, new merchandise, and firearms. Averages up to a capacity of 900 vendors. Snacks and hot meals are served on the premises. Run by the VFW Grover King Post 1115. There is a large gun show held along with the flea market. ATM machine, public phones on the premises.
RATES	$55 per 9'×20' space, with town license. Reserve at least a year in advance; there may be a waiting list.
CONTACT	Joseph B. Semones, 2421 Airport Road, Hillsville, VA 24343-8581.

PHONE   (703) 728-7188; day of market call (703) 728-2911; for information about the gun show, call (703) 728-9810.

NORFOLK: The Flea Market of Norfolk

WHEN   Every weekend, from 7:00 A.M. to whenever. In operation since 1989.
WHERE   At 3416 North Military Highway, near the airport.
ADMISSION   Free admission; free parking for up to 250 cars; indoors and outdoors, rain or shine.
FEATURES   Full spectrum of antiques and collectibles, new and used merchandise, new and vintage clothing, kitchenware, crafts, and fresh produce; specialities include dolls, electronics, records, CDs, videos, rugs, army suplus, auto parts and accessories, and sporting goods. Averages 100 to 300 vendors. Snacks and hot meals are served on the premises. Claims to be the largest indoor/outdoor flea market in the Norfolk–Virginia Beach area.
RATES $10 per table per day; call for monthly rates. Reservations are on a first-come, first-served basis.
CONTACT   Robert L. Ingram, 3416 North Military Highway, Norfolk, VA 23518.
PHONE   (757) 857-7824 or (757) 855-3331
FAX   (757) 853-8393

RICHMOND: Bellwood Flea Market

WHEN   Every weekend, 5:30 A.M. to 4:30 P.M. In operation since 1970.
WHERE   At 9201 Jefferson Davis Highway, at Willis Road, at the drive-in theater. Take exit 64 off I-95 south of Richmond.
ADMISSION   Admission $1 per person; free parking for up to 1,200 cars; outdoors, weather permitting.
FEATURES   Antiques and collectibles, books, new and vintage clothing, coins and stamps, kitchenware, crafts, furniture, jewelry, new and used merchandise, porcelain, fresh produce, and toys. Averages 100 to 300 vendors. Snacks and hot meals are served on the premises.

RATES $14 per 20'×20' space per day. Reservations are not required.

CONTACT Belinda Riddle or Julie Campbell, 9201 Jefferson Davis Highway, Richmond, VA 23237.

PHONE (800) 793-0707 or (804) 275-1187

RICHMOND: Superflea

WHEN Every weekend, 9:00 A.M. to 6:00 P.M. In operation since 1988.

WHERE At 5501 Midlothian Turnpike, a mile east of Chippenham Parkway.

ADMISSION Free admission; paved, free parking for 1,000 cars; indoors and outdoors, rain or shine.

FEATURES New and used merchandise (including computers and electronics) and "outlet" stuff. Averages 250 to a capacity of 355 vendors. Food is served on the premises. Over 100,000 square feet of display area.

RATES $210 per 10'×12' booth per month, $165 per 6'×12' booth; table setups at $15 per day ($25 for two). Reservations are on a first-come, first-served basis.

CONTACT Kathy Freiburger or Fred, 5501 Midlothian Turnpike, Richmond, VA 23225.

PHONE (804) 233-2512 or (804) 231-6687

FAX (804) 231-3170

E-MAIL ppns0010@aol.com

 NFMA Member

Seattle

OLYMPIA

WASHINGTON

SEATTLE: Fremont Sunday Market

WHEN	Every Sunday, 10:00 A.M. to 5:00 P.M. In operation since 1989.
WHERE	At the corner of Evanston Avenue and North 34th, in the central parking lot behind the Red Door Tavern by the Fremont Bridge, about a mile north of the Space Needle.
ADMISSION	Free admission; free parking; indoors year-round and outdoors from May through October, weather permitting.
FEATURES	Used merchandise, crafts, used furniture, jewelry, treasures and collectibles, and fresh produce. Averages 120 to a capacity of 175 vendors. Snacks and hot meals are served on the premises.
RATES	$25 per space per day for flea market items, $25 for crafts and imports. Reservations are not required except in December (Christmas season).
CONTACT	John Hegeman, Manager, or Marcia Hunt, Member Coordinator, 3416 Evanston, Seattle, WA 98103.
PHONE	(206) 781-6776 or (206) 784-2753
E-MAIL	jon@hotmail.com
WEB	www.fremarket.com

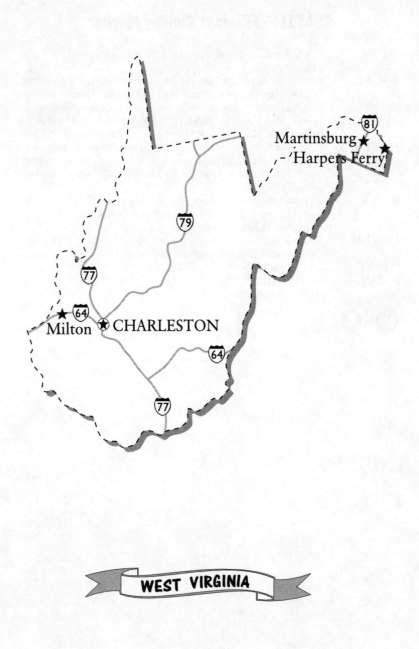

WEST VIRGINIA

CHARLESTON: Capitol Flea Market

WHEN	Every Friday, Saturday, and Sunday, 8:00 A.M. to 5:00 P.M. In operation since 1991.
WHERE	Near the Capitol High School. Take exit 99 off I-64, or the Greenbrier (State Capitol and Airport) exit off I-77, then proceed 3.6 miles on Route 114 South; or take exit 5 (Big Chimney exit) off I-79, then go 3.6 miles on Route 114 South.
ADMISSION	Free admission; paved parking for up to 500 cars; indoors and outdoors, year-round.
FEATURES	Wide range of new and used merchandise. Averages 100 to 250 vendors. Hot meals are available on the premises. Tour buses welcome.
RATES	$31 per 10'×14' space for three days. Reserve approximately three weeks in advance.
CONTACT	Frances Brown, 24 Meadow Brook Plaza, Charleston, WV 25311.
PHONE	(304) 342-1626
FAX	(304) 342-1339

HARPERS FERRY: Harpers Ferry Flea Market

WHEN	Every weekend from mid-March through October, dawn to dusk. In operation since 1983.
WHERE	On the site of the former Fort Drive-In, on Route 340, Dual Highway, one mile past the entrance to Harpers Ferry National Park, on the left. One hour from Washington, D.C.; take Route 270 North to Frederick, then pick up Route 340 West.
ADMISSION	Free admission; five acres of free parking; outdoors, rain or shine.
FEATURES	Antiques and collectibles, yard-sale stuff, new and vintage clothing, coins and stamps, kitchenware, crafts, furniture, jewelry, and new merchandise. Averages 140 to 200 vendors. Snacks and hot meals are served on the premises. Nicknamed "the Outdoor Mall" and billed as the largest flea market in the area. In a tourist area near a national park, horse and car racing, whitewater rafting, fishing, hiking on the Appalachian Trail, biking along the C & O Canal, nearby antiques shops, etc.
RATES	$11 per space per day; electricity is available at $3 per day. Reservations are not required.

CONTACT   Ron Nowell or Dan Barnett, 904 Oregon Trail, Harpers
          Ferry, WV 25425.
PHONE   (304) 725-0092 (Dan) or (304) 725-4141 (Ron); day of mar-
          ket call Ron or Dan at (304) 535-2575.

MARTINSBURG: I-81 Flea Market

WHEN   Every Friday, Saturday, and Sunday, plus selected holiday
           Mondays, 8:00 A.M. to 5:00 P.M. In operation since the
           1980s.
WHERE   On Route 11 at Spring Mills Road. Take exit 20 off I-81, go
           east to Route 11, then go right approximately 2,000 feet and
           market will be on the right.
ADMISSION Free admission; ample free parking; outdoors, weather per-
           mitting. (The market lost its indoor space to fire in 1995.)
FEATURES   Antiques and collectibles, books, new and vintage clothing,
           coins and stamps, kitchenware, crafts, furniture, jewelry,
           new merchandise, porcelain, fresh produce, and toys.
           Averages 125 to 250 vendors. Hot meals (including soups),
           sandwiches, and grocery items.
RATES $5 per 8'×12' table (provided) on Friday, $11 on Saturday or
           Sunday. Reservations are recommended.
CONTACT   Sam Pannuty or Betty Kline, Route 2, Box 230,
           Martinsburg, WV 25401.
PHONE   (304) 274-1313 or (304) 274-3387

MILTON: Milton Flea Market

WHEN   Every Friday, Saturday, and Sunday, 8:00 A.M. to 5:00 P.M.
           In operation since 1989.
WHERE   At 1215 U.S. Route 60, a half mile east of Milton and one
           mile from the Milton exit off I-64.
ADMISSION Free admission; free parking for up to 500 cars; indoors and
           outdoors, rain or shine.
FEATURES   Antiques and collectibles, books, new clothing, crafts, furni-
           ture, jewelry, new merchandise, fresh produce, and toys.
           Averages up to a capacity of 300 vendors. Snacks and sand-
           wiches are available on the premises.
RATES $8 per 10'×20' space outdoors under shed per weekend, or

$6 per space in open air. Reservations are not required for outdoor spaces; waiting list for indoor spaces.

CONTACT Boyd L. Meadows, P.O. Box 549, Milton, WV 25541.
PHONE (304) 743-1123 or (304) 743-9862

NFMA Member

★Hayward

★Ladysmith
★
Saint Croix Falls

Shawano★

★Adams

MADISON ★
Mukwonago★   Milwaukee
Elkhorn★   ★
      Caledonia

WISCONSIN

ADAMS: Adams Flea Market

WHEN	Weekends, May through October plus Memorial Day, July Fourth, and Labor Day, 6:00 A.M. to 4:00 P.M. In operation since 1981.
WHERE	At 556 South Main (Highway 13), twenty-five miles north of Wisconsin Dells.
ADMISSION	Free admission; free parking for up to 400 cars; indoors and outdoors, rain or shine.
FEATURES	A good mixture of antiques and collectibles, new and vintage clothing, furniture, hardware, household items, jewelry, and produce. Averages close to 75 vendors. Hot and cold sandwiches, soda, coffee, and snacks on the premises. This is a growing market with a country look and a friendly atmosphere.
RATES	From $7 to $10 per day for one table (provided) or from $14 for two tables, but no limit on size of space; also yearly rentals of inside space. Reservations are not required.
CONTACT	Irene Steffen, 2151 State Highway 13, Adams, WI 53910-9711.
PHONE	(608) 339-3192; day of market call Irene Steffen at (608) 339-9223.
FAX	(608) 339-3079

CALEDONIA: Seven-Mile Fair Flea Market

WHEN	Every weekend, plus holidays. Summer hours (April through October): 7:00 A.M. to 5:00 P.M.; winter hours (November through March): 9:00 A.M. to 5:00 P.M.
WHERE	At 2720 West Seven Mile Road at intersection of I-94 (use Seven Mile Road exit), fifteen miles south of Milwaukee and twenty-five miles north of the Illinois state line.
ADMISSION	Admission $1.25 per person; free parking; indoors and outdoors, year-round.
FEATURES	Antiques and collectibles, crafts, new and used merchandise, and fresh produce—"everything under the sun." Averages up to several hundred vendors. Restaurant on the premises. Billed as the granddaddy of all indoor and outdoor flea markets.
RATES	Outdoors: free on Friday, $10 on Saturday, and $15 on Sunday or holidays for a regular 12'×24' space (one vehicle or trailer allowed per space). Reservations are on a first-come, first-served basis.

CONTACT   Manager, P.O. Box 7, Caledonia, WI 53108.
PHONE   (414) 835-2177
FAX   (414) 835-2968

NFMA Member

ELKHORN: Antique Flea Market

WHEN   Five events a year, in May, June, July, August, and
            September, 7:00 A.M. to 3:00 P.M. In operation since 1981.
WHERE   At the Walworth County Fairgrounds on Highway 11 East.
ADMISSION   Admission $2 per person; children are admitted free; ample
            free parking; indoors and outdoors, rain or shine.
FEATURES   Antiques and collectibles only. Averages 500 to 700 vendors.
            Food is available on the premises. This is a big market and a
            good one for collectibles, and vendors come from all over.
RATES   Call for rates. Reservations are recommended.
CONTACT   Manager, c/o N. L. Promotions, P.O. Box 544, Elkhorn, WI
            53121.
PHONE   (414) 723-5651

HAYWARD: Hayward Fame Flea Market

WHEN   Every Tuesday and Wednesday from June through August,
            9:00 A.M. to 3:00 P.M.; added weekend dates in summer
            months (call for dates). In operation since 1978.
WHERE   At the junction of Highway 27 South and County Highway
            B, across from the National Fishing Hall of Fame.
ADMISSION   Free admission; free parking; indoors and outdoors, weather
            permitting.
FEATURES   Antiques and collectibles, new and used merchandise, and
            fresh produce. Averages 50 to a capacity of 85 vendors.
            Snacks and hot meals are served on the premises.
RATES $8 per 12'×25' space per day. Reservations are recom-
            mended.
CONTACT   Jan Thiry, 10556 N. Sunnyside Avenue, Hayward, WI
            54843.
PHONE   (715) 634-4794

LADYSMITH: Van Wey's Community Auction and Flea Market

WHEN   Several weekends plus Memorial Day, July Fourth, and Labor Day weekends (call for dates), 6:30 A.M. to whenever; auction begins at 10:00 A.M. In operation since 1926; the auction has been running since the mid-1970s.

WHERE   At W-10139 Van Wey Lane, on Highway 8, four miles west of Ladysmith (or four miles east of Bruce).

ADMISSION Free admission; parking for over 1,000 cars at 50¢ per car; indoors and outdoors, rain or shine.

FEATURES Antiques and collectibles, books, new and vintage clothing, kitchenware, crafts, furniture, jewelry, new merchandise, porcelain, fresh produce, toys, and "many other items too numerous to mention." Averages up to 100 vendors. Snacks (French fries, hot sandwiches, etc.) are available at a coffee shop on the premises. This family-owned business, now in its third generation, calls itself the "flea market capital of the northland" and claims to be the biggest flea market and consignment auction in the state.

RATES $8 per 12'×30' space per day. Rentals are on a first-come, first-served basis; consignment items are accepted until noon of the preceding day.

CONTACT   Mark or Judy Van Wey, W-10139 Van Wey Lane, Ladysmith, WI 54848.

PHONE   (715) 532-6044

MILWAUKEE: Rummage-O-Rama

WHEN   Generally thirteen weekends per year, in all months except June through August, 10:00 A.M. to 5:00 P.M.—call for dates. In operation since 1974.

WHERE   At the State Fair Park, 84th Street and Greenfield Avenue, just south of I-94 at 84th Street exit (exit 306).

ADMISSION Admission $1.75 per person; discounts for seniors and children; acres of free parking (75,000-car capacity); indoors, year-round.

FEATURES Antiques and collectibles, new clothing, books, coins and stamps, crafts, porcelain, fresh produce, spices, closeouts, vacuum cleaners and supplies, jewelry, school and office supplies, household items, toys for all ages, pet supplies, and tools. Averages up to 500 vendors. Snacks and hot meals are served on the premises. Claims to be Wisconsin's only (and the Midwest's largest) "high-class" indoor flea market. Average attendance is 14,000 to 19,000 per weekend. Well advertised. Motels and camping facilities are nearby. Police protection of vendors' property left on grounds over Friday and Saturday nights.

RATES
From $68 to $84 per 10'×10' space per weekend; tables are extra. Reserve at least a month in advance; spaces are reserved on a first-paid basis.

CONTACT
Walter Rasner, P.O. Box 510619, New Berlin, WI 53151.

PHONE
(414) 521-2111

MUKWONAGO: Maxwell Street Days

WHEN
The second weekend in June and September and the third weekend in July and August, 8:00 A.M. to 5:00 P.M. In operation since the 1950s.

WHERE
At Field Park, with entrances on Highway 83 and Highway "NN." Take I-43 to Highway 83 North to the north end of the village, located in the southwest corner of Waukesha County.

ADMISSION
Free admission; parking for more than 1,000 at up to $3 per car; outdoors, weather permitting.

FEATURES
Antiques and collectibles, books, new clothing, kitchenware, crafts, used furniture, jewelry, fresh produce, toys, and used merchandise. Averages close to its capacity of 685 vendors. Snacks and hot meals are served on the premises. Sponsored by the American Legion.

RATES
$33 per space per two-day event. Reserve two weeks in advance.

CONTACT
Mukwonago Community American Legion Post #375, P.O. Box 152, Mukwonago, WI 53149-0152.

PHONE
(414) 363-2003

SAINT CROIX FALLS: Pea Pickin' Flea Market

WHEN
Every weekend (plus holidays) from the third weekend in April through the third weekend in October, 6:00 A.M. to 5:00 P.M. In operation since the late 1960s.

WHERE
On Highway 8 East, five miles east of Saint Croix Falls (fifty

miles northeast of Twin Cities, Minnesota). Take Highway 35W North to Highway 8 East.

ADMISSION Free admission; free parking for up to 300 cars; indoors year-round and outdoors, weather permitting.

FEATURES Antiques and collectibles, books, new and vintage clothing, kitchenware, crafts, used furniture, jewelry, new merchandise, toys, fresh produce, frozen meats, sausage, cheese, and honey. Averages up to 75 vendors. Snacks and hot meals are served on the premises.

RATES $9 per twelve-foot frontage for one day (with room to park vehicle in space); vendors may stay overnight on weekends. Reservations are recommended one week in advance from June through August.

CONTACT Steve D. Hansen, 1938 Little Blake Lane, Luck, WI 54853.

PHONE (715) 857-5479 or (715) 483-9460

SHAWANO: Shawano Flea Market

WHEN Every Sunday, April through October, 6:00 A.M. to 5:00 P.M. Two added Saturdays in May and July; special three-day market on Memorial Day weekend. In operation since 1972.

WHERE At the Shawano County Fairgrounds on Highway 29/47, half an hour west of Green Bay.

ADMISSION Admission $1 per person; free parking for 1,500 cars; outdoors, rain or shine.

FEATURES Antiques and collectibles, baseball cards, books, bottles, coins and stamps, comics, old toys, kitchenware, crafts, used furniture, jewelry, knives, porcelain, and fresh produce. About 80 percent antiques and collectibles. Averages 150 to 200 vendors. Snacks and hot meals are served on the premises. Northeast Wisconsin's largest weekly flea market.

RATES $21 per day for twenty-foot frontage; discount on sellers' space in April. Reservations are recommended.

CONTACT Bob Zurko, Zurko's Midwest Promotions, 211 West Green Bay Street, Shawano, WI 54166.

PHONE (715) 526-9769

FAX (715) 524-5675

E-MAIL vatabat@aol.com

WEB www.zurkoantiquetours.com

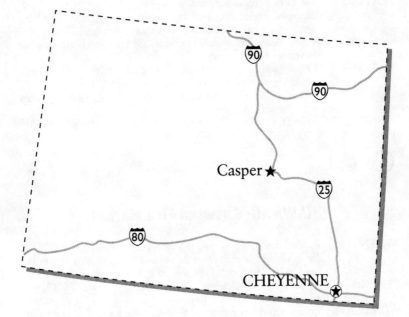

Casper ★

CHEYENNE ★

WYOMING

CASPER: Casper Super Flea

WHEN Two events in August and mid-November (call for dates; smaller events in June and October), Saturday, 10:00 A.M. to 5:00 P.M., and Sunday, 10:00 A.M. to 4:00 P.M. In operation since 1974.

WHERE At the Central Wyoming Fairgrounds on Route 220 in the southwest part of the city. Come in via Cy Avenue.

ADMISSION Admission 50¢ per person; ample free parking; indoors, rain or shine.

FEATURES Antiques and collectibles of all kinds plus various new and used merchandise. Averages close to 50 vendors. Snacks and hot meals are served on the premises. Sponsored by Casper Antique and Collectors Club; claims to be the largest in Wyoming.

RATES $20 per table per event. Reserve several months in advance; there may be a waiting list.

CONTACT Bruce B. Smith, 1625 South Kenwood Street, Casper, WY 82601-4049.

PHONE (307) 234-6663

Appendix: Brief Listings

Alabama

Attalla: Mountain Top Flea Market. Every Sunday. At 11301 U.S. Highway 278 West, six miles west of Attalla. Free admission; indoors and outdoors. Averages up to 1,000 vendors. Draws nearly 2 million visitors annually. Contact Janie Terrell at (800) 535-2286 (reservation office hours are Monday, 12:30 P.M. to 4:00 P.M. and Tuesday, 8:00 A.M. to 4:00 P.M. E-mail: mtopflea@hopper.net. Web: www.lesdeal.com. NFMA member.

Birmingham: Farmers Flea Market. Daily. At 344 Finley Avenue West, at Fourth Street. Take Finley Avenue exit off I-65 North (between Montgomery and Nashville). Free admission; indoors year-round and outdoors. Averages 40 to 60 vendors year-round (capacity 30 indoors plus 25 outdoors). Contact Cathy Cwine at (205) 254-9852 or (205) 251-8737, ext. 13.

Birmingham: Jefferson County Farmers Market. Daily. At 344 Finley Avenue West. Contact Danny Jones, Manager, at (205) 251-8737.

Dothan: Jed's Country Mall and Flea Market. Every Friday, Saturday, and Sunday. Highway 231, ten miles south of Dothan and three miles north of the Alabama–Florida state line. Free admission; indoors and outdoors. Averages 75 to 100 vendors (capacity 138 indoor booths plus 46 acres outdoors). Formerly J. Hooter's. Market is now developing several specialty shops. Contact Jim Easterly at (334) 677-7234.

Elmore: Elmore Flea Market. Every Thursday through Sunday. On Route 143. Contact Marty Greer at (334) 567-7731.

Foley: Foley Flea Market. Every Friday, Saturday, and Sunday. On Highway 59, fifteen miles south of I-10. Free admission; indoors and outdoors. Averages up to a capacity of 195 vendors. Contact Pam Harding, Manager, at (334) 943-6349.

Guntersville: All-American Trade Day. Every weekend. At 11190 U.S. Highway 431, between Albertville and Guntersville. Free admission; indoors, outdoors, and under cover. Averages 400 to 700 vendors (capacity over 800). Well advertised with over 30,000 shoppers daily. Contact Margaret Parks at (256) 891-2790.

Hammondville: I-59 Flea Market. Every weekend. On I-59, at exit 231 (Hammondville/Valley Head), ten miles north of Fort Pine and forty miles south of Chattanooga. Free admission. Averages up to its capacity of 386 vendors on fifty-two acres. Call (256) 635-6899.

Killen: Uncle Charlie's Flea Market. Every weekend (plus Labor Day and the Friday after Thanksgiving). On Highway 72 West, thirty miles west of Athens and seven miles east of Florence, Alabama. Exit off I-65 Highway 72. Free admission; indoors year-round and outdoors. Averages 100 to 150 vendors (capacity 200). Contact Tom Mabry at (800) 542-2848 or (256) 757-2256.

Lookout Mountain: World's Longest Flea Market. Annually in August. Runs along Route 127 for 350 miles. Free admission; outdoors. Vendors line the road for miles. Contact Lloyd Wagnon at (256) 549-0351.

Phenix City: Valley Flea and Farmers Market. Every weekend. At 3864 U.S. Highway 80 West. Free admission; indoors, outdoors, and under cover. Averages 100 to 155 vendors. Acres and acres of bargains at this market, which is under new management as of the late 1990s. Call (334) 298-728.

Scottsboro: First Monday Trade Day. First Monday of every month and the preceding Sunday. On the courthouse square; use Routes 72 and 79 to downtown Scottsboro. Free admission; outdoors. Averages 250 to 500 vendors. Contact Gayle Moore at (256) 574-4468 (office hours are Monday through Friday, 8:00 A.M. to 4:30 P.M.).

Tuscaloosa: Tuscaloosa County Flea Market. Every Friday, Saturday, and Sunday. On Kicker Road (call for directions). Free admission; indoors. Averages up to a few dozen vendors. Contact Orman L. Corbin at (205) 533-9206 or (205) 556-2113.

Westover: Westover Flea Market. Every Friday, Saturday, and Sunday. At 12000 Highway 280. Call (205) 678-6729.

Arizona

Glendale: Glendale 9 Drive-in Swap Meet. Every weekend. At 5650 North 55th Avenue (western part of Phoenix) at Bethany Home Road. Admission 50¢ per person or carload; outdoors. Averages 110 to 300 vendors (capacity 450). Call (602) 931-0877 or (602) 939-9715; for the main office in San Francisco, call (415) 448-8400.

Kingman: Historic Route 66 Flea Market. Every Friday, Saturday, and Sunday. On Historic Route 66, three miles off I-40 on Eastbound 66. Free admission; outdoors. Averages 50 to 80 vendors. Smallish, but maybe worth a pass. Call (520) 692-1428.

Phoenix: Indoor Swap Mart. Every Friday, Saturday, and Sunday. At 5115 North 27th Avenue. Admission $1 per person; indoors. Averages close to 500 vendors. Contact Michelle Leslie at (602) 246-9600.

Quartzsite: The Main Event. Shops open daily year-round, but the "Main Event" spans three weekends (sixteen days) every year—generally the last two weeks of January (call for dates). On I-10, milepost 17 in La Paz County. Free admission; outdoors and under cover. Averages up to a capacity of 1,500 vendors during the "Main Event." Quartzsite's "Annual Gemboree," one of the largest flea markets in the country (and probably the largest gem show), attracts over a million visitors. Contact Howard or Marilyn Armstrong at (520) 927-5213.

Scottsdale: Scottsdale Swap Meet. Every weekend. At 8101 East McKellips, on the corner of Hayden at the Scottsdale Drive-in Theatre. Free admission; outdoors. Averages 50 to 150 vendors (capacity 300). Call (602) 994-3709.

Surprise: Surprise Swap Meet. Every Thursday. At 12910 Santa Fe Drive, across the railroad tracks from Grand Avenue (Highways 60 and 89), east of Dysart Road. Free admission; indoors and outdoors. Averages close to 300 vendors (capacity 350). Contact R. Vukanovich at (602) 583-616.

Tucson: Marketplace U.S.A. Every Friday. At 3750 East Irvington Road. Take exit 264-B off I-10. Free admission; indoors. Averages 50 to 400 vendors during special events (gun shows, gem shows, etc.—call for details and dates). Call (520) 745-5000.

Yuma: Avenue 3-E Swap Meet. Every Thursday through Sunday from September through April. At 4151 South Avenue 3-E. Admission 25¢ per person; outdoors. Averages 3 to 250 vendors. Call (520) 344-2399.

Arkansas

Eureka Springs: Front Porch Antiques and Collectibles. Daily. At 5579 Highway 23 North. Free admission; indoors. Averages close to 22 vendors. Run by the owner of the former Old Town Flea Market, this is on the antiques-mall end of the flea market spectrum, with long-term dealers only. Call (501) 253-6557.

Fort Smith: Fort Smith Flea Market. Every Friday, Saturday, and Sunday. At 3721 Towson Avenue. Free admission. Call (501) 646-0410 or (501) 698-9909.

Greenbrier: Springhill Flea Market. Daily. On Highway 65, just north of the intersection of Routes 65 and 287. Take exit 125 off I-40 at Conway, then go north seven miles to market (on the east side of the highway, on the way to Branson, MO). Free admission; indoors and outdoors. Averages 12 to 25 vendors (capacity from 50 to 75). Contact Bill R. Wisler at (501) 679-9106.

Hot Springs: Snow Springs Flea Market. Every Friday, Saturday, and Sunday, plus any holidays that fall on Thursday or Monday. At 3628 Park Avenue, two miles from the intersection of Route 5 and Highway 7 North (five miles from downtown). Free admission; outdoors. Averages 15 to 50 vendors (capacity more than 60). Contact J. L. Long at (501) 624-7469 (624-SHOW).

Little Rock: Carrie's Flea Market. Every Monday through Saturday. At 8717 Geyer Springs Road. Averages close to its capacity of more than 600 vendors on 76,000 square feet of selling area. Contact Henrietta Grainger at (501) 562-8088 or (501) 562-1019. NFMA member.

Little Rock: Little Rock Expo. Weekends of the second and fourth Saturdays of each month. At 13000 I-30. From Memphis, take I-40 to I-30 to exit 128, then continue west one mile, and market will be on the right. From Texarkana, take I-30 to exit 126 crossover, then continue east, and market will be on the left. Admission $1 per person; indoors and outdoors. Averages 200 to 300 vendors (capacity 800). "The big one." Contact Jim Hembree, General Manager, at (501) 455-1001 or (501) 455-1646. E-mail: ppns0010@aol.com. NFMA member.

Pleasant Plains: Pleasant Plains Flea Market. Every Friday, Saturday, and Sunday. On Highway 167, fifteen miles south of Batesville and eighteen miles north of Bald Knob. Free admission; outdoors and under cover. Averages 40 to a capacity of 65 vendors. Call (501) 345-2720 or (870) 668-3434.

Rogers: Rose Antique Mall. Daily. At 2875 West Walnut (Highway 71). Free admission; indoors. Averages close to 150 vendors. Call (501) 631-8940.

Springdale: Discount Corner Flea Market Mall. Daily. At 418 East Emma, across from Layman's. Free admission. This "flea market mall" doesn't have multiple sellers but they put out other people's stuff for sale. Call (501) 756-0764.

Springdale: Oak Grove Flea Market. Every weekend. At the corner of Elm Springs and Oak Grove Roads. From Springdale, turn to Huntsville, approximately four miles on left. From Route 71 Bypass, take Elm Springs exit and turn left, then go approximately one-half mile, and market will be on the left. Free admission; indoors and outdoors. Averages 50 to 75 vendors. Contact Ramona or Bob Wallis at (501) 756-0697.

West Memphis: West Memphis Flea Market. Every Thursday through Sunday. At 512 East Broadway. Easy access from I-55 or I-40. Take Seventh Street to Broadway, then right on Broadway about two blocks and market is on the right. Free admission; indoors and outdoors. Averages close to 60 vendors. Call (870) 735-9332 or (870) 735-1644.

California

Anaheim: Anaheim Swap Meet. Every weekend. At 1520 North Lemon Street, off the 91 Freeway. Admission $1 per person. Call (714) 680-0986.

Antioch: Antioch Trader Jack's Swap Meet. Every Friday, Saturday, and Sunday. At 10th and L. Free admission. Averages 125 to 150 vendors (capacity 210). New management. Call (510) 778-6900 or (925) 706-0502.

Arlington: Van Buren Cinema Three Swap Meet. Every Thursday, Saturday, and Sunday. At 3035 Van Buren Boulevard, a half mile south of the 91 Freeway. Admission 50¢ per person (free on Thursday); outdoors. Call (909) 688-2829 or (909) 688-2360 (drive-in).

Bakersfield: Pacific Theater Swap-O-Rama. Every Sunday. At 4501 Wible Road. Admission 75¢ per person; outdoors. Averages up to 350 vendors. Contact Gary Rollins, Manager, at (661) 831-9346.

Bloomington: Bel-Air Swap Meet. Every weekend. On Valley Boulevard. Admission 50¢ per person. Call (909) 875-3000.

Campbell: Second Saturday Flea Market. Second Saturday of every month. At 1769 South Winchester Boulevard, at the Campbell Center. Take the Hamilton exit off Highway 880, then west approximately four blocks to Winchester Boulevard, then left, and go half a block on the right at the shopping center. Free admission; outdoors. Averages 50 to 70 vendors (capacity 80). Friendly and clean atmosphere; many of the vendors have been selling at the market for years. Contact Karl H. Miller at (408) 374-1415 or (408) 370-2144.

Canoga Park: Valley Indoor Swap Meet. Every Friday, Saturday, and Sunday. At 6701 Variel Avenue. Admission $1 per person; indoors. Call (818) 340-9120.

Chico: Silver Dollar Swap Meet. Every weekend (except when the fairgrounds are in use—call for dates). At the Silver Dollar Fairgrounds, at Fair Street and Park. Free admission; indoors. Averages up to 50 vendors. Formerly known as Cal's Flea Market. Call (530) 892-9205.

Clearlake: Clearlake Flea Market. Every Friday, Saturday, and Sunday. At 16080 Davis Street, off Highway 53. Follow the County Landfill signs off Highway 53 to Davis Street. Free admission; indoors and outdoors. Averages close to 75 to 100 vendors year-round (capacity 125 on an acre and a half, including 35 permanent indoor shops). Under new ownership—"largest shopping village and flea market in Lake County." Contact Beatrice or Leslie at (707) 998-3522.

Clovis: Old Town Clovis Nostalgic Peddlers Fair. Three days a year, in spring and fall around the end of March and the beginning of October (call for dates). In downtown Clovis (east of Fresno). Take Herndon exit off southbound Highway 99, then east to Clovis Avenue; northbound, use Clovis Avenue exit, then north to downtown Clovis. Free admission; outdoors. Averages close to 250 vendors (capacity 350). An antiques and collectibles street fair sponsored by the Business Organization of Old Town. "If you collect anything, you should be here." Contact Dick Clarke at (559) 683-2537.

Concord: Solano Flea Market. Every weekend. At 1611 Solano Way, at the junction of Highway 4. Admission 25¢ on Saturday, $1 on Sunday. Averages up to several hundred vendors. Thousands of shoppers show up for this one. Call (925) 687-6445 or (925) 825-1951.

Daly City: Doelger Senior Center Flea Market. Second Sunday of the month from June through October. At 101 Lake Merced Boulevard. Averages 50 to 75 vendors. Benefits the Senior Center. Call (650) 991-8012.

Escondido: Escondido Swap Meet. Every Wednesday through Sunday. At 635 West Mission Avenue. Take I-15 to Valley Parkway East, then left on Quince, then left onto Mission. Admission 50¢ on Wednesday, free on Thursday, 75¢ on Saturday, $1 on Sunday; indoors and outdoors. Contact Lee Porter at (760) 745-3100.

Eureka: Redwood Flea Market. Approximately fifteen weekends spread throughout each year (call for dates). At 3750 Harris Street, in the main Exhibit Building at the fairgrounds. Admission 25¢; free for children age twelve and under; indoors. Averages 80 to 125 vendors (capacity 150). Contact Larry or Amanda Plant at (707) 839-3049 or (707) 442-8770.

Folsom: Annual Peddlers Faire and Flea Market. Every September (call for dates). On Sutter Street. Free admission; outdoors. Call (916) 985-7452.

Fresno: Sunnyside Swap Meet. Every weekend. At the Sunnyside Drive-in, at 5550 East Olive Street. Admission 25¢ per person on Sunday, free on

Saturday; outdoors. Averages close to 300 vendors. Their motto is "People pleasing people." Call (559) 255-7469 (255-SHOW).

Galt: Galt Wholesale/Retail Flea Market. Every Wednesday. At 890 Caroline Avenue. Take the Central Galt exit off Highway 99, turn left on Fairway and follow the green signs to the market, with entrances off Caroline and Chabolla. Free admission; outdoors. Averages close to its capacity of 860 vendors year-round. Contact City of Galt at (209) 745-2437 (enter 0 at the tape) or (209) 745-4695 (City Hall).

Huntington Beach: Golden West College Swap Meet. Every weekend. On Golden West Street, a mile south of the 405 Freeway, in the parking lot. Free admission; outdoors. Call (714) 898-2289 (898-2BUY) or (714) 898-7927 (898-SWAP) or (714) 895-9737.

King City: King City Rotary Annual Swap Meet. Annually, the first Sunday in April or the last Sunday in March. On the Salinas Valley Fairgrounds, at 626 Division. Admission $2 per person; indoors and outdoors. Contact Diane Schabel at (831) 385-1978.

Lodi: Lodi District Chamber of Commerce Retail Merchants' Semi-Annual Flea Market. Twice annually (call for dates). In downtown Lodi. Contact Lodi District Chamber of Commerce at (209) 367-7840 (office is open Monday through Friday, 8:30 A.M. to 5:00 P.M.).

Los Altos Hills: Los Altos Hills Electronic Swap Meet. Second Saturday of every month from March through September. At 12345 El Monte Road (Foothills College). Free admission. Averages close to 200 vendors. Flea markets meet Radio Shack; sponsored by the Perham Foundation, a pro-electronics group. Call (408) 734-4453.

Marin City: Marin City Flea Market. Every weekend. At 147 Donahue (at Drake), just off Highway 101 at the Marin City/Sausalito exit, twelve miles north of San Francisco. Free admission; outdoors. Averages 100 to 150 vendors. Draws from 1,700 to 2,000 customers per day on average. Contact Gene Clark, Manager, at (415) 332-1441 (office hours are Monday through Thursday, 2:00 P.M. to 4:00 P.M., and Friday, 10:00 A.M. to noon).

Montclair Pomona: Mission Drive-in Swap Meet. Every Wednesday, Friday, Saturday, and Sunday. At 10798 Ramona, on the corner of Mission. Fifty cents on weekdays, $1 on weekends; outdoors. Averages 300 to 500 vendors. Call (909) 628-7943.

Napa: Napa Valley Antiques and Collectibles Market. Third Sunday of every month from May through October. 3285 California Boulevard, near the Trancas exit off the interstate. Admission $1 per person; outdoor. Call (707) 253-1599.

National City: National City Swap Meet. Every weekend. At 3200 D Avenue. Contact Elizabeth Gomez, Manager, at (619) 477-2203.

Newport Beach: Orange County Market Place. At 504 South Bay Front. Contact Robert Teller at (949) 723-6660. NFMA member.

Niles: Niles Antique Flea Market. Annually, the last Sunday in August. On the streets of Niles. Free admission. Contact Flea Market Committee at (510) 792-8023 from Tuesday through Friday, 11:00 A.M. to 1:00 P.M.

Novato: New Marin Flea Market. Reopened in April 1999. At Hamilton

AFB. Claims to be the only flea market in Marin County. Contact Anita Macourbrie at (415) 898-6276 (898-MART).

Oakhurst: Mountain Peddlers Fair. Twice annually, on the Saturday and Sunday preceding Memorial Day and Labor Day. On Route 41 East. From Merced, take Route 140 to Maripose, then Route 49 South to Route 41E in Oakhurst. Free admission; outdoors. Averages close to its capacity of 400 vendors. Sponsored by the Eastern Madera County Chamber of Commerce. Contact Eastern Madera County Chamber of Commerce at (559) 683-7766 or (209) 642-4244.

Oakland: Jack London Square Antiques Mart. First Saturday of every month (except July: call for date). At Jack London Square, by the waterfront. Free admission. Averages close to 100 vendors. Call (510) 652-5728.

Oceanside: Oceanside Swap Meet. Every Friday, Saturday, and Sunday, plus holiday Mondays. At 3480 Mission Avenue. Take I-5 to Mission Avenue, then go east two miles. Admission 35¢ on Friday, 50¢ on Saturday, 75¢ on Sunday; indoors and outdoors. Contact Gil at (760) 757-5286 or (760) 745-3100 (main office).

Pasadena: Pasadena City College Flea Market. First Sunday of every month. At 1570 East Colorado Boulevard. Take Freeway 210 to Pasadena and exit on Hill Boulevard heading south; go six blocks, then left on Del Mar and park in the lot on the left. Free admission; outdoors. Operating at close to its capacity of 500 vendors, this is one of the largest flea markets in the area, besides the Rose Bowl. Call (626) 585-7906.

Petaluma: Petaluma Fairground Flea Market. Every weekend (except from June through mid-July). On the Sonoma-Marin Fairgrounds, at the intersection of East Washington and Payron Streets (about a half hour drive north of San Francisco). Free admission; indoors year-round and outdoors. Averages up to 56 vendors under cover plus another 75 tables outdoors. Contact John Letinich, Treasurer, at (707) 763-0931 (fairground) or (707) 763-1242.

Pico Rivera: Fiesta Swap Meet. Every weekend. At 8452 East Whittier Boulevard (at Paramount). Admission 50¢ per person. Contact Rick Millet, Chamber of Commerce, at (310) 949-5918.

Pomona: Valley Indoor Swap Meet. Daily except Tuesday. At 1600 East Holt Boulevard. Take the Indian Hill exit off Freeway 10 and go south to Holt. Free admission; indoors. Averages close to its capacity of 350 vendors year-round. There is also an outdoor street fair and farmers market four times a year—call for dates. Contact Robyn Gordon at (909) 620-4792 or (909) 620-5083 (office hours are Friday, Saturday, and Sunday, 10:00 A.M. to 6:00 P.M., and Thursday, 9:00 A.M. to noon).

Porterville: Porterville College Swap Meet. Every Saturday. At 100 East College Avenue. Admission 50¢ per person; outdoors. Averages close to 275 vendors (capacity 400). Contact Bill Goucher at (209) 781-3130, ext. 254. NFMA member.

Roseville: Denio's Roseville Farmers Market and Auction. Every Friday through Sunday. At 1551 Vineyard Road. Pronounced "Deny-oh," this one's old and big. Contact Denio at (916) 782-2704 (after 1:00 P.M.)

San Fernando: San Fernando Swap Meet. Every Tuesday, Saturday, and Sunday. At 585 Glenoaks Boulevard, at the corner of Arroyo. A hundred thousand bargains. Call (818) 361-1431.

San Luis Obispo: Sunset Drive-in Theatre Swap Meet. Contact Larry Rodkey, Manager, at (805) 544-4592.

San Ysidro: San Ysidro Swap Meet. Every Wednesday through Sunday. At 2383 Via Segundo, on the west side of I-5, between Dairy Mart Road and the Via de San Ysidro. Admission 50¢; indoors and outdoors. Averages 250 to 375 vendors (capacity 480). Call (619) 690-6756. NFMA member.

Santa Ana: Orange Coast College Swap Meet. Every weekend. In the parking lot (Fairview Street). Free admission; outdoors. Call (714) 432-5866 (714) 432-5880, ext. 1.

Santa Cruz: Antiques Fair. Second Sunday of every month. On Lincoln near Cedar. Free admission; outdoors. Contact Santa Cruz Downtown Association at (408) 429-8433 or (408) 477-1374 (Jeremy).

Santa Cruz: Skyview Drive-in Flea Market. Every Friday through Sunday. At 2260 Soquel Drive. Admission 50¢ per person on Friday, $1 on Saturday, $1.50 on Sunday. Averages up to 500 vendors. Contact Marcy, Manager, at (408) 462-4442.

Santa Fe Springs: Santa Fe Springs Swap Meet. Every Wednesday, Thursday, Saturday, and Sunday. At 13963 Alondra Boulevard. Take Santa Ana Freeway (Route 5) south of Los Angeles approximately twenty-five miles; Valleyview Boulevard exit, north on Valleyview to Alondra Boulevard, west on Alondra. Admission 50¢ on Wednesday, 75¢ on Thursday night; 75¢ on Saturday and Sunday; outdoors. Averages 150 to a capacity of 721 vendors (varies according to season and market day). Contact Rick Landis at (310) 921-4359; reservation office is closed Monday and Tuesday.

Santa Monica: Airport Outdoor Antique and Collectibles Market. Fourth Sunday of every month. At the Santa Monica Airport. Free admission; outdoors. Call (323) 933-2511.

Santee: Santee Swap Meet. Every weekend. At 10990 Woodside Avenue North. Take the Riverford exit off Route 67 North, then go left to Woodside. Admission 50¢; outdoors. Averages close to 50 vendors. Call (619) 449-7927 or (619) 745-3100 (main office).

Simi Valley: Moore Park Swap Meet. Every Sunday. Call for new location in 2000. Admission $1 per person over fourteen years old; outdoors. Averages 310 to 390 vendors (capacity 500). Contact John Blazej, Manager, at (805) 579-7899 or (805) 526-6048.

Slauson: Slauson Indoor Swap Meet. Daily. At 1600 West Slauson Avenue. Free admission; indoors. Averages close to 140 vendors. Barely a flea market but colorful (junky). Call (323) 778-6055.

Stanton: Indoor Swap Meet of Stanton. Daily except Tuesday. At 10401 Beach Boulevard (at Cerritos), between Route 91 and Freeway 22, two miles south of Knotts Berry Farm. Free admission; indoors. Averages 70 to 75 vendors (200 indoor spaces). Contact Jila Ilami or Avo Dakessian at (714) 527-1234 or (714) 527-1112.

Stockton: Stockton Flea Market. At 2542 South El Dorado. Averages up to 400 vendors. Contact Tae W. Oh, Manager, at (209) 465-9933.

Stockton: Stockton Open-Air Mall. At 3550 N. Wilson Way. Contact Glenn Marzion at (209) 478-1192. NFMA member.

Tulare: Open Country Flea Mart. Every Sunday. At 23090 Road 152. Take Tulare Central exit off Freeway 99, then three and a half miles east to Road 152; market is on the corner. Admission 50¢; free admission for children; outdoors and under cover. Averages close to 400 vendors. Call (209) 686-9588.

Ukiah: Ukiah Flea Market. Every weekend. At 1055 North State Street, on the Redwood Empire Fairgrounds. Take Highway 101 north to North State Street exit and then south one-half mile. Free admission; indoors. Averages 40 to 60 vendors (capacity 75). A country-style market serving the Redwood Empire. Contact Bob Bazzano at (707) 468-4626.

Vernalis: Orchard Flea Market. Every weekend. At Vernalis and Highway 132. Call (209) 835-8972.

Yountville: Peddlers Faire. First Saturday of every month (but call to confirm as dates are not consistent). At the Yountville Veterans Home, off Highway 29. Call (707) 944-4941.

Colorado

Englewood: Arapahoe Flea Market. Every weekend. At 3400 South Platte Drive in the Denver suburb of Englewood, at the Cinderella City Drive-in Theatre. Admission $1 per person; outdoors. Averages 100 to 500 vendors (capacity 600). Contact R. L. Lunders at (303) 789-2710 (weekends only).

Fort Collins: Fort Collins Indoor Flea Market. Daily. At 6200 South College Avenue (Route 287), 1.8 miles south of Fort Collins. Free admission; indoors. Averages close to 84 vendors year-round. Contact Vince or Joy Barnhart at (303) 223-6502.

Lafayette: Lafayette Indoor Flea Market. Daily. At 130 East Spaulding. From Highway 287, turn east onto Spaulding, and the market is on that corner just behind the Conoco gas station. Close to Denver and Boulder. Free admission; indoors. Averages close to 115 vendors. Formerly called the Boulder Valley Indoor Flea Market. Contact Bill Hopkins at (303) 665-0433.

Northglenn: Collectors Corner. Daily. At 10615 Melody Drive in Northglenn (in the greater Denver area). Free admission; indoors. Averages 125 to 150 vendors. More like an antique mall atmosphere. Call (303) 450-2875.

Pueblo: Sunset Swap Meet. Every Friday, Saturday, and Sunday. On the Colorado State Fairgrounds, at 2641 I-25 North (use exit 104). Free admission; indoors and outdoors. Averages 110 to 190 vendors (capacity 200 in summer). Advertised statewide as southern Colorado's largest swap meet. Contact John Musso at (800) 647-8368 or (719) 584-2000.

Connecticut

Canton: The Cob-Web Outdoor Flea Market. Every Sunday from May through September. At the junction of Routes 44 and 202, near Route 179. Free admission; outdoors. Averages up to 50 vendors. Clean and green. Indoor shop on the grounds. Contact Dolly Rudder at (203) 693-2658 (answering machine will pick up during the week).

Naugatuck: Peddlers Market. Every Sunday from May through October. At 100 Church Street. Contact Thomas Murray, Creative Fabrics, at (203) 729-6339 or (203) 729-7762.

New Haven: Boulevard Flea Market. Every weekend. At 500 E. T. Grasso Boulevard. Free admission. Call (203) 772-1447.

Torrington: Wright's Barn. Every weekend. Off Route 4 (on Wright Road), between Torrington and Goshen. Take exit 44 off Route 8 to Route 4, Look for easy-to-find large signs. Free admission; indoors. Averages 25 to 35 vendors on two floors of selling area. A pleasant New England market with something for everyone—"all kinds of treasures from Grandma's attic and Grampa's out-back barn." Contact Millie Wright, Manager, at (203) 482-0095.

Delaware

Laurel: Route 13 Market. Every Friday, Saturday, and Sunday. At the intersection of Routes 462 and 13. Free admission; indoors. Call (302) 875-4800.

District of Columbia

Washington: French Open-Air Market. Every Sunday in May. Along the streets near the Friendship Heights Metro Station. Free admission; outdoors. This Washington outdoor exposition of fine antiques has a nice streety feel to it. Call (800) 948-4009 or (202) 364-4600. E-mail: info@antiquesdc.com. Web: http://www.antiquesdc.com.

Florida

Arcadia: Auction Barn. Every Saturday in wintertime; auction house is open daily. At the old drive-in theater on Highway 17. Averages close to 15 vendors. This market is dwindling every year due to competition from shopping centers, says the owner. Contact Anthony DiLiberto, Manager, at (941) 494-2321.

Belleview: Flea City U.S.A. Antique Shop and Swap Meet. Every weekend. At 12180 Highway 441, a mile south of Belleview. Also known as Flea City U.S.A. Call (352) 245-3532 (245-FLEA).

Bradenton: Roma Flea Market. Every weekend. At 5715 15th Street East (old Highway 301). Take I-75 to State Road 70 and go west to Old 301 Boulevard, then turn left and head south to 57th Avenue East, first traffic light. Free admission; indoors and outdoors. Averages 20 to 80 vendors (capacity about 100). An old-fashioned flea market. Call (941) 756-9036.

Brooksville: Airport Mart Flea Market. Every weekend. At 17375 Spring Hill Drive. Free admission; indoors and outdoors. Averages up to 300 vendors (capacity 450, including 300 outdoors under cover). Contact Scott or Jennifer Barker at (352) 796-0268.

Clearwater: Forty-niner Flea Market. Every weekend. At 10525 49th Street North, near 105th Avenue North. Call (727) 573-3367.

Crestview: Crestview Huge Flea Market. Every weekend. On Highway 85 and I-10 (just off exit 12), directly in from the Wal-Mart Supercenter. Free admission; indoors. Averages close to 500 vendors. Call (850) 683-1117 (office hours are Wednesday through Friday, 8:00 A.M. to 4:00 P.M.)

Dade City: Joyland Swap Shop and Theatre. Every weekend. At 2224 North Highway 301, in the parking lot of the Joyland Drive-In. Free admission; outdoors. Call (352) 567-5085.

De Funiak Springs: De Funiak Flea Market. Every Friday; Saturday, and Sunday. On Route 90. Go north from I-10 on Route 331, then right at stoplight onto Route 90 to the market. Free admission; indoors and outdoors. Contact Chuck at (850) 892-3668.

Delray Beach: Delray Swap Shop and Flea Market. Every Thursday and Friday. At 2001 North Federal Highway. Call (561) 276-4012.

Delray Beach: Delray Indoor Flea Market. Every Thursday through Sunday (plus every Wednesday from November through April). At 5283 West Atlantic Avenue. Take exit 42 (Atlantic Avenue exit) off I-95 and go west three miles, or take the Delray Beach exit off the Florida Turnpike and go east two miles. Free admission; indoors. Averages close to 180 vendors year-round. Calls itself a flea market though there is no used, collectible, or antique merchandise, and no accommodations are made for transient vendors; specializes in name-brand merchandise at discount prices. Call (561) 499-9935.

Fort Myers: Ortiz Avenue Flea Market. Every Friday. At 1501 Ortiz Avenue. Take exit 24 off I-75 onto Luckett Road, go to stoplight at the end of Luckett, then left to market. Free admission; outdoors and under cover. Averages 150 to 450 vendors. Contact Mrs. Collins, Manager, at (941) 694-5019.

Homosassa: Howard's Flea Market. Every weekend. At 6373 South Suncoast Boulevard (Route 19), approximately three miles south of Homosassa Springs. Free admission; under cover. Contact Tom and Alice Cushman, Managers, at (352) 628-3437.

Jacksonville: ABC Flea Market. Every Thursday through Sunday. At 10135 Beach Boulevard. Free admission; indoors and outdoors. Averages up to a dozen vendors. This has become mostly a furniture store, but a few vendors still set up; as a flea market it's not what it used to be. Contact Bill Lucas, Manager, at (904) 642-2717.

Jacksonville: Jacksonville Marketplace. Every Saturday and Sunday. At 614 Pecan Park Road. Take Exit 128 (Pecan Park exit) off I-95 (one exit north of airport). Free admission; under cover. Averages up to its capacity of more than 900 vendors. Billed as the largest in Jacksonville. Call (904) 751-6770.

Key Largo: Key Largo Flea Market. Every weekend. At 103530 Overseas Highway (Route 1, at mile marker 103.5), three-fourths of a mile north of

Pennekamp State Park. Free admission; indoors. Averages close to 50 vendors year-round. Call (305) 451-0677 or (305) 451-0922.

Lake City: Webb's Antiques. Daily. On U.S. 41-441; take exit 80 off I-75. Conveniently located between Lake City and High Springs. Free admission; indoors. Averages close to 200 vendors. Formerly known as Grandpa's Barn Flea Market, Webb's is really an antique mall with long-term dealers, but there's quite a bit to see. Call (904) 758-5564.

Lake Worth: Trail Drive-in Swap Shop. Every Thursday, Saturday, and Sunday. On Lake Worth Road between Congress Avenue and Military Trail, at the Trail Drive-in Theatre. Call (561) 965-4518.

Maitland: Ole Red Barn Flea Market. Every weekend (produce market open daily). At 8750 South Highway 17/92. Free admission; outdoors and under cover. Averages 20 to 25 permanent vendors. An old-fashioned, small flea market. Contact Betty L. Smith at (561) 789-3945.

Margate: Margate Swap Shop. Every Tuesday, Saturday, and Sunday. At 1000 North State Road 7. Take the Coconut Creek exit off the Florida Turnpike to Route 441, then south about one block, and market is on the east side. Free admission; indoors and outdoors. Averages 350 to a capacity of 600 vendors. Big on produce. Contact Alex Gusman at (305) 971-7927.

Miami: Flea Market U.S.A. Every Wednesday through Sunday. At 3013 Northwest 79th Street at 30th Avenue. Take 79th Street exit off I-95 and go west to 30th Avenue. Free admission; indoors and outdoors. Call (305) 836-3677.

Miami: Liberty Flea Market. Daily except Sunday and Monday. At 7900 Northwest 27th Avenue at 79th Street, in the Northside Shopping Center. Take the Northwest 79th Street exit west off I-95 to 27th Avenue. Free admission; indoors. Averages 60 to a capacity of 400 vendors. In what used to be a Sears department store; expanding to a new floor that will bring its total selling area to 155,000 square feet. More of a "merchandise mart" than a true flea market, but a good place for bargains. Call (305) 836-9848.

Micanopy: Smiley's Antique Mall. Daily. At Road 234 (exit 73 off I-75). Free admission; indoors. Averages close to 200 vendors. Contact Jamie Housewright, Manager, or Ben Campen, Jr., at (352) 466-0707 or (352) 331-2999. NFMA member.

Milton: I-10 Flea Market. Every Friday, Saturday, and Sunday. One-half mile south of exit 8 off I-10. Free admission; indoors. Averages up to 130 vendors. Call (850) 623-6349.

Naples: Naples' Big Cypress Flea Market. Contact Keith Basik at (941) 262-4622. NFMA member.

North Miami: North Miami Flea Market. Daily except Monday and Tuesday. At 14135 Northwest 7th Avenue. Call (305) 685-7721.

North Miami Beach: Oakland Park Flea Market. Call (305) 651-9530.

Oak Hill: Oak Hill Flea Market. Every Tuesday, Friday, Saturday, and Sunday. At 351 North Highway 1. Go east off I-95 onto State Road 442 to Route 1, then go south eight miles; or take Oak Hill/Scottsmoor exit off I-95 and go east to Route 1, then north eight miles, and market will be on your right, just beyond a flashing yellow light. Free admission; indoors. Averages up to a capacity of 100 vendors. Trash to treasures. Contact Sue Perry at (904) 345-3570 or (904) 428-9544 (Coronado Real Estate).

Okeechobee: Cypress Hut Flea Market. Every weekend. At 4701 Highway 441 South, seven miles south of downtown Okeechobee. Free admission; indoors and outdoors. Averages 100 to 400 vendors. Call (941) 763-5104.

Palmetto: Midway Flea Market. Every Wednesday, Saturday, and Sunday. At 10816 U.S. Highway 41 North. Take Route 75 to exit 45 west to Highway 41, then north one-half mile and market will be on the right. Free admission; indoors, outdoors, and under cover. Averages up to a capacity of 1,000 vendors. Billed as a clean and modern market with old-fashioned prices. Call (941) 723-6000.

Plant City: Country Village Market Place. Every Wednesday, Saturday, and Sunday. At 3301 Highway 39 North. Take exit 13 off I-4, then turn north on State Road 39 and go a mile to first stoplight, and market will be on the left. Free admission; outdoors and under cover. Averages 200 to a capacity of 400 vendors (filled in winter months). During the week a wholesale produce market operates on part of the property. Contact Ferris Waller at (813) 752-4670 or (813) 752-7088.

Port Charlotte: Rainbow Flea Market: Every Friday, Saturday, and Sunday. At 4628 Tamiami Trail (Route 41) in Charlotte Harbor, at the corner of Kings Highway. Under new management (formerly Poor Jed's Flea Market). Contact Loretta Meegan at (941) 629-1223 or (813) 629-2259.

Port Charlotte: Sun Flea Market. Every Friday, Saturday, and Sunday. At 18505 Paulson Drive, at the intersection of U.S. Routes 41 & 776. Well promoted (advertised on local radio). Contact Berinda or Ken Levy at (941) 255-3532 (255-FLEA). NFMA member.

Riviera Beach: Riviera Beach Swap Shop. Every Wednesday, Friday, Saturday, and Sunday. At the Riviera Beach Drive-In. Call (561) 844-5836.

Rockledge: Carnival Mall. Daily. On Route 1, one-half mile south of Route 520 (close to Kennedy Space Center). Free admission; indoors. Averages close to 51 vendors. More like a mall than a flea market. Contact Dennis Sheppard at (407) 636-4200.

Saint Augustine: Saint John's Marketplace. Every weekend. At 2495 S.R. 207. Contact John Alexon or Bob Hunter at (904) 824-4210 or (904) 824-9840.

Tampa: Golden Nugget Flea Market. Every weekend. At 8504 Adamo Drive East (Highway 60). Call (813) 621-0045.

Thonotosassa: North 301 Flea Market. Every weekend. At 11802 U.S. Highway 301 North. Averages close to 25 vendors. Call (813) 986-1023.

West Palm Beach: Uptown-Downtown Flea Market. At 5700 Okeechobee Road. Contact Beverly Koplowitz at (561) 640-7283. NFMA member.

Georgia

Albany: Kitty's Flea Market. Every Saturday and Sunday. At 3229 Sylvester Road (Route 82), north of town. Free admission; outdoors. Averages up to several hundred vendors. Call (912) 432-0007.

Atlanta: Mall at 82 Peachtree. Monday through Thursday. At 82 Peachtree Street Southwest. Free admission; indoors. Averages close to 80 vendors. Formerly the Five Points Flea Market. Call (404) 681-9439.

Barnesville: M and M Flea Market. Every weekend. At 341 Industrial Drive (Highway 341), between Griffin and Barnesville. Free admission; indoors and outdoors. Averages 20 to 30 vendors (capacity 50). Contact J. B. Moss at (404) 358-1724.

Brunswick: Brunswick Flea and Farmers Market. Every Friday, Saturday, and Sunday. At 204 Old Jesup Road, a mile and a half southeast of exit 7A or 7B off I-95. Take route 341 South to Community Road east to Old Jesup Road. Free admission; indoors year-round and outdoors. Averages 25 to 40 vendors (capacity 150). Contact Tom or Barbara Schuh, Managers, at (912) 267-6787.

Calhoun: New Town Flea Market. Every weekend. On New Town Road, right off I-75 (take Red Bud exit). Free admission; indoors, outdoors, and under cover. Averages 25 to 50 vendors (capacity 100). Most vendors are the one-time yard-sale type. Contact Earl Abernathy at (706) 625-1157.

Cartersville: North Atlanta Flea Market. Contact Lisa Hamilton at (770) 606-9063. NFMA member.

Chamblee: Buford Highway Flea Market. Every Friday and Saturday. At 5000 Buford Highway, one mile inside Perimeter (I-285) in the northern area of the city of Atlanta. Free admission; indoors. Averages up to a capacity of 265 vendors. Good for bargain hunters chasing discounts on new products. Call (770) 452-7140.

Cleveland: Charlie's Red, White, and Blue. Every weekend and holidays. On Highway 129, 75 miles north of Atlanta. Free admission; indoors. Averages up to a dozen or so vendors. Formerly Henry's Mountain Flea Market. Contact Charlie or Genie at (888) 451-2267 (reservations only) or (704) 865-1716.

Conyers: All Star, Inc. At 1777 Old Camp Trail. Contact John Gallman or Kathe Renfroe at (770) 760-7727 or (770) 483-4141. E-mail: 8liner@bellsouth.net. NFMA member.

Decatur: Kudzu Flea Market. Every Friday, Saturday, and Sunday. At 2874 East Ponce de Leon. Contact Emily at (404) 373-6498.

East Point: Greenbriar Flea Market. Daily except Tuesday and Wednesday. At 2925 Headland Drive. Take Route 166 exit off Route 285 (in southeast part of Atlanta) to Greenbriar Parkway, then turn at the second stoplight to Headland Drive; or take 75/85 South to 166 West to Campbellton Road to Greenbriar Parkway to Headland Drive. Free admission; indoors. Averages close to its capacity of 150 vendors. Call (404) 349-3994.

Forest Park: South Atlanta Flea Market. Every Friday. At 4140 Jonesboro Road, a half mile south of exit 40 off I-285. Free admission; indoors. Averages close to 45 vendors year-round. Contact Betty Ratledge at (404) 363-6694.

Gainesville: Gainesville Flea Market. First weekend of every month. At 3600 Atlanta Highway (Highway 13 South). Take exit 4 off I-95, then turn right and go past three traffic lights, then right onto Highway 13 South, and the market will be a quarter mile away on the right—look for signs at the building. Free admission; indoors year-round and outdoors. Averages close to its capacity of 70 vendors year-round. Contact Johnny Benefield at (770) 536-8068.

Lake Park: Bargainville Flea Market. Every weekend. Take exit 2 off I-75 and go east, then right at the Hardee's, then one and a half miles farther on the left. Free admission; outdoors and under cover. Averages 50 to 70 vendors (capacity 150). Contact Terry Herndon or Rich Lewis, c/o Park Mark Properties at (912) 559-0141 or (912) 559-5192.

Norcross: Georgia Antique Center and International Market. Every Friday. At 6624 I-85 North Access Road. Take exit 36 (Pleasantdale exit) off I-85 northbound from Route 285, then go approximately one and a half miles on the access road, and market will be on the right. Free admission; indoors. Averages close to 200 vendors year-round, on 100,00 square feet of selling area. More like an antiques mall than a flea market but boasts a varied selection of antiques and collectibles. Call (770) 446-9292.

Norcross: The Gwinnett Flea Market and Antique Gallery. Every Wednesday and Thursday. At 5675 Jimmy Carter Boulevard, at exit 37 off I-85. Free admission; indoors. Averages close to its capacity of 70 vendors. Contact Anne Osmerg at (770) 449-8189.

Pennville: Ye Old Trading Grounds. Every Tuesday and Saturday. On Route 27 Tyron and Summerville. Free admission. Contact Larry or Jane at (706) 857-1433 or (706) 862-2442.

Thomasville: Rose City Flea Market. Every Friday, Saturday, and Sunday. At 2069 County Line Road. Free admission; outdoors and under cover. Averages up to 10 vendors. Contact Charlie (Manager), or Virginia Bossier at (912) 574-5373 or (912) 941-2356.

Thomson: The Market Place Flea Market. Every Friday, Saturday, and Sunday. At the corner of State Road 223 and Harrison Road. Take Route 150 exit off I-20, then go southwest, then left at the first four-way signal, then one mile, and market will be on the right. Free admission; indoors and outdoors. Averages up to a few dozen vendors. Contact Barbara Reid at (706) 595-9875. NFMA member.

Tifton: Tifton Flea Market. Every Friday, Saturday, and Sunday. On Route 82/319 (east of I-75). Call (912) 386-1734 or (912) 386-1449.

Waycross: Chrystal's Flea Market. Every weekend: Saturday. At 1631 Genoa Street. Admission $1 per person; indoors. Averages close to 75 vendors. Contact Jimmy Langford at (912) 283-9808.

Idaho

Boise: Spectra's Flea Market. On the Fairgrounds. Contact Spectra Productions at (208) 939-6426, ext. 21.

Ketchum: Antique Peddlers Fair. Twice a year in summer (call for dates). At the ski resort. Contact Jan Perkins at (208) 368-9759.

Illinois

Amboy: Amboy Flea Market. Third Sunday of every month from February through November. At the Lee County Fairgrounds. Admission $1 per person. Contact Bill Edwards, Manager, at (815) 626-7601 or (815) 857-3488.

Centralia: Don's Flea Market. Every Friday through Monday. At the intersection of Route 161 and I-57. Free admission; indoors and outdoors. Averages three to four vendors. Over 7,000 square feet indoors plus outdoor space; two antiques shops next door. Contact Don Mercer at (618) 533-2778.

Fairmont: Fairmont City Flea Market. Every weekend. Route 40 and 111. Free admission; indoors and outdoors. Averages close to 70 vendors. Call (618) 271-9885.

Laura: Outdoor/Indoor Flea Market. Third Sunday of every month (except the last Saturday in July) from April through November. At Millbrook Township Center on Route 78 about twenty-five miles northwest of Peoria. Free admission; indoors and outdoors. Averages 30 to 50 vendors. Contact Karen Megan or Gwen Pumphrey at (309) 446-3619 (Karen) or (309) 639-2738 (Gwen).

Peotone: Antique Show. Fourth Sunday of every month. At the fairgrounds. Contact Robert W. Mitchell, Sr. at (815) 857-2253 or (815) 284-9216.

Princeton: Second Sunday Flea Market. Second Sunday of every month. On the Bureau County Fairgrounds at Routes 6 and 34. Contact Tony Martin, Manager, at (815) 872-1601 or (815) 875-1948 (fairgrounds).

Indiana

Bunker Hill: North Drive-in Flea Market. Every weekend. On Highway 31. Free admission; indoors and outdoors. Averages 50 to 300 vendors, depending on the weather. Under new ownership. Contact Dennis or Parrisha Miller at (765) 689-9432 (office) or (219) 699-7760 (home). E-mail: dbtow@aol.com.

Centerville: Big Bear Flea Market. Every weekend from April through October. At 2131 North Centerville Road; take exit 145 off I-70. Free admission; outdoors. Averages close to a dozen vendors. Contact Ed Newman at (765) 855-3912.

Evansville: Diamond Flea Market. Every weekend. At 1250 Diamond Avenue (Highway 66 West) at the corner of Business Highway 41. Free admission; indoors and outdoors. Averages 30 to 70 vendors. Contact Mike Johnson or Barbara Staub at (812) 464-2675.

Fort Wayne: Fort Wayne Flea Market. Every Friday, Saturday, and Sunday. At 6901 South Hanna Street. From I-30, take 469 South to exit 11, then go north. At 6901 South Hanna Street; indoors. Call (219) 447-0081.

Indianapolis: Indiana Flea Market. Monthly on Friday and Saturday (call for dates). On the Indiana State Fairgrounds, at 1202 East 38th Street. Free admission; indoors. Contact Stewart Promotions at (317) 927-7500 or (502) 456-2244.

Laporte: Wildwood Park Flea Market. Every weekend from April through October. Call (219) 879-5660.

Lawrenceburg: Tri-State Antique Market. First Sunday of every month from May through October. At the Lawrenceburg Fairgrounds, on U.S. Route 50, a mile west of exit 16 off I-275 (Cincinnati Beltway). Billed as

America's Largest "Antique and vintage only" flea market. Contact Bruce Metzger, Manager, at (513) 738-7256.

Monticello: Twin Lakes Flea Market. Every Friday, Saturday, Sunday, and holidays from the first weekend in May through Labor Day. At 3016 West Shafer Drive. Take Route 24 to Sixth Street, one mile. Free admission; indoors and outdoors. Averages up to 35 vendors on six acres of selling area. Located in a resort community visited by over a million vacationers each summer. (Market is one mile from Indiana Beach Resort.) Contact Guy Harrison at (219) 583-4146.

Reelsville: Croy Creek Traders. Selected dates from May through November (call for dates). On Pinkley Street, seven miles east of Brazil and five miles southwest of Reelsville, Indiana. On twenty acres of selling area. Family owned and operated. Contact John Lynch at (812) 986-3075 or (765) 672-4862. E-mail: croycreek@businesscents.com.

South Bend: Thieves Market. Every weekend. At the corner of Edison and Ironwood, near the Notre Dame campus. Free admission; indoors and outdoors. Averages 30 to 35 vendors (capacity 45). Specialty is estate and distinctive jewelry. Contact David Ciesiolka at (219) 272-2030.

Iowa

Bentonsport: Flea Market and Craft Show. Irregular schedule (call for dates). Free admission; outdoors. Contact Greef General Store at (319) 592-3579.

Davenport: Mississippi Valley Flea Market. Last Sunday of every month (except in July—inquire for July date). At 2815 West Locust, on the Mississippi Valley Fairgrounds. Take I-80 to I-280 and look for Locust Street exit in Davenport. Admission $1.50 per person; indoors year-round and outdoors. Averages close to 60 vendors year-round (large outdoor vendor capacity). Contact Robert H. Balzer at (319) 323-2319 or Fairgrounds office (319) 326-5338.

Des Moines: Fairgrounds Flea Market. Every month from October through April (call for dates). In the 4-H Building at the State Fairgrounds. Run by the Simpson Methodist Church. Contact Earl Sigmund at (515) 262-4504 between 8:00 A.M. and 2:00 P.M.

Milford: Treasure Village Flea Market. About four three-day events annually, on the major holidays plus a (two-day) weekend in August (call for dates). At 2033 Highway 86. Free admission; indoors and outdoors. Averages close to 80 vendors. Contact Garth at (712) 337-3730.

Kansas

White Cloud: White Cloud Flea Market. Twice a year, in May and September. Contact Sally Wagner at (785) 595-6683.

Kentucky

Bowling Green: Flea Land of Bowling Green: At 1100 Three Springs. Contact Grant Lewis at (502) 843-1978. NFMA member.

Corbin: Cumberland Gap Parkway Flea Market. Every weekend. At exit 29 off I-75 and Cumberland Gap Parkway. Free admission; indoors. On over

80,000 square feet of shopping area. Billed as the best shopping in south-eastern Kentucky. Contact Bill Hamblin at (606) 526-9712 or (606) 528-5034. NFMA member.

Covington: 450-Mile Outdoor Market. Annually. Along Highway 127. Contact at (800) 225-8747 (225-TRIP).

Flemingsburg: Flemingsburg Monday Court Days. Second Monday of every October, plus the preceding Saturday and Sunday. All over town. Free admission; outdoors. The whole town swells with stuff—food, garage-sale vendors, etc.—a fun experience if you're in the area. Contact Fleming County Rescue Squad at (606) 845-8801.

Georgetown: Country World Flea Market. Every Friday, Saturday, and Sunday from April through November. On Route 460 East, within sight of I-75; southbound: take exit 126 off I-75 to Route 62, then go right toward Route 460, then left to market entrance about one-third of a mile down the road; northbound: take exit 125 off I-75 to Route 460, and market entrance. Free admission; outdoors. Averages up to 200 vendors (capacity 450). Billed as one of Kentucky's largest weekly outdoor flea markets. Call (502) 863-1557.

Guthrie: Southern Kentucky Flea Market. Every Wednesday through Sunday. At 52 Waste Water Road, off Dixie Beeline Highway (Highway 41), about a half mile out of town. Take exit 4 off I-24 onto Route 79 to Route 41. Free admission; indoors. Averages close to 110 vendors. Call (270) 483-2166.

Leitchfield: Bratcher's Flea Market. Every Saturday. On Highway 62 East. Contact Gladys Bratcher or Carol at (502) 259-5948 or (502) 259-3571.

Louisville: Kentucky Flea Market. Several shows every summer, Friday through Sunday (call for dates). At the Kentucky Fair and Exposition Center. Free admission; indoors. Averages close to 2,000 vendors. Big. Contact Stewart Promotions at (502) 456-2244 (Monday and Wednesday, 10:00 A.M. to 4:00 P.M.; Thursday, 10:00 A.M. to 2:00 P.M.; closed Tuesdays).

Maceo: Hog Heaven Flea Market. At 8424 Highway 60 East. Contact Leslie Bittle at (502) 264-4420 or 729-4949.

Paducah: Great American Flea Market. Third weekend of every month. At the Bluegrass Downs Racetrack. Contact Dottie Stout, Manager, at (502) 443-5800.

Winchester: Winchester Flea Market. Every weekend. At 4400 Oliver Road. Take exit 94 off I-64. Free admission; indoors and outdoors. Averages close to 50 vendors year-round (capacity 200). Contact Raymond C. Huls at (606) 744-1179 or (606) 745-4332.

Louisiana

Baton Rouge: Merchant's Landing Flea Market. Every weekend. At 9800 Florida Boulevard, three blocks east of Airline Boulevard, at the Broadmoor Shopping Mall. Free admission; indoors. Averages up to 75 vendors. Call (225) 925-1664.

Lacombe: 190 Trading Post Flea Market. Every weekend. At 31184 Highway 190 West, six miles west of Slidell. Take Lacombe exit off I-12 to Highway 190. Free admission; indoors and outdoors. Averages 20 to a capacity of 30 vendors. Contact Harold Fayard or Mary Fayard at (504) 882-6442 or (504) 641-3476.

Maine

Leeds: Red Roof Flea Market. Every weekend in warm months. On Route 202, behind the Red Roof Store. Free admission; outdoors. Averages up to about a dozen vendors. This is a small but nice market. Contact Ed Frost at (207) 933-4533 or (207) 375-6291.

Newcastle: Foster's Flea Market and Antique Hall. Every weekend from May through October. On Route 1—watch for the big sign. Free admission; indoors year-round and outdoors. Averages up to 30 vendors. This one's good for old-fashioned stuff. Contact Robert L. Foster at (207) 529-5422.

Portland: Portland Expo Flea Market. Every Sunday. At the Portland Exposition Building, 239 Park Avenue. Take exit 6A or Exit 7 off the Maine Turnpike, and follow I-295 to exit 5A (Congress Street), then turn left at the first set of lights to St. John Street, then go right at the next set of lights to Park Avenue. Free admission; indoors. Averages close to its capacity of 152 vendors. Call (207) 874-8200.

Searsport: Hobby Horse Flea Market. Every Friday, Saturday, and Sunday from May through mid-October (antique mall open daily). On Bangor Road (Route 1), three miles north of central Searsport thirty miles south of Bangor and ten miles north of Belfast). Free admission; indoors and outdoors. Averages up to 30 vendors (capacity 36), plus 20 shops. Contact Mary E. Harriman at (207) 548-2981.

Maryland

Columbia: Columbia Antiques Market. Every Sunday, from late April through late October. Across from the Columbia Mall, between Baltimore and Washington, D.C. Take exit 175 (Columbia exit) off I-95. Flea market operates in the parking lot, near the Sears (and almost 200 other shops). Free admission; indoors, outdoors, and under cover. Averages up to 125 vendors (capacity 300). Contact Hubert, c/o Bellman Corporation at (410) 329-2188 or (410) 679-2288.

Edgewood: Bonnie Brae Flea Market. Every weekend. At 1301 Pulaski Highway (Route 40), between Routes 152 and 24 (twenty miles out of Baltimore on the way to New York). Free admission; mainly outdoors. Averages 10 to 50 vendors (capacity 60 to 70). Indoor antiques shop specializes in glassware. Contact Angil Reynolds or Juanita A. Merritt at (410) 679-6895 (shop) or 679-2210 (residence).

Saint Leonard: Chesapeake MarketPlace. Every Friday through Sunday. Contact Sharon, Manager, at (410) 586-3725.

Massachusetts

Brimfield: Crystal Brook Flea Market. Three three-day events annually in May, July, and September, timed to coincide with the other major Brimfield events (call for dates). On Route 20 just west of town. Free admission. Another piece of the gigantic Brimfield puzzle. Contact Richard and Maureen Ethier at (413) 245-7647.

Brimfield: May's Antique Market. Three three-day events anually in May, July, and September, timed to coincide with the other major Brimfield events (call for dates). On Route 20. There's always a crowd at May's during the big events. Contact Richard or Laura May at (413) 245-9271.

Douglas: Douglas Flea Market. Every Saturday. Off Routes 16 and 146 at the Uxbridge/Douglas town line. Take 146 South to East Douglas exit or Lacky Dam; travel on Lacky Dam to four corners, then left; then first left over a bridge. Market will be a quarter mile farther, on the left. Free admission; indoors and outdoors. Averages up to a capacity of 25 vendors. Located on the historic Bosma Farm. Contact Marlene Alsop Bosma at (508) 278-6027. Web: www.wccvb#99.com.

Ludlow: Ludlow Flea Market. Every Sunday. At 1099 Center Street (Route 21 North), three miles from exit 7 off the Massachusetts Turnpike. Free admission; outdoors. Contact Jack or Grace Machado at (413) 589-0419.

Lynn: Mass. Merchandise Mart. Every Wednesday through Sunday for the indoor market, plus outdoors on the weekends. At 800 Lynn Way. Free admission; indoors and outdoors. Averages close to 40 vendors indoors, plus as many as 80 outdoors. Call (781) 598-5450.

Malden: Malden Flea Market. Every weekend. At the corner of Route 60 and Ferry Street. Admission 50¢ per person; indoors. Contact Stanley Krigman at (781) 321-9374 or (781) 324-9113.

New Bedford: Whaling City Festival. Annually, the Friday, Saturday, and Sunday of the second weekend in July. In the Veterans Memorial Button Wood Park. From the north: take Route 24 south to Route 140, then south to junction with Kempton Street (Route 6), and park is beyond intersection on the left. From the west (Providence) or east (Cape Cod): take I-195 to Route 140 South. Free admission; outdoors. Averages up to 300 vendors (capacity 320). Contact Louis Oliveira at (508) 996-3348.

North Brookfield: Brookfield Orchards Flea Market. Flea market every weekend from May through August (farm stand is open year-round). At 12 Lincoln Road, right off Route 9 (from East Brookfield). Free admission; outdoors. Averages 7 to 10 vendors. The farm stand also has crafts and some collectible items in addition to fresh produce. Call (508) 867-6858 or (508) 885-7719.

North Oxford: Flea Market. Every weekend during summer season, plus holidays. On Route 20, five hundred feet west of Route 56. Free admission; outdoors. Averages up to 40 vendors. Call (508) 987-5098 or (508) 987-5011.

North Quincy: Naponset Flea Market. Every weekend. At 2 Hancock Street. Contact David Stanton, Manager, at (617) 472-3558.

Wilmington: Jolly Jim's Extravaganza. Two weekends annually, in November and December (call for dates). At the Shriner's Auditorium on Fordham Road. Take exit 39 off Route 93. Admission $4 per person; indoors. Averages 200 to 250 vendors on 50,000 square feet of selling area. There is good variety here, and bargains. Contact Show Promotion, Inc., at (800)

759-7469 (759-SHOW) or (508) 687-1010. E-mail: info@showpromotion.com. Web: www.showpromotion.com. NFMA member.

Michigan

Centreville: Caravan Antiques Market. Five Sundays a year, May through October. On the Saint Joseph County Grange Fairgrounds, at 1510 North Hoyne. Use M-86 to Centreville, near Three Rivers and Kalamazoo. Admission $3 per person; indoors and outdoors. Averages up to 650 vendors. Billed as one of the best antiques markets in the state. Call (773) 227-4464.

Detroit: Metro Flea Market. Every Friday, Saturday, and Sunday. At 6665 West Vernor. Take I-75 to Livernois, then go one mile to Vernor. Free admission; indoors year-round and outdoors. Averages close to 70 vendors year-round. Contact Ralph Najor at (313) 841-4890.

Ionia: Ionia Antique and Collectible Market. Selected Sundays (call for dates). On the Ionia Fairgrounds, on South M-66. Admission $2 per person; indoors year-round and outdoors. Contact Judith Kramer at (517) 593-3316 (evenings 6:00 to 10:00 P.M.).

Kalamazoo: Bank Street Market. Every Wednesday and Friday from May through September. At the Kalamazoo City Market, at 1205 Bank Street. Free admission; outdoors and under cover. Averages up to 120 vendors.

Kalamazoo: Fairgrounds Flea Market. Every Tuesday, Wednesday, and Thursday from October through April, except first week in March, plus some weekends (call to confirm dates). At the Kalamazoo County Fairgrounds. Contact Kalamazoo County Parks at (616) 383-8778.

Lexington: Harbor Bazaar Antiques Mall. Every weekend. At 5590 Main Street (Route 25), two blocks south of the stoplight. Free admission; indoors. Averages close to its capacity of 200 vendors. Contact E. R. Kinsley II at (810) 359-5333 or (810) 359-5819. E-mail: bazaar@greatlakes.net.

Marshall: Cornwell's Flea Market. Selected weekends between May through September (call for dates). On 15-Mile Road, about six miles west of Marshall. Free admission; outdoors. Averages up to 150 vendors. Call (616) 781-4293.

Muskegon: Golden Token Flea Market. Every Saturday. At 1300 East Laketon Avenue, a block from U.S. Route 31. Call (616) 773-1137.

Muskegon: Select Auditorium Flea Market. Every Saturday. At 1445 East Laketon Avenue. Free admission; indoors during winter, outdoors in summer. Call (616) 726-5707.

Paw Paw: Busy Bea's Flea Market. Every weekend (plus holiday Mondays). On Red Arrow Highway. Take Paw Paw exit off Route 94, then left at light. Contact Bea Key, Manager, at (616) 657-6467. NFMA member.

Port Huron: Wurzel's Flea Market. Every weekend. At 4189 Keewahdin Road. Free admission; indoors and outdoors. Averages close to 40 vendors. Call (810) 385-4283.

Taylor: Gibraltar Trade Center. Every Friday, Saturday, and Sunday (daily from the Friday after Thanksgiving until Christmas): Friday. At 15525 Racho Road. Take exit 36 (Eureka Road) off I-75. Admission $1.50 per carload; indoors, outdoors, and under cover. Averages up to a capacity of 1,200 vendors (but this is said to be a large market). A large and well-advertised market; see also its "sister" market in Mount Clemens, Michigan. Contact Jeff Turner, General Manager, or Susan Lenz, President, at (734) 287-2000.

Warren: Michigan Flea Market. Every Thursday and Friday. At 24100 Groesback Highway. Free admission; indoors. Call (810) 771-3535.

Minnesota

Hinckley: Hinckley Flea Market. Every Thursday through Sunday from the last weekend in April through the first full weekend in October. On Highway 48 and I-35, between Famous Tobie's Restaurant and the Grand Casino. Take exit 183 off I-35 (midway between Minneapolis and Duluth), then go four blocks east on Highway 48, and market will be on the left—look for five large red and white buildings. Free admission; indoors, outdoors, and under cover. Averages up to 180 vendors (capacity 200). Minnesota's most modern flea market is well promoted, with approximately 30,000 to 50,000 shoppers passing through each day. Contact Walter "Micky" Nilsen at (715) 394-3526.

Oronoco: Olmstead County Gold Rush. Second weekend in May and third weekend in August. At the Olmstead County Fairgrounds. Call (507) 367-4405.

Mississippi

Amory: Big Bee Waterway Trade Days. On the first Monday of every month, plus the preceding Friday, Saturday, and Sunday. At 30211 Highway 371 North. Call (601) 256-1226.

Canton: Canton Flea Market. Twice annually, in May and October. On the Court House Square. Call (601) 589-8057.

Pass Christian: A-1 Trade World. Every weekend. Off 1-10 at exit 24 (Menge Avenue exit). Free admission; outdoors and under cover. One of the larger flea markets along the Gulf Coast. Call (228) 452-0590. NFMA member.

Tupelo: Tupelo Gigantic Flea Market. At 18799 North Coley Road. Contact Debbie Griffin at (601) 842-4442. NFMA member.

Missouri

Asbury: Stateline Trade Center. Every Thursday, Friday, Saturday, and Sunday (noon to 6:00 P.M.). On Highway 171, twenty miles north of Joplin on the Kansas-Missouri state line. Free admission; indoors. Averages 30 to a capacity of 35 vendors. Contact Donna or Gary Lair at (417) 642-5850.

Branson: Coffelt's Country Flea Market and Craft Village. Daily from April through October. At 673 Highway 165, one-half mile south of Highway 76, three miles west of Branson. Free admission; indoors, outdoors, and under cover. Averages 25 to 30 vendors. The atmosphere is Ozarks rustic, but this farm village doesn't accept weekend vendors—it's just permanent sellers, but there's a variety of offerings. Contact Gerald Coffelt at (417) 334-7611 or (417) 334-1282.

Farmington: Farmington Flea Market. Every weekend. At 4062 Highway 67. Free admission; indoors, outdoors, and under cover. Averages 80 to 120 vendors (capacity virtually unlimited). Draws a large crowd from as far away as Saint Louis. Call (573) 756-1967.

Joplin: Joplin Flea Market. Every weekend. At 12th and Virginia Avenue, one block east of Main Street. Free admission; indoors and outdoors. Over 40,000 square feet of indoor selling area. Contact La Verne Miller at (417) 623-3743 or (417) 623-6328.

Sedalia: Sho-me Flea Market. Three weekends a year (call for dates). At the State Fairgrounds. Contact Pat Klatt at (660) 530-5600 (State Fairgrounds).

Montana

Great Falls: Great Falls Farmers Market. Every Wednesday and Saturday. Free admission. Mostly crafts and fresh produce. Call (406) 761-3881.

Great Falls: Senior Citizens Center Flea Market. Usually on the first Saturday of the month in the fall and spring seasons (call for dates). At 1004 Central Avenue, at the Senior Citizens Center. Free admission; indoors. Averages 5 to 10 vendors. Call (406) 454-6995.

Terry: Prairie Flea Market. Twice annually, in the summer (call for dates). At the Prairie Drive-in Theatre (visible from the Terry exit off I-94). Free admission; outdoors. Averages up to a couple of dozen vendors. This market is near the Lewis and Clark Trail and is growing every year. Call (406) 635-4000.

Nebraska

Grand Island: Great Exchange Indoor Flea Market. Daily except major holidays. At 3235 South Locust Street at the intersection of Highway 34. Take exit 312 off I-80 onto Route 281 and go north five miles to Highway 34, then two miles east to South Locust Street; or go four miles north from exit 318 to Highway 34 and then four miles. Free admission; indoors. Averages close to its capacity of 60 vendors year-round. Billed as Nebraska's best antiques and collectibles flea market. Contact Andrea or Pat Lee at (308) 381-4075.

Kearney: Buffalo County Antique Flea Market. Monthly (call for dates). On the fairgrounds. Contact Cynthia Svarvari, Manager, at (308) 987-2633.

Lincoln: Flea Market Emporium. Every Monday through Saturday. At 3235 South 13th Street, between High and Arapahoe (Indian Village Shopping Center). Free admission; indoors. Averages up to 50 vendors. Contact Ruth Trobee, Owner, at (402) 423-5380.

Lincoln: Sunrise-Sunset Flea Market. First and third weekend of every month. At the fairgrounds. Call (402) 467-4836 or (402) 466-0334.

South Sioux City: Siouxland Flea Market. Monday through Saturday. At 2111 Dakota Avenue. Free admission; indoors. Averages close to its capacity of 200 vendors year-round. Contact Jim or Bobbie Gallup at (402) 494-3221 or (712) 259-0174.

Nevada

Las Vegas: Gemco Swap Meet. Every Friday, Saturday, and Sunday. At 3455 Boulder Highway. Contact Mike Levy at (702) 641-7927.

New Hampshire

Davisville: Davisville Barn Sale and Flea Market. Every Sunday from May through October. Take exit 7 off I-89 (twelve miles north of Concord, New Hampshire), then east on Route 103 one-half mile. Look for signs. Free admission; indoors. Contact Toby Nickerson at (800) 662-2612 or (603) 746-4000.

Londonderry: Londonderry Gardens Market Place. Contact Pete Sapatis at (603) 883-4196. NFMA member.

New Jersey

Edison: New Dover United Methodist Church Flea Market. Every Tuesday from the third Tuesday in March through the second Tuesday in December. At 690 New Dover Road. Take exit 131 (Iselin exit) off the Garden State Parkway and turn right onto Route 28 South, then one block to Wood Avenue, then right (north) on Wood Avenue two miles to New Dover Road (at second stoplight), then turn left (west). Free admission; indoors and outdoors. Averages 20 to a capacity of 55 vendors. Call (732) 381-7904 (market information) or (732) 381-9478 (church office).

Hackensack: Packard's Variety Market. Daily. At 630 Main Street. Free admission. Contact Philip LaPorta at (201) 489-8809.

Lambertville: Golden Nugget Antique Flea Market. Every weekend. On Route 29. Call (609) 397-0811.

Meyersville: Meyersville Grange Antique Market. Every Sunday, from the first Sunday in October through the last Sunday in April. On Meyersville Road. Free admission; indoors. Averages up to a capacity of 37 vendors. Contact Ron Miller at (908) 689-5188 or (908) 464-1598.

Rahway: Rahway Italian-American Club Flea Market. Every Wednesday. At 530 New Brunswick Avenue, at the Italian-American Club. Call (732) 574-3840.

Vineland: U-Sell Flea Market. Every Friday, Saturday, and Sunday. At 2896 South Delsea Drive. Call (609) 691-1222.

Warren: Warren Market. Every Sunday from Easter through Christmas. Take exit 36 off Route 78, then go south two miles to Big Flags, then right, and market will be a third of a mile on the left; or take Route 22 West to Warenville Road, then go one mile north to Big Flags, then left, and market will be a third of a mile on. Free admission; outdoors. Averages close to its capacity of 150 vendors. Supports the Washington Valley Volunteer Fire Company. Contact Jerry Boschen at (732) 469-2443.

Woodstown: Cowtown Farmers Market. Every Tuesday and Saturday. On Route 40. Contact Bob Becker at (609) 769-3000 or (609) 769-3202.

New Mexico

Bosque Farms: BJ's Flea Market. Every Friday, Saturday, and Sunday during summer. At 1775-A Bosque Farms Boulevard. Free admission; outdoors. Averages 20 to 40 vendors (capacity 75). Good country flea market. Contact Bennie J. Garcia at (505) 869-6995.

New York

Bronx: Fordham Plaza Flea Market. Every Wednesday through Thursday. On Fordham Plaza, right next door to Sears and across from the Fordham University Metro North station. Free admission; outdoors and under cover. Averages 30 to 50 vendors in a busy shopping area right across the street from the university. This is a market to pass through quickly, but you may find a bargain.

Bronx: Saint John's School Flea Market. Every Saturday, September through June. At 3030 Godwin Terrace. Call (718) 543-3003.

Brooklyn: Cadman Plaza/Columbus Park. Every Friday from April through Christmas. On Court Street between Montague and Johnson Streets, at the Brooklyn Civic Center. Free admission; outdoors. Averages up to a few dozen vendors. Sponsored by the New York City Department of Parks and Recreation. Contact Gio Art, Inc., at (212) 809-5000.

Brooklyn: Seventh Avenue Flea Market (at P.S. 321 Recycling Center). Every weekend. At 180 Seventh Avenue, in front of the school, between First and Second Streets in Brooklyn's Park Slope section. Free admission; outdoors. Averages 35 to a capacity of 54 vendors. Contact Fred Stern at (718) 833-9864, Monday through Friday, from 5:00 P.M. to 8:00 P.M.

Clarence: Antique World and Marketplace. Every Sunday. At 10995 Main Street. Contact Katy, Manager, at (716) 759-8483.

Claverack: Bryant Farms Antique and Flea Market. Every weekend. On Routes 9H and 23, six miles east of Hudson, New York, and ten miles east of the New York State Thruway (I-87). Free admission; indoors year-round and outdoors. Averages 25 to 30 vendors (capacity 50). Contact Giulio DeLaurentis at (518) 851-9061 or (212) 851-3817.

Corinth: Corinth Bluegrass Festival Flea Market. Annually in August (call for dates). At 635 Main Street (Route 9N). Free admission; outdoors. Averages up to several dozen vendors on twenty-five acres of selling area. Vendors set up during the music festival. Contact Winona Sitts at (518) 654-9424.

Ithaca: Ithaca Farmers Market. Every Saturday. At Third Street and Route 13, near the Steamboat Landing. Free admission; outdoors. Call (607) 273-7109.

Jamaica/Queens: Saint Nicholas of Tolentine Outdoor Flea Market. Every Saturday from March through November. At 150-75 Goethals Avenue. Take Grand Central Parkway to 168th Street, then to Parsons Boulevard and Union Turnpike; or take Long Island Expressway to 164th Street to Union Turnpike. Free admission; indoors. Averages 75 to a capacity of 85 vendors. Contact Saint Nicholas of Tolentine Church at (718) 969-3226 or (718) 591-1815.

Levittown: Tri-County Flea Market. Every Thursday and Friday. At 3041

Hempstead Turnpike. Free admission; indoors. Averages up to 400 vendors year-round. Four levels of air-conditioned indoor shopping. Contact Barbara Eve at (516) 579-4500.

Maspeth/Queens: Knights of Columbus Flea Market. Every Friday and Saturday. At 69–60 Grand Avenue at 69th Lane. Free admission; outdoors. Averages 10 to 15 vendors. Contact Harvey Hyman at (718) 446-4973 (7:00 P.M. to 10:00 P.M. is best).

Massapequa Park: Busy Bee Compartment Store. Daily except Tuesday and Wednesday. At 5300 Sunrise Highway. Free admission; indoors. Averages up to a capacity of 300 vendors. For bargain hunters looking for cheap new stuff. Call (516) 799-9090.

Maybrook: Maybrook Flea Market. Every Sunday. On Route 208. Call (914) 427-2715.

New York City: Battery Park Market. Every Thursday from April through Christmas. In Battery Park, on State Street between the waterfront and Battery Place. Free admission; outdoors. Averages up to a few dozen vendors. Focus on multicultural crafts. Sponsored by the New York City Department of Parks and Recreation. Contact Gio Art, Inc., at (212) 809-4900.

New York City: Bowling Green Plaza. Every Tuesday and Friday from April through Christmas. At the corner of Broadway and State Streets in lower Manhattan. Free admission; outdoors. Averages up to a few dozen vendors. Focus on multicultural crafts. Sponsored by the New York City Department of Parks and Recreation. Contact Gio Art, Inc., at (212) 809-5000.

New York City: Eleventh Street Flea Market. Every weekend from about April through October. On First Avenue between 11th and 12th Streets, in a vacant lot in Manhattan's East Village. Free admission; outdoors. Averages up to 25 vendors. Contact Manager, c/o Mary Help of Christians Church, at (212) 254-0058.

New York City: Fulton Street Plaza. Every Wednesday from April through Christmas. On Cliff Street between Fulton and Beekman Streets, near lower Manhattan's South Street Seaport. Free admission; outdoors. Focus on multicultural crafts. Sponsored by the Pearl Street Park Association. Contact Gio Art, Inc., at (212) 809-5000.

New York City: The Grand Bazaar. Every weekend. In a lot on 25th Street, between Broadway and Avenue of the Americas (Sixth Avenue). Free admission; outdoors. Averages a dozen to a capacity of 125 vendors. Sometimes odd, interesting things turn up here, but it's small and unpredictable, being overshadowed by the much larger Annex market on Sixth Avenue. Contact Andrew Lackowitz at (914) 273-1578.

New York City: Jan Hus Flea Market. At the Jan Hus Church, 351 East 74th Street (between First and Second Avenues) on Manhattan's Upper East Side. Contact Bobby, Manager, at (212) 288-6743.

New York City: P.S. 41 Schoolyard Flea Market. Every Saturday. On Greenwich Avenue between Sixth and Seventh Avenues, just west of 8th Street. Free admission; outdoors. Averages up to a dozen vendors. Contact Cedric at (212) 751-4932.

383 · APPENDIX: North Carolina

New York City: Spring Street Market. Daily. At 43 Spring Street, in the lot (at the corner of Wooster Street in the heart of SoHo). Free admission; outdoors. Averages up to 15 vendors year-round. This tiny little thing, which has held on surprisingly amidst a real estate boom in SoHo, is worth a quick detour for budget fashion hounds (not antiquers). Contact Irwin Yesselman at (718) 273-8702; day of market call (917) 837-5941.

New York City: Thomas Payne Park. Every Wednesday from April through Christmas. At Worth and Centre Streets, at the Civic Center in lower Manhattan. Free admission; outdoors. Averages up to a few dozen vendors. Focus on multicultural crafts. Sponsored by the New York City Department of Parks and Recreation. Contact Gio Art, Inc., at (212) 809-5000.

New York City: Tower Records Flea Market. Every weekend. At 688 Broadway, in the lot next to Tower Records at 4th Street. Free admission; outdoors. Averages 50 to a capacity of 75 vendors. Contact Irwin Yesselman at (718) 273-8702 or (917) 860-1217.

Plattsburgh: Bargaineer. Daily. At 39 Bridge Street. Free admission; indoors. Averages 6 to 10 vendors on 2,200 square feet on two floors. Fewer than a dozen vendors but mainly collectibles and antiques. Contact John Silver at (518) 561-3525.

Queens: Bingo Hall Flea Market. Every Sunday. At 117-09 Hillside Avenue (at Myrtle Avenue) in Richmond Hill, Queens. Free admission; indoors. Contact David Gross at (718) 847-1418.

Saratoga Springs: Stan's Flea Market. Every weekend from April through October. On Route 9, three miles north of town. Free admission; outdoors. Averages 45 to 60 vendors (capacity 80). Contact Stanley Akers at (518) 584-6938; day of market call (518) 584-4339.

Schenectady: White House Flea Market. Every Wednesday through Sunday. At 952 State Street (Route 5), close to exit 25 off the New York State Thruway (I-87). Free admission; indoors. Averages close to 35 vendors. Contact Rudy or Jeanette Fecketter at (518) 346-7851.

Westbury: Roosevelt Raceway Flea Market. Every Sunday year-round, every Saturday in November and December, and every Wednesday from April through December. At the Roosevelt Raceway on Old Country Road, accessible from the Long Island Railroad or by car from the Long Island Expressway. Free admission; indoors and outdoors. Averages 1,500 to 2,000 vendors. Contact Jeff Lake at (516) 222-1530. NFMA member.

Whitehall: Whitehall Flea Market. Every Sunday. At 259 Broadway (Route 4) in Whitehall, twenty-five miles west of Rutland, Vermont, and sixty-five miles north of Albany, New York. Free admission; indoors year-round and outdoors. Averages up to 80 vendors. Run by the local Chamber of Commerce. Contact Nicholas Deutsch, c/o Whitehall Chamber of Commerce, at (518) 499-2292.

North Carolina

Albemarle: Albemarle Flea Market. Every Friday and Saturday. At 40818 Stony Gap Road. Free admission; indoors. Averages close to 40 vendors. Contact Lyman Jones at (704) 982-5022.

Andrews: Hillbilly Mall. On Highway 19/74 Bypass. Free admission. Capacity over 1,000 vendors. Contact Jeff or Theresa at (828) 321-2386. Web: www.hillbillymall.com.

Asheville: Dreamland Flea Market. Wednesday, Friday, Saturday, and Sunday. At 91 South Tunnel Road. Call (704) 255-7777 or (704) 254-7309.

Baker's Creek: Aunt Fanny's Flea Market. Every Friday, Saturday, and Sunday. On Highway 74, (Great Smoky Mountain Highway) between Sylva and Cherokee. Free admission. Hardly competes with Uncle Bill's, which is directly across the highway. Call (704) 586-1413; after hours call (704) 586-4822.

Baker's Creek: Uncle Bill's Flea Market. Every Wednesday through Sunday. On Route 441-N and 74, between Dillsboro and Cherokee, on the Great Smoky Mountain Highway. Free admission; indoors year-round and out-doors. Averages up to 150 vendors (capacity 200). Eighteen thousand square feet of permanent antiques and crafts, plus 14,000 square feet of covered flea market area, right alongside the Tuckaseegee River (where there's rafting and tubing). Contact Ben or Sonnia Seay at (828) 586-9613 (office closed on Tuesday).

Cherokee: Gateway Flea Market. Every Friday, Saturday, and Sunday. On Highway 74, between Sylva and Cherokee (three miles west of Uncle Bill's Flea Market. Small, but okay. Contact Steve or Gail Cooper at (704) 497-9664.

Durham: Starlite Drive-in Flea Market. Every weekend in summertime. At 2523 East Club Boulevard, two blocks from exit 179 off I-85. Free admission; outdoors. Averages 75 to 100 vendors (capacity 150). Call (919) 688-1037.

Eden: Eden Flea Market. Every Friday, Saturday, and Sunday. At 122 North Van Buren Road. Free admission; indoors and outdoors. Averages 150 to 300 vendors. Call (336) 627-9440.

Forest City: 74 Bypass Flea Market. Every Friday, Saturday, and Sunday except Christmas (produce market every Wednesday and Thursday). At 180 Frontage Road. Market is visible from exit 180 (Forest City) off 74 Connector. Free admission; indoors year-round; outdoors and under cover. Averages 60 to a capacity of 150 vendors. Contact Gary Hardin at (828) 245-7863.

Franklin: Franklin Flea and Craft Market. Every Friday, Saturday, and Sunday from April through November (store is open daily, year-round). At 867 Highlands Road (Route 64). Free admission; indoors and out-doors. Averages close to 100 vendors, plus 15 permanent stores. Contact Julie Capaforte at (828) 524-6658 (office hours are 8:00 A.M. to 5:00 P.M., Thursday through Sunday).

Goldsboro: Wayne County Flea Market. Every weekend. At the fair-grounds, on Highway 70. Call (919) 731-2854.

Hickory: Hickory Flea and Farmers Market. Every Thursday. At 951 Cloninger Road Northeast (Route 1). Free admission. Call (704) 324-7354.

Kill Devil Hills: Indoor Flea Market. Every Saturday. At 306 West Lake

Drive, across from Kentucky Fried Chicken. Turn west off U.S. Route 158. Free admission; indoors. Averages 15 to 50 vendors (capacity 80 or more). Contact Fred Bear at (252) 441-8830.

Lexington: Farmers Market and Flea Market and Wholesale Alley. Every Tuesday, plus holiday Mondays. Take I-85 to Business 85 to Old 64 West, then one mile; look for signs. Free admission; outdoors. Averages 300 to 500 vendors. There is also a wholesale market with 200 vendors every Monday from 11:00 A.M. to 7:00 P.M. and every Tuesday from 7:00 A.M. to 1:00 P.M. (this part of the market is not open to the public). Contact Sam Fritts at (336) 248-2157.

Lumberton: Traders Station Flea and Farmers Market. Every Friday, Saturday, and Sunday. On Route 41 East. Take exit 20 off I-95 and follow signs to Route 41 East, then three miles on the right. Free admission; indoors and outdoors. Averages close to 12 vendors. Call (910) 618-0004 or (910) 739-4268.

Mount Airy: Greyhound Flea Market. Every weekend. At 2134 West Pine Street (Highway 89); from I-77 (go east on 89 for two and a half miles). Free admission; indoors. Averages 25 to 30 vendors. Twenty thousand square feet of selling area in a new building. Contact Nancy Dixon at (336) 789-0417.

Statesville: Sharon's Discount Flea Market. Daily. On Highway 21. Take exit 151 off I-40, then go north a mile and a half on Highway 21; or take exit 54 off I-77 and go a mile south on Highway 21. Free admission; indoors year-round and outdoors. Averages 40 to its capacity of 60 vendors. Contact Sharon or William Fuller at (704) 838-0940 or (704) 873-5352.

Wilmington: Good Stuff Flea Market. Daily except Monday (Saturday is when sellers set up). At 5318 Carolina Beach Road. Free admission; indoors and outdoors. Averages 5 to 15 vendors, plus 15,000 square feet of indoor space in the shop. This very small market might offer a surprise or two. Contact the Brewers at (910) 452-0091.

Ohio

Brooklyn: Memphis Flea Market. Every Wednesday, Saturday, and Sunday from April through October. At 10543 Memphis Avenue, at the Memphis Triple Drive-in. Take exit 13 (Tiedeman) off Route 480 and go north on Tiedeman to Memphis and turn left. Admission 75¢ per person; outdoors. Averages up to 400 vendors (capacity 450). Contact William H. Applegarth at (216) 941-2892.

Canton: Old Stark Antique Faire. One weekend a month. On the Stark country Fairgrounds, at 305 Wertz Avenue, in the Exhibition Building and Art Hall. Free admission; indoors and outdoors. Averages close to 200 vendors. Call (330) 794-9100.

Cincinnati: Village Flea Market. Every weekend. At 2095 Seymore Avenue, near the Cincinnati Garden. Free admission; indoors and outdoors. Averages 15 to 20 vendors. Call (513) 351-3151.

Cleveland: The Bazaar. Every Friday, Saturday, and Sunday. Free admission; indoors. Averages up to 200 vendors on 37,000 square feet of selling area. Call (216) 362-0022.

Cleveland: I-X Center Super Flea Mall. At 6200 Riverside Drive. Contact James Kostas at (216) 265-2623. NFMA member.

Columbiana: Theron's Country Flea Market. Every Sunday. At 1641 State Route 164, one mile south of Columbiana county line. Take Ohio Turnpike to North Lima, then south on Route 164. Free admission; indoors and outdoors. Averages 45 to 55 vendors. Go-kart race every Sunday; auction for miscellany on Saturdays at 6:30 P.M. Contact Joann at (330) 482-4327.

Cuyahoga Falls: Oakwood Antiques and Collectibles. Every Friday, Saturday, and Sunday. At 3265 Oakwood Drive at the corner of Fillmore, one block south of Graham Road, off Routes 8 or 59 or 77 North. Free admission; indoors and outdoors. Averages up to 10 vendors. A small operation. Contact Bill Kern at (216) 923-7745.

Dayton: Olive Road Flea Market. Every weekend. At 2222 Olive Road. Contact Mr. or Mrs. Richard Jackson at (937) 837-3084 or (513) 836-2641. NFMA member.

Fremont: Fremont Flea Market. Generally the second weekend of every month. At 821 Rawson Avenue, at the Fremont Fairgrounds, four miles south of the Ohio Turnpike (exit 6). Free admission; indoors and outdoors. Averages 120 to 300 vendors (capacity 500). Call (419) 332-6937.

Johnstown: Johnstown Lions Flea Market. Every Memorial Day. On the Johnstown Public Square in the center of town, at the intersection of Routes 62 and 37. Free admission; outdoors. Averages up to 50 vendors (capacity 80). Contact Dick Scovell at (740) 967-1279.

Lima: Lima Antique Show and Flea Market. First full weekend of January, March, April, May, October, November, and December. At the Allen County Fairgrounds. Take 309-E off I-75 to the fairgrounds, approximately one and a half miles. Admission $1 per person; indoors. Averages close to 50 vendors. Contact Aubrey L. Martin at (419) 228-1050 or (419) 339-7013.

Proctorville: Proctorville Flea Market. Every Friday, Saturday, and Sunday. At the foot of the East End Bridge (Route 7). Call (614) 886-7606.

Springfield: Freedom Road Center Flea Market. Every Friday, Saturday, and Sunday. At 1100 Sunset Avenue. Take exit 54 off I-20, then right at bottom of exit ramp, then right at first stoplight, then left at second stoplight, then left again at first stoplight, and market will be on the right. Free admission; indoors. Averages 25 to 40 vendors (capacity 80). Contact Elizabeth Kish at (993) 722-5555.

Springfield: Springfield Antique Show and Flea Market. Generally on the third weekend of every month during summertime (call for dates), with an extravaganza weekend annually in September. At the Clark County Fairgrounds. Take exit 59 off I-70. Admission $2 per person ($3 for extravaganza); children under twelve free. Averages up to 2,500 vendors during extravaganza. Contact Bruce Knight at (937) 325-0053.

Xenia: Heartland Flea Market. Every weekend. At 457 Dayton Avenue (Route 35) in Xenia, ten miles east of Dayton. Take Route 71 from Columbus or Cincinnati. Free admission; indoors. Averages 45 to 50 vendors (capacity 200). Contact Jason May at (937) 372-6699.

387 • APPENDIX: Oregon

Oklahoma

Del City: Cherokee Flea Market and Snack Bar. Daily. At 3101 Southeast 15th Street. Take Sunny Lane exit off I-40, then go right to Southeast 15th Street, then right to Bryant, and market is on the corner. Free admission; indoors and outdoors. Averages close to its capacity of 40 vendors. A small but friendly market—to "buy, sell, and trade." Contact K. O. Jose at (405) 677-4056.

Muskogee: Good Stuff Flea Market. Daily. At 2541 South 32nd Street. Free admission; indoors and outdoors. Averages close to its capacity of 35 vendors. Call (918) 682-9226.

Oklahoma City: Old Paris Flea Market. Every weekend. At 1111 Southeastern Avenue; take Eastern exit off I-40 and go south onto Southeastern Avenue. Free admission; indoors and outdoors. Family owned and run. Contact Wise and Wise at (405) 670-2611 or (405) 670-2612.

Ponca City: Fran's Flea Market. Every weekend. At 3501 North 14th Street. Call (580) 762-6501.

Tulsa: Admiral Flea Market. Every Friday, Saturday, and Sunday. At 9401 East Admiral, at the corner of Mingo. Free admission; indoors and outdoors. Averages up to 250 vendors. Call (918) 834-9259.

Tulsa: Tulsa Flea Market Saturday (call to confirm). At the Fairgrounds. Free admission; indoors. Call (918) 744-1113.

Oregon

Cloverdale: Red Barn Flea Market and RV Park. Daily in summer (April or May through September or October). At 33920 Coast Highway 101 South, two miles south of Hebo, Oregon. Free admission; outdoors. Averages up to 27 vendors (very small). Indoor barn is open year-round and has 3,000 square feet of shopping area. Contact Nancy Altman, Owner/ Manager, at (503) 392-3973 or (503) 392-3846 (evenings). E-mail: redbarn@wcn.net.

Hillsboro: Banner Flea Market. Every Friday, Saturday, and Sunday. At 4871 S. E. Tualatin Valley Highway. Call (503) 640-6755.

Lincoln City: Stuffy's Flea Market. Every weekend. At 1309 Northwest 12th Street. Admission 25¢; indoors. Averages 30 to 40 vendors (capacity 78 tables). Contact Stuffy Stone at (541) 994-7711.

Salem: Salem Collectors Market. Generally the second and fourth Sundays of each month (but not every month), plus several two-day events (call for dates). On the State Fairgrounds, at 17th Street and Silverton Road. Take the Market Street exit off I-5 and follow signposts. Admission $1 per person; 50¢ for senior citizens; free for children under twelve; indoors. Averages 500 to 600 vendors. Special dates featuring such items as vintage radios and phonographs, glassware, clocks and watches, ephemera, fifties collectibles, toys, and dolls. Contact Karen or Greg Huston at (503) 393-1261.

Pennsylvania

Bloomsburg: Pioneer Village Sales Market. Every weekend from April through October. On Route 11 North. Free admission; indoors and outdoors. Averages close to 50 vendors. Contact Ted Birk at (570) 784-5008.

Carlisle: Northgate Antiques. Daily. At 725 and 726 North Hanover Street. Take exit 14 off Route 81, then go north a mile and a half on Route 11; or, take exit 16 off the PA Turnpike, then go south approximately two and a half miles, and market will be on the left. Look for the yellow sign. Free admission. Carlisle's oldest and finest quality market (good for antiquers but not for transient vendors). Call (717) 243-5802.

Collegeville: Power House Antique and Flea Market. Every Sunday. At 45 First Avenue, on Route 29, three miles north of Route 422, near Valley Forge. Free admission; indoors. Averages close to 40 vendors year-round. Closer to an antique mall than a true flea market, but the merchandise is good. Contact Janet McDonnell at (610) 489-7388.

Gilbertsville: Zern's Farmers Market and Auction. Every Friday. On Route 73, one mile east of Boyertown. From New York, take the New Jersey Turnpike to the Pennsylvania Turnpike; then take exit 23 to Route 100 North for nineteen miles to Route 73 (Boyertown exit), then turn right and go one-half mile. From Washington, D.C, take I-95 to Wilmington, Delaware, then follow Route 202 toward West Chester, then get on Route 100 North and go eight miles north of Pottstown to Route 73 (Gilbertsville exit), then turn right and go half a mile; market will be on the right. Free admission; indoors and outdoors. Averages 280 to a capacity of 472 vendors. The world's largest dutch treat. Miles of aisles. Nowhere else has so many unusual departments! Auctions of livestock and nursery items (Saturday at 6:30 P.M.), automobiles (Friday at 6:30 P.M.), and general merchandise (Friday at 5:00 P.M. and Saturday at 1:00 P.M. every weekend). Contact Kim Klein at (610) 367-2461.

Hulmeville: Old Mill Flea Market. Every Thursday and Friday. At the intersection of Bellevue Avenue, Trenton and Hulmeville Roads, at Fricke's Mill. Near exit 28 off the Pennsylvania Turnpike and Business Route 1; take Route 1 exit off I-95. Free admission; indoors. Housed in an authentic Bucks County grist mill (built in 1881 and in operation as a mill until 1970). Billed as Lower Bucks County's oldest indoor flea market. Contact Kathy Loeffler at (215) 757-1777.

Kulpsville: Kulpsville Antique and Flea Market. Every weekend, plus holidays. At 1375 Forty Foot Road (Route 63). Take first two left turns from exit 31 (Lansdale) off the Northeast extension of the Pennsylvania Turnpike. Free admission; indoors. Averages 40 to 60 vendors. Contact Dawn Myers at (215) 361-7910 or (215) 256-9600.

Lancaster: Black Angus Antique Market. Every Sunday. On Route 272. Averages 200 to 300 vendors. Especially good for antiques. Contact Carl Barto, Manager, at (717) 569-3536 or (717) 484-4385.

Lancaster: Jockey Lot. Every Thursday through Monday. On Route 272, twelve miles south of Lancaster. Two buildings full. Contact Manager, Rhoda Fisher, at (717) 284-4984 or (717) 284-4965.

Marshalls Creek: Pocono Bazaar Flea Market. Every weekend, plus major holidays. On Route 209, five miles north of I-80 (use exit 52) and the Delaware Water Gap, near the New Jersey border. Free admission; indoors and outdoors. Averages 200 to 600 vendors. Contact Kevin Hoffman at (717) 223-8640. NFMA member.

Menges Mills: Colonial Valley Flea Market. Every Sunday. On Colonial Valley Road, off Route 116 between York and Hanover. Free admission; indoors and outdoors. Averages up to 30 or so vendors. Contact Betty Staines at (410) 472-2701.

Morgantown: Clocktower Plaza. Every Friday. At the intersection of Routes 10 and 23. Take exit 22 off the Pennsylvania Turnpike. Free admission; indoors year-round and outdoors. In the heart of scenic Pennsylvania Dutch country. Call (610) 286-0611.

New Hope: New Hope Country Market. Every Tuesday through Sunday. On Route 202, one-half mile from town and the intersection of Route 179. Free admission; outdoors. Averages 30 to 70 vendors (capacity 100). Intimate market in the center of a good antiques area with shoppers from all around (many come from Philadelphia and New York areas). Call (215) 862-3111. NFMA member.

Perkiomenville: Perkiomenville Flea Market. Every Monday. On Route 29. Contact Bob Landis, Manager, at (215) 234-4733.

Pittsburgh: Superflea Flea Market. Contact Ed Williams at (412) 673-3532 (673-FLEA). NFMA member.

Saylorsburg: Blue Ridge Flea Market. Every weekend from April through December. At the Blue Ridge Drive-in. Call (717) 992-8044.

Schuykill Haven: Renninger's Market. Every weekend. Contact Tommy Renninger, Manager, at (717) 336-2177 or (215) 267-2177.

Waynesboro: Annual Antiques and Collectibles Market. Annually in June (call for dates). On Main Street. Free admission; outdoors. Contact Greater Waynesboro Chamber of Commerce at (717) 762-7123.

Rhode Island

Ashaway: Ashaway Flea Market. Every weekend. At 1 Juniper Drive. Free admission; indoors and outdoors. Small but varied. Contact John Marley at (401) 377-4974.

Providence: Big Top Flea Market. Every weekend. Free admission; indoors. Call (401) 274-0060.

Woonsocket: Blackstone Valley Flea Market. Every weekend. At 401 Clinton Street. Free admission; indoors. Averages 8 to 50 vendors. Contact CAP Promotions at (401) or 762-9101 (508) 677-2244.

South Carolina

Lexington: Smiley's Flea Market. Every Thursday, Friday, Saturday, and Sunday. On Highway 302, nine miles south of Columbia Airport. Free admission; indoors and outdoors. Billed as Carolina's finest indoor/out-door market. Call (803) 955-9111. NFMA member.

North Charleston: All New Palmetto State Flea Market. Every weekend. At 7225 Rivers Avenue, just south of Ashley Phosphate Road. Take exit 209

(Ashley Phosphate Road) off I-26. Free admission; indoors and outdoors. Averages up to 300 vendors. Contact Ruth Silverman at (843) 553-8030.

Springfield: Springfield Flea Market. Every Saturday and Monday. At the intersection of Highways 3 and 4, one mile east of Springfield. Free admission; indoors and outdoors. Averages 500 to 750 vendors (capacity 1,000). This well-established, old-fashioned market attracts crowds in excess of 8,000 customers on nearly every Saturday (the biggest of the three market days). Contact W. Henry Cooper at (803) 258-3192.

Travelers Rest: Foothills Flea Market. Every Friday, Saturday, and Sunday. On Route 25 North, north of Travelers Rest. Free admission; indoors and outdoors. Averages up to a few dozen vendors. Very sleepy. Contact Macie Blackwell, Manager, at (864) 834-2021.

Westminster: Traders Junction. Every weekend. On Highway 11 South. Call (864) 882-3775.

South Dakota

Sioux Falls: Cliff Avenue Flea Market. Every day except Wednesday. At 3515 North Cliff Avenue, about a mile and a half south of the Cliff Avenue exit off I-90. Free admission; indoors year-round and outdoors. Averages six to ten vendors (with big displays) year-round. Contact Naomi Carman at (605) 338-8975.

Tennessee

Baxter: C & M Flea Market. Every weekend. At 6501 Flea Market Road. Take exit 280 off I-40 and go north 100 yards, then turn right. Free admission; outdoors and under cover. Averages 75 to a capacity of 150 vendors. Under new management. Contact Mary Hall at (615) 868-5152.

Clarksville: Carol's Flea Market. At 1690 Guthrie Highway. Contact Carol Atkins at (615) 552-1952.

Dickson: Log Cabin Antiques and Flea Market. Every Thursday through Sunday of the first Saturday of every month (except January, July, and August), plus Monday of Labor Day weekend. At 1635 Highway 46 South. Take exit 172 off I-40, then right onto Highway 46 and go approximately two and a half miles and market will be on the right, beside the Log House. Free admission; outdoors. Averages 6 to 60 vendors (capacity 72). Contact Wayne or Reba Harris at (615) 446-4438.

Jonesborough/Telford: Jonesborough Flea Market. Every Sunday. On Highway 11 East toward Greeneville. Support your local flea market. Call (615) 753-4241 or (615) 753-4999 or (615) 753-4115.

Knoxville: Green Acres Flea Market. Every weekend. On Highway 129. Free admission; indoors and outdoors. Contact Nina Franklin at (423) 681-4433.

Lawrenceburg/Pulaski: Green Valley Flea Market. Every weekend, plus holidays (Memorial and Labor Day Mondays). On Route 64, halfway between Lawrenceburg and Pulaski. Free admission; outdoors. Contact Morris D. Williams at (931) 363-6562.

Lebanon: Gracie T.'s Flea Market. Every weekend, plus holidays. At 1024 Murfreesboro Road. Take exit 238 off I-40, then go south one-half mile on Highway 231 and market will be on the right. Free admission; indoors year-round and outdoors. Averages 35 to 55 vendors (capacity 65). Contact Twenty Five, Inc., at (615) 444-5177 or (615) 444-2440.

Memphis: Cleveland Street Flea Market Mall. Every weekend. At 438 North Cleveland, across from the old Sears building. Free admission; indoors. Averages 15 to 30 vendors. The atmosphere is a bit sleepy (we visited on July 4, 1999), but it's worth a quick perusal; we got an automatic numbering machine in perfect shape, marked at $10, for $7 (they go for more than $50 new), so you never know. Call (901) 276-3333.

Memphis: Friendly Frank's Flea Market. Third weekend of most months (call for dates). At the Memphis Fairgrounds (home of the Liberty Bowl every December). Follow signs (well posted). Free admission; indoors and outdoors. Averages close to 600 vendors year-round. Contact Betty Mullikin at (901) 755-6561.

Monteagle: I-24 Flea Market. Every weekend plus holidays. At exit 134. Free admission; indoors, outdoors, and under cover. Averages close to 200 vendors. Call (931) 924-2227.

Mount Juliet: P. J.'s Flea Market. Daily. At 11520 Lebanon Road. Take exit 226B off I-40 and go five miles to dead end, turn left and go a block and market will be on the left. Free admission; indoors and outdoors. Averages close to its capacity of 50 vendors year-round. Twenty minutes from Opryland and downtown Nashville (no transient sellers here, just permanent dealers). Contact Ruth or Paul Johnson at (615) 754-6232 or (615) 754-9291.

Mount Juliet: Rawlings Flea Market. Daily. At 13338 Lebanon Road (Highway 70). Take exit 226 off I-40 to Highway North to Highway 70 and then head west about a mile and market will be on the right. Free admission; indoors. Averages close to its capacity of 60 vendors. No transient sellers here, just permanent dealers. Contact Managers at (615) 754-7457.

Nashville: Nashville Flea Mart and Liquidation Center. Every Friday. At 1364 Murfreesboro Pike near the airport, one-half mile east of Briley Parkway, between Highways I-24 and I-40. Free admission; indoors. Averages 200 to 240 vendors (capacity 240). Located in an old Zayre's store near the airport, this is a deep-discount outlet, not a flea market. Contact the de Jaeger Family, Managers, at (615) 360-7613 or (615) 366-4907.

Texas

Abilene: Old Abilene Town Flea Market. Every Friday, Saturday, and Sunday. At 3300 East IH-20 (exit 390), just east of Loop 322. Call (915) 675-6588.

Alvarado: I-35 West Flea Market and Auto Swap Meets. Every Friday, Saturday, and Sunday. Near exit 30 (F.M. 917) off I-35 West, four miles north of Alvarado, between Cleburne and Dallas. Free admission; indoors and outdoors. Averages 75 to 300 vendors (capacity 1,000). Contact Fred, A.A.T.F.M. Shows at (817) 783-5468.

Amarillo: Historic Route 66 Flea Market. On Route 66. Contact Manager, c/o Amarillo Chamber of Commerce at (800) 692-1338.

Aransas Pass: Shrimp Capital Flea Market. Every weekend. On Route 35, next to the lumber company. Contact Mary Manning, Manager, at (512) 758-5812.

Belton: Bell County Antique and Collectible Fair. Twice a year (call for dates). At the Bell County Expo Center. Take exit 292 off I-35. Free admission; indoors. Averages 90 to 100 vendors. Contact Christopher Dwyer at (512) 441-2828 or (877) 840-3829. E-mail: citywide@onr.com Web: www.cwgs.com

Bonham: Bonham Trade Days. The weekend following the first Monday of every month, plus the Thursday and Friday preceding. Call (903) 583-2367.

Buffalo Gap: Buffalo Gap Flea Market. Weekend of the third Saturday of each month. On Highway 89. Call (915) 572-3327.

Burleson: All-American Texas Flea Market. Every weekend. On I-35 West, five miles south of Burleson. Free admission; indoors and outdoors. Averages up to 300 vendors (capacity 500). Call (817) 783-5468.

Channelview: White Elephant Flea Market. Every weekend. At 15662 East Freeway. Contact Manager's Office at (281) 452-9022 (office hours are Monday through Friday, 8:00 A.M. to 4:30 P.M.)

Cleveland: Frontier Flea Market. Every weekend. At 18431 Highway 105. Free admission; indoors and outdoors. A well-established market. Call (281) 592-2101.

Coldspring: Courthouse Square Trade Days. Fourth Saturday of each month from March through November. At the square in the historical Old Town; from Shepherd, take F.M. 150 off Highway 59; or take F.M. 190 off Highway 45, then go right onto 156. Free admission; outdoors. Averages 36 to 45 vendors (capacity 75). This market is run by the San Jacinto County Heritage Society in the historical Old Town. Contact Jane Guissinger or Billie Jo Trapp at (409) 653-2009 or (409) 653-2184 or (409) 653-2255.

Dallas: Big T Bazaar. Daily: every Sunday through Wednesday. At Ledbetter and I-35. Contact Kenneth Lee, Manager, at (214) 372-9173.

Denton: 380 Flea Market. Every Friday, Saturday, and Sunday. On Route 380, about three miles east of Denton. Contact John Lillard, Owner, at (817) 383-1064 or (817) 566-5060.

Dibol: Olde Frontier Town Traders. Daily. On Highway 59. Free admission; indoors and outdoors. Averages close to half a dozen vendors. Contact Kevin Bentley at (409) 632-8696.

El Paso: Bronco Swap Meet. Every weekend. At 8408 Alameda Avenue. Free admission; outdoors. Averages close to 300 vendors. Contact Sandoval, Manager, at (915) 858-5555.

Garland: Vikon Village Flea Market. Every weekend. Contact C. J. Piercy at (972) 271-0565.

Lubbock: Flea Market. Every weekend. At 2323 Avenue K at 24th Street in downtown Lubbock. Free admission; indoors and outdoors. Averages 200 to a capacity of 300 vendors year-round. Contact Nan Young, Manager, at (806) 747-8281 or (806) 747-8281.

Lubbock: National Flea Market. Every Wednesday through Sunday. At

1808 Clovis Road, a block west of Avenue Q. Free admission; indoors and outdoors. Averages up to 125 vendors. Call (806) 744-4979.

McAllen: McAllen Flea Market. Contact H. C. Gunter at (956) 687-4513. NFMA member.

Odessa: Henry's Flea Market Mall. Every weekend. At 7715 Andrews Highway (Highway 385), across from County Airport north of Odessa. Free admission; indoors year-round and outdoors. Averages close to 40 vendors year-round, depending on the weather (capacity 30 indoors, plus hundreds more outdoors). Five acres of family fun. Contact Frances or Ray Henry at (915) 366-8189.

Pearland: Cole's Antique Village and Flea Market. Every weekend. At 1014 North Main (Route 35/Telephone Road). Admission $1 per person; indoors and outdoors. Averages close to 100 vendors. Contact E. J. Cole at (281) 485-2277.

Rockport: Rockport's Pirate's Cove Flea Market. Every Friday, Saturday, and Sunday. On Austin Street in downtown Rockport. Free admission; indoors. Averages up to 21 vendors. Contact Bradley or Maryjane Knight or Gordon Ansell at (361) 790-8658 or (281) 337-1946. E-mail: mjkrd@pyramid3.net NFMA member.

Rosenberg: Fort Bend County Antique and Collectible Fair. Twice a year (call for dates). At the Fort Bend County Fairgrounds. Admission $3 per person (children under twelve are admitted free); indoors. Averages 75 to 85 vendors. Contact Christopher Dwyer at (512) 441-2828 or (877) 840-3829. E-mail: citywide@onr.com Web: www.cwgs.com

San Antonio: Mission Flea Market. Call (210) 923-8131.

Seven Points: Abner's Flea Market. Every weekend. On Highway 334, two miles east of the stoplight in Seven Points. Free admission; indoors and outdoors. Averages close to 100 vendors year-round. Contact Earlene Abner at (903) 432-4067.

Waxahachie: Waxahachie Flea Market. Every weekend. On Howard Road (F.M. 877). Take exit 399-A off I-35 South, cross the freeway, and then turn right at the first stoplight, and the market will be exactly one mile ahead on the right. Free admission; indoors and outdoors. Averages 40 to 60 vendors (capacity 90 vendors indoors alone). Contact Shirley Peel at (972) 937-4277.

Utah

Salt Lake City: Redwood Swap Meet. Every weekend. At 3600 South Redwood Road, at the Redwood Drive-in Theatre. Take the 33rd Street South exit off I-15, and go west to 1700 West (Redwood Road), then turn left to the market. Admission 50¢ per person; indoors year-round and outdoors. Averages 200 to a capacity of 600 vendors (winter is low season). Call (801) 973-6060.

Vermont

Manchester: Manchester Flea Market. Every Saturday from the third week of May through October. On Routes 11 and 30, three miles from the traffic light in Manchester Center. Free admission; outdoors. Averages up to

35 vendors (capacity 40). Primarily an antiques market that steers away from "plastic garbage and cheap clothes." Contact Wessner's Auction Surplus and Flea Market at (802) 362-1631.

Waterbury Center: Stowe Road Flea Market. Every weekend from June through the foliage season. On Stowe Road (Route 100), four miles east of the Waterbury/Stowe exit off I-89. Free admission; outdoors and under cover. Averages up to 30 vendors (capacity 85 vendors on five acres). Along a heavily traveled tourist route near the gorgeous peaks of Vermont's Green Mountains. Contact the Woodwards or the Flatows at (802) 244-8879 (Barbara and Richard Woodward) or (802) 244-8817 (Walter and Marie Flatow).

Virginia

Altavista: First Saturday Trade Lot. First Saturday of every month, plus preceding Friday. On Seventh Street. Take Business Route 29 (Main Street) into the center of town and go one block west to Seventh Street. Free admission; outdoors. Averages 100 to 120 vendors (capacity 296 vendor spaces). Profits support of the bands in the Altavista schools. Contact Carl Davis (by mail only), c/o Altavista Band Boosters, P.O. Box 333, Altavista, VA 24517.

Bridgewater: Mossy Creek Flea Market. Every Thursday through Saturday. At 205 South Main Street (Route 42). Take exit 240 off Route 81 and go left onto 257 to Route 11, then right on Route 11, then left on 257 West to Bridgewater, then left onto Main Street at the stoplight. Free admission; indoors. Averages close to 20 vendors. Contact Bruce or Betty Knicely at (703) 828-3924.

Chantilly: D.C. Big Flea. Four weekends a year in March and July (call for dates). At 4320 Chantilly Expo Center (near Dulles Airport). Admission $5 per person; indoors. Averages close to 600 vendors. For the intensive flea experience in an indoor environment. Call (703) 802-0066 or (757) 431-9500.

Charlottesville: C.W. Investments. Contact Mac Walter at (804) 977-2705. NFMA member.

Edinburg/Woodstock: The Flea Market. Every Friday, Saturday, and Sunday (plus Memorial Day and Labor Day; closed Easter Sunday and Christmas Day). Just off Route 11, between Edinburgh and Woodstock. Take exit 279 off I-81 and go east on Stoney Creek Boulevard to Edinburg; then turn left on U.S. Route 11 (Old Valley Pike) and go about a mile and a half north; turn left on Landfill Road, and market will be on the right (next to Shenandoah Self-Storage). Free admission; indoors. Averages 45 to 50 vendors. Billed as Shenandoah County's oldest and biggest flea market. Contact Jessica Rush or Clayton Fadeley at (540) 984-8771 or (540) 984-8618.

Roanoke: Happy's Flea Market. Every weekend. At 5411 Williamson Road Northwest. Call (703) 563-4473.

Rustburg: Big B Flea Market. Every weekend. On Route 1. Free admission; indoors and outdoors. Contact Clyde at (804) 821-1326.

Verona: Verona Antique and Flea Market. Every Thursday through Sunday. On Route 11, directly across the street from the firehouse. Free admission; indoors. Averages close to 20 vendors. Call (540) 248-3532 (248-FLEA).

Winchester: Shen Valley Flea Market. Every weekend from March through November. On Route 522, south of town. Call (540) 869-7858 or (540) 635-7023.

Washington

Everett: Puget Park Swap. Every weekend, April through October. At 13026 Meridian Avenue South. Take exit 128 (128th Street S. W. exit) off I-5; coming from the north, take a left off exit; coming from the south, take a right off exit; then onto Third Avenue S. E., then right. Admission $1 per person; outdoors. Averages up to 230 vendors (capacity 255). Contact Dan Sutton at (425) 337-1435 or (425) 455-8100 (Sterling Realty), 8:00 A.M. to 3 P.M., Monday through Friday.

Kent: Midway Swap 'N' Shop. Every weekend. At 24050 Pacific Highway South. Contact Frank Wilson, Manager, at (206) 878-1802.

Pasco: Pasco Flea Market. Every weekend from March through November. At the corner of Highway 12 and East Lewis Street. Admission $1 per carload; outdoors. Averages up to 300 vendors. There are definitely bargains to be had here—vendors are less cutthroat than in the big-city areas; but still, this one has lots of good stuff—it's advertised as the largest open-air flea market in eastern Washington. Contact Bill Robinson, Jr., at (509) 547-7057 or (509) 547-5035.

Prosser: Harvest Festival Flea Market. Annually in September. In downtown Prosser. In conjunction with the balloon festival. Contact Chamber of Commerce at (800) 408-1517 or (509) 786-3177.

Tacoma: Star-lite Swap 'N' Shop. Every Tuesday through Friday (indoors). At the Star-lite Drive-in Theatre, 8327 South Tacoma Way at 84th, one-half mile west of I-5. Admission $1 per person, 75 for juniors and seniors; free for children under twelve; indoors and outdoors. Averages 315 to 565 vendors (capacity 600). Call (253) 588-8090.

West Virginia

Bluefield: Bluefield City Flea Market. Every Saturday. At the Parking Building (a large blue structure) on Princeton Avenue (Route 19) in downtown Bluefield. Free admission; indoors. Averages up to 175 vendors (capacity 250). Managed by the City Parking Commission. Call (304) 327-2401 or (302) 327-8031.

Morgantown: Riverfront Antique and Flea Market. Every Thursday through Sunday. At 1389 University Avenue (Route 119) and the intersection of University and Beechurst Avenues and Fayette Street. Take the University Avenue exit off I-68 onto University Avenue, then north about three miles, and market will be on the left. Free admission; indoors. Averages close to 20 vendors. Under new management in 1996; renovated in 1998. Contact Joan Evanoff at (304) 292-9320.

Pipestem: Sun Valley Flea Market. Every Sunday. On Route 20, at the Pipestem Drive-In, approximately seven miles north of Athens. Free admission; outdoors. Call (304) 384-7382.

Pockview: Pineville Drive-in Theatre Flea Market. Every Thursday. On Route 10. Free admission. Call (304) 732-7492 from Friday through Sunday after 7:00 P.M.

Wisconsin

Cedarburg: Maxwell Street Days. On Maxwell Street. Call (414) 375-7630 (Fire Department) or (414) 377-8412 or (414) 778-7733.

Janesville: Janesville Flea Market. Every weekend. At 3030 Prairie Avenue (intersection of Route 351 and Country Trunk G). Call (608) 755-9830 or (608) 752-7264.

Kenosha: Kenosha Flea Market. Every Friday. At 5535 22nd Avenue, at the corner of 56th Street. Take exit 342 (Highway 158) off I-94 and go east to 22nd Avenue, then right on 22nd Avenue and go four blocks. Free admission; indoors. Averages 20 to a capacity of 40 vendors. Contact Beth or Don Goll at (414) 658-3532 (658-FLEA).

Wautoma: Wautoma Flea Market. Every Sunday from April through November. On Route 21. Free admission. Contact Milt Sommer at (414) 787-2300.

Wyoming

Cheyenne: Avenues Flea Market. Daily. At 315½ East 7th Avenue, at Evans Avenue. From I-25 South, take Central Avenue South exit and go to 8th Avenue, then turn left past airport terminal (street bears right and becomes Evans Avenue); or take Central Avenue North exit off I-80. Free admission; indoors. Averages close to its capacity of 50 vendors. Contact Darla Wellman at (307) 635-5600.

Cheyenne: Bart's Flea Market East. Daily. At the corner of Lincolnway and Evans. Free admission; indoors. Averages close to 35 vendors. Contact Mike, Manager, at (307) 632-0063.

Cheyenne: Bart's Flea Market West. Daily. At 415 West Lincoln. Free admission; indoors. Averages 35 to 40 vendors. Contact Manager, Mike, at (307) 632-0004.

Jackson Hole: Mangy Moose Antique Show and Sale. Twice a year, in July and August (call for dates). Contact Jan Perkins, Manager, at (208) 345-0755.

Laramie: Bart's Flea Market. Daily. At 2401 Soldier Springs Road. Free admission; indoors. Averages close to 30 vendors. Call (307) 632-0004.

Laramie: Golden Flea Gallery. Daily. At 725 Skyline Road. From downtown, go out Third Street and take a left. Free admission; indoors. Averages close to 125 vendors. Call (307) 745-7055.

Canada

Kingston, Ontario: Professor Flea. Every weekend. At the corner of Beth Boulevard and Gordimer Road. Free admission; indoors. Averages up to 100 vendors; 92,000 square feet of selling area. Contact Jeff Holmes at

(613) 548-7136 or (613) 561-0536. E-mail: j.holmes@sympatico.ca. NFMA member.

Oakville, Ontario: Dr. Flea's Flea Market. Every weekend. At 8 Westmore Drive. Take Route 401 to Dixo Road, then to Highway 27 North. Averages up to a capacity of 400 vendors indoors, plus dozens more outdoors. Contact Allen Koffman at (416) 745-3532 (745-FLEA). E-mail: drfleas1aol.com NFMA member.

Oshawa, Ontario: Courtice Flea Market. Every weekend. At the Courtice Road exit off Highway 401, between Oshawa and Bowmanville. Free admission; indoors and outdoors. Averages 150 to 250 vendors. Contact Randy Henry at (905) 436-1024. E-mail:randih@istar.ca NFMA member.

Stouffville, Ontario: Stouffville Country Market. Every weekend. Take Stouffville Road exit off Highway 404 North, go right to 10th Line, then go north to market. Free admission; indoors and outdoors. Averages 150 to 300 vendors (averages 250) in two buildings and forty-seven acres of outdoor selling area. Contact Gary Rouse at (905) 640-3813. NFMA member.

Index